'ANCIENTLY A MANOR'

'ANCIENTLY A MANOR'

Excavation of a medieval site at Lower Putton Lane, Chickerell, Dorset

Clare Randall

with contributions by
Tara Fairclough, Cheryl Green, Richard McConnell
Wendy Carruthers, Lorraine Mepham and Jörn Schuster

Illustrations by
Tara Fairclough, Liz James and JG O'Donoghue

Dorset Natural History and Archaeological Society Monograph Series No. 24
2020

© Dorset Natural History and Archaeological Society 2020

Dr Clare Randall, Editor Dorset Natural History and Archaeological Society.
Dorset Museum, High West Street, Dorchester, Dorset, DT1 1XA.

ISBN 978-0-900341-61-8

Design and layout by Frabjous Books ~ www.frabjousbooks.com

Printed by Short Run Press, Exeter, UK

CONTENTS

LIST OF FIGURES

LIST OF TABLES

PREFACE

The investigation at Putton Lane began nearly twenty years ago when it was first being promoted for development. An archaeological desk-based assessment was initially undertaken followed by a geophysical survey. After a hiatus, evaluation through trial trenching followed in 2010 and while this identified some medieval activity it sadly failed to locate the buildings. On the basis of the limited results, it was determined that targeted monitoring and recording of development groundworks would be an appropriate archaeological strategy. It was at this point, that Context One Heritage & Archaeology was engaged to carry out the investigation. Soil striping began under archaeological supervision in the spring of 2016 and almost immediately revealed the outline of a building on higher ground. Further soil removal exposed additional walls and stone spreads and it soon became clear that the site incorporated a number of separate buildings and walls. Similar soil stripping on the opposing side of the slope exposed lines of ditches and several small structures. At this stage the significance of the discovery was still unclear so a 'strip, map and record' exercise was agreed to elucidate the remains. However, as the investigation progressed it was soon superseded by a more detailed but targeted approach as the importance of the medieval remains revealed themselves. Throughout the summer of that year, we unpicked the archaeology, disentangling rubble spreads from foundation and wall lines, and exploring the associated relict field systems. By the time we reached Autumn, high ground water and flooding prompted the decision to postpone the excavation until the following Spring. Thankfully, this fitted with the development schedule. With the weeds cleared and the site cleaned, we set about our final season of excavation and ultimately completed our task in October of 2017.

Along the way, we were assisted by numerous volunteers who were unstinting through rain and shine to trowel swathes of soil; clean walls; wash finds; metal detect; and generally help with those unsung back office tasks that are so vital to the smooth running of any excavation. The results were richer for their involvement. We were pleased to host a site visit as part of the Mayor of Chickerell's Civic Day in July 2016 as a prelude to an Open Day in August 2016 which included site tours as well as a display of finds and information panels in Willowbed Hall. We welcomed hundreds of visitors throughout the day and it was a delight to share the site with so many. Community involvement in the project was recognised with an award for us and the developer, C G Fry & Son Ltd, as Joint Runner-up in the Dorset Archaeology Awards in 2019.

This monograph charts the story of the medieval manor of Putton through archaeological evidence and historical records. Together, they paint an extraordinary picture of feudal aspiration, land management, animal husbandry and human endeavour during a pivotal time in manorial evolution and the shaping of the political and socio-economic framework in medieval England. Ultimately however, this is a story about people and their lives, about their survival, their hopes and dreams, and the challenges they faced. Our challenge has been to bring their story to life, to draw together the strands of physical evidence from our excavation and flesh this out with the surviving historical documents. The following chapters are the result of that endeavour, and one that demonstrates a painstaking and forensic examination of the evidence befitting this important and rare discovery of a complete medieval manor in Dorset.

Richard McConnell
Director, Context One Heritage & Archaeology
East Stour, 28 October 2020

ACKNOWLEDGEMENTS

As is usual with a project of this scale the results presented here and the ideas which have been developed out of them have only been possible due to the effort and support of a large number of people.

Context One Heritage and Archaeology were employed by C G Fry and Son Ltd who funded the work. They were patient when the project proved to be more complicated than had been anticipated, and enthusiastic about a programme of public engagement. We would particularly like to thank David Lohfink (Land & Planning Director, C G Fry and Son Ltd) for his interest and support throughout the project. We are grateful to Chickerell Town Council for making us welcome at the Willowbed Hall for the display of artefacts and information during an open day, and subsequently housing an interpretation panel explaining the site, also funded by C G Fry and Son Ltd. The manor of Putton will as a consequence hopefully remain alive in the memories of local people. Context One would like to thank Steve Wallis, Senior Archaeologist, Dorset Council for his support throughout the project.

The project was directed, managed and led by Richard McConnell (Director, Context One) and the fieldwork team was supervised by Stuart Milby, with Context One senior staff Cheryl Green, Tara Fairclough and Clare Randall providing specialist on-site assistance and advice. The fieldwork team also included Nel Barnes, Issy Bentley, Eve Cottrell, Kerry Ely, Peter Fairclough, Barry Hennessey, Steve Legg, Sean O'Regan, Matt Palmer, Rachel Pender-Cudlip, Nick Plunkett, and Orlando Prestidge. The Context One team were joined for part of the work by volunteers and work experience placements who enabled us to examine more of the site than would have been feasible in the time available. They included Stuart Ackerman, Sue Cullinane, Millie Goswell, Racquel Lopez, Rosemary Maw, Kirsty McDonald, Zoe Owlett, Brian Popple, Alan Prentice, David Rhodes, and John Singleton. Members of the Weymouth and Portland Metal Detecting Club, led by Karen Brown, also provided us with an invaluable service during the stripping and mapping of the site and in checking spoil. We would also like to thank Ciorstaidh Hayward-Trevarthen, the Dorset Portable Antiquities Scheme Finds Liaison Officer who has dealt with the administration associated with the discovery of the gold and rock crystal brooch under Treasure Act provisions.

Richard McConnell oversaw the project from start to finish and was instrumental in honing the text and photographic images. Cheryl Green was the post-excavation manager for the project, whilst also being responsible for grappling with the medieval buildings and proof-reading the publication. This volume would not have been the same without the maps and illustrations produced by Tara Fairclough. She has not only provided clear figures to present and interpret the archaeology but was actively involved in discussing all of the elements of the text as it developed. Context One thanks Liz James for her stunning, detailed finds drawings. JG O'Donoghue brought the site to life, turning the list of 'must haves' that he was provided with into a fascinating visualisation of how the manor may have looked and functioned.

Thanks are due to Wendy Carruthers, Lorraine Mepham and Jörn Schuster for their active engagement and ongoing conversations during the project about the various classes of finds and ecofacts. These interactions made a huge difference in unravelling the potential nuances of the site. Jörn Schuster would like to thank the following colleagues for discussion and advice: Mechthild Schulze-Dörrlamm and Stephan Patscher (RGZM,

Mainz); Richard Hobbs and Richard Abdy (BM, London), Richard Henry (Salisbury); Anthony Camp and Bruce Eagles (Salisbury); Lynn Wootten, Lorraine Mepham (Wessex Archaeology, Salisbury); S. E. James (Salisbury); Sally Worrell (UCL, London).

We are also grateful to Claire Pinder, Senior Archaeologist, Dorset Council for assistance in providing HER data and tracking down unpublished reports. The staff at Dorset History Centre were as efficient and knowledgeable as usual. Particular thanks also go to staff at the Wiltshire and Swindon History Centre for locating something which was supposed to no longer exist. Anna Butler is thanked for her phenomenally rapid turn-around of the copy editing, whilst Val Lamb and Julie Blackmore of Frabjous Books have been a delight to work with in making this volume a reality. Michael Costen was an inspiring correspondent during the 2020 covid-19 lockdown; his clarifications and corrections of the author's ignorance of aspects of the earlier medieval period have made this report both more interesting and potentially less embarrassing. Iain Hewitt, Bournemouth University, also pointed the author in the right direction with respect to the medieval period in Dorset. Context One are also hugely grateful to the reviewer who most generously gave of their time to read this volume. It has benefited enormously from the feedback received. Of course, any residual glitches, inconsistencies or nonsense remain entirely the responsibility of the author.

SUMMARY

Development for residential housing of land located off Lower Putton Lane, Chickerell, provided the opportunity to archaeologically investigate an area of open land which had been historically associated with the medieval settlement of Putton. Extant earthworks, avoided by the development, attested to the likely presence of archaeology on the site, whilst there had been past finds of Roman material in the general area, particularly in the former location of Putton Brickworks. The site was situated to the south-east of the centre of Chickerell, a settlement *c.* 6km to the west of Weymouth and Melcombe Regis. It is a lowland area of gently rolling slopes, on variable geology. Streams in the area run west to east, draining into the River Wey as it opens out into Radipole Lake. Putton was located beside one of these. To the south-west lies the Chesil Bank, with the Fleet lagoon enclosed behind it. The area therefore affords a range of probable resources as well as access to routeways and the sea.

This volume presents the results of the archaeological investigations carried out by Context One Heritage and Archaeology (C1) during 2016–2017. An initial strip map and record exercise was superseded by the targeted excavation of a complex of stone-built medieval buildings and contemporary land boundaries on the facing slope. Evidence of prehistoric use of the landscape was seen in a general scatter of flint within colluvial and alluvial deposits. A small amount of Romano-British pottery and a handful of other finds attest to probable agricultural use of the area during that period. In neither case were contemporary features identified. A small selection of finds dating to the 9th–11th centuries, recovered from later deposits, attest to the beginnings of the medieval settlement, although no structural evidence of it was identified.

Most significant was the excavation of a large part of the plan of a manorial settlement of the 12th–14th centuries. Originating in the later 12th or early 13th century, this initially consisted of three buildings arranged around a roughly square courtyard, open on its east side. It included a chamber block and a ground-floor open-hall, supplemented by a further stone building which might have been a kitchen. This arrangement was at least partly enclosed with a substantial boundary ditch, whilst the Chickerell stream ran on its southern side. During the later 13th century, the hall went out of use, to be replaced just to the north by a cross-passage house. The chamber block and ancillary building remained in use, but the overall organisation of the settlement was changed, presumably reflecting altering social considerations.

The artefacts and ecofacts from the site provide a glimpse of both daily life and the underpinning manorial economy. The faunal and plant remains, considered in relation to the development of 13th–14th century field boundaries and availability of local resources, indicate responses to changing land pressure. A wide range of objects provided glimpses of the activities carried out at the manorial centre, but also attested to the potential status and connections of the people who lived there, as well as the status of Putton relative to other manors in the wider Dorset landscape. Finds included an important high-quality gold and rock crystal brooch of mid-11th to early 12th century date with continental origins. This volume also explores the documentary records associated with Putton to place the archaeology within the picture provided of the land holders. It suggests some reasons for the eventual demolition of the manorial buildings, probably in the early 15th century.

Part of the site was re-used during the 15th–16th centuries, with the construction of at least one building. This was ephemeral and its nature could not be fully ascertained. Subsequently, post-medieval structures were built overlying part of the medieval chamber block. This activity probably dated to the 17th–18th centuries, but the full ground plans of these buildings could not be recovered. By the end of the 18th century the map evidence implies that the entire area had returned to agricultural use as a field associated with Putton Farm.

1

THE EXCAVATION

By Clare Randall with contributions by Cheryl Green

INTRODUCTION

The excavation of a medieval manorial centre on land situated off Lower Putton Lane, Chickerell, Weymouth was undertaken during 2015 and 2016 by Context One Heritage and Archaeology on behalf of C G Fry and Son Ltd. The work was carried out in advance of residential development of a field which formed part of a total development area of 10.41 hectares. Lower Putton Lane formed the northern boundary to the site, whilst Putton Lane lay to the west. The excavated part of the site was *c.* 0.8 hectares and occupied the north-western corner of the development. It lay over two slopes, one north-east facing, one south-west facing, on either side of a stream which had been altered during the 20th century to provide a culvert (Fig. 1.1).

Background and previous work

The overall development area encompassed the known location of an apparent deserted medieval settlement (RCHME 1970a, 41; HER Ref. MDO 871 and MWX2923; Fig 1.1). This has long been associated with the manor of Podington known from documentary sources, 'Putton' being a contraction of the original name (Fägerstern 1978, 153). A previous archaeological watching brief carried out on the route of a gas pipeline (Higgins 1998), had suggested a wider zone of potentially contemporary activity with medieval material recognised as being spread across three fields 200m to the north-east of the site.

On the ground, and in aerial photographs, features recorded as the deserted settlement are visible as the earthworks of a holloway and associated boundaries (Fig. 1.2). The holloway was oriented north–south, almost parallel to the northern part of Putton Lane, situated to the west, and at its southern extent meeting a point where the lower stretch of Putton Lane changes direction. Two adjoining east–west aligned banks were identified as closes, and the aerial photography suggests that on the west side of the holloway these may have been further subdivided by north–south aligned boundaries. The earthworks were surveyed in 1980, with the plan produced shown in Fig. 1.3 (following Cotswold Archaeology 2005).

The RCHME noted (1970, 41) that pipe trenches immediately to the north of the earthworks had produced 14th and 15th century pottery. The location of this pipe trench is not recorded. Subsequent geophysical surveys comprising both gradiometer and earth resistance provided results which corresponded with the location of the known earthworks (GSB 2003). They also identified potential archaeological features surrounded by the earthworks, although it was suggested that features in the area were largely limited to those which could be identified on the ground. There do not appear to be any smaller enclosures or areas identifiable as house platforms. As the area of the earthworks was not to be disturbed, none of these possible features

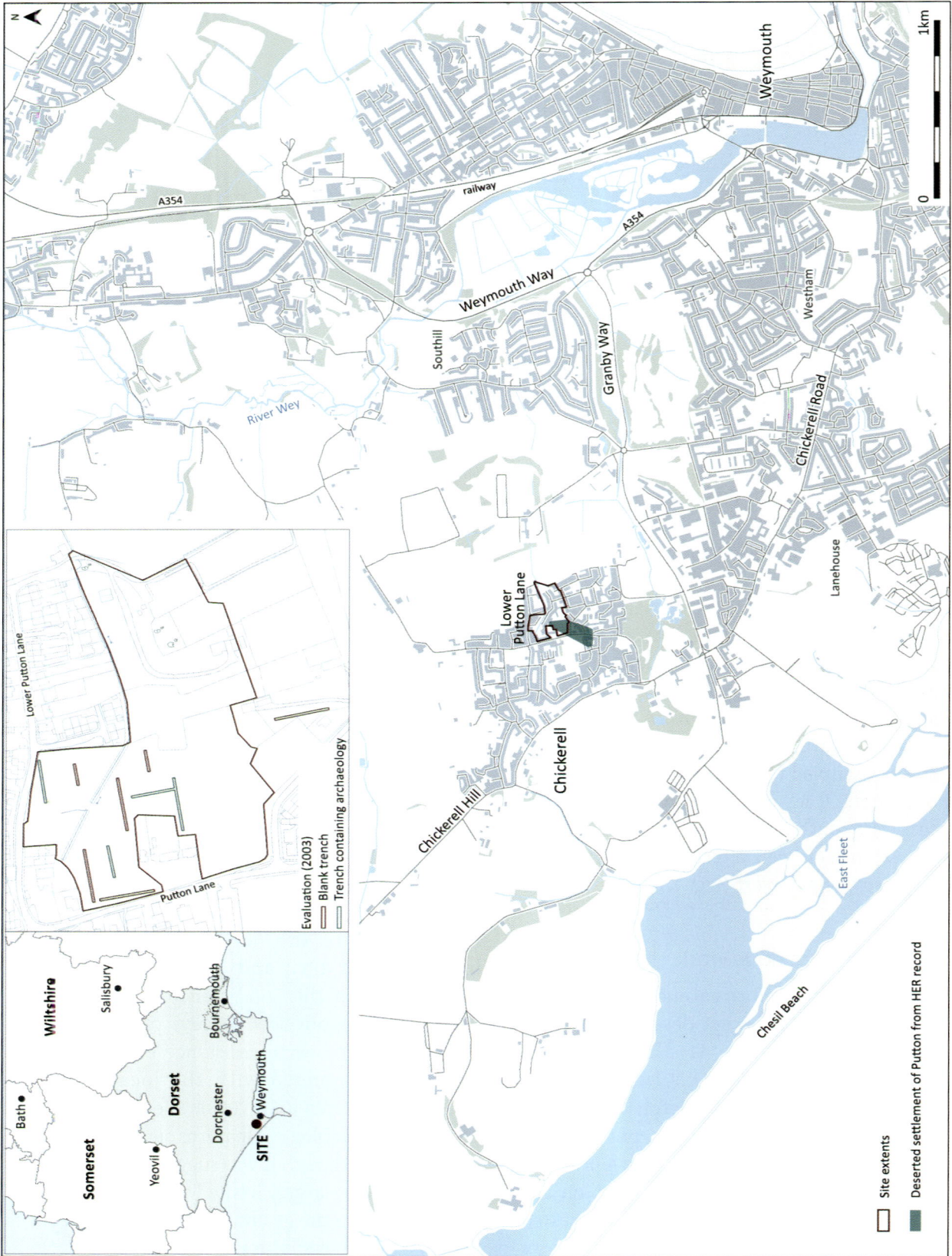

Fig. 1.1 The location of the site at Lower Putton Lane, Chickerell.

Evaluation (2003)

Blank trench

Trench containing archaeology

Site extents

Deserted settlement of Putton from HER record

Fig. 1.2   Detail of 1947 vertical aerial photograph showing the holloway earthworks.

has been subject to further investigation. To the north of the earthworks the geophysical surveys suggested there was some archaeological potential. A desk-based assessment was carried out by Cotswold Archaeology in 2003 which was updated (Cotswold Archaeology 2005) following an archaeological field evaluation (Cotswold Archaeology 2003) (Inset, Fig. 1.1).

The 2003 evaluation of the site explored the potential archaeological features identified in the geophysical surveys (Cotswold Archaeology 2003). This covered geophysical anomalies situated to the south and north of the earthworks, as well as checking areas which had no apparent activity. A total of 10 trenches were concentrated across the north-west corner of the proposed development area. A trench situated to the south-east of the earthworks did not identify any archaeology. In the area to the north of the earthworks, a trench positioned across the course of the Chickerell stream as seen on 19th century maps failed to locate it. Prior geophysical survey had suggested the presence of a palaeochannel, but no recognisable feature was identified. A further evaluation trench did however identify a 'modern' linear c. 10m to the north of where the old river course had been expected, and the overlying deposits

indicated frequent inundation in the past (Cotswold Archaeology 2003, 7).

Archaeological features were observed in four of the evaluation trenches, including the profile of the earthwork holloway. In the latter case, no cut or structural features were identified, other than the surface which provided a profile across the holloway, and largely reflected the profile of the ground surface. This was covered with a deposit containing 14th and 15th century pottery which merged into the alluvium seen in an adjacent trench and was regarded as having derived from hillwash from upslope to the south. Pottery of 13th to 15th century date was present in a shallow ditch and a pit situated in the area c. 20m to the north-west of the most northerly visible part of the earthworks The ditch that was seen could possibly relate to an extension of the eastern side of the holloway (Cotswold Archaeology 2003, 7; fig. 2).

Shallow ditches were also identified in one trench on the western slope, whilst three shallow pits were recognised in another trench in the northernmost part of the site on the eastern slope. In both cases the features contained medieval pottery. The finds from the north part of the site were regarded as suggestive of domestic refuse, whilst the ditches on the western slope were seen as potentially related to drainage or demarcation of cultivation plots (Cotswold Archaeology 2003). This evaluation suggested that there was potential for further archaeology in areas which had not been identified by the gradiometry survey and that there was some potential for the survival of archaeological remains to the north of the extant 'settlement' earthworks (Cotswold Archaeology 2005). The housing development was therefore designed to take this into account, to avoid and preserve the earthworks. The archaeological features and deposits situated outside of this area were allowed for during the planning process and when the site subsequently came forward for development, a programme of archaeological work was put in place. On the basis of previous findings, this was designed as an archaeological monitoring and recording project, but the strategy was upgraded to targeted excavation when it became clear that the remains were more substantial and extensive. The site archive will be deposited with Dorset Museum.

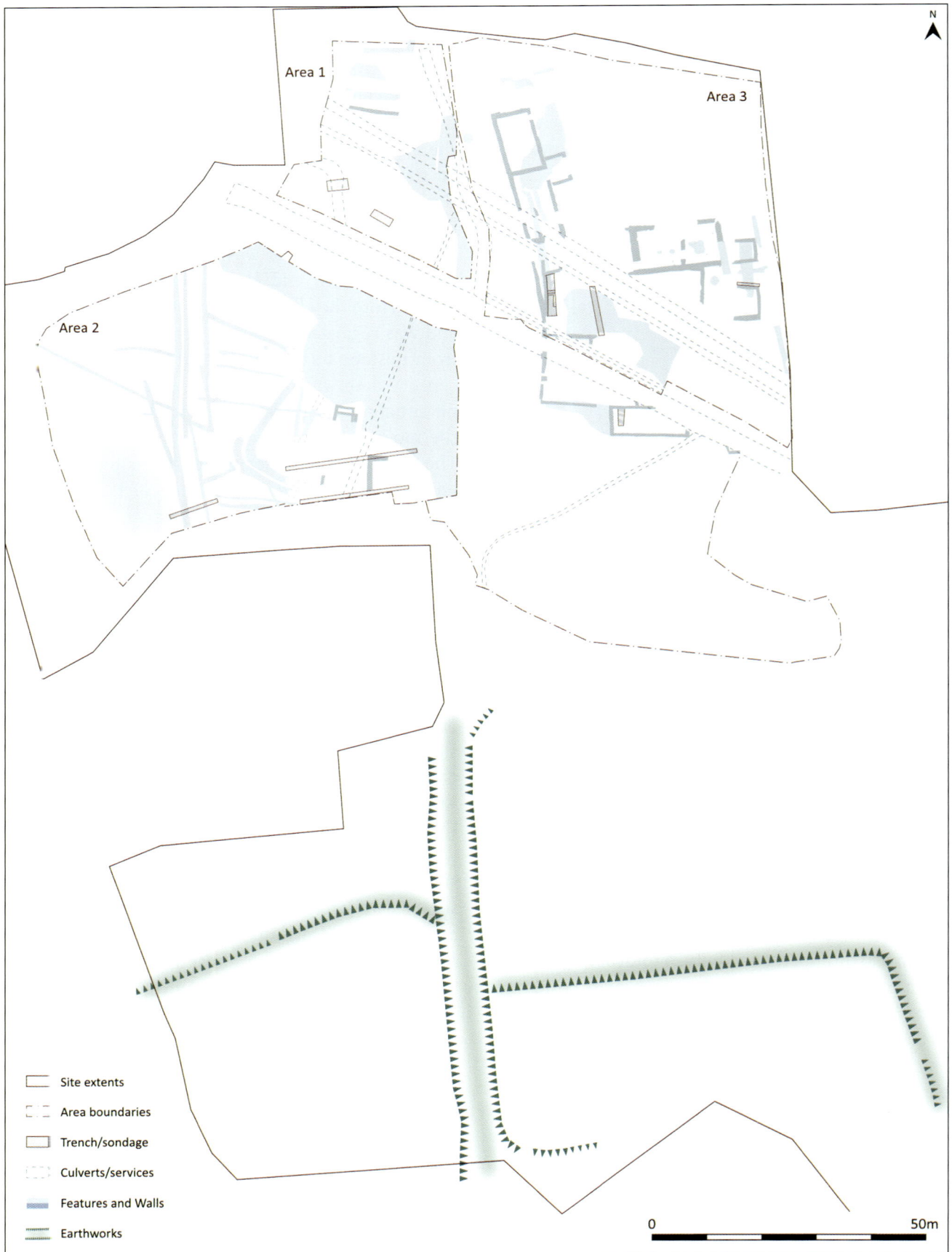

Area 1

Area 3

Area 2

N

Site extents

Area boundaries

Trench/sondage

Culverts/services

Features and Walls

Earthworks

0   50m

Fig. 1.3   The site showing the excavated areas in relation to the extant earthworks.

Current research questions in medieval archaeology

Archaeological research and excavation of medieval sites has tended to prioritise high status and ecclesiastical sites (castles and abbeys) and urban deposits. There is in general terms a lack of extensively excavated rural settlements in southern Britain. Much fieldwork has related to non-invasive earthwork and geophysical surveys of abandoned and partly abandoned settlements or, where excavated, has involved individual houses and small hamlets. It remains the case that nationally there are still only a handful of extensively explored and subsequently published sites, with prominent examples such as Wharram Percy (Yorkshire), West Cotton, Raunds (Northamptonshire), Potters Lyveden (Northamptonshire), Great Linford (Buckinghamshire) and Hatch Warren (Hampshire) (Christie and Stamper 2012).

Medieval settlements and manorial centres are therefore still relatively poorly understood, not least because they frequently lie beneath current settlements. Where settlements exist as earthworks, they are often protected by Schedule and there is no necessity to disturb them. Settlements and manors seem highly variable in their genesis, chronology, layout, function and status, and their relation to the variety of land types, land use and land holding arrangements. These are currently mainly understood from landscape studies and documentary evidence. It is clear from the historical sources that certain locations, even as manorial centres, held greater or lesser importance (which also changed over time) depending on how they functioned in relation to a wider pattern of landholding by an individual or family. However, archaeological evidence which is able to elucidate these gradations in type, status between places, or indeed the degree to which they were used as primary or secondary residences is still limited. The value of excavation in comparison with reliance on written sources has been extensively demonstrated by work on Wharram Percy and West Cotton (Wrathmell 2012; Chapman 2010). These have shown that there is a great deal of localized variation which is not indicated by documentation alone. Construction methods, land holding patterns, and agricultural organisation and

practice, are all regionally and locally variable and are themselves still only partly understood.

The questions that remain at both a regional and national scale are extensive. These include the relationship of building type and settlement layout to the land holding type and farming regime; hierarchy of settlement within manors; spatial organization of functions and status within settlements; spatial organization of functions and status within individual buildings; understanding the relative status and social role between buildings, and between the structures and their surroundings; local construction methods over time; how settlements developed and contracted from the Saxon to the end of the medieval period; subsistence methods and practices (arable agriculture, the role of wild food, including fishing, and other resources, animal husbandry etc). The number of animal bone, charred wood, plant macrofossil and other environmental proxy assemblages available for study from rural sites of this period is regionally limited, and locally almost entirely absent. Similarly, the ceramic sequence for the medieval period is still relatively poorly understood due to the lack of well stratified sequential assemblages. Whilst the site at Lower Putton Lane has its limitations in all these areas, it provides the first comprehensive examination of a manorial centre in Dorset, more data to build towards a rationalised ceramic framework to assist interpretation of other local sites and assemblages, and provides environmental proxies which may be used to examine localised nuances in the economic base of manorial units in the region.

Issues that have a specific Dorset focus, but which feed into discussions of wider economic and population trends, include the pattern, chronology and extent of expansion into previously un-utilised or arguably under-utilised spaces such as the east Dorset heaths, the heavy valley soils of West Dorset and the expansion and contraction of occupation on the chalk, and how that may or may not relate to the wool trade. Whilst Lower Putton Lane may not be directly related to the development of these areas, the trajectory of its establishment and growth is part of the texture of settlement and agricultural change. Connections between the creation of villages in the

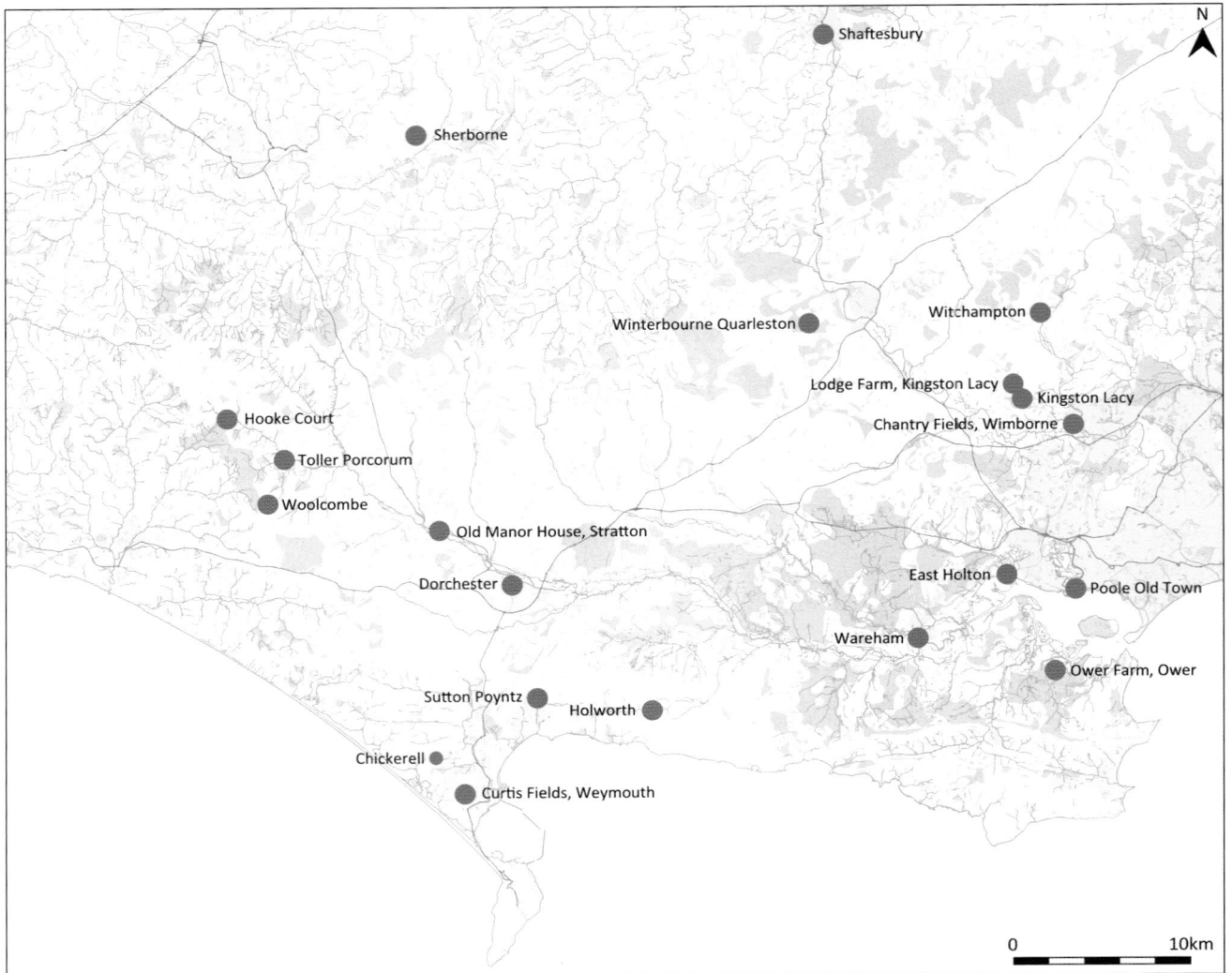

Fig. 1.4 Places mentioned in Chapter 1.

Late Saxon and medieval period and the adoption of open field agriculture borrowed from models developed for the English midlands (e.g. Hall 1993, 121) may hold up in specific Dorset cases, but do not allow for a range of trajectories which we do not currently have the data to understand. Planned or planned settlements do occur in the south of England, with Holworth, Purbeck (Fig. 1.4) providing a local example, but there has been no systematic study of this phenomenon within Dorset. The variability of adoption of the open-field system has been discussed by Costen (1992) with areas which were not suitable continuing to have a range of patterns of land exploitation. Achieving a better understanding of strategies for land use during this period in individual cases is informative in understanding the wider picture.

The current state of play in medieval settlement studies in Dorset

In Dorset, a limited understanding of the archaeological resource together with a lack of research into medieval rural settlement meant that no site in the county achieved a mention in the medieval chapter of the *South West Archaeological Research Framework* (Webster 2008). The issue is referred to in the following terms:

'*Research into the post-Conquest medieval period has proved (with a few notable exceptions) to be one of the weaker areas of archaeological activity in the South West. There appears to have been very little work in the eastern counties of Dorset and Wiltshire with the exception of some development-led work in towns.....The evident gaps in our current knowledge need to be addressed to test if they are evidence of real variations in the past or the results of fieldwork bias and this is a period where the lack of synthetic work is clearly hampering research*' (Webster 2008, 270).

This general picture does not appear to have changed greatly in the decade since the SWARF was composed. The SWARF does, however, identify that in general terms across the south west there is a particular need for integrated studies in lowland areas and identifies Dorset in particular as an area needing work to address spatial and temporal bias under its Research Aim 3 (m). More work is also needed generally on the diagnostic material culture and good contextual material relating to the transitional periods from early to later medieval and the later medieval to post-medieval periods (Research Aim 10 (f)); environmental data linked to land use (RA 21 (d), 22 (k)); the development of villages (RA 33); improved understanding of medieval farming (RA 42); and economy trade, technology and production (RA 47, particularly (b) with a focus on coastal sites) (Webster 2008, 198, 277, 280, 284–5, 287, 290–291). These are all areas where the site at Lower Putton Lane makes a valuable contribution.

In Dorset, some work has focused on large scale land ownership/tenure issues and extant earthworks (Hinton 2012). Whilst the county lies within the central zone of England where open field agriculture associated with villages came into being (Rippon 2008; Rippon et al. 2014) the limited degree of study of the various aspects of this mean that the extent to which this occurred is unclear. Dorset is fortunate in that the Royal Commission on Historic Monuments included earthworks in its various volumes published between 1970 and 1975, although there has been little to supplement that work since. There is as yet no substantial synthetic consideration of the use of the landscape in the medieval period. There has to date only been one substantial published excavation of a medieval settlement and that was carried out in the 1950s. Holworth, to the east of Ringstead, in the Isle of Purbeck (Fig. 1.4) comprised a series of houses and plots, dating from the 12th–15th centuries and apparently represented a planned settlement imposed by the landowner, Milton Abbey. That excavation demonstrated that the layout seen in the extant earthworks was only part of the story and there had been numerous changes in the organisation of the buildings and settlement over

time. Whilst some of the buildings had stone footings, they made extensive use of timber construction (Rahtz 1959), and the layout and construction styles can already be seen to be radically different at Lower Putton Lane. Whilst the pottery assemblage at Holworth consisted of more than 14,000 sherds, it has not been fully analysed to produce a type series, intended to be part of what Rahtz hoped in 1959 was the beginning of research into medieval settlements in Dorset, but which has never actually taken place.

Many archaeological interventions carried out in Dorset have either been on a small scale or the medieval component was incidental to other features. In both cases this often results in the medieval elements having poor wider context. As far as understanding manorial buildings and their organization is concerned, there are a number of standing buildings in Dorset which incorporate fabric of this period (e.g. Moigne Court, Owermoigne [RCHME 1970a; 184–6]), but they do not appear to have received a great deal of consideration. Limited investigations were undertaken by Time Team at the moated site of Hooke Court (Wessex Archaeology 2006). Small scale investigations located medieval buildings and other features including a midden and fishpond at Woolcombe, the site of a later farm (Poulsen 1983; Hunt 1984; 1985; 1986; 1990; 1991; 1992); this probably represents a manorial centre. Investigations were also undertaken within the nearby village of Toller Porcorum (Hunt 1990; Gale 1991; 1992; 1993) but were not fully published. Excavation at Quarleston Farm, Winterborne Stickland, adjacent to the earthworks associated with Winterborne Quarleston, included pits containing 12th and 13th century pottery (Butterworth 2003). Small scale excavations in Witchampton elucidating the date of establishment of the village settlement were undertaken in the 1950s and 1980s (Hall 1993) but were not comprehensively published.

Excavation at Sutton Poyntz in the 1980s revealed part of a possible chapel of the 12th–14th century (Rawlings 2007) but was not extensive enough to locate other complete buildings in a supposed manorial complex. There has been small scale and limited investigation of the manorial buildings at Kingston Lacy (Papworth 1997; 1998), and within the Kingston Lacy estate at Lodge Farm (Papworth

1994). Parts of the ancillary buildings to the Old Manor House at Stratton have been demonstrated to relate to activity between the 12th and 15th centuries (Maw 2015) but are typically limited by the presence of later building on the site. Previous excavations in the area during the 1980s remain unpublished (Iain Hewitt pers. comm.). Excavation at Curtis Fields, Weymouth located agricultural activity of the 13th–14th century, but no associated buildings (Randall 2019). Boundaries were located at Chantry Fields on the outskirts of Wimborne (Heaton 1992). Even urban interventions have been limited. Some medieval elements were encountered at Greyhound Yard (Woodward et al. 1993); in Shaftesbury (Nash 2003), and Sherborne (Brown 2001). There have been a number of small interventions within Wareham (e.g. Harding et al. 1995; Milward 2017). The most extensively explored medieval town is arguably Poole (e.g. Horsey 1992; Watkins 1994). Buildings and a shell midden were explored at Ower Farm, on the south side of Poole Harbour (Cox and Hearne 1991). A medieval farmhouse and ancillary buildings were also excavated at East Holton, Wareham St Martin (Hewitt et al. 2002; 2004; 2005). Recent exploration of earlier medieval salt works on the southern fringes of Poole Harbour (Pitman et al. in prep), are to be welcomed.

The potential of Lower Putton Lane

The site at Lower Putton Lane consisted of substantial medieval buildings and associated features and deposits which represented a large proportion of the core of a manorial settlement. This had multiple phases of construction, buildings serving different purposes that subsequently evolved, apparent relationships with adjacent land division and agricultural areas, and evidence of inhabitants of some status. The range of material culture therefore allows us to consider the chronology, function and relative status of the complex as a manorial centre. It also lends some insight into access to goods from further afield and links between rural settlements and towns. The economic and environmental material offers some understanding of husbandry and consumption of livestock, the exploitation of fish and other marine resources as well as the residues of arable agriculture which provide insight

into land use. Combined with this, there is a useful documentary record, which facilitates exploration of some of the wider questions raised above.

Site location

Chickerell lies c. 6km to the north-west of Weymouth town centre. The site (centred on NGR SY 64877 80471) is located on the east side of the village, c. 200m east of Chickerell Primary School and with Putton Lane forming the western boundary of the site, Lower Putton Lane the northern boundary and recent residential development to the south and east. The area discussed in this publication was situated on two slopes either side of a water course (now a drainage channel); the west side sloped down from the south-west to the north-east at an average height of c. 26m to c. 21m above Ordnance Datum (aOD) and the eastern side sloped from the north-east to the south-west at an average height of c. 23m to c. 22m aOD. The site also straddles two geologies (BGS 2020). The northern third is Cornbrash Formation limestone with superficial deposits of alluvium comprising clay, silt, sand and gravel. An area of alluvium was previously identified in the north-west part of the site (Cotswold Archaeology 2005). The soils are characterised as lime-rich loamy and clayey soils with impeded drainage. The rest of the site is on Kellaways Formation interbedded mudstone and sandstone. The soils are characterised as slowly permeable seasonally wet slightly acid but base-rich loam and clay (CSAI 2020).

The structure of this publication

A detailed description of the structural evidence revealed by the excavation is presented below. Detailed reports on the various categories of artefacts are presented in turn with the pottery, ceramic building material and stone architectural fragments forming Chapter 2, and other artefacts and human remains within Chapter 3. The ecofactual evidence for the economic basis and environmental background of the site is within Chapter 4, whilst Chapter 5 examines the documentary evidence. These strands are then discussed in the final chapter with respect to the nature of the buildings and layout of the complex in comparison to local and other contemporary examples; the aetiology of the manorial unit; the occupation and use of the site and its economy; and the site in its wider setting.

THE EXCAVATION

The machine stripping of the area immediately to the north-west of the earthworks (Fig. 1.3) was observed, but the area was heavily contaminated with post-medieval and modern rubble and had been subject to considerable disturbance. Two ditches were noted but were of recent origin, and no further work was undertaken in this area.

The focus of fieldwork was therefore directed towards the north-western extent of the development area (Fig. 1.1; Fig. 1.5). Soil stripping here identified the two slopes facing each other across the culvert, and in particular the eastern side as areas of archaeological interest. In response to the anticipated density of archaeological features suggested by the 2003 evaluation it had been agreed with Dorset Historic Environment Service that a programme of 'strip, map and record' across the north-western extent of the site would be the most appropriate archaeological response for identifying and then excavating any archaeological remains. This strategy was implemented between March and September 2015. However, the discovery of extensive and complex archaeological remains necessitated a hiatus to the work over the winter due to difficulties caused by the higher water table, particularly in the central part of the site. The site was re-opened in March 2016 and focussed on excavation of the key areas of interest. Site work was completed in November 2016.

The site was first soil stripped with machine excavation continuing until archaeological features or natural geology was encountered. The site was also subject to a metal detecting survey carried out, under archaeological supervision, by volunteers from Weymouth and Portland Metal Detecting Club. Once machine work had been completed, three broad areas of archaeological interest were identified, and labelled as Areas 1, 2, and 3 (Fig. 1.5). The reduced surfaces were cleaned using hand tools, and features and deposits were mapped to create a pre-excavation plan. Archaeological features/deposits were then

identified for subsequent sampling. Small discrete features were fully excavated; larger discrete features were half-sectioned (50% excavated); and long linear features were sample excavated.

The deposits and features encountered during the excavation are described in the narrative below and the full details are accessible within the site archive. In the text, context numbers for cuts appear in square brackets, e.g. [1-004]; layer and fill numbers appear in standard brackets, e.g. (1-002). Numbers are generally prefixed with the recorder's personal identifying number; where this is not the case, it is because the context was recorded during the initial clearance phase of works. Features were also assigned a feature number which appear here prefaced with an F, with wall numbers prefaced with a W and building numbers with a B. The location of sections illustrated in this chapter is shown in Fig. 1.6.

GENERAL SEQUENCE AND CHRONOLOGY

The topsoil across the site was generally a dark greyish brown to brown soft silty clay with small cornbrash generally of 0.25–0.30m depth. Occasional building rubble, dominated by stone and roof tile, also occurred in the topsoil in Area 3. The subsoils across Areas 1 and 2 comprised similar very dark grey to very dark greyish brown silty clays with common cornbrash and occasional concentrations of building rubble and was generally 0.25m in depth. This overlay a 0.13m deep very dark grey to black clay loam, which in places covered a yellowish brown, grey to greyish brown clay loam containing sparse pottery and animal bone. In Area 3 the deposit sequence beneath the topsoil comprised numerous localised spreads and deposits of very dark greyish brown to dark greyish brown friable to firm silty clay loam containing frequent to abundant building rubble. Distinct areas of extensive rubble spreads were situated over the footprints of a series of seven stone-built buildings. The underlying natural deposits in Area 3 comprised fractured and weathered cornbrash, which in places had been terraced and built onto directly. The surface of the solid geology was uneven with areas of weathering as a consequence of exposure, while in places it was

Fig. 1.5 Excavation areas, building numbers, features and deposits discussed in the text.

Fig. 1.6   Location of section drawings described in the text, and illustrated.

overlain by colluvial deposits comprising yellow compacted silt with fine sand and clay.

It is worth noting that understanding of the relationships of features and deposits between (and in some cases within) the excavation areas was affected by modern culverts and services. Areas 1 and 3 were divided from Area 2 by a wide culvert which ran across the entire site from north-west to south-east. A second culvert joined the first one at its south end and ran north to south between Areas 1 and 3, severing them from each other. Further complication was introduced by two parallel service trenches situated c. 11m to the north of the main culvert. These ran through Areas 1 and 3 disrupting the potential to understand the relationships between deposits in Areas 1 and phases of building in Area 3. A further sewer trench had been constructed at a 90 degree angle from the first one on a north-east to south-west orientation across the eastern part of Area 1 and 2. In the latter case it severed deposits between the buildings in the southern part of Area 2, and hampered understanding of their relationship. None of these services appears to have attracted any archaeological monitoring during their installation.

The chronology of the site is largely dependent on the pottery and to a lesser degree, the other dateable finds. Sequentially the main phases have been identified as follows:

Phase 1 – Pre-medieval activity
Phase 2 – Initial medieval phase – pre-building features (c. 10th–12th centuries AD)
Phase 3 – The initial building phase (c. 13th century AD)
Phase 4 – The re-building phase (c. Late 13th–14th centuries AD)
Phase 5 – The demolition of the manorial buildings (c. 14th century AD)
Phase 6 – Late medieval phase (c. 14th–16th centuries AD)
Phase 7 – Post-medieval (c. 17th–19th centuries AD)
Phase 8 – Modern

THE STRATIGRAPHIC NARRATIVE

Phase 1 Pre-medieval

No features clearly pre-dating the medieval period were identified. Where underlying subsoils were observed they contained medieval material, so it

seems that earlier occupation may have been masked or reworked by later activity. This is particularly the case with respect to Area 1 and the lower lying parts of Area 2 which were covered by a spread of soils which appear to have derived from medieval refuse redistributed by ploughing. In Area 3 the construction of the main manorial buildings, including terracing into the hillslope, may have removed any evidence of underlying features or deposits. Despite this, earlier activity in the general area is evident from the range of dateable material culture. This included a spread of worked flint incorporating several flint artefacts, with further material recovered from a wide range of contexts across Areas 1–3 but dominated by debitage. These contexts are dated to the medieval period or later, with the flint particularly notable in deposits which appeared to relate to alluvial deposition and potential inundation of the lower lying parts of the site. The flint is therefore residual and possibly found at some distance from the original location of deposition. As such, the flint assemblage has not been subject to analysis within this publication although it has been retained in the site archive. Two undiagnostic pottery sherds with a later prehistoric fabric were also recovered. Romano-British activity in the area is attested by the presence of a handful of Roman coins and a copper alloy needle of Romano-British type (Schuster, Chapter 3) and 18 sherds of pottery, largely Black Burnished ware (BB1), but including a single sherd of Oxfordshire colour-coated ware (Mepham, Chapter 2). These were also all residual in later contexts.

Phase 2 – The initial medieval phase (c. 10th–12th centuries AD)

The earliest medieval activity on the site is attested by a small selection of Saxo-Norman pottery and several finds recovered by the metal detecting survey. These include a coin of Aethelred II, a fragment of a probably 10th century equal-arm or ansate brooch and a gold and rock crystal brooch dated to the mid-11th to early 12th centuries which originated in central Europe. These are discussed in Chapters 2 and 3.

Features and deposits beneath Building 4
In the southern part of Area 3, three approximately west-east aligned ditches were located beneath B4 (Fig. 1.7). They all extended the full length of the

Fig. 1.7 Phase 2.

building, cutting the underlying colluvium, although their full eastward extent could not be established as they converged with the main culvert. To the west they were buried beneath an extensive rubble spread F46, in an area which was susceptible to repeated flooding from the culvert. It was not possible to establish whether they had been cut by the construction of B4. The most northerly of the three ditches, F101, had concave sides of a steep gradient and a flat base [9-135], measuring 0.40m wide and 0.35m deep (Fig. 1.8a). The fill (9-136) contained pottery dated to the 11th–12th centuries, flint and ceramic building material (CBM). Ditch F99 was positioned slightly south of and parallel to F101, with steep concave sides and a flat base [9-126] /[9-132], measuring 0.70m–0.80m wide and 0.30–0.38m deep (Fig. 1.8a). It contained silty clay fills which differed along its length, with (9-127) at the western end containing infrequent charcoal, pottery dated to the 12th century and animal bone whilst to the east (9-133) contained pottery, CBM and oyster shell.

Ditch F98 was seen in interventions [9-124] and [9-130], situated further south of F101 and F99 and curving away slightly towards the south-east, with steep concave sides and a flat base, and measuring 0.80–0.83m wide and 0.32–0.38m deep (Fig. 1.8a). In intervention [9-124] the basal fill (9-125) and secondary fill (9-128) had infrequent charcoal inclusions. The upper fill (9-129) contained pottery, CBM and oyster shell. The pottery included two 12th century sherds and a residual sherd of samian ware. In the second intervention [9-130] there were two fills (9-131) and (9-134), the latter containing pottery flecks, oyster shell and CBM.

These closely parallel ditches differ in character from the agricultural boundaries on the western slope. Interpretation of function is difficult given that the full extent could not be established, although their form and location parallel to the base of the slope suggests they were associated with water management. However, their position in relation to the later courtyard orientation of the subsequent phase (see below) may indicate that they represent an early attempt to define an occupied space. They appear to represent a series of episodes of re-establishment from the 11th and into the 12th century. Across the south-western portion of B4,

and running under its north, west and south walls to include an area outside of the building, was a deposit (15-115) of very dark grey silty clay with some burnt sandstone. It also included pottery, animal bone and CBM, and was in some respects similar to a midden spread (10-108) in Area 1 and 2 ascribed to Phase 3. However, the pottery could be dated to the 12th century and clearly pre-dated B4. Beneath this were colluvial deposits (15-113) and (15-114), yielding flecks of pottery and bone as well as flint, and deposit (9-139). These deposits and the three ditches are clearly dated to the 12th century, and as such are probably amongst the earliest features on the site.

Area 3

Ten features in Area 3, comprising ditches and pits, were assigned to the medieval period but were situated beneath the main medieval structural phases represented by B5 and B2. As B5 was the earlier of these two buildings, those features beneath it represent some of the earliest stratigraphic components, whilst a more limited number of features and deposits beneath B1 may also relate to this phase. Some of the dateable material recovered from these features supports the inception of activity during the 11th or 12th centuries. However, no individual features can be assigned specifically to this date. Some of them may relate to activity in the 12th century, whilst others contain 13th century material consistent with being created or used immediately prior to the establishment of the Phase 3 structures.

DEPOSITS PRE-DATING BUILDING 5

In the area to the north of B5, east of its contemporary boundary wall W42, the bedrock was characterised by natural hollows and fissures (Fig. 1.9). Immediately overlying this was a silty clay deposit (13-120) with infrequent rubble which varied in depth where it filled the undulations in the rock surface. It contained pottery of 13th century date and was covered by three similar layers (13-119) (13-118) and (13-117) with no dateable finds but some charcoal. They extended beneath W6 (which represents the only evidence for a north end to B5) and W42. This series of deposits may have been associated with ground clearance ahead of construction of B5, but also created a flatter terrace. A number of features either cut or related to this series of deposits, and these are described below. A

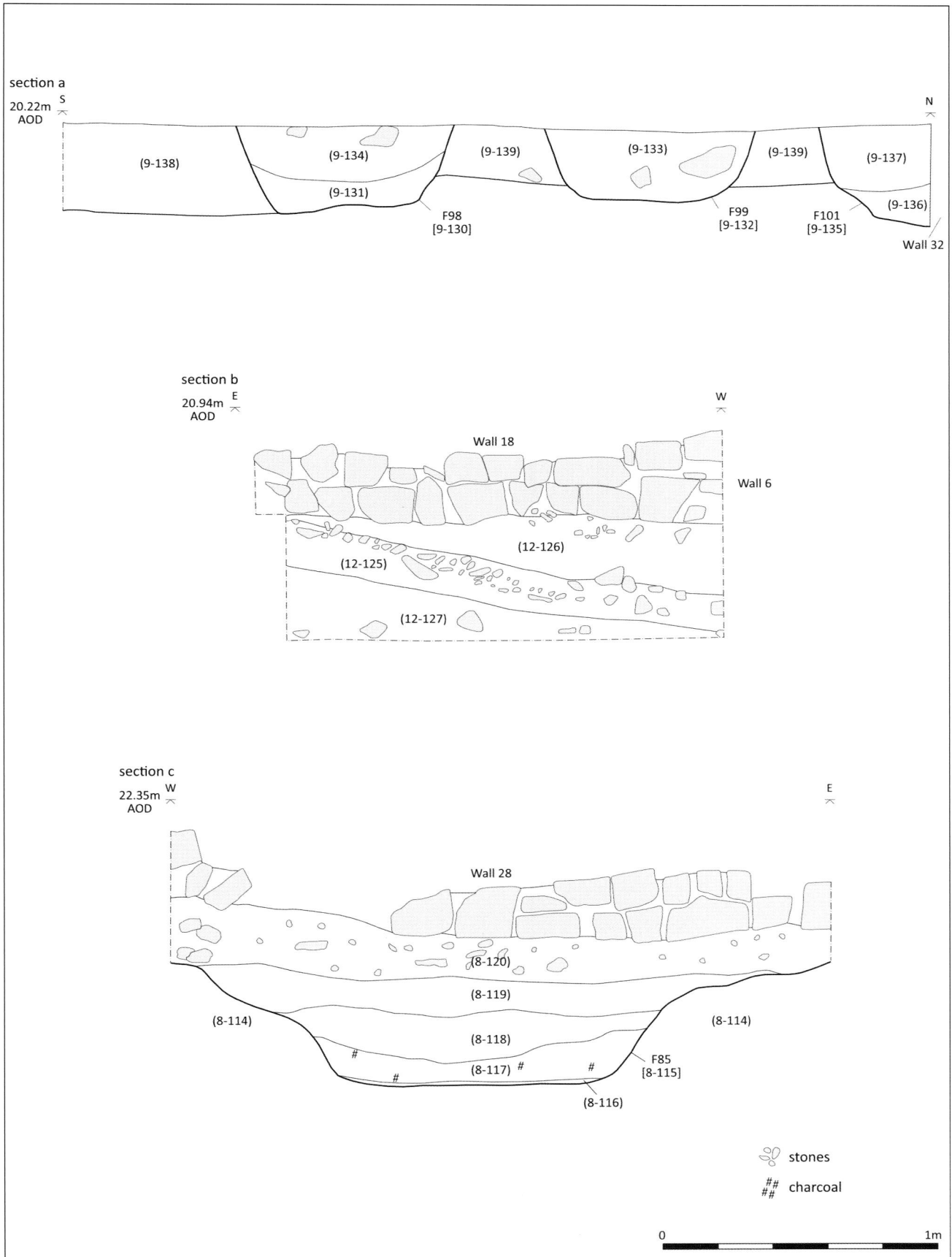

section a
20.22m
AOD

S

N

(9-138)

(9-134)

(9-139)

(9-133)

(9-139)

(9-137)

(9-131)

(9-136)

F98
[9-130]

F99
[9-132]

F101
[9-135]

Wall 32

section b
20.94m
AOD

E

W

Wall 18

Wall 6

(12-126)

(12-125)

(12-127)

section c
22.35m
AOD

W

E

Wall 28

(8-120)

(8-119)

(8-114)

(8-114)

(8-118)

(8-117)

F85
[8-115]

(8-116)

stones

charcoal

0   1m

Fig. 1.8   Section drawings showing features under B4, B5 and ditch F85.

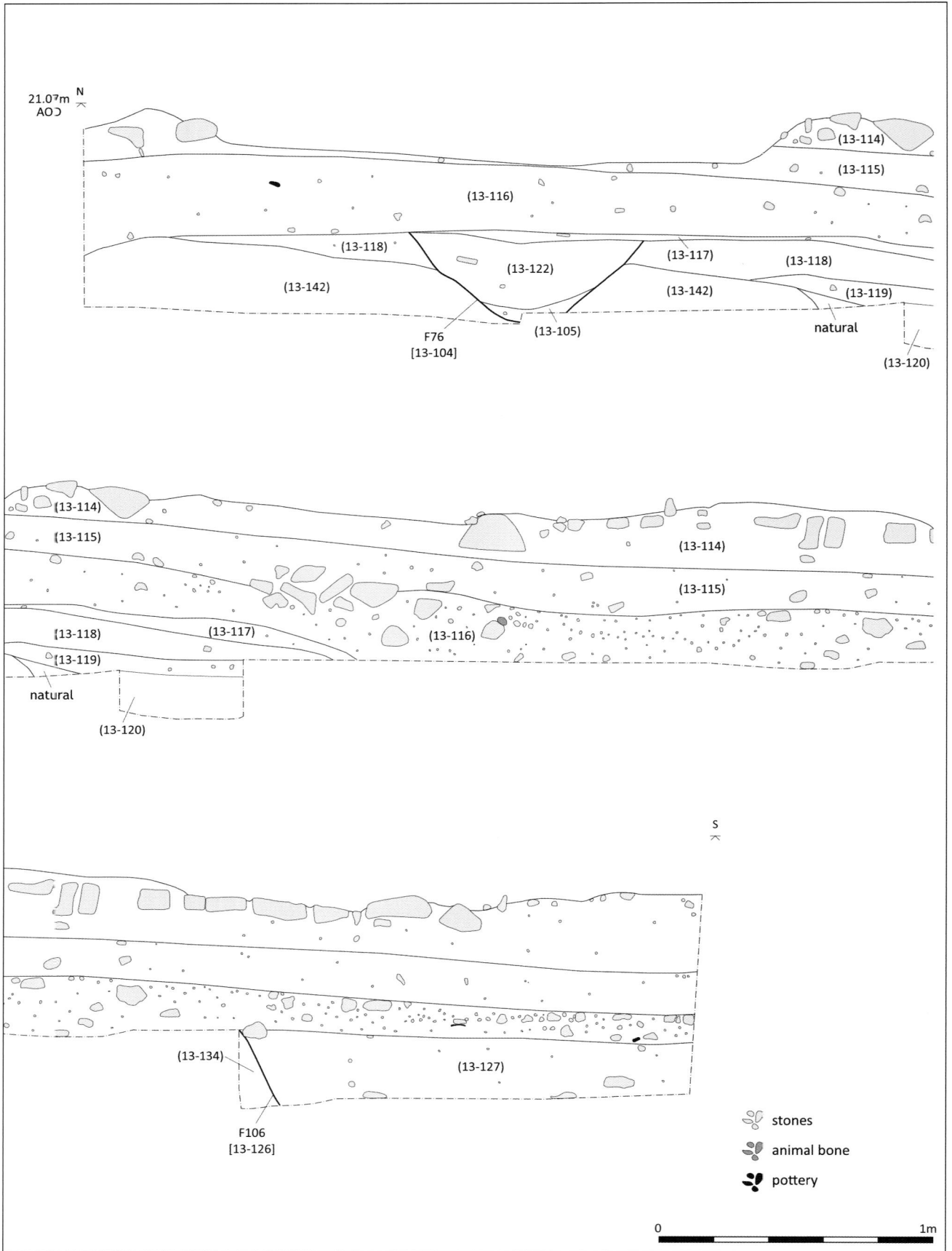

21.07m
AOD

N

(13-114)

(13-115)

(13-116)

(13-118)   (13-117)   (13-118)

(13-122)

(13-142)   (13-142)   (13-119)

natural

F76
[13-104]   (13-105)

(13-120)

(13-114)

(13-115)

(13-114)

(13-115)

(13-118)   (13-117)

(13-119)

(13-116)

natural

(13-120)

S

(13-134)

(13-127)

F106
[13-126]

stones

animal bone

pottery

0   1m

Fig. 1.9   Section drawing of deposits beneath B5.

further layer (13-116) was also present both within the footprint and to the north of B5. This was an extensive, 0.30m thick deposit comprising silty clay with frequent small to large limestone rubble. Although it contained no dateable finds, it sealed the pits at the north end of B5 and may have been a make-up layer associated with both the internal surfaces and exterior yard of the building.

Situated in the area of W18 (belonging to B5), were a sequence of deposits (12-127), (12-125) (12-126) and (12-138) of compacted silty clay with frequent small rounded and sub-rounded cornbrash. They ran under W18 with the lowest (12-127) measuring up to 0.28m thick and overlying the limestone natural (Fig. 1.8b). These deposits were very similar and can be regarded as equivalent to the deposits underlying W6 and W42 and might also be interpreted as levelling layers. Contexts (12-125) and (12-138) contained pottery dating to the 12th–13th century, which supports a date no earlier than the 13th century for B5.

Cut features pre-dating Building 5

Pit F110 was unclear in overall plan as it was obscured by the boundary wall (W42) associated with B5 and had been cut by the bedding trench [13-111]. However, it survived to a depth of c. 0.30m and had steep straight sides and a flat base [13-136]. It had a fill (13-137) of silty clay with frequent small limestone rubble but did not yield any dateable material. In turn, F110 seems to have cut a levelling deposit (13-120) which contained 13th century pottery. Pit F105 also had a cut [13-123] which could not be defined fully because it had been cut by pit F107. Pit F105 was at least 0.80m across and was 0.28m deep. Its primary fill (13-125) contained Saxo-Norman pottery of 10th–12th century date as well as oyster shell and animal bone, but this was most likely redeposited material. The upper fill (13-124) of silty clay contained frequent limestone rubble. Pit F107 was similarly undefined in plan but had moderate concave sides [13-128], although the base was not seen. It was 1.20m across and more than 0.10m deep, and contained a single fill (13-129), which contained pottery, animal bone, flint and oyster shell, with two pottery sherds of 11th–12th century date. Over this was deposit (13-116), a c. 0.30m deep silty clay layer with frequent small to large limestone rubble which may represent a levelling layer. Pit F108 cut

through this layer, and although it was unclear in plan it was probably sub-circular with sloping sides and a flat base, 0.60m wide and 0.40m deep. The primary fill (13-131) contained animal bone and metal whilst the secondary fill (13-132) had no finds. Stratigraphically, pit F108 was directly beneath the subsoil but given its location it is unlikely to have been open during the use of B5 and is more likely to predate it.

Pit F109, like F107, was also covered by the levelling layer (13-116). It also had an unclear overall plan but had steep concave sides [13-133] and was at least 0.40m deep. It contained a single fill (13-134) with no dateable finds but given its location and stratigraphic position it is likely to be broadly contemporary with F107. Pit F106 was similarly stratigraphically situated to the east of W42 (Fig. 1.10). Its plan was not recoverable but measured at least 0.80m across with moderate convex sides [13-126]; the base was not fully excavated below the water table (Fig. 1.9). The single fill (13-127) contained pottery, animal bone and oyster shell, the pottery providing a date in the 12th century.

Pit F77 was a shallow sub-rectangular cut [13-106] aligned north–south with steep straight and concave sides and a flat base and measured 0.70m wide and 0.13m deep. It had a single fill (13-107) containing redeposited limestone and animal bone. In turn, F77 cut pit F76 on its western side, which in turn cut the layers (13-118) (13-119) and (13-120) discussed above. F76 was sub-circular with concave sides of moderate gradient and a concave base [13-104], measuring 0.85m in diameter and 0.35m deep (Fig. 1.10). It contained a thin primary fill (13-105) of soft clayey silt with a couple of pieces of limestone but was rich with charcoal. This contained pottery dated to the 12th–13th century, and a notable concentration of amphibian remains in this primary fill suggests it was at least damp if not waterlogged when initially open (see Randall, Chapter 4). The upper fill (13-122) was a silty clay. Pit F78 was situated just to the south of pits F77 and F76, and also cut pre-building deposit (13-120). In plan, it had an irregular oval shape, aligned north–south with concave sides of a gentle gradient [13-108]. The base was concave, 0.80m in diameter and 0.14m deep. This contained a primary fill (13-109) which contained pottery, animal

Fig. 1.10   Pits F106 and F107 on east side of boundary W42 and beneath rubble layer, looking east (1 x 0.5m, and 1 x 1m scales).

bone, flint and oyster shell. The pottery dated to the 13th–14th century, although fully consistent with an earlier 13th century date. The secondary fill (13-110) contained 12th century pottery and animal bone. This shallow feature could quite easily have been cut from a higher level, and the contents of the upper fill may be re-deposited or residual. It is however likely that it was exterior to B5 during Phase 3 and may relate to that phase of activity.

It appears from the sequence and dateable material that there was an initial phase of activity in this area which certainly involved pit F105 and, if not contemporary, pit F106 was created soon after during the 11th–12th century. These were succeeded after what appears to have been a short time by pit F107, which produced material of 12th century date, with pits, F108, F109 and F110 following in quick succession. Pits F76 and F77 seem to be

broadly contemporary with these features with pit F78 appearing to be slightly later and dated to at least the 13th century. This activity was sealed by deposits associated with the construction of B5 and its associated boundary wall (W42) (Fig. 1.10), which provided similar dates. These features attest to an ill-defined but protracted period of occupation.

FEATURES AND DEPOSITS BELOW BUILDING 1
Several cut features lay within the footprint of B1, but as there were no interior floor deposits present it was difficult to establish any relationships. However, in all cases where dateable material was present, that material was earlier than the overlying deposits. Within the eastern end of the building a large shallow irregular pit F84 around 2m across contained pottery of the 11th–12th century and was directly overlain by deposits from the collapse of B1. A single circular post-hole F75 was also stratigraphically lower than the

southern wall (W9) but produced no dateable material. It was cut into the fractured limestone geology [14-102], measured 0.33m in diameter and 0.20m deep, and was filled with a firm clay (14-103). As such it is the only clear structural element pre-dating B1.

Two circular pits in the western half of B1, F82 and F83, measured 0.72m and 1.02m in diameter and 0.30m and 0.35m deep respectively. The upper fill of F82 (8-110) contained pottery of the 12th–13th century whilst the lower fills (8-106) and (8107) of F83 contained pottery consistent with a 13th century date. Given the lack of stratigraphic relationships and the dating of the material within these two pits they may well be either earlier than B1 or contemporary with the construction or use of the building. The case for their being contemporary with the building relates to their position relative to each other and to the walls of B1. Their location suggests that they were aligned in parallel with the south wall (W9) and located almost half-way across the width of the building. Whilst unprovable, it is possible that these two features represent large post-pits which were either related to the structure of B1 or possibly derived from an earlier structure on a similar footprint (discussed below).

The limited number of deposits immediately below B1 occurred in the irregularities of the underlying limestone bedrock, including (9-117) and (9-119) beneath W19, whilst (9-120) was located under W9 and overlying the redeposited natural (9-118). These deposits were silty clays and although they contained no dateable material the presence of sparse charred material and degraded marine shell suggests they had been derived from anthropogenic sources. They probably represent levelling layers for the construction of B1. An area of heat affected natural (520) appears to predate the existence of a floor within B1.

THE BOUNDARY DITCH
On the eastern side of Area 3 (located beneath B6 and B7) was a north–south aligned ditch F85 with straight sides of moderate gradient and a flat base [8-115], measuring 2.40m wide and 0.80m deep (Fig. 1.8c). It narrowed to 0.80m wide and 0.50m deep providing a rounded end [8-121], and therefore terminated to the south of W26 of the post-medieval building B7.

The basal fill (8-116) in intervention [8-115] was a very thin (0.01m) wash of clay which must represent initial silting of the open feature. Over this, fills (8-117) (8-118) and (8-119) had accumulated and contained 12th century pottery and animal bone. In the terminal [8-121], the basal fill (8-122) also contained 12th century pottery. Above this was a fill (8-123) containing pottery assigned to the 12th–13th century. However, upper fills (8-119) and (8-124) contained pottery of the 13th–14th centuries indicating that F85 was filling during Phase 3 and after. Pit F100 cut linear F85, under W26 of B7. It was sub-circular in plan with concave sides of a steep gradient and a flat base, measuring 1.20m long by 1.85m wide and 0.85m deep. Its fills (16-109) and (16-110) contained no dateable material. Cutting F85 at a right angle, on a west-east alignment and between B6 and B7, was an undated linear feature F87 which in turn was cut by the similarly undated pits F88 and F89. These features may relate to later medieval activity and clearly must pre-date the post-medieval re-use of the area to the east of B1.

This large linear was a significant landscape feature, potentially providing an eastern boundary to the area containing the buildings and creating a courtyard area. The location of the terminal suggests the presence of an entryway to the south-east of B1. It could not be reliably traced to the north, and a matching ditch was not seen downslope where the main modern culvert ran through. It is worth noting that this ditch lay in a parallel orientation to both B1, the current eastern field boundary, and F80 which may have been the western court boundary, suggesting a relationship between the organisation of the buildings and the wider landscape. The initial silts of the boundary ditch exclusively contained pottery of the 12th century, which suggests that it was a feature associated with the initial laying out of the complex. The subsequent fills indicate that it was filling with material during the first stone-built phase of the complex, and that once the layout had been established it was no longer maintained.

Phase 3 – The first building phase – Buildings 1, 4 and 5 (c. 13th century AD)

The buildings in Area 3, by Cheryl Green
Buildings 4 and 5 appear to be the earliest recognizable

stone-built structures on the site, positioned at right-angles and flanking the remains of a cobbled limestone surface (F51) (Fig. 1.11; Fig. 1.12). This survived across an area measuring at least 25m long from west to east and 10m from north to south, the full extent removed by the modern service trenches and culvert. It probably relates to a yard, with B1 situated along the north side and completing a loose three-sided inner courtyard arrangement. A further yard area may have existed between the west end of B4 and the south end of B5, however this was difficult to differentiate from the overlying rubble (F46) that abutted the walls. Nevertheless, the juxtaposition of B4 and B5 indicates that they functioned as a unit, even though they were not structurally adjoined and not precisely aligned.

Detailed discussion of the possible purpose of these buildings is presented below (see Green, Chapter 6) and is summarised here. Building 5 has the hallmarks of a ground-floor open hall with a service wing to the south (low end) and a possible chamber to the north (high end); if the north chamber did not exist then an alternative might be a 'prototype' tripartite plan, comprising hall and service end. The function of B4 is unknown, although given the depth of the walls they are unlikely to have carried a first floor. The proximity of this building to the service end of B5 might suggest it housed the kitchen, the high risk of fire dictating that these were free-standing structures. The manorial residence, the chamber block, is represented by B1, the substantial and wide foundations indicating a building of two-storeys comprising an undercroft for storage with accommodation above.

Inevitably, the functions of these buildings would have evolved in response to the changing needs of the manor, particularly following the construction of B2 in Phase 4 encompassing a new hall and accommodation. Also, they would have been supplemented by a host of further structures serving other purposes, possibly all wooden although several sections of disembodied and undated walling were recorded during the excavations. Detailed accounts of the three main buildings are provided below.

BUILDING 5

Building 5 was situated at the base of the south-west facing limestone slope, with the stream on its western side. It comprised a series of discontinuous segments of wall, having suffered more extensive truncation and damage than elsewhere on the site (Fig. 1.13). As discussed above, a series of deposits and pits beneath B5 and the boundary wall contained material dated to the 10th–12th centuries and the 13th century, suggesting an earliest construction date during the 13th century. Indeed, the pottery associated most closely with the walls of the southern portion of the structure have a date range between the 13th–14th centuries.

The superimposition of walling relating to B2 of the subsequent Phase 4 over walling associated with B5 provides phasing evidence, even though there was a substantial gap between the buildings themselves. A well-constructed and substantial rubble wall (W42) ran northwards from near the possible north-west corner of B5, the southern section visible for a length of 9.40m with further intermittent sections extending up to 10m to the north. This was underlain by pits and deposits as discussed above and had been built within a 1.40m wide ditch F80 which may represent one side of the manorial boundary, subsequently formalised by W42 (Fig. 1.14). This ditch F80 contained a silty clay fill with cornbrash (13-112) and 13th century pottery. The orientation of W42 was slightly skewed from that of B5 but together they appear to have delineated the western side of the complex. This boundary W42 ran below three Phase 4 walls, the south end (W24) of B2, and two walls (W17 and W7) which shared the same orientation as B2. The southern end of the later boundary W7 bisected the northern part of B5, adding further weight to the argument that not only was B5 earlier than B2, but that B5 along with W42 were removed before B2 was constructed.

Two or possibly three separate elements are identifiable within B5, a large square central room, a narrow rectangular room to the south, and possibly a northern rectangular room. The evidence for the latter is solely derived from the short stretch of W6 extending northwards by 1.00m from W18 of B5 and overlain by the later boundary W7 (Fig. 1.15). This wall was deeper than W18, and therefore more akin to the main west wall (W39) with a slightly projecting plinthed foundation; as the upper courses had been removed by W7 it was not possible to ascertain if

Fig. 1.11 Phase 3.

Fig. 1.12   Aerial view across the medieval buildings, looking east.

W6 had been keyed-in to W18. Between W18 and the southern extent of the boundary W42 there would have been space for a northern room measuring *c.* 3.00m long internally, which is identical to the south room. However, the argument against the existence of the north room lies in the swathe of cobbling F51 sweeping in from the courtyard and covering this area, although the cobbling was not precisely dateable and may relate to Phase 4, after B5 had been demolished.

By excluding this postulated northern room, W18 would represent the north end of B5 as opposed to an internal partition, in which case the rectangular building would have measured 12m long internally. The width between the two side walls is 7.50m, however the short stub of the eastern W30 might relate to later modifications; comprising only a single course of stones, the inset position and the narrow width of 0.65m suggests it is more likely to be a later

adaption. As such, an alternative internal width of 8.00m might be derived from W18 itself.

All of the walls were faced with coursed limestone slabs and rubble around a core comprising small limestone rubble, bonded with firm soil. They generally survived from between a single course up to a height of four courses. Neither W18 nor the possible east W30 had any foundations, although W18 was substantial at 0.80m wide.

The large central room is of sufficient dimensions to be a square or approximately square hall; this was defined by a west wall (W39) measuring 1.00m wide with a slightly projecting external foundation within a cut. The foundation plinth widened to 0.30m at the north end (Fig. 1.16) and may relate to a buttress or structural support for a feature such as a lateral fireplace. The north end of the wall had been removed by a culvert therefore the

N

boundary wall

wall 42

ditch
F80

cobbled courtyard
F51

wall 6

?chamber

wall 18

wall 18

?later wall

wall 30

Building 5

wider
foundation
plinth

wall 39

hall

doorway

cross passage

wall 38

?counter

service rooms

wall 31

rubble
F46

?yard

0   5m

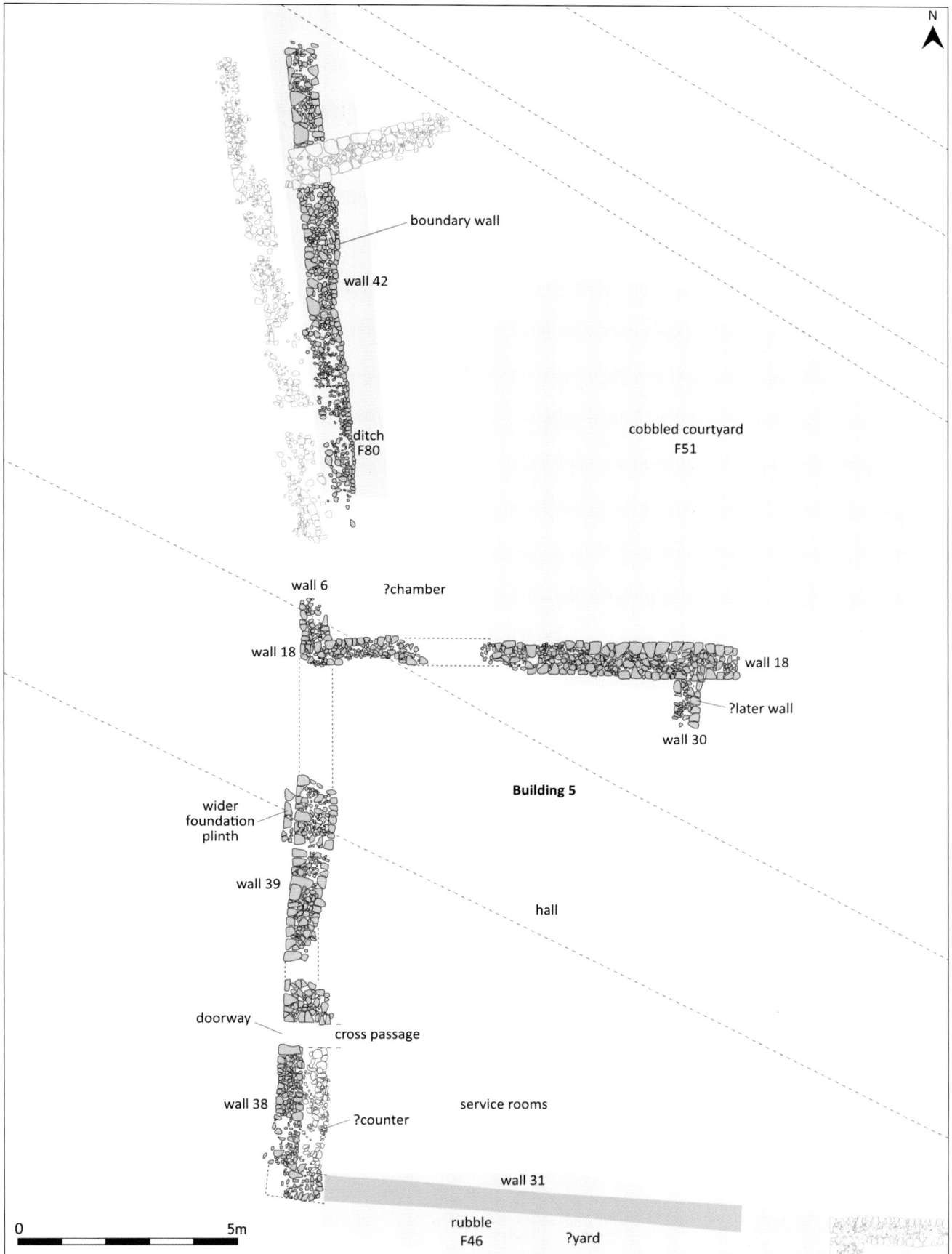

Fig. 1.13   Building 5 plan.

wall 5 — section a

20.96m
AOD

W

E

wall 6

(14-109)

(14-107)

F79
[14-106]

(14-104)

(14-110)

F80
[14-108]

(14-111)

section b

21.15m
AOD

N

S

wall 3

(9-104)

(9-103)

(9-105)

(9-106)

section c

21.?3m
AOD

N

S

section d

21.55m
AOD

WNW

ESE

(12-111)

(12-112)

(12-110)

(12-113)

F19
[12-108]

(12-109)

(12-114)

(12-115)

wall 3

(12-116)

section e

E

21.81m
AOD

W

(13-103)

(13-103)

(13-101)

F9
[13-100]

(13-102)

section f

21.34m
ACD

NE

SW

(12-101)

(12-102) #

(12-103)

F16
[12-100]

section g

22.20m
AOD

N

S

(12-105)

F11
[12-104]

stones

animal bone

pottery

roof tile

charcoal

mortar

0   1m

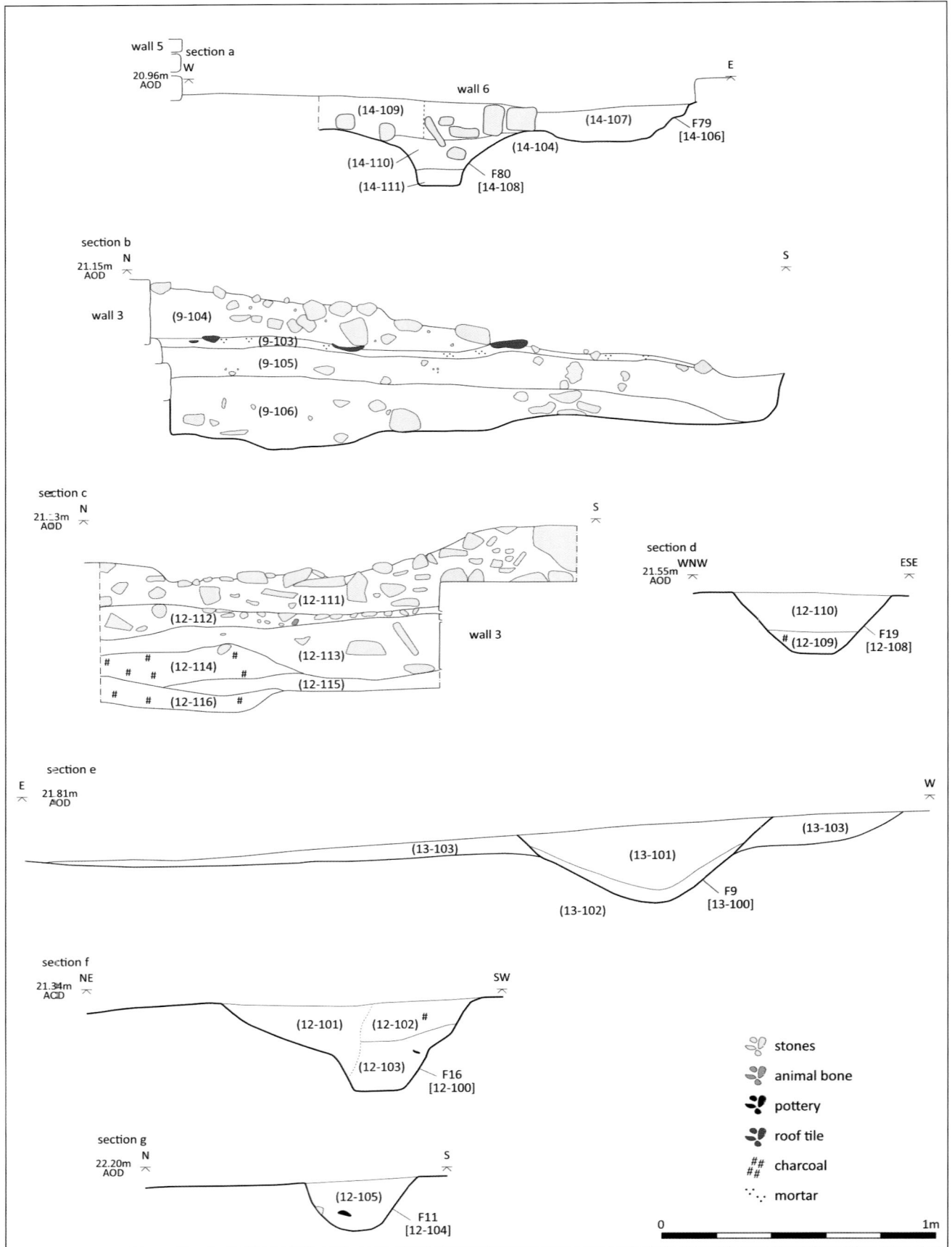

Fig. 1.14   Section drawings showing features and deposits beneath and within B5, B2 and ditches in Area 2.

Fig. 1.15 Detail of B5 showing W18 and W6 below W7, looking south-south-east (1 x 0.5m and 1 x 2m scales).

relationship with W18 could not be established. Nevertheless, the top of the foundation plinth indicates the internal floor level confirming that W18 was constructed at a slightly higher level, the inference being that the north end was raised. A short eastern return at the south end is evidenced by a lined face, directly opposite the faced side of W38 of the south room (Fig. 1.16 and Fig. 1.17). This relates to an entrance, albeit very narrow at only 0.50m wide.

The west wall (W38) of the south room was narrower, measuring only 0.67m wide, and utilized slightly smaller stones for the rubble facing. The difference in construction might suggest that the south room was either added to provide a service end or that the build was different, such as a lean-to. The south wall (W31) continued for a short distance, eastwards from W38 and although the remainder had been robbed the rubble spread F46 delineated the line of this wall. Another wall ran along the full length of the western side of the south room. As this was contained by the south wall W31, it is suggested that this may have

formed the base of an internal structure, perhaps for a counter; this would be in keeping with a buttery or pantry which were typically accommodated within the service end. Alternatively, it may have provided a foundation for a staircase.

Despite being able to establish the level of the floor horizon within B5, the overlying deposits were difficult to associate with its primary use. This might be because it was superseded by B2, with the immediate area put to some other use. The only deposit linked with collapse or demolition within B5 was an area of rubble (12-137), lying to the north of and probably derived from W18, containing fragments of stone roof tile and pottery dated to the 13th–14th centuries.

BUILDING 4
Building 4 co-existed with Building 5 and was probably constructed within the same period, forming the south side of the inner courtyard. This fits with the dating evidence provided by a deposit (15-115) underlying B4 which contained 12th century

pottery, along with 12th–13th century pottery associated with the north wall (W32).

With the exception of the north-east corner which had been removed by the modern culvert, the plan was intact outlining a simple rectangular stone building aligned precisely east to west (Fig. 1.18). Internally this measured 13.22m long and 4.55m wide giving a length to width ratio of c. 3:1. The lateral walls (W32 and W34) measured between 0.55m and 0.66m, and the end walls (W33 and W37) between 0.66m and 0.77m. The masonry was keyed-in at the three surviving corners and relates to a single construction phase. They were all neatly built of coursed limestone slabs and rubble around a core comprising small limestone rubble bonded with clay soil and survived up to six courses (Fig. 1.19). An external plinth, three courses deep, was present along the exterior of W34 alone indicating the presence of a foundation, although the other three walls extended to the same depth and therefore also had foundations (Fig. 1.20). These rested directly above the natural colluvium with no evidence of foundation trenches.

A short stub of wall (W35) measuring 0.60m wide abutted the north lateral wall (also cut through by the culvert) and probably relates to the west side of a small porch situated slightly west of centre, the opposing side having been lost. This did not have the same depth of footings, resting on pebbly material which may have been an earlier ground surface. The walling immediately east of W35 was lower and probably relates to the threshold. Two drainage openings had been constructed within the base of the foundation for the south wall (W34), capped by stone slabs.

The external foundation plinth of W34 indicates the level of the internal floor horizon. No traces of this floor remained, the accumulated soils within the building directly overlying the earlier ditches that ran beneath the building, with no apparent interior divisions. The finds were similar to those recovered from the other buildings, and do not assist with interpreting the function of this building. However, the possible yard between the west end of B4 and the south side of B5 might suggest the two buildings were connected by a working area or perhaps even a covered walkway.

Another possible wall (F48) was located to the east of Building 4. It may represent the south-west corner of another building which had been largely removed by the modern culvert. Despite the fragmentary remains and the absence of dateable finds, it appears to share the same orientation as B4 and therefore may be associated with the manorial courtyard.

BUILDING 1
Building 1 was a substantial structure situated on the upper part of the sloping ground towards the eastern side of the Site and enjoyed a dominant position within the courtyard overlooking B4 and B5 (Fig. 1.21). Material from beneath B1 indicates that it was constructed no earlier than the 13th century, matching the broad dates for B4 and B5. A small rectangular building B6 dated as post-medieval was situated immediately east of B1, with a cobbled path along the east side, and constructed on the same alignment (Fig. 1.22 and Fig. 1.23). A robber trench F104 meant it was impossible to ascertain if the buildings were connected however it certainly appears as if B6 was added to B1 or at least respected it. The implication is that B1 was extant for several centuries, proving that it co-existed with the Phase 4 B2, although it must have been a ruin prior to the construction of B3 which ran across it. Although none of the buildings is depicted on historic maps (the earliest dating to 1792), the recovery of 19th–20th century pottery from within the backfill of the robber trench F104 suggests that some walling was either still extant until modern times or was perhaps causing an obstacle.

The rectangular plan was relatively intact with internal measurements of 14.30m long and 7.22m wide, giving a length to width ratio of c. 2:1 (Fig. 1.21). The approximate east to west alignment was skewed very slightly anti-clockwise from B4 and B5. The lateral walls (W8 and W9) measured 0.83m–0.97m deep, the west end wall (W19) was very deep at 1.25m–1.38m, while the east end wall had mostly been robbed (F104) but appears to have had a considerable depth of 1.11m. The walls comprised a rubble core faced with random coursed limestone with silty clay bonding material. Only W20 appeared to have a shallow foundation within a construction cut [16-103] filled with silty clay (16-

Fig. 1.16 West side of B5 showing area of widened plinth foundation and narrow doorway into service end, looking south-east (1 x 1m and 1 x 2m scales).

112) and producing pottery assigned to the 13th century. The rest of the walling lay directly on the natural underlying colluvium or bedrock, or some undated deposits.

The north wall (W8) survived to two courses high, although most of the central part was missing. The south wall (W9) was extant for up to six courses; the removal of walling associated with a later building (B3) across W9 exposed an approximately centrally placed ground level entrance c. 1m wide (Fig. 1.24). Despite the absence of walling along much of the north side of the building, it seems unlikely that there was another door accessing the undercroft. The upper floor would probably have been accessed from an external staircase, of which no firm evidence remains. A small remnant of pitched stones alongside the exterior eastern side may provide a tentative

indication for a stair foundation, but this could equally relate to structural support for a lateral fireplace.

The west wall (W19) was only three courses high, with part of the south end removed by an evaluation trench. By contrast, W20 was extant for up to seven courses, with the lower couple of courses relating to the foundation. With the exception of the north-east and south-east corners of the building, which had been subject to robbing (F104), the walls were keyed-in to one another and therefore of one construction phase. All four walls incorporated occasional heat-affected stones, some of which displayed quarry marks, suggesting the material was derived from another building possibly on the site itself. To the west of W19 were two abutments (510) and (511) measuring 0.70m and 1.38m long respectively, and up to 0.70m wide. These may represent lateral buttresses as opposed to an additional room at the west end of B1; although the southern projection was cut through by a modern service trench, there was no evidence that the northern projection continued any further to the west.

No internal floor was identified within B1 although the underlying bedrock was close to the surface in places and would have provided a natural base. The horizon at which an infant burial (F74) was cut from indicates the floor was not far off, even though the burial was slightly truncated (see below). There were no apparent interior divisions although if F82 and F83 were contemporary with B1 (see above) they may have related to supports for a first floor. A further single post-hole F75 below (W9) was located beside the western side of the south doorway and provides the tantalising possibility that B1 replaced an earlier timber structure.

The deposits and features, by Clare Randall
AREA 3

The most significant feature associated with B1 was a small circular cut F74 [14-100] dug into the underlying natural deposits, most likely through the original floor level of B1, close to the southern wall (W9). Within this, the lower portion of a pottery vessel (14-101) remained *in situ*. The vessel can be dated to the 13th century and contained the remains of an infant (Fig. 1.25 and Fig. 1.26; Randall, Chapter 3). Along the eastern side of W8 and running parallel, offset from it to the north by 0.30–0.40m, was a gully F111. The cut [16-104] had convex sides and a tapered base measuring 2.00m long by 0.25m wide and 0.05m deep. It cut the natural bedrock, and was overlain by subsoil, contained no dateable material and had no stratigraphic relationship with W8, but may have served a drainage function channelling water away from the wall.

On the exterior of B1, were layers of compacted cornbrash pebbles (516), (517) and (518) on the north, west and south sides of the building respectively. Rounded on the upper surface, these appear to have provided a partly cobbled surface or pathway which wrapped around the building, stratigraphically later, but probably contemporary with its use. It was not observed on the eastern side, but this may relate to it having been destroyed or obscured by the later

Fig. 1.17 West side of B5 showing narrow doorway between hall and service end, looking north-east (1 x 1m and 1 x 2m scales).

wall 37

drainage opening

Building 4

wall 34

drainage opening

wall 35

?porch

wall 32

wall 33

F46

yard

N

0 5m

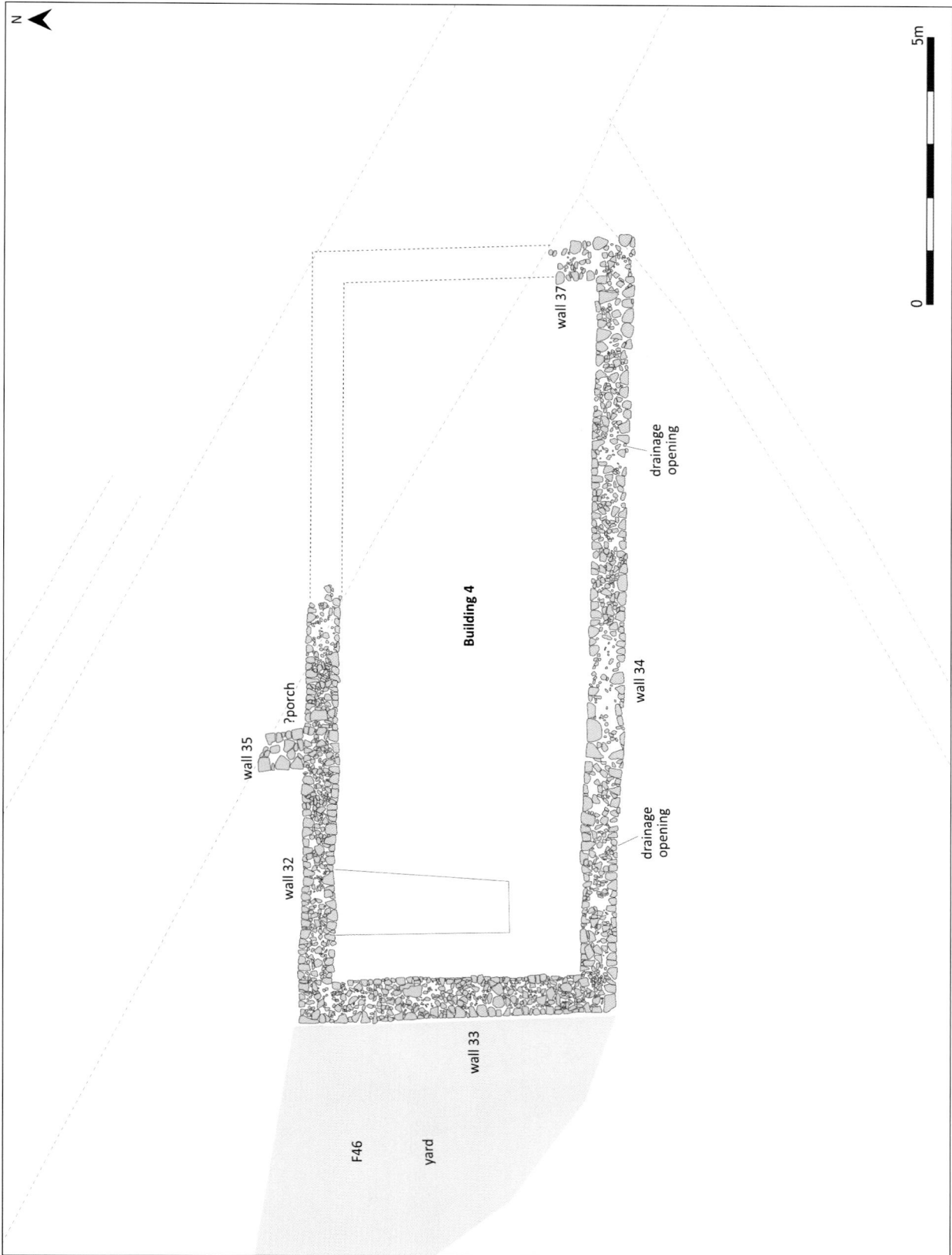

Fig. 1.18 Building 4 plan.

Fig. 1.19 B4 with porch and door threshold indicating approximate level of floor, looking west (1 x 1m and 1 x 2m scales).

Fig. 1.20 B4 showing foundation plinth along south wall looking north-east (1 x 2m scale).

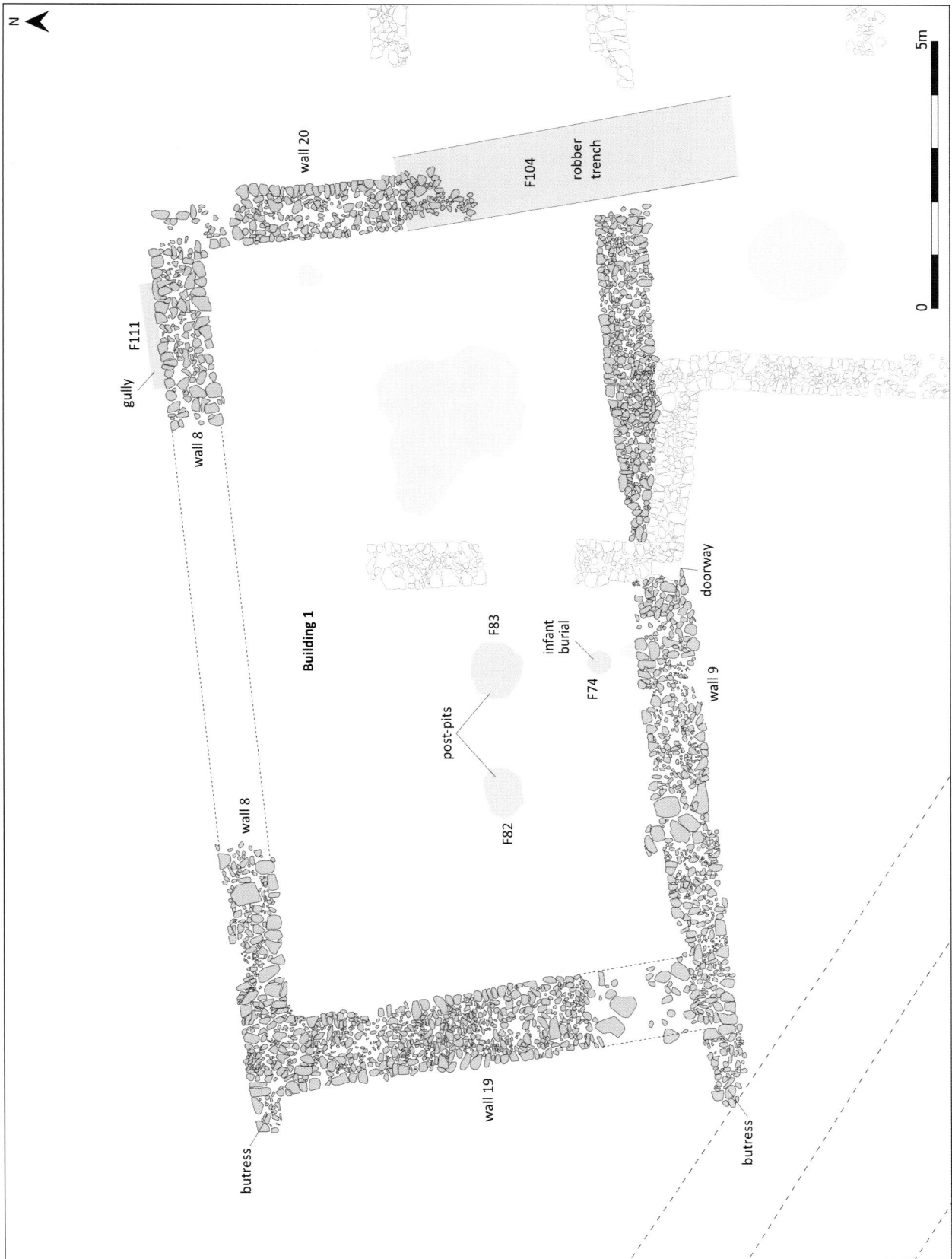

Fig. 1.21 Building 1 plan.

Fig. 1.22 Aerial view of B1 and later buildings.

structures built in this area. A round pit F102 was situated to the south of the east end of B1, cutting a pocket of colluvium overlying the cornbrash natural but with no stratigraphical relationship with nearby deposits. It measured almost 2m in diameter and c. 0.30m deep with gently sloping convex sides and a rounded base. The single fill contained no finds and it is not clear which of the neighbouring buildings it may have been associated with or what its function may have been. It was possibly related to the construction of B1, which is why it has been included here.

Nearer the western side of the manorial complex, a gully (F81) ran south-westwards from the west side of the northern end of ditch F80 and might represent a drainage feature. At the northern end of F80/boundary W42, immediately to the east and running parallel, was a linear F79 with concave sides and a flat base measuring 0.95m wide. The fill (14-107) produced pottery dating to the 13th–14th

century, animal bone, metal, CBM and oyster shell. This may have been a pathway alongside the wall, although it is possible that it represents one side of another structure (perhaps wooden), certainly earlier than B2.

To the north of B5, a series of deposits appear to have formed during the period of its use, also underlying B2. At the base of the observed sequence was a very dark grey and yellowish-brown silty clay (12-116) with frequent charcoal, at least 0.10m thick. It contained pottery of the 12th–13th centuries, bone and marine shell fragments, and was waterlogged. It may represent an accumulation of refuse within a hollow in the underlying geology. Above this was a thin, greyish-brown silt clay layer (12-115) with no artefactual material which may represent an episode of flooding. This was overlain by a charcoal rich silty clay layer (12-114) varying between 0.02m and 0.13m thick and containing pottery that was no earlier than the 13th century. The uppermost deposit comprised

Fig. 1.23   View across B1 with post-medieval building B6 and adjacent cobbled path in foreground, looking west (1 x 1m and 1 x 2m scales).

Fig. 1.24   Position of south door in B1, with B3 cutting through, looking west-north-west (1 x 1m and 1 x 2m scales).

extensive degraded cornbrash and greyish sandy clay (12-113) with a variable depth (c. 0.06–0.32m), yielding animal bone and pottery of a similar date. A similar deposit (9-106) was seen beneath a possible floor in the southern room of B2, adjacent to W3, also containing pottery of 12th–13th century date and possibly equivalent to the deposits seen on the north side of the wall.

AREA 2, THE WESTERN SLOPE

The western slope contained numerous cut features. This was dominated by ditches, with a small number of pits on the lower slope and a number of other deposits. A total of 20 ditches were mapped and nine excavated. Some of these (e.g. F13, Fig. 1.5) crossed the length of the site, whereas there were other shorter and more ephemeral sections. All of the excavated examples appear to be medieval in date and were similar in character. They were generally of modest width, shallow depth, with concave sides and sloping bases, and backfilled with greyish brown or yellowish-brown silty clays, usually with sparse stone inclusions, which often had diffuse boundaries with the surrounding subsoil. They were consistent with agricultural boundaries. The small amounts of pottery recovered from the fills indicates activity dating from the 12th–13th centuries onward, suggesting an inception of boundary provision which was probably broadly contemporaneous with the initial building phase. The complexity of the boundaries, and the inclusion of ceramics of the 13th–14th centuries indicates that elements of the system continued in use through the later phase of the manorial centre. The contents of this network of boundaries and its total period of use therefore spans Phases 3 and 4. Dating is in some cases tentative as there were only small quantities of dateable material from within well sealed contexts.

Ditch F16 [12-100] was aligned north-west to south-east with undulating sides of a steep gradient and a flat base, measuring 1.2m wide and 0.48m deep (Fig. 1.14). The sequence of fills was more complex than most with a series of three silty clays (12-103), (12-102) and (12-101) defined only by slight colour differences. The lower two fills contained a small amount of exclusively 12th or 12th–13th century pottery. At its northern end this ditch met

F9, although the stratigraphic relationship was not discerned. This ditch [13-100] (Fig. 1.14e) was aligned north–south with concave sides of gentle to moderate gradient and a concave base, measuring 0.85m wide and 0.28m deep. This contained two fills (13-102) and (13-101) similar to those within F16, and a small quantity of 13th century pottery.

Ditch F1 ran across almost the entire width of Area 2 on a north-west to south-east orientation. It was not sampled during the excavation but measured 1.20m wide and was recorded during the evaluation by Cotswold Archaeology as feature [507]. That was described as having shallow, gentle sides, being 0.74m in width and 0.08m deep, with a single fill (506) of light to mid grey-brown silty clay with very occasional small sub-rounded quartz and flint pebbles (Cotswold Archaeology 2003, 10). This yielded two sherds of pottery assigned to the 12th–13th century (Cotswold Archaeology 2003, 6), and a small amount of 13th century pottery was recovered from the surface of F1 during the excavation. At its southern end it was intersected by ditch F10, also unexcavated but examined during the Cotswold Archaeology evaluation as feature [505]. Aligned north–south, it was described as having moderately sloping sides, being 0.66m in width and 0.21m in depth, with a single fill (504) of firm mid grey-yellow silty clay with charcoal flecks and occasional flint nodules which contained eight sherds of pottery of 11th century to mid-13th century date. It was noted that the similarity of the fills meant that it was not possible to ascertain which of the two ditches was the earlier feature (Cotswold Archaeology 2003, 6). It was apparent from the surface that F10 was a recut or extension to ditch F9, which contained 13th century pottery. The close dates of the material from these features does not assist in providing a sequence, but instead suggests that these features were in some cases contemporary or represent short-lived reorganisation of the landscape.

A substantial ditch F21 was visible as two sides positioned at right angles to each other. The northern part was aligned north-north-east to south-south-west and was traceable for 24.70m, with a rounded return towards the south-east of at least 12.50m long. It had concave sides of moderate gradient and a concave base [11-100] and was 1.25m

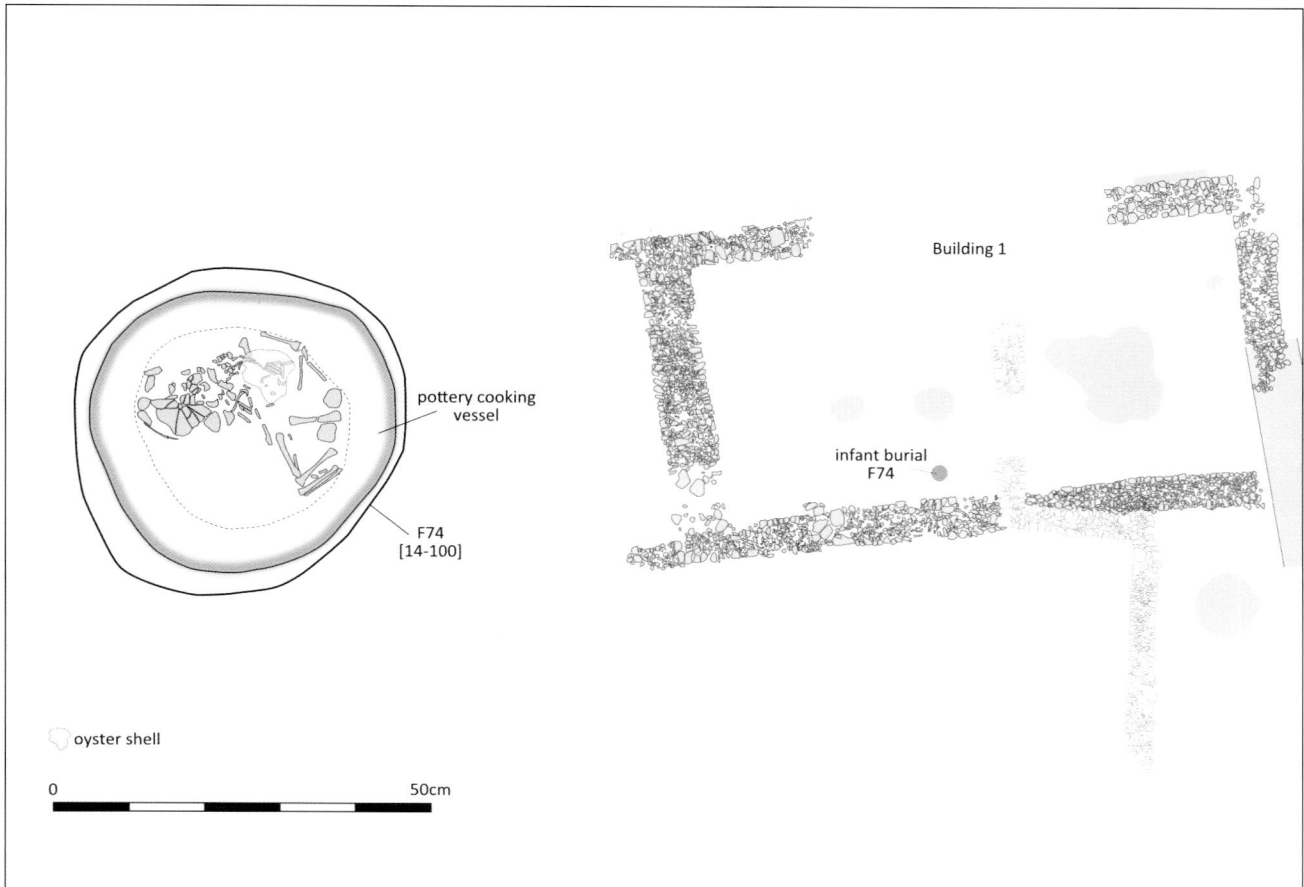

Fig. 1.25   Plan identifying the location of the infant burial within B1.

wide and 0.4m deep. The basal fill (11-102) included rare, weathered flint gravel, 0.25m deep. The upper fill (11-101) was similar and contained flecks of degraded medieval pottery and animal bone. F73 was visible on the surface as a linear, running parallel with and to the south of the southern portion of F21 with a gap of 0.60m. The cut [11-110] had irregular edges and irregular sides and base, 0.50m wide and generally less than 0.10m deep. It contained a single fill (11-111) which contained residual flint and a small amount of pottery of 13th–14th century date. Given the irregularity of the feature, it seems that rather than representing a deliberately cut feature, this may be a hollow formed by animal trampling around the outside of F21 creating a routeway.

Situated in the south-western corner of Area 2, at the top of the rise was F70. This was a rectangular terrace [10-116] aligned north–south with a concave west edge, where the ground had been terraced into the

hillside leaving a relatively flat base. It was roughly 12.24m by 20.56m in extent and the soils which filled it were c. 0.40m deep. This accumulation (10-117) of silty clay contained rare flint and limestone gravels. It was noted that the fill was darker towards the base, and the irregularity of the surface and diffuse boundary with the subsoil was suggestive of either bioturbation or trampling. This fill contained pottery of 13th century date and a single Romano-British sherd. The orientation of this terrace accords with the alignment of F13 and parallel ditches. The relationship of this area to the field boundaries is difficult to discern, as it seems to have had no direct stratigraphic relationships with any of the medieval linears. It was defined on its eastern side by ditch F2, but whether this was the original arrangement or F2 came to define it cannot be established. It may have been a feature of some longevity, as it appears to have remained on the 'outside' of the area of more intense activity.

Fig. 1.26 Infant burial within pottery vessel, inside B1 (looking S).

North–south aligned ditch F13 [20-103] ran the entire length of Area 2, exiting the north and south edges of the site. It appears to be a significant organising feature. A section through the ditch at the north end indicated that it had steeply sloping sides and a rounded base, measuring c. 0.40m wide and c. 0.40m deep. It contained a single fill (20-101) of dark brown silty clay. Pottery dated to the 13th century was recovered from this location and further sherds dated to the 13th–14th century were collected from the surface of F13 elsewhere. Undated ditch F12 ran closely parallel to F13 immediately on its east side, measuring 0.60m wide and 0.40m deep, with concave sides and a rounded base [20-104]. The single fill (20-102) was very similar to that in ditch F13, which is only 0.50m to the west, but given the lack of stratigraphic relationship or dateable material it may represent an earlier or later version of F13, although a tentative later date might be postulated from its apparent extension at the southern end as ditch F3.

Ditch F11 [12-104] was aligned approximately west-north-west to east-south-east with undulating sides of moderate gradient and an irregular base, measuring 0.4m wide and 0.2m deep (Fig. 1.14g). The single fill (12-105) comprised firm silty clay with rare stones, yielding a small amount of 13th century pottery. Ditch F19 intersected with F11, aligned south-south-west to north-north-east with concave sides of moderate gradient and a sloping base [12-108], measuring 0.57m wide and 0.22m deep (Fig. 1.14d). The initial fill (12-109) contained undiagnostic flint. The upper fill (12-110) contained more flint and a single sherd of pottery of 12th–13th century date.

Ditch F8 shared the same alignment as F11 and was located on the western side of F13, intersecting with it but not continuing beyond it. This feature was not excavated, but it contained highly similar clay silt fills to those in F13 and was 1.35m wide. On the eastern side of F9 was ditch F14, measuring 1.20m wide and positioned on exactly the same alignment and therefore probably a continuation of F8. At its eastern end it was obscured by the fringes of the midden spread (10-108). Just to the north of F14 was ditch F15, another parallel linear of 1.10m width. This also seemed to originate to the west of F9 and

ended to the west of the midden spread. Neither of these features were excavated and remain undated.

Adjacent to the southern edge of the site were two parallel ditches aligned approximately east–west and 1.25m apart. F5 had concave sides of moderate gradient and a concave base [11-107] and measured 0.75m wide and 0.30m deep. It had a single fill (11-108) of firm silt clay with rare flint gravel and manganese flecks and yielded an undated metal object. F6 had concave sides of moderate gradient and a flat base [11-105], measuring 1.04m wide and 0.23m deep. The single fill (11-106) contained a few sherds of medieval pottery of 13th century or later date. There were also a few residual sherds of Black Burnished ware.

Ditches F2 and F3 extended northwards from the southern boundary of Area 2. F2 was generally aligned north-north-west to south-south-east, altering to a more southerly course near the excavation baulk where it appeared to recut F13. It measured c. 1.10m wide and 0.50m deep, with irregular gently sloping sides and an irregular base [20-105], and a single fill (20-106) of silty clay with occasional gravels and rare larger limestones. F3 ran for 33.20m on a north-north-west to south-south-east orientation, largely parallel to F2 and separated from it by 7.55m. It was c. 1.40m wide and c. 0.40m deep, with irregular gently sloping sides and a flat, but irregular base [20-107] with a single fill (20-108). No finds were recovered from either feature. About halfway along the length of F3 it was met at right-angles by ditch F4, which was not excavated. At its northern end it intersected with ditches F12 and F1 at the point where those two features met.

Two pits were identified in Area 2. An isolated pit F18 situated south of F16 was sub-circular in plan, with undulating sides of moderate gradient and a sloping base [12-106] and measuring 0.41m by 0.70m and 0.07m deep. The single fill (12-107) contained no dateable material. To the south-east and apparently cut by ditch F23, pit F20 remained unexcavated. The full extent of this feature was not seen as, at its north end, it intersected with the midden spread (10-108) and to the south the rubble deposits associated with B8. F23 was on a north-north-east to south-south-west alignment which differed from the other linears. However, it is worth noting that it would have intersected with F1 on a right angle if it extended far enough. The relationship with ditch F11, the eastern end of which it crossed, was unclear and no finds were attributed to it.

The eastern third of Area 2 (extending into the southern part of Area 1) contained a deep and extensive deposit (2005)/(10-108). This was located across the base of the slope through the valley base. It was deepest at the lowest point of the valley and had been divided by the modern culvert, which both delineated it to the east, and cut through it between Area 1 and 2. As such, the extent was difficult to discern but it covered an area of at least 33.80m by 79.30m. It was shallower towards its edges, blending with surrounding deposits and subsoils, and appeared to have been spread from a point of origin in the centre of the site. The deposit itself was a dark yellowish grey firm silty clay containing frequent charcoal flecks and comminuted ceramics, shell and bone. The pottery from this deposit can be dated to the 13th and 13th–14th centuries. Three test pits were excavated through this deposit in the valley base and in places it was seen to be c. 0.70m deep. The deposit had the appearance of a midden accumulation, with a mixture of bone, pottery and charred organic components. The highly comminuted microartefacts and bone suggest a heavily reworked deposit (Randall, Chapter 4). This should be considered alongside the way in which the material appears to have been spread through the base of the valley, including into the remains of what may have been the northern extension of the holloway, creating a level surface which peters out at the edges where the subsoil rises up the slope. The density of finds was greater than one would expect from a manured agricultural soil. The best explanation for this deposit is that it is the remnant of a midden heap contemporary with but situated outside of both the complex of buildings and the cultivated land. It subsequently spread through the valley base, possibly by ploughing but also probably during flooding episodes.

SUMMARY
While more than one phase of activity can be discerned across Area 2, the relatively narrow date range of the ceramics associated with some of the features, and the general presence of this pottery across the area, makes it difficult to assign individual features to more clearly defined phases. The undated ditches and gullies are all likely to be medieval in date and should be considered in relation to the excavated features which provide some dateable material. There is tentative evidence for the inception of this activity in the 12th–13th centuries, but the exact pattern, phasing and contemporaneity of particular features is unclear. What does seem to be the case is that the nature of the fills and density of finds within them is consistent with the type of silting of field ditches with manured soils from the ploughzones of the enclosures. This implies that whatever the nuances of subsequent arrangements, the use of these bounded enclosures ceased probably during the 14th century or shortly after.

Having accepted the limitations of the dating of individual elements, some observations can be made. Both square and narrow strip enclosures are suggested at different times as well as what appears to be a more specific type of enclosure. Some putative ideas of how the arrangements may have changed over the course of Phases 3 and 4 are shown at Fig. 1.27. This is suggested from the limited stratigraphic and dating evidence and on the possibilities of relationships based on alignment and orientation.

When considering the entire network of features the north–south oriented ditches F13 and F9 and associated features appear to dominate the layout. However, they may not represent the earliest organisation. Whilst the stratigraphic relationships were not entirely clear, there are reasons to suspect that two parallel linears F1 and F16, may constitute the initial phase of boundary making (Fig. 1.27 Stage 1). Whilst the dating evidence from F1 and F16 is limited, they did contain pottery of the 12th–13th centuries. The two features were on a north-west to south-east alignment, suggesting that they were contemporary. Ditch F16 appeared attached to F9 but did not seem to cross it. The stratigraphic relationship between the two was not established. The stratigraphic relationships of F1 are also unclear despite it intersecting with several features associated with the north–south arrangement (F13, F12, F3 and F10, discussed below). If those linears defined a trackway, the eastern extent of F1 appears to have run across it and so could not be contemporary with its use. However, if F1 was an earlier feature in its entirety, it could have influenced the orientation of later boundaries. The western extent of F1 could have remained in use, even if a track was imposed over its eastern extent. If F1 provided an early organising principle the fragmentary and undated F23 could have formed a right angle creating a subdivision between F1 and F16.

The alignment of F1/F16 also appears to have influenced the layout of the isolated right-angled enclosure F21. The southern side of F21 respects the alignment of F1, although there is no evidence that F1 extended as far as F21. It seems unlikely that F23 could have existed at the same time as the enclosure, so it could be that F21 is a slightly later imposition. The irregular sided F73 which ran around the outside of F21 may have something to add to the understanding of the relationship between features. It was shallow and irregular in both plan and its surface, which is strongly suggestive of it having developed from animal trampling rather than a deliberately cut feature. It appears to have developed as a routeway around the outside of the area defined by F21. It could be envisaged as feeding into a system of enclosures, and if followed to the south-east, would intersect with the valley bottom holloway. The rectilinear enclosure itself might be most understandable as some form of corral. It is in this light that we should perhaps consider the large terrace F70, situated to the west towards the top of the rise. This also had indications of trampling by livestock. A functional relationship might therefore be suggested between these features.

In Stage 2 (Fig. 1.27), the substantial ditch F13 which crossed the entire length of Area 2 on a north–south alignment, seemed to provide the major organising element. F13 ran largely along the contour but it was also parallel with the base of the valley.

It was on the same orientation as the holloway F28 identified in Area 1, which is most likely the northern continuation of the holloway preserved in earthworks to the south of the excavation area (Fig. 1.28). To the east of F13 was the parallel ditch F9 (possibly recut in its southern extent as F10). It was separated from F13 by 6.35m. Together they could have defined a track, oriented on a parallel alignment to the earthwork/F28 holloway, located c. 50m to its western side. It is possible that F16 and the western extent of F1 could have continued in use after the creation of the central trackway. It is also possible that the enclosure F21 continued in use during this second stage, as the routeway F73 would have funnelled traffic towards the north–south track.

A complicating factor is the further parallel feature, the undated ditch F12. This could have been either an earlier version of F13 or a re-establishment of this alignment. It is suggested here that the latter may be the case (Fig. 1.27 Stage 3) due to the relationship of F12 with a possible extension at the southern end, F3. Considerable rearrangement appears to have occurred at the southern extent. This includes the potential re-cutting of F9 by F10 and the appending of F3 to the southern end of F12. These features seemed to reflect a slight change in orientation. The right-angled ditch F4 which was attached to the side of F3 may indicate a small pen or paddock, possibly representing a change in farming approach.

Further elements probably represent another reorganisation as they were on a clearly different orientation. The limited dating material available from this group of features, has a range covering the 13th–14th centuries, tentatively suggesting that this arrangement may be late in the sequence (Fig. 1.27 Stage 4). Ditches F8 and F14 are on the same alignment. F8/F14 are parallel with F15 to the north and F11 to the south. F11 seems to have an associated right-angled boundary, F19. This series of boundaries are also arranged in parallel with F5 and F6 near the southern edge of Area 2. Between them this group of features seems to represent a series of small land parcels arranged in strip form, running across the slope and downhill, possibly aligned between a trackway defined by F9/F10, and the holloway in the base of the valley (Fig. 1.28).

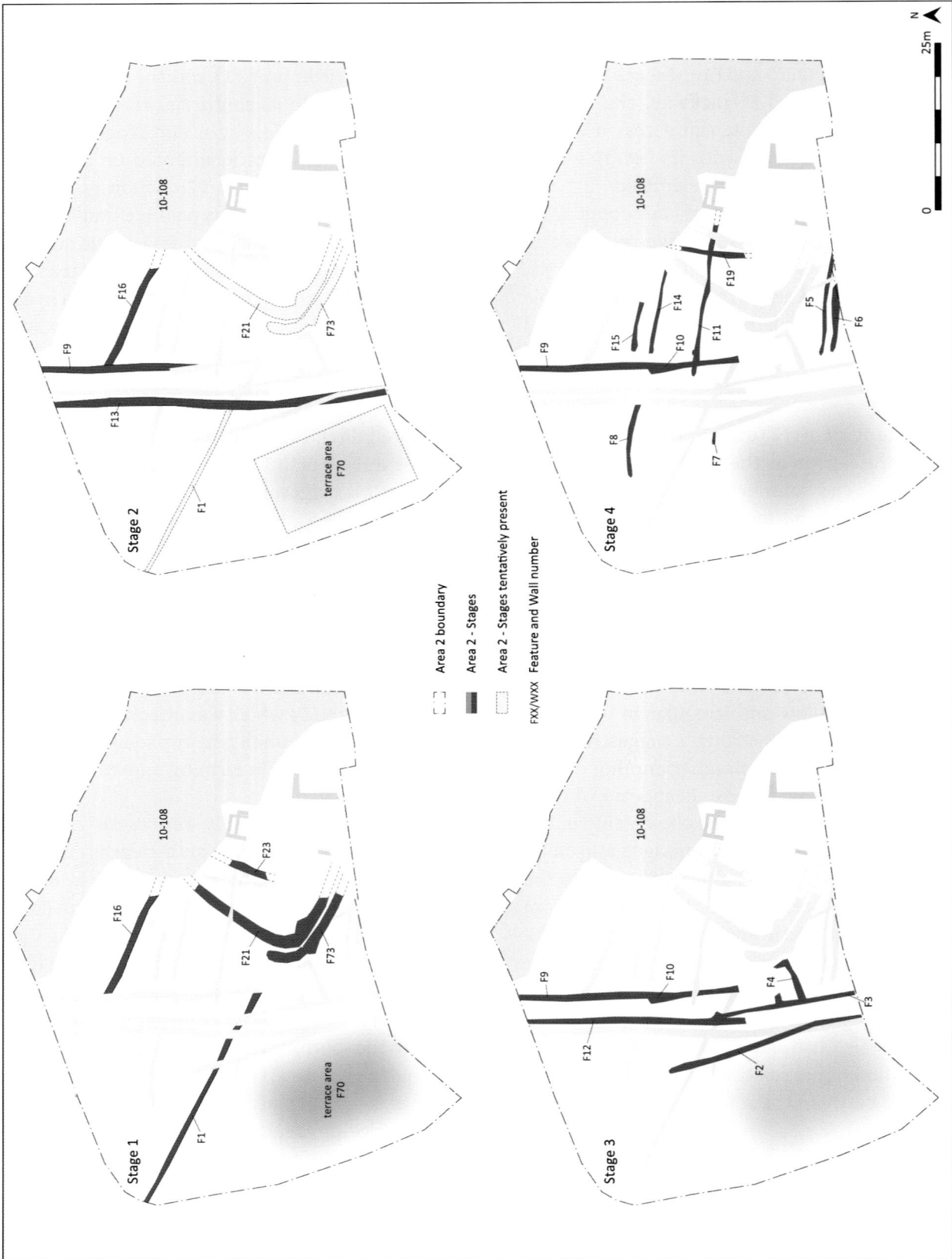

Fig. 1.27   Suggested stages of development of agricultural boundaries in Area 2.

If something on this broad sequence occurred between the 12th and 14th centuries, we might imagine an initial arrangement of fairly widely spaced linear parcels, added to by an area suitable for livestock handling. This may have been added to or replaced by spaces dependent on the north–south trackway. A re-organisation or re-establishment of boundaries may then have occurred, with the addition of at least one smaller pen or paddock. This then seems to have been replaced by more narrowly arranged strip cultivation. One thing which does seem clear is that there was an imperative to alter the way in which this relatively small patch of agricultural landscape was used several times within a limited duration, and this included consideration of the needs of livestock husbandry as well as cropping.

Phase 4 – The re-building phase – Building 2 and continued use of Buildings 1, 4 and agricultural boundaries (*c*. Late 13th–14th centuries AD)

The buildings in Area 3, by Cheryl Green

Building 2 is the last recognisable building dated to the medieval period. Constructed northwards of the Phase 3 buildings B5 and B4, but downslope from the chamber block B1, it represents expansion of the manor in that direction (Fig. 1.29). It was positioned slightly westwards of and at a skewed angle to the former west range (B5), which it is argued was demolished prior to the construction of B2. The presence of a water channel and what appears to have been a holloway would have prevented any significant expansion westwards. Detailed discussion of the possible purpose of this building is presented in Chapter 6 and is summarised here. The plan comprises two equally sized rectangular rooms divided by a cross-passage formed against a solid dividing wall, the eastern entrance enclosed by a grand porch (Fig. 1.30). Finds from underlying deposits and features (see above) indicate an earliest possible construction date in the 13th century. Assuming that the larger, southern room would have been sub-divided, B2 typifies the later medieval houses that began to appear in the late 13th and 14th centuries, bringing the functions of hall and accommodation under one roof.

The building had an elongated rectangular plan on a north-north-west to south-south-east alignment with internal dimensions of 20m long and 5m wide, giving a length to width ratio of 4:1 (Fig. 1.31). A substantial dividing wall (W3) separated the north and south rooms (Fig. 1.32), with an adjacent 1.67m wide doorway leading from the porch (Fig. 1.33). A lined face at the west end of the cross-passage wall and the absence of walling above foundation level at the north end of the west wall (W5) indicates an opposing narrower doorway, leading to a cobbled pathway which hugged the exterior of the building (Fig. 1.34). This seems to be supported by a large flagstone found *in situ* immediately outside the supposed threshold. These doorways suggest the presence of a cross-passage, the south side presumably provided by a timber partition for which no evidence survived. This would have screened off the southern room and would have meant it was approximately equal in size to the north room (*c*. 9m long).

The porch doorway was undoubtedly the main entrance, and the porch provided a room of sufficient dimensions (*c*. 3.60 wide internally and projecting about 2.60m eastwards from the door) to have served as a waiting room. Indeed, the north side may have accommodated a bench, set against the north room, or perhaps a narrow internal staircase to the first floor of the north room. Although the east wall of the porch had been truncated, leaving discolouration where the foundation rested on the ground, the entrance is presumed to have been on this side providing direct access from the courtyard. The porch walls abutted the main walls of B2 which might suggest it was a later addition, although this may just relate to the construction sequence as the fabric of the walls was similar. Notwithstanding this, some particularly large blocks had been used as underpinning support in the south-east and south-west corners of the porch.

A further entrance might possibly be suggested by a gap in the east wall (W4) of the south room, however with no lined faces this could not be proven (Fig. 1.35). Similarly, the southern end of the building had been cut through by two modern service trenches, destroying any evidence there may have been for a centrally placed entrance within the south wall.

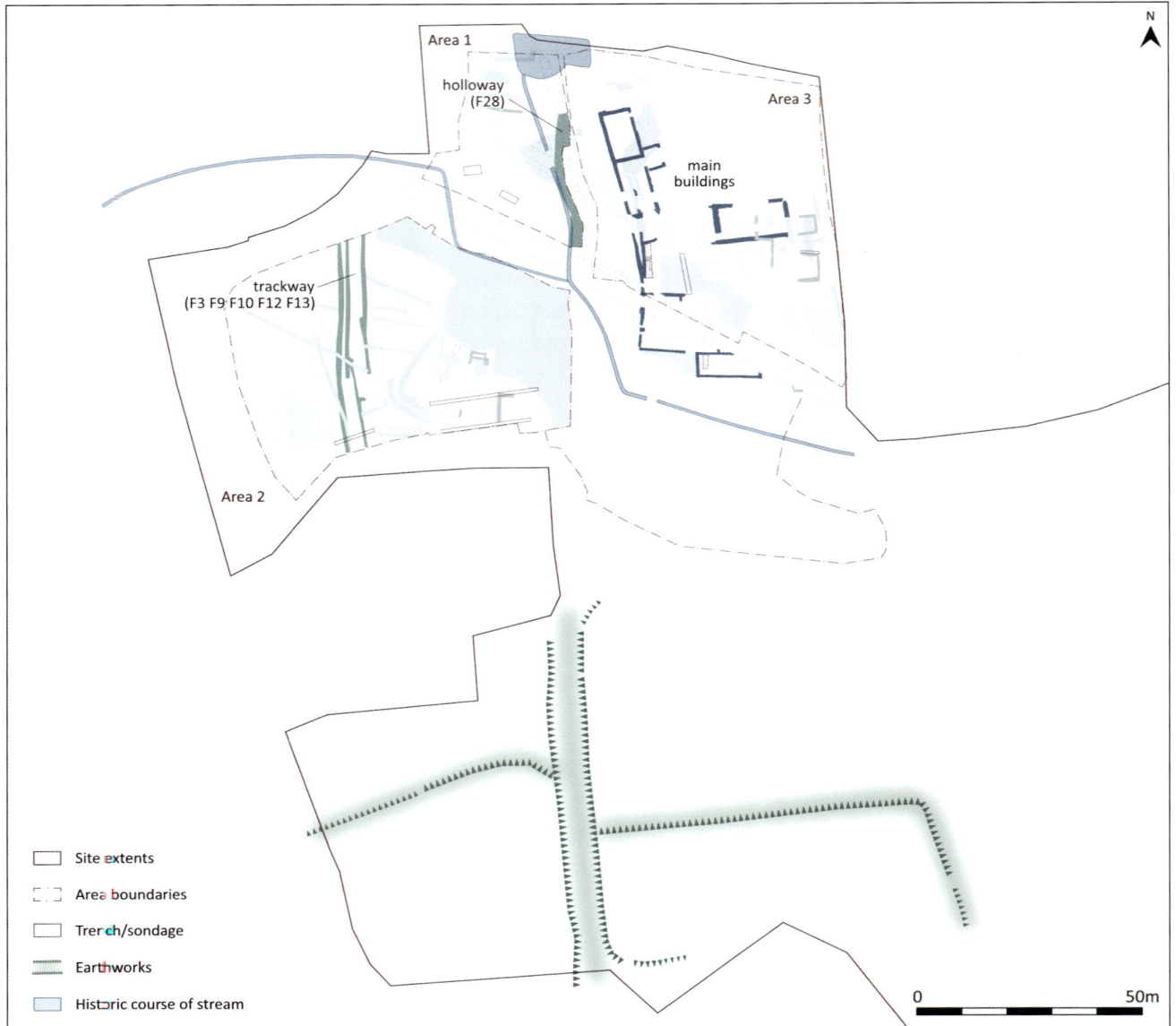

Fig. 1.28   Location of earthworks in comparison with associated excavated features.

The walls of the north room (W16, W15 and W1) were keyed-in to one another, with W16 also keyed-in to the cross-passage wall (W3). However, a tiny gap existed between the east wall (W1) and the cross-passage wall, perhaps suggesting that construction began and ended in this corner. The main eastern doorway meant there was no continuity in walling between the north and south rooms, and it is assumed that a stone threshold once occupied the flattened and compacted ground within the gap. By contrast, the foundation of the west wall (W5) of the south room joined the foundation of the cross-passage wall (W3). In conjunction with the porch,

which tied the two elements of the building together, this proves the construction was of a single phase.

The walls of B2 were constructed of random coursed limestone with clay bonding. These had faced and squared blocks on both sides with a rubble infill. The bonding material within the west wall (W16) included rubble fragments, implying reused materials perhaps derived from B5. The walls varied in thickness, with the north room walls measuring up to 0.95m wide, expanding in the north-eastern corner to 1.34m. The cross-passage wall (W3) was 0.92m thick. Within the

Fig. 1.29 Phase 4.

Legend:
- Site extents
- Area boundaries
- Trench/sondage
- Culverts/services
- Phase 4
- FXX/WXX Feature and Wall number
- BX Building number

wall 15

northern room

quarrying

F91

Building 2

wall 16

wall 2

?seat

cobbled floor

doorway

cobbled path

wall 3

porch

cross passage

doorway

wall 2

wall 5

southern room

wall 4

doorway

wall 5

wall 4

wall 24

garden wall

wall 17

boundary wall

wall 7

N

0   5m

Fig. 1.30   Building 2.

south room, W5 was 0.97m wide, standing up to six courses high and almost identical to W16, of which it was effectively a continuation. W24 was

Fig. 1.31   Aerial view of B2.

1.24m wide, providing a robust gable end wall. W4 was 0.90m wide and survived up to four courses high. Where investigated, the exterior walls had stepped foundations, while the cross-passage wall (W3) had a substantial masonry foundation with walling above.

A further two walls (W7 and W17) situated to the south were associated with this phase of construction. W7 was a courtyard boundary wall approximately aligned with the western wall of B2, although the presence of the modern service trenches meant a relationship could not be established. It was constructed of random coursed and squared random limestone with firm clay bonding material, 0.72m wide and standing to 0.48m. The lower two courses forming the foundation protruded by up to 0.07m and were constructed of larger stones, while the upper courses of the superstructure utilized smaller stones. As discussed within Phase 3 above, at its southern end it ran over the western wall of B5 and was associated with the later re-configuration of the space. Its southern extent could not be established due to another modern service and the main culvert. However it was not present within the hall of B5.

At right angles to W7 was a short wall (W17), orientated almost parallel to the southern end wall of B2. This was constructed of a single course of random coursed limestone with clay bonding, 0.75m wide and surviving to a height of 0.20m. Re-used stone appears to have been incorporated into this wall, with faced stones incorporated within the rubble core. W17 also overlay W6a, the boundary wall associated with B5. This may represent the wall of an ancillary structure to B2, such as a kitchen, although the less substantial character might suggest a subdivision of the courtyard space for a garden, stalling or enclosed yard.

The deposits and features, by Clare Randall
Area 3
Prior to the construction of B2 there had been an episode of quarrying (F91, [14-114]), which removed rock on the upslope, eastern side. This may have been originally undertaken to extract building stone but it also created a more level terrace to accommodate the northern end of B2. This quarry cut the north end of linear feature F79, associated

Fig. 1.32   B2 from the north-north-west, with cobbled path along west side of room, looking south-south-west (2 x 2m scales).

Fig. 1.33   B2 looking across the porch, main door and cross-passage, looking west-south-west (4 x 1m scales).

Fig. 1.34 B2 looking through the west door, through the cross-passage and towards the porch, looking east-north-east (4 x 1m scales).

Fig. 1.35 B2 from the south-south-west showing earlier W42 running underneath, looking north-north-west (2 x 2m scales).

with B5 (see above). The fill of the terrace/quarry (14-116) consisted of re-deposited natural silts and contained a single sherd of 12th–13th century pottery. Several deposits (12-113), (12-114), and (12-116), most likely associated with the use of B5 (see above), lay beneath the central wall (W3) of B2. These deposits contained 12–13th century pottery, including some examples which could not date earlier than the 13th century, providing the earliest possible date for the construction of B2. Pottery closely associated with the deposits overlying the walls of B2 provided similar dates (excluding small numbers of 17th–18th century and modern sherds, which were probably intrusive).

An area of cobbled floor F39, was located in the northern room of B2, adjacent to W3, although its full extent was not uncovered. This comprised cornbrash cobbles set in silty clay (12-112), and was stratigraphically later than W3, but best understood as the original floor level in this part of the building. It included pottery dated no earlier than the 13th century and overlay a series of deposits which were probably contemporary with the use of B5 (see above). Within the southern room, adjacent to the cross-passage wall (W3) (and thereby, probably within the cross passage itself) was a compacted surface (9-105), which was covered by building collapse. This surface was of silty sandy clay with stone fragments, probably derived from re-deposited natural silts. It was uniformly 0.20m deep across the area adjacent to the wall, but became deep to the south, where it would have been part of the southern room of the building. Beneath this was deposit (9-106), which probably predated B2.

The overall layout of the complex has in places been difficult to refine, partly given the limitations with deciphering which features were contemporary. How it articulated at different dates with the wider landscape is also problematic. One element of this is the recognition of a lower lying wide linear north–south feature, F28, in Area 1 but severed from the complex on the eastern slope by the north–south culvert. This was not excavated, but in its southern extent it blended with the spread of material F31 which can be identified with the midden spread (10-108) in Area 2. Whilst it was not fully characterised, its position and alignment would suggest that it

was a routeway through the base of the valley, possibly alongside an existing stream, aligned with the holloway preserved in the earthworks to the south of the excavation area (Fig 1.28). As such it would have provided both the western boundary to the manorial complex and the routeway linking the buildings of the manor core with the southern extent of the manorial holding.

Phase 5 – The demolition/collapse of the manorial centre (c. 14th century AD)

Extensive and complex deposits of collapsed masonry and rubble filled the footprints of Buildings 1, 2 and 3. This also extended into the areas around these buildings, often covering the walls. The character of these deposits reflected the composition of the buildings, largely comprising limestone rubble of varying concentrations and stone sizes with silty clay infills. The deposits within and around B2 also contained frequent limestone roof tile fragments and fragments of clay ridge tiles (e.g. F50) (Fig. 1.33, Fig. 1.34 and Fig. 1.36). However, there was a distinct lack of worked building stone in all these deposits, suggesting deliberate removal (see Green, Chapter 2). Most collapse/demolition and levelling deposits within and around the buildings also contained frequent artefacts and ecofacts, with the vast majority of pottery and other artefacts of 13th–14th century date. Small amounts of 17th–19th century material in some areas seem to have been largely derived from the upper layers of deposits or have intruded into these rubbly layers, possibly during a piecemeal process of robbing stone or levelling. However, a clear hiatus in activity is indicated across the site which seems to have occurred at some point in the 14th century.

The overburden above B1 was relatively thin, and this may explain the widespread and even distribution of demolition derived deposits which covered the footprint of the building and the areas surrounding it. Clay loams with frequent limestone rubble surrounded B1, which included pottery, animal bone, marine shell, ceramic building material and metal objects, designated (506) on the north side, (507) on the south side and (508) on the west side. All three contained small amounts of post-medieval pottery (mainly 17th–18th century), with the great majority dating from the 12th–14th century. On the north side of W8, a clay loam deposit containing oyster shell (515) had formed over part of the probable path (516). Over this was a collapsed section of W8, (513) 1.60m long and 1.70m wide, retaining the stacked pattern of the exterior facing material. The dimensions of the deposit indicate that the walls had stood to a considerable height for some time, rather than having been demolished immediately. This potentially has a bearing on the apparent later orientation of post-medieval building B6. To the east of B1, an extensive 0.36m deep deposit (15-112) covered a further 0.41m deep deposit (15-116), located over the boundary ditch F85 and beneath B6 for which it may have served as a levelling layer.

Within the footprint of B1, rubbly layers (501) in the western portion and (601) in the eastern part contained finds of the same date range. In the north-eastern corner of B1 a similar deposit (16-107) contained two patches of heat-affected rubble (16-105) abutting the interior faces of W8 and W20. These burned areas were localized within the demolition deposits and may have related to the disposal of materials. At the eastern end of B1 were a number of deposits which may also relate to demolition or have been introduced or redistributed in association with the construction of the post-medieval structures above, B3 and B6. An undated rubble deposit (9-123) within the footprint of B1, lay beneath W10 of B3. The rest of the interior of B1 was covered by rubble layers (15-106) to (15-110) with stones of varying sizes within a silty clay matrix. These may have been levelled for the later construction of B3.

The rubble deposits associated with B3 itself (see below) also generally contained 12th and 13th century pottery, implying that they were largely derived from the occupation of B1. Rubble deposits to the south of B1 could not be related to a particular phase of construction or demolition, but most likely formed contemporaneously with the series of deposits within the building footprint. This included a clay loam (605) with common sub-angular cornbrash rubble, containing pottery of 12th century date, sparse oyster shell, and animal bone. This deposit overlay a clay loam (606) with common sub-angular cornbrash containing shell and pottery of similar date.

The deposits associated with B2 were the most extensive and deepest and this should be seen in the light of its position at the base of the slope and the deeper overlying deposits; this contrasts with the shallower overlying deposits in the area of B1 which may have led to greater re-working of the demolition layers. On the north-east side of the building, overlying walls W1 and W2, was an extensive rubble deposit (12-129) of 0.21m depth, comprising roof tiles and building stone. It overlay a silty clay with degraded cornbrash (12-130), which was located in a part of W2 which had been entirely robbed out and resembled the bonding material of the wall with bits of mortar. It may therefore be the residue of the core of the wall once re-useable material had been removed. Further rubble deposits (12-124) were located within the northern room, against W2.

Within the south room of B2 against, and possibly originating from, the cross-passage wall (W3) was a spill of rubble (9-104) (Fig 1.34). This covered a deposit of limestone roof tiles (9-103), some of them with mortar still adhering. Beneath this was the apparent interior floor surface of the southern room. If these deposits are indicative of the sequence of collapse, it seems that the roof fell in before the central wall collapsed over it. A deposit of limestone roof tiles and fragments (12-121) was also present in the north-east corner of the room between W3 and W4. This covered an area exceeding 3m wide and was 0.07m deep, yielding pottery of the 12th–13th century, animal bone and marine shell. It was similar to, and may have derived from, the same episode of collapse as (9-103), although the underlying sequence suggests a different order of events. Thin silty clay deposits (12-121) and (12-122) may represent an initial levelling layer, as it was situated above a further rubble deposit (12-123) sealing the underlying natural deposits. This rubble incorporated largely broken roof tiles with some mortar. Burning was evident in some places but a number of roof tiles had sooting only to one side, suggesting this accumulated as a result of exposure to smoke from an open hearth.

A very compacted dump of building debris (14-109) was situated in the central part of the southern room of B2, above the location of earlier linear

Fig. 1.36   Rubble layers against W3 of B2, looking east (1 x 0.2m and 1 x 0.5m scales).

F79 and covering gully F81 which was associated with boundary wall W42 It mostly comprised stone rubble and stone roof tiles but included glazed ceramic ridge tile fragments, which would equate to about three or four whole tiles. This indicates the presence of a decorative ridge, although the general paucity of ceramic tiles implies that the majority had been carefully removed for reuse. The deposit also contained pottery of 13th century date, animal bone, nails and oyster shell.

The walls of B4 had been reduced but not robbed out completely at any location around the perimeter, and the only rubble spread was F46 to the west of B4. This was contained within the alluvium and was jumbled with no coherent composition. It seems most likely to have derived from the southern end of wall W31 of B5, the line of which could be deciphered in places. However, the dispersed nature of the deposit would also be explained by the action of flooding. Overall, the lack of rubble around B4 appears to indicate that the superstructure was either not entirely of stone construction or that deconstruction may have been more systematic. Instead of a covering of rubble like the other buildings, the area of B4 was buried in an extensive alluvial deposit (9-138) of dark grey soft silty clay both within the footprint and outside of the structure. It appears to have been deposited by the flooding of the stream over this lowest lying area of the complex.

Phase 6 – Late Medieval (c. 14th–16th centuries AD)

There appears from the dateable material culture to have been a hiatus in activity in Area 3 after the 14th century. A single probable candlestick fragment (see Schuster, Chapter 2) dating to the 14th–15th centuries came from deposits overlying the western side of B5; deposit (509) in the same area contained a few pottery sherds of probable 15th–16th century date. Several sherds of 14th–15th century date came from clearance layers in Area 1, and over both B1 and B4. All of this could be explained by a low level of manuring as the land continued in use. Other activity which might be assigned to a late medieval re-purposing of the site was observed in the south-eastern corner of Area 2. This part of the site contained a series of rubble scatters and dumps of varying coherence which were clearly later than the medieval linears. One extensive limestone rubble scatter (F61) was related to the collapsed walls of B8 (Fig. 1.37). The ditches in Area 2 (discussed above) with their origins in Phase 3, defined an area which had been manured with household refuse during Phase 4 and had fully silted up. Ditches F11, F21 and F73 ran under the rubble scatter and walls of B8.

The structure of B8 was highly fragmentary although the overall dimensions could be ascertained from short stretches of walls, and partly coherent rubble. Part of the west wall of B8 (W12, F62 and F69) and the northern end of the building (W40, F60) survived, indicating a long narrow structure measuring 3.75m wide and in excess of 20m long. This might imply that it was not a domestic dwelling but that it had some agricultural purpose. Where observable, the walls comprised irregular uncoursed rubble with no evident bonding material and incorporated burnt stone and occasional ceramic tile fragments, clearly derived from an earlier structure.

The most coherent element of W12 extended for a length of 2.25m and measured 0.63m wide, although a line of small rubble fragments extended the length of the wall. The medieval pottery associated with this section was largely residual but included some sherds dating to the 15th–16th century. The northern end of B8 was formed by W40, which shared the same 0.63m width as W12 implying that they were contemporary. A plinthed foundation was present below W40 whereas W12 had no foundation. The majority of the pottery in the deposits surrounding B8 was medieval in origin with some dated to the 15th–16th centuries. A major structural change to B8 suggests the building had

some longevity of use. Another wall (W41) of similar construction crossed the northern end of B8 from east to west, widening the building to 4.25m. It was also 0.63m wide, presumably to facilitate reuse of the side walls. The presence of fallen rubble (F61) over this wall, within which pottery of 14th–15th century date was recovered, combined with the rubbly construction of the wall itself made it difficult to define, but it certainly represents a foreshortening of the original building. It appears to be slightly offset towards the east, indicating a change in orientation and suggesting that it was a rebuild as opposed to a modification of the existing structure. B8 was covered in one of the dumps of rubble which occurred in patches across this part of the site, immediately below the subsoil. The overlying and extensive surrounding silts provided medieval pottery although this was ubiquitous, likely deriving at least in part from the adjacent midden deposit (10-108).

To the east and downslope from B8 was B9, which appears to have been a north–south oriented structure represented by W13. The north wall measured 7.5m long by 1m wide and the southern return was visible for c. 3.75m, although the north-western corner had been robbed out. The construction of W13 was much more coherent than the walls comprising B8, with a bedding course including some shaped limestone, and a single course of faced limestone blocks constructed directly onto the subsoil. The outer surface of the wall was faced in larger stones whilst the core incorporated rubble with no evident bonding material. It was covered by the southern portion of the extensive spread (10-108) described above, but there were no associated finds directly associated with this wall. However, pottery dated as 13th–15th century (with a few sherds dated to the 17th–18th centuries) was recovered from the deposits at the eastern, downslope, end of a sondage through this area. Nearby, pottery of the 14th–15th centuries and possibly the 16th century was recovered in modern service trenches dug at the north end of the holloway earthworks (RCHME 1970, 41).

The walls of B8 were of a different character to the clearly defined buildings in Area 3, as also noted for the structural remains in Area 1 (see below),

Fig. 1.37 Phases 6 and 7.

whereas the solid construction of B9 has greater similarity to the clearly medieval structures in Area 3. Both buildings utilized recycled materials, with B8 overlying the silted medieval ditches, and in conjunction with the dating evidence from the pottery are likely to represent a late phase of medieval activity, or occupation of the land, after the abandonment of the manorial complex.

Phase 7 – Post-medieval buildings and activity (c. 17th–19th centuries AD)

Material dateable to the post-medieval period was recovered from overlying deposits across Areas 1–3, with the majority of the material coming from Area 1. Fragmentary rubble walls in Areas 1 and 3 did not constitute a recognisable ground plan and were either late in the stratigraphic sequence or insecurely dated. While there is some potential for them to be later medieval/early post-medieval, they have on balance been included in this section (Fig. 1.37).

In Area 1 a single wall (W14) ran west to east, over a distance of around 10m and 1.0m wide. It comprised random uncoursed irregular limestone bonded with the surrounding soil matrix, which probably filtered into the gaps between the stones, with only one course consistently present. It was covered with the alluvial deposit (10-113) recorded across this area, which contained small amounts of medieval pottery, but is likely to have been transported by flooding and later agricultural operations. The underlying deposits were characterized by homogenous brown silty clay. Running parallel with W14 and c. 2m to the north was a rubble spread F35 comprising similar material, which may have derived from W14 and from a stub of wall (F36) which was situated at its western end. Although this is likely to be contemporary it was not possible to identify a coherent structure. F35 was covered by a similar alluvial deposit (10-114) containing pottery of the 12th–15th century as well as post-medieval material.

A further rubble spread F33 was noted in the northern part of the area covering an area around 10m long by 4.5m wide, together with a possible wall (F32) which lay at the northern edge of the site running west to east for c. 9.5m with a north return at its eastern end. This wall comprised a single course or layer of irregular limestones with no apparent bonding. In addition, a spread of stone F31 in the eastern part of Area 1 yielded medieval pottery and was adjacent to the possible medieval holloway F28. It may have been contemporary with these apparently later walls and stone deposits or possibly derived from the medieval buildings to the east. In all cases, the survival of only one or two poorly constructed courses suggests structures that were more akin to the post-medieval structures in Area 3. Whilst the overlying silts contained medieval pottery, this was spread over a wide area and probably ultimately derived from the midden deposit along the west side of the modern culvert.

In the eastern part of Area 3, B3 overlay the Phase 3 B1 (Fig 1.22 and Fig. 1.24). It consisted of three sections of wall (W10, W11, and W25) partially outlining a ground plan. The structure was at least 15m long, and the walls consisted of a rubble core faced with random coursed limestone with silty clay bonding material. The walls were 0.60m–0.80m wide and survived up to four courses high. Whilst B1 was covered and surrounded by debris from its demolition (see above), some of these deposits may have been reworked or introduced in order to level up the area for the construction of B3. An example of this was a rubble deposit (514) situated within the south doorway of B1 and through which W10 and W25 passed; this suggests that (514) was a deliberate infill supporting these walls. W10 overlay a layer of demolition rubble (9-122) within B1 (see above). However, a similar deposit (9-107) of silty clay with frequent medium to large angular rubble situated within and alongside the walls of B3, appeared to be later than W11. It also contained frequent oyster shell and largely medieval pottery as well as five sherds of residual Romano-British pottery. Pottery associated with deposits immediately around W11 was largely of the 13th–14th century.

An area 4.89m long and 2.87m wide of slightly rounded and angular cobbles (15-111) was set in clay silt on the south side of B1. Associated with 17th–18th century, and some modern pottery, it may represent external hard standing for B3. It overlay (15-103), (15-104) and (15-105), all silty clay deposits with stones, which provided bedding and levelling layers. The overwhelmingly medieval date of material from deposits surrounding the walls of B3 might indicate a medieval date for the structure, but most of these relate to the demolition of B1, possibly re-deposited at a later date. Given the stratigraphic relationship with B1, the different style of the apparent ground plan, total lack of respect for the alignment of B1, and the less massive dimensions and coherent structure of the wall itself, B3 is most likely post-medieval in date.

Further to the east, B6 (Fig. 1.22 and Fig. 1.23) consisted of three walls (W21, W22 and W28), forming three sides of a structure. W21 was aligned on B1, so that W28 appeared as an extension of that building's southern wall (W9). It demarcated a space broadly 5m square and about half the width of B1. However, neither the north wall (W21) or south wall (W28) extended far enough west to have a relationship with B1, the robber trench F104 having removed the eastern wall of B1. The eastern wall (W22) was 3.15m long which indicates the width of the structure. These walls were of different construction than those of B1, generally 0.50m wide and represented by only a single layer of limestone rubble with a small area of W28 surviving to two courses.

The alignment of B6 in relation to B1, as well as evidence from the rubble deposits on the north side of B1, suggests that at least some walls of B1 remained standing from which the orientation of B6 was based. An area in the central portion of W28 showed an inconsistency in the coursing, perhaps suggesting a blocked doorway or area of damage. This might even suggest that B6 utilised a standing wall in some way. The 19th and 20th century material within the robber trench F104 raises the possibility that the end wall of B1 was at least visible until relatively recently, although the building was no longer extant (see below).

All three walls of B6 were situated over an extensive 0.36m deep layer of silty clay (15-112) with occasional medium to large angular stones and interpreted as a make-up layer albeit undated. W21 and W22 both ran over medieval ditch F85. The pottery directly associated with W21 and W22 was generally 17th and 18th century in date, with a few medieval sherds. Clay pipe fragments were also associated with W22, whilst no finds were attributed to W28. With the cobbled path F44/F103 (see below) which produced

18th century pottery situated immediately to the east, running north–south, and abutting W22, it seems that this was a post-medieval structure.

The eastern end of a further building, B7, was situated to the south-east of B3 (Fig. 1.22). This comprised a north wall (W26), an east wall (W29) and a south wall (W23), encompassing an extant space of approximately 5m by 7m, but not providing a complete ground plan. The walls were generally 0.60m wide and constructed of random coursed limestone. W29 was constructed directly onto natural stone (16-102) and covered directly by topsoil. Whilst the pottery associated with W26 is assigned to the 13th century, this was most likely derived from the adjacent deposits associated with B1. Sharing the same alignment as B3, a post-medieval date seems most likely.

Although physically and stratigraphically un-connected, structures B3, B6 and B7 probably belong to the same phase of activity and represent a re-purposing of this eastern part of the site. Immediately to the east of B6 and B7 was a cobbled path, F44/F103 running parallel with the eastern boundary of the site as well as the eastern end wall of medieval building B1, and thence B6. Associated with 18th century pottery, this path was just below the topsoil and consisted of a surface of limestone cobbles and pebbles (8-127) set within a soil matrix (Fig. 1.23). This appeared to have incorporated re-used stone from the buildings, and it was stratigraphically later than W22 of B6. Further south, F38 was a similar but more fragmentary curved path and was most likely a continuation of F44/F103. The point at which these structures went out of use is unclear. Several 19th century objects were recovered from across this area. However, the earliest map which dates to 1792, does not show buildings here (see Chapter 5), which implies that they had ceased to function before the end of the 18th century. The rubble footings of a fragment of wall (F52), situated to the north of B2 were associated with material in the overlying topsoil dating to the 19th and 20th century, and may represent the remnant of a recent small farm building too insignificant to depict on historic mapping. A well F47 was located at the western edge of Area 3, close to B2. This was circular in plan, with an interior diameter of *c*. 0.80m. It was constructed of random limestone rubble in rough courses with a range of stone sizes included up to 0.40m. This was excavated to *c*. 1.2m before it became flooded. While undated it is assumed that it is post-medieval in date, as there are several wells in this area shown on 19th century maps (see Chapter 5).

According to the later 19th and earlier 20th century maps, the Chickerell stream ran broadly west to east through the field, but originally it undertook two right-angled turns in the centre of the site. The course of the stream is first shown on the 1st edition Ordnance Survey map, and remained unaltered until at least the 1960s. At some point shortly after that, it appears that it was straightened into a north-west to south-eastern course. Alluviation appears to have been on-going after this time, given the deposits observed in the evaluation trenches over the original course of the stream (Cotswold Archaeology 2003, 7). It was also in the latter half of the 20th century that several services were also installed running through the site. During the 20th century the site area has been in agricultural use, a continuation from preceding centuries (see Chapter 5). In recent years it has been used as rough grazing.

2

POTTERY, CERAMIC BUILDING MATERIALS AND ARCHITECTURAL STONE

THE POTTERY, By Lorraine Mepham

Introduction

The combined pottery assemblage recovered from the site, from the initial clearance and subsequent excavation, amounts to 5204 sherds, weighing 42,039 grammes and representing a maximum of 4548 vessels. The majority of the assemblage is of medieval date, but there is also material of prehistoric, Romano-British and post-medieval/modern date.

The condition of the assemblage ranges from fair to poor. The assemblage is markedly fragmentary, and sherd size is generally small. There are very few reconstructable (partial) profiles, and in general context groups appear to represent small parts of numerous vessels rather than single-vessel sherd groups. Medieval and earlier sherds have suffered surface and edge abrasion. Mean sherd weight overall is 8.1g; this rises slightly to 8.3g for Romano-British sherds and falls to 7.4g for medieval sherds, with the harder-fired and better preserved post-medieval/modern wares having a mean sherd weight of 14.2g. The condition of the material suggests that a significant proportion has been reworked and redeposited, and therefore is likely to represent secondary rather than primary refuse. This is supported by the provenance: a relatively low proportion of the assemblage appeared to derive from well-stratified feature fills or other deposits.

Methods of analysis

Analysis has involved a detailed examination of fabric and vessel form, with details of surface treatment, decoration, vessel dimensions and presence of residues also recorded. Quantification has been by sherd count and weight. The level of recording corresponds to the 'detailed record' advocated by national standards (Barclay et al. 2016, section 2.4.6), and the definition and description of vessel forms follows nationally recommended nomenclature (Medieval Pottery Research Group 1998). Estimated Vessel Equivalents (EVEs) have not been used here as the proportion of measurable rim sherds is very low (6.5%), and Estimated Number of Vessels (ENV) has been calculated instead, counting conjoining sherds, or groups of sherds almost certainly from the same vessel, as 1. The total ENV for the assemblage of 4548 emphasises its fragmentary nature.

Prehistoric pottery

Two sherds have been identified as late prehistoric, both recovered from a possible levelling layer adjacent to W18 of B5. One is in a coarse flint-tempered fabric (sparse, poorly sorted inclusions), and the other is in an oolitic-tempered fabric. Both are undiagnostic body sherds, dated solely on fabric grounds to the Late Bronze Age to Early Iron Age. Both are clearly residual sherds here.

Romano-British pottery

Eighteen sherds were recorded as Romano-British; again, all these are likely to be residual sherds in later contexts; all are small and abraded. No concentration was noted in the distribution. The majority are in Black Burnished ware (BB1), unsurprising given the predominance of this ware type in the region from at least the 1st century BC and throughout the Romano-British period. Identifiable vessel forms amongst this small group comprise a bead-rimmed jar, an everted rim jar, a straight-sided 'dog dish' and a dropped-flange bowl; overall these suggest a date range spanning the Romano-British period. The single sherd of Oxfordshire colour-coated ware is from a mortarium, while the four sherds of samian are all tiny flakes from vessels of uncertain form. The New Forest colour-coated ware and sandy greyware of uncertain source likewise included no diagnostic sherds.

Medieval pottery

The medieval material makes up the bulk of the recovered assemblage, and the wares represented conform to the expected range for the area. These consist very largely of wares probably made within the county; the presence of a small proportion of imported wares is of interest, but not unexpected given the coastal location of the site. The wares fall into four groups, with a fifth group of miscellaneous wares. Fabric totals are given in Table 2.1.

Table 2.1   Pottery by fabric type.

	Fabric type	No. sherds	Weight (g)	MNV
Prehistoric	Grog-tempered	1	2	1
	Oolitic-tempered	1	1	1
	Sub-total prehistoric	*2*	*3*	*2*
Roman	Black Burnished ware	11	84	11
	New Forest colour coated ware	1	22	1
	Oxon colour coated ware	1	34	1
	Sandy greywares	1	5	1
	Samian	4	4	4
	Sub-total Roman	*18*	*149*	*18*
Medieval: Saxo-Norman wares	E400 (Cheddar-type ware)	31	250	31
Medieval: West Dorset sandy wares	E425A	2406	15150	2012
	E425B	339	2909	274
	E425E	29	220	20
Medieval: Wessex coarsewares	E422A	101	1052	97
	E422B	219	2127	158
	E422C	187	1639	180
Medieval: Poole Harbour whitewares	E426A	49	594	45
	E426B	2	25	2
Medieval: Imports	E515 (Normandy Gritty)	3	44	3
	E520A (Saintonge whiteware)	48	376	45
	E520B (Saintonge bright green-glazed)	3	11	3
	E520C (Saintonge polychrome)	4	4	4
	E530 (Iberian coarsewares)	6	44	5

	Fabric type	No. sherds	Weight (g)	MNV
Medieval: Other coarsewares	C400	41	423	37
	C401	35	167	31
	C402	4	28	4
	F400	321	2615	306
	F401	253	2537	242
	Q400	56	331	51
	Q401	32	212	32
	Q402	38	225	37
	Q403	143	1101	141
	Q404	284	2340	258
	Q405	6	74	6
	Q407	9	105	8
	Q408	27	170	15
	Q409	1	4	1
	R400	10	73	10
	Sub-total medieval	*4687*	*34,850*	*4058*
Post-medieval	Creamware	1	4	1
	English stoneware	6	109	5
	Frechen stoneware	3	29	3
	Jackfield ware	1	2	1
	Late white-slipped redware	9	134	8
	Pearlware	8	78	7
	Post-medieval redware	282	4108	270
	Porcelain	1	2	1
	Refined whiteware	39	232	39
	Staffordshire-type slipware	1	4	1
	White salt glaze	2	6	2
	Verwood-type earthenware	141	2317	129
	Westerwald stoneware	2	7	2
	Buff/yellow ware	1	5	1
	Sub-total post-med/modern	*497*	*7037*	*470*
	Overall total	**5204**	**42039**	**4548**

Saxo-Norman wares

E400: Cheddar-type ware; hard-fired, wheelthrown; moderate, poorly sorted quartz <1mm; rare limestone <2mm, mostly leached out.

A small number of sherds, mostly small and abraded, have been tentatively identified as Saxo-Norman, on the basis of fabric type. All these sherds appear to be from wheelthrown vessels, in a fabric containing mixed inclusions; this can be paralleled amongst wares from the Saxon royal palaces at Cheddar, although the poor condition of the sherds renders a precise match somewhat uncertain – there are points of similarity with several (Rahtz 1979, 310, fabrics CC, E, EE). There are five jar rims, one finger-impressed (Fig. 2.1); the rims are sharply everted, with simple

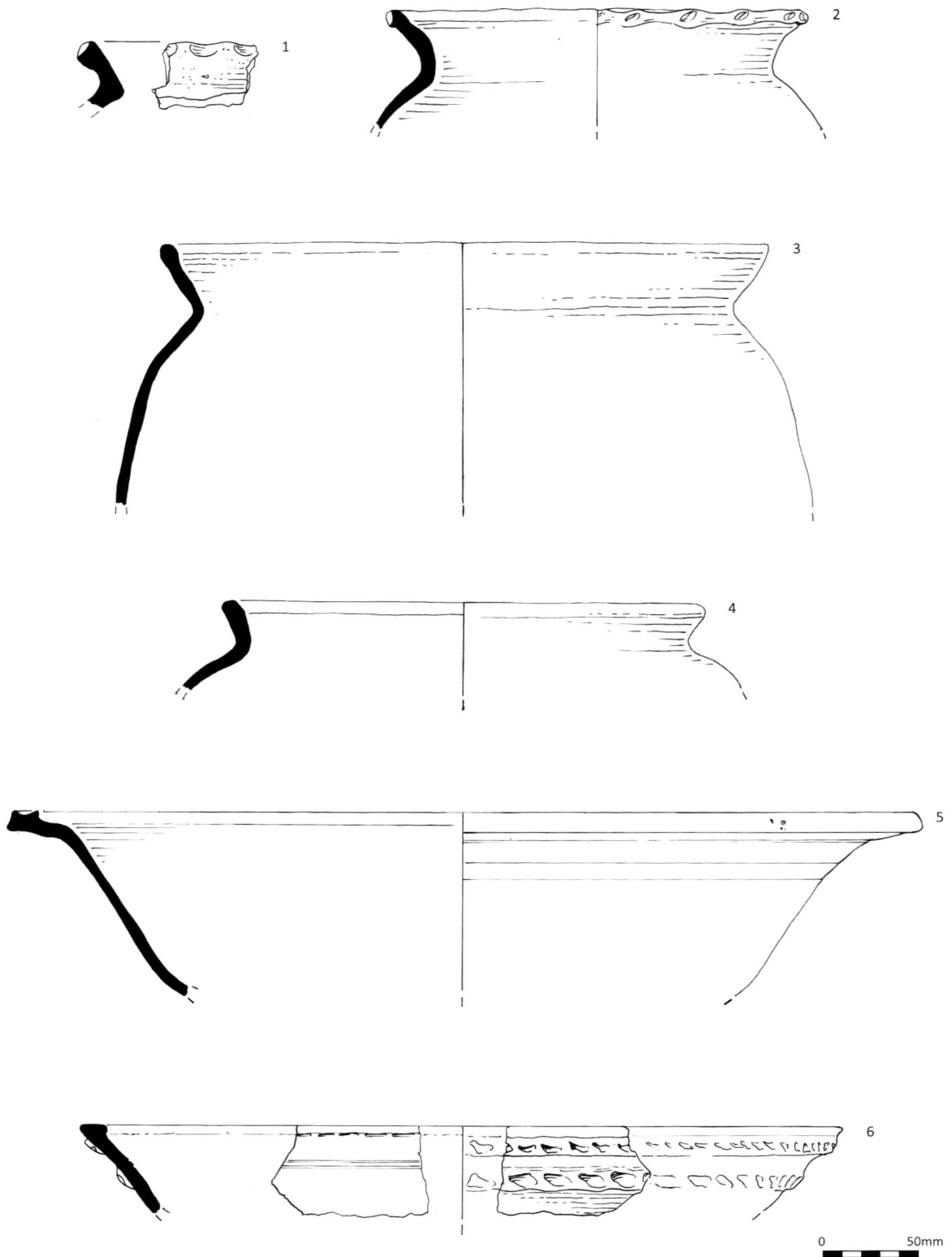

Fig. 2.1 Pottery. 1. Jar rim, classic Saxo-Norman form; fabric E400. PRN [Pottery Record Number] 1582, unstratified over Wall 32 (B4). 2. Jar rim, Wessex coarseware (E422c); finger impressed rim. PRN 1636, F85 (8-117); courtyard boundary ditch. 3. Jar rim, West Dorset sandy ware. PRN 345, construction cut for W20 (B1). 4. Jar rim, West Dorset sandy ware. PRN 1679, W11 (9-107); rubble deposit over B3. 5. Flanged bowl, West Dorset sandy ware. PRN 157, F35 (1006); alluvial deposit. 6. Flanged bowl, West Dorset sandy ware; impressed 'collar' around rim and thumbed applied strip below. PRN 1224, 501; rubble deposit to west of B1. Drawings © Liz James.

rounded profiles, a form particularly characteristic of the Saxo-Norman period.

Cheddar-type wares are found widely across the south-west, although none as yet in this part of Dorset. Examples have been recorded at Stratton Old Manor (Maw and Mepham in prep), Ilchester (Pearson 1982, 170, type A4, fig. 80, 555–60) and Winterborne Stickland (Mepham 2003, fabric QU400). More recent research has matched some of the Cheddar-type wares (Rahtz's fabrics C and CC) with the Upper Greensand-derived wares produced around the Blackdown Hills in south Somerset (Allan et al. 2010, 171), although another type (fabric E) may have been made in south or central Wiltshire (Allan et al. 2010, 168; Vince 1984, ch. 11, 12–16). There is no sign here of the calcareous Saxo-Norman wares noted at sites such as Stratton and Winterbourne Stickland, but some of the sherds amongst the Wessex coarsewares may also fall into this date range (see below).

No significant concentration was noted in the distribution of the Saxo-Norman sherds, although four were found in and around B1. All sherds appear to be residual; the majority (21 sherds) came from unstratified, topsoil and clearance layers

West Dorset sandy wares

E425A: the most common variant is hard-fired, ranging from a bright orange-red to buff-brown in colour, sometimes with a pale grey core; well sorted, subrounded quartz <0.25mm; smooth, slightly powdery texture. Equivalent to Sutton Poyntz fabric Q401 (Mepham 2007) and Sherborne Old Castle fabric Q404 (Mepham 2015).

E425B: as E425A but containing rare subangular flint inclusions <1mm and occasional limestone; equivalent to Sutton Poyntz fabric Q402.

E425E: texturally as E425A but with less powdery feel; glazed more evenly; possibly late medieval.

Relatively fine-grained sandy wares, frequently but not invariably oxidised, are found across west Dorset and are known to have been produced at the excavated kiln at Hermitage, dated to the 13th century on typological grounds (Field 1966), although more recent review has picked out 14th or early 15th century vessel forms amongst the published products (Allan 2003, 76 n. 2). Certainly the evidence from, for example, Sherborne Old Castle suggests that West Dorset wares are likely to have continued in use into the late medieval period (Mepham 2015, 165–6), and at Chickerell a possible later medieval component has been recognised on the basis of both fabric and a few distinctive forms.

Variants of the main type have now been identified on a few sites: fabric E425B, with rare flint inclusions, has been found at Sutton Poyntz and Stratton Old Manor. Other subdivisions (E425C and E425D) defined at Stratton cannot be sustained here, but fabric E425E, less powdery and more evenly glazed, could be a late medieval variant; it has proved difficult to distinguish from post-medieval redwares (and may therefore be under-represented) but is generally thinner-walled and glazed externally. A similar hard-fired variant was seen at Sherborne Old Castle (Mepham 2015, fabric Q426), but on the basis of vessel form could not be convincingly separated chronologically from the main West Dorset variant. There is still a question as to how far the fabric variants represent chronological development and how much might be variation between different sources – given the prevalence of these wares across west Dorset it is likely that Hermitage was not the only source (Spoerry 1990, 10).

Whatever their source(s), the West Dorset sandy wares formed a significant proportion of the medieval assemblage (52.4% by sherd weight). The repertoire of vessel forms is relatively limited (see Table 2.1) and consists almost entirely of jars (Fig. 2.1, 3–4), bowls (Fig. 2.1, 5–6) and jugs. Few vessel profiles could be reconstructed even partially, but jars appear to conform to the rounded or convex profiles seen in the Hermitage kiln assemblage. The very fragmentary remains of the lower part of one jar was found in feature [14-100], containing an infant burial (see Fig. 1.25 and Fig. 1.26). One jar rim is finger-impressed. Bowls are invariably flanged, with a slight angle change in the vessel wall; three examples have applied thumbed strips around the neck. Both jar and bowl rims are in almost every case internally bevelled; the distinction between jars and flanged bowls is therefore not always obvious where orientation of small rim segments is uncertain, and many rims have been defined broadly as jar/ bowl. Jugs are strap-handled, the handles generally slashed; several vessels carry applied thumbed strips around the rim. The occurrence of a single tripod foot is of interest as this could have belonged to a tripod pitcher; if so, this could extend the potential date range of West Dorset sandy wares back into the 12th century. Tripod feet were also found at Stratton Old Manor (Maw and Mepham in prep.).

Apart from the applied strips and finger-impressed rim already mentioned, decoration is restricted to some horizontal rilling on jug necks, a handful of body sherds with linear or curvilinear combing, and one body sherd with white painted slip. Glaze is generally thin and patchy, although slightly thicker and more even on sherds of fabric E425E.

Less common forms include shallow dishes (the five examples in Table 2.2 may in fact be from a single vessel) and cisterns, represented by bunghole spouts. There is one possible dripping dish (a rim from a shallow vessel lacking any discernible curvature), and a probable candlestick (Fig. 2.2, 7). An unusual lid-seated rim from a handled vessel (Fig. 2.2, 8) is of uncertain form. This vessel, together with the cisterns (a form introduced after the mid-14th century) and the candlestick, form a demonstrable late medieval component amongst the West Dorset wares.

Wessex coarsewares

E422a: coarsest variant as defined in Salisbury (Mepham 2000a), with quartz grains <1mm and deep scratch-marking.

E422b: medium-grained variant; quartz grains <0.5mm and shallower scratch-marking.

E422c: finest variant; quartz grains <0.25mm, and scratch-marking reduced to shallow brushing.

These coarsewares, characterised by fabrics abundantly tempered with rounded quartz grains and with very few other macroscopically visible inclusions, have a distribution extending across the eastern half of the county (Spoerry 1990, ware C1). Visually similar to the Laverstock-type coarsewares of south-east Wiltshire, they probably had an alternative source somewhere in the Purbeck/Poole Harbour area, and possibly also in the Verwood area, acting as a precursor to the post-medieval industry there. Petrological work has so far failed to convincingly distinguish separate groups amongst the overall south-east Wiltshire/east Dorset distribution, although the only large-scale survey (Spoerry 1990) was based on an early and relatively crude form of chemical analysis which could undoubtedly now be refined. Chickerell lies on the western edge of the distribution area (Spoerry 1990, fig. 6), but the proportion of Wessex coarsewares

Table 2.2   West Dorset sandy ware vessel forms (maximum number of vessels).

Vessel form	Profile	Rim	Foot	Handle	Spout	Total
Bowl		20				20
?Candlestick	1					1
Cistern					4	4
Dish		5				5
Dish/bowl		2				2
?Dripping dish		1				1
Jar	1	29				30
jar/bowl		97				97
Jug		17	1	33		51
Uncertain		12				12
Total	2	183	1	33	4	223

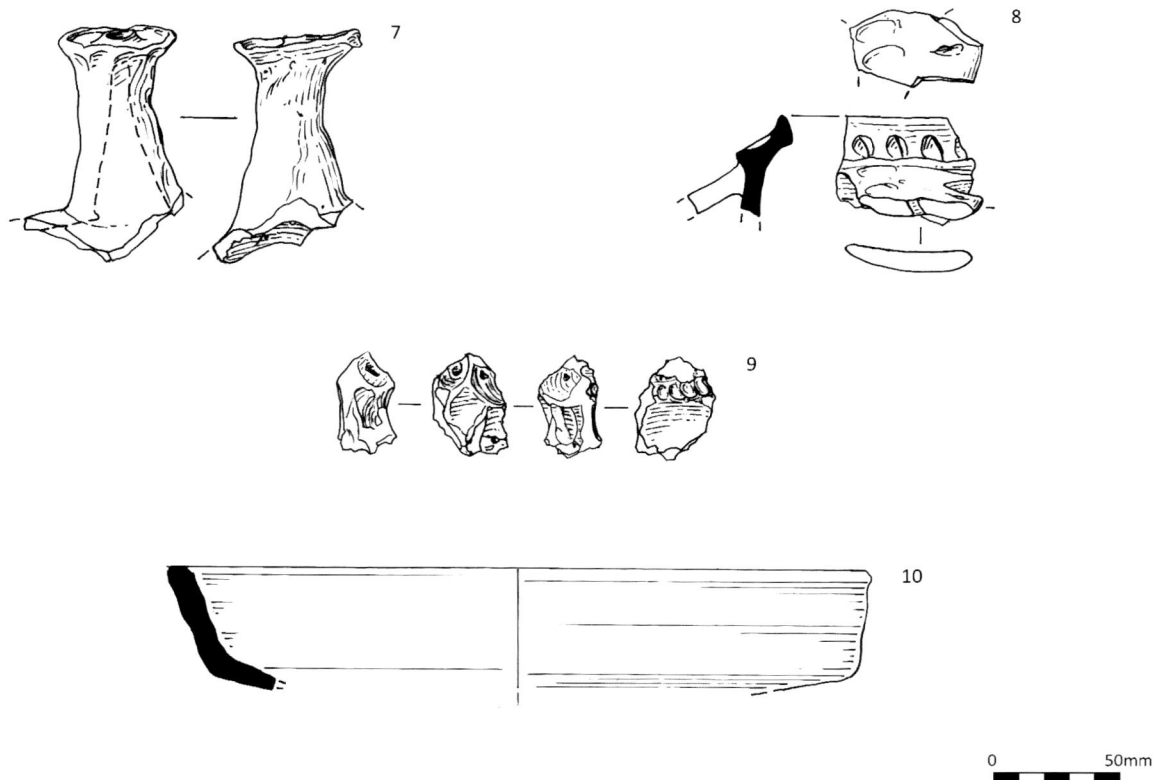

Fig. 2.2   Pottery. 7. Possible candlestick, West Dorset sandy ware; partially glazed. PRN 1629, F63; rubble over south-west corner of B5. 8. Inturned, lid-seated rim from vessel of uncertain form, West Dorset sandy ware; applied strap handle with cut-outs; fingertip impressions around lid-seating; partially glazed. PRN 1630, unstratified over W18 (B5). 9. Applied decorative element, possibly zoomorphic; Poole Harbour whiteware; green glazed. PRN 1613, F24 (10-115); subsoil, Area 3. 10. Dish profile, fabric F401. PRN 1565, unstratified over W32/35 (B4). Drawings © Liz James.

(12.5% by weight of the medieval assemblage) is almost identical to that seen at Sutton Poyntz (12.9%; Mepham 2007, table 10).

Recent work has pushed the origins of this ceramic tradition back to the mid–late Saxon period (Mepham 2018), but their *floruit* was from the 12th to 14th centuries. Analysis of the coarsewares in Salisbury has suggested a somewhat arbitrary three-fold division into coarse-grained, medium-grained and fine-grained, and this subdivision is followed here. While a simple chronological progression from fine to coarse cannot always be sustained, and there are substantial overlaps in the use of the three subdivisions, it is generally the case that the coarsest variant (E422A) tends to occur earlier in the sequence (up to the 12th century) while the finest variant

(E422A) appears in the 13th century and continues in use thereafter. The medium-grained E422B overlaps with the use of both of these and is the variant most frequently used for the distinctive tripod pitchers of the late 11th–12th century. Vessels are frequently scratch-marked, although the proportion of scratch-marked sherds seen at Chickerell is relatively low.

Vessel forms seen here support a date range focusing on the 13th–14th century, although there is a suggestion of some earlier material. Jars constitute the most common vessel form (see Table 2.3), and rim profiles conform to the typology seen elsewhere. Four forms are represented here:

1   Simple everted (Musty et al. 1969, fig. 7, type I); four examples

Table 2.3 Wessex coarseware vessel forms (maximum number of vessels).

Vessel form	Handle	Rim
?Curfew		1
Dish		1
Jar type 1		4
Jar type 2		7
Jar type 3		15
Jar type 4		9
Jar type unspec		3
Jar/bowl unspec		1
Jug	3	5
?Tripod pitcher		1
Total	3	47

2   Everted with slight lid-seating (Musty et al. 1969, type II); eight examples

3   Externally expanded (Musty et al. 1969, type III/IV); 15 examples

4   Short and stubby with a squared profile, sometimes grooved along the top (Musty et al. 1969, fig.10, 38); nine examples.

The first three forms have a date range of 12th–13th century, and the fourth from 13th–14th century. One of the type 3 jar rims is finger-impressed (Fig. 2.1, 2). There is only one possible example of a dish, while jugs are represented by five rims (one with a rod handle) and three separate strap handles. Some of the jugs have a patchy external glaze; none of the diagnostic sherds is decorated, but two slip-decorated body sherds (one with painted red slip, one with an applied slip pellet) almost certainly belong to jugs. There is also one possible curfew – a heavy, flattened rim from an open form. All these vessel forms could be accommodated within a date range of 13th–14th century although some of the type 1–3 jars could fall earlier. The only other sherds which could date prior to the 13th century are two in fabric E422B that have been tentatively identified as belonging to tripod pitchers. These comprise one rim sherd, and a glazed body sherd with combed decoration; if the identifications are correct, these date to the late 11th or 12th century. Good parallels for all of these forms can be seen in assemblages from around Poole Harbour, for example from Poole and Wareham (Barton et al. 1992; Hinton and Hodges

1977), and a smaller group was found at Sutton Poyntz (Mepham 2007).

Poole Harbour whiteware

E426A: White to pale pink, medium-grained (subrounded quartz grains <0.5mm); handmade; generally glazed (yellow or green).

E426B: White-firing, fine-grained, wheelthrown fabric; subrounded quartz grains <0.5mm.

The glazed tableware component of the medieval assemblage was supplied by whitewares of Poole Harbour type (Jarvis 1992a, fabrics 4 and 5). There is some variation in these wares; colouring ranges from off-white to pale pink, and glazes from yellow to green. Although whitewares have been found in some quantity across south Dorset, particularly in Poole (Jarvis 1992a, fabrics 4 and 5; Barton et al. 1992), little detailed work has been directed towards defining their variety and possible source(s). The range in colouring, for example, suggests the exploitation of different clay sources, although the pale-firing clays accessible in the Poole Harbour/ Purbeck area, outcropping in lenses of different colours and textures, could account for the variety, and this putative source area has recently been confirmed by the excavation of a kiln site in Wareham. Wasters from the site (which may include the products of more than one kiln dumped into the backfill of another) indicate the manufacture of jugs characteristic of the 13th and early 14th century, but also some baluster forms which appear later (14th or 15th century) (Blinkhorn n.d.). There is also a distinction to be made in manufacturing techniques: the majority of vessels found on consumption sites appear to be handmade, although the Wareham kiln wares are apparently wheelthrown. A small proportion of whitewares from Stratton Old Manor have been found to be wheelthrown (Maw and Mepham in prep), and in Southampton, where these wares are defined as 'Dorset whitewares', they are apparently all wheelthrown (Brown 2002, 16–17).

Jug forms are overwhelmingly predominant, and constitute the only vessel form seen at Chickerell, with one possible exception. No jug profiles could be reconstructed, but there is only one possible 14th–15th century baluster base, and it seems likely that most of the jugs conformed to the range of 13th–14th century rounded or pear-shaped profiles as seen, for example, in Poole. They are invariably glazed, generally with a clear lead glaze appearing yellow on the pale-firing fabric, but less commonly green-glazed. A number of sherds carry slipped decoration, generally in the form of vertical strips and/or pellets. The strip-and-pellet decorative scheme, together with other simple linear motifs, are common amongst the Poole assemblage (e.g. Barton et al. 1992, fig. 63, 650), and have also been seen at Sutton Poyntz and Stratton Old Manor (Mepham 2007, fig. 28, 7; Maw and Mepham in prep).

The only other possible vessel form here is represented by two small decorative elements; these are identical and although from separate contexts (clearance layer 1101, subsoil 10-115) almost certainly belonged to the same vessel. These decorative 'finials' (Fig. 2.2, 9) could have formed part of a highly decorated jug, but are more likely to have come from a less common form such as an aquamanile.

Other wares

All wares are handmade unless otherwise stated.

F400: Hard-fired, fine sandy matrix (rounded/subrounded quartz <0.25mm) containing rare subrounded quartz <1mm; sparse subangular flint <3mm.

F401: Hard-fired, slightly micaceous, slightly coarse matrix containing moderate rounded/subrounded quartz <1mm; rare to sparse subangular patinated flint <2mm.

C400: Hard-fired, fine sandy matrix (rounded/subrounded quartz <0.25mm) containing sparse to moderate, poorly sorted calcareous inclusions (crushed chalk/limestone) <2mm; rare subrounded quartz <1mm; rare subangular flint <2mm.

C401: Hard-fired, moderately coarse matrix containing sparse rounded/subrounded quartz <0.5mm; sparse irregular crushed calcareous material (chalk/limestone), mostly leached out, <2mm.

C402: Hard-fired, fine sandy matrix (rounded/subrounded quartz <0.25mm) containing sparse, well sorted oolitic limestone <0.5mm.

Q400: Hard-fired, slightly micaceous matrix containing sparse rounded/subrounded quartz <0.5mm; rare greensand < 1mm; rare subangular flint <2mm.

Q401: Hard-fired, slightly micaceous matrix containing moderate to common, rounded/subrounded quartz <0.5mm; rare patinated flint <1mm.

Q402: Hard-fired, fine sandy matrix (rounded/subrounded quartz <0.25mm) containing rare to sparse subangular flint <3mm and greensand <2mm.

Q403: Hard-fired, fine sandy matrix (rounded/subrounded quartz <0.25mm) containing rare subangular flint <2mm (finer variant of F400).

Q404: Hard-fired, fine sandy matrix (rounded/subrounded quartz <0.25mm); rare subangular flint <1mm; fairly smooth texture.

Q405: Hard-fired, slightly micaceous silty matrix containing moderate, poorly sorted subrounded quartz <2mm (mainly <1mm); evenly oxidised pale orange.

Q407: Hard-fired, slightly micaceous sandy matrix (subrounded/subangular iron-stained quartz <0.25mm); firing pale orange-red with pale grey inner surface; patchy clear glaze

Q408: Hard-fired matrix containing sparse, well sorted subrounded quartz <0.25mm; evenly oxidised (orange-red) with slightly darker surfaces; wheelthrown.

Q409: Hard-fired fine sandy matrix (?glauconitic sand); firing pale grey with pale orange interior; glazed; possibly wheelthrown.

R400: Hard-fired matrix containing sparse, poorly sorted subangular greensand <2mm; slightly soapy texture.

The remaining 15 fabrics form a miscellaneous group, although most are likely to be of at least relatively local manufacture. They contain varying quantities of patinated flint/chert, quartz, limestone and greensand. There is not as yet a clear understanding of the various coarsewares in use across south Dorset, apart from those already discussed, and this is not helped by the lack of detailed fabric descriptions in some published reports. There is no reason why pottery manufacture should not have taken place here, as there were abundant supplies of raw materials, although in more isolated pockets than elsewhere, and there must have been important concentrations of potential consumers in boroughs such as Dorchester and Weymouth. Evidence for manufacture, however, is confined to a few isolated documentary references such as personal names and field names (Spoerry 1988, 34).

The flint/chert-gritted wares (F400, F401) seem to have affinities to the west; only one such sherd was identified at Sutton Poyntz, but they comprise the dominant coarsewares in Bridport (Mepham 2000b, 116–7), and at Putton Lane they form 12.3% of the medieval assemblage by sherd count. Rim forms are often indeterminate between jars and bowl but given that no bowl profiles were definitively identified they probably do mostly belong to jars (a maximum of 54 vessels based on number of rims). Dating for these flint-/chert-gritted coarsewares remains vague, but their appearance at Putton Lane in Phase 2 (pre-building) contexts suggests that they have an origin at least as early as the 11th or 12th century. Rim profiles here vary between internally bevelled and (less frequently) dished, suggesting a date range that spans the 12th to 13th centuries but which is perhaps focused towards the earlier end (the dished rim seems to have appeared in the south-west c. 1200); there are also two simple everted rim profiles that suggest a Saxo-Norman date (one of which came from a Phase 2 deposit under B4). There is also a glazed strap handle that might belong to a tripod pitcher, although this is by no means certain. Other vessel forms are confined to five shallow dishes (Fig. 2.2, 10).

Of the other fabrics, the quantities of Q403 and Q404 also suggest a local origin. Vessel forms show a strong similarity to those in the flint-/chert-gritted wares – mainly jars, a number of indeterminate jar/bowl rims, with a mixture of internally bevelled and dished rim profiles. There are also two jug handles and a flanged bowl. However, here the emphasis is more on the dished profiles (26 out of 45 jar rims), suggesting a slightly later chronological focus, although a few sherds of Q403 did occur in Phase 2 contexts.

The range of vessel forms is replicated in other less commonly occurring fabrics (Q400, Q401, Q402, C400, R400); sherds of Q400, Q401, Q402, Q403, C400 and C402 occurred in Phase 2 contexts. Fabrics Q405 and Q406, for which there no diagnostic sherds, do not appear until Phase 4. Fabrics Q407, Q408 and Q409 are probably later medieval wares (14th–15th century). Most of the sherds of fabric Q408 came from the area of B8 and may belong to a single vessel with wet sgraffito decoration in the Donyatt style; another sgraffito-decorated sherd was found in subsoil (10-115) in Area 3. These sherds do not precisely match the fabric descriptions given for the medieval Donyatt wares (Coleman-Smith and Pearson 1988, 103–4).

Imports

E515: Normandy Gritty

E520A: Saintonge whiteware

E520B: Saintonge Bright Green-glazed ware

E520C: Saintonge Polychrome

E530: Iberian redware: hard-fired, fine sandy fabric (rounded/subrounded quartz <0.25mm), visibly micaceous, wheelthrown; evenly oxidised (pale orange-red)

Five imported ware types are present, comprising 64 sherds and representing a maximum of 60 vessels. The majority are Saintonge wares, which have been subdivided into three here following the Southampton typology (Brown 2002, 27–8): whiteware, bright green-glazed ware and polychrome ware. Most of the sherds from Chickerell are unglazed (31 sherds), and so have been classified as the standard whiteware by default, although a smaller proportion have a dull mottled green glaze. Most of the diagnostic sherds are in this ware type and include jug rims (one with a pulled spout) and strap handles. Four sherds carry a bright green glaze (E520B), and these include another strap handle. Polychrome ware is represented by three small body sherds only.

No sherds of North French whitewares (a relatively common early 13th century imported type found in the ports of the south coast and on 'higher status' sites in the hinterland) have been identified. This is perhaps surprising and is unlikely to have a chronological explanation as the ceramic sequence covers the early 13th century. A few sherds were identified at Sutton Poyntz (Mepham 2007). There are three sherds of Normandy Gritty ware, all undiagnostic body sherds. This is a type with pre-conquest origins, although it did continue to be produced into the 15th century; in Southampton it has a chronological focus in the late 11th and 12th centuries (Brown 2002, 22).

There are six sherds in visibly micaceous redwares, falling within the group usually termed 'Merida-type ware', although it is now recognised that this group can also encompass coarsewares made elsewhere on the Iberian peninsula (Gerrard et al. 1995, 288). Diagnostic sherds here include a small rod handle and a base, possibly from a standing costrel; the latter was found in the Phase 4 midden deposit. The ware was imported from the 13th century onwards, but a wide range of forms became common in the 16th and 17th centuries; it is impossible to pin these sherds down any more closely within this wide date range. Merida-type wares have previously been recorded from south Dorset, but only around Poole Harbour (Gerrard et al. 1995, 288., fig. 20.5c).

Post-medieval/modern pottery

Post-medieval/modern wares make up 9.6% of the total by sherd count and 16.8% by weight; the discrepancy is explained by the preponderance of larger, thicker-walled sherds amongst the earthenwares, which dominate this chronological group (85.2% by sherd count). These coarsewares provided the utilitarian component of the domestic repertoire – vessels for use in kitchen and dairy. They include two main groups: red-firing wares and the paler-firing wares characteristic of the Verwood area industry of east Dorset. The redwares are not so easily attributable to source, and indeed there are likely to be several represented, including Donyatt in south Somerset, operating throughout the post-medieval period (Coleman-Smith and Pearson 1988), and Holnest in north Dorset. The latter centre, for which documentary references are known from the 17th century (Spoerry 1988, 32) is a possible source for a few sherds with sgraffito slip decoration in 'West Country' style, whose fabric does not appear to match that of the Donyatt products (Dawson et al. 2018, 32), nor that of the mid-18th century kiln at Lyme Regis (Draper 1982). Slipware wasters have been found at Holnest (author's examination of sherds found by the late Penny Copland-Griffiths).

The dating of the earthenwares is necessarily broad; they were produced throughout the post-medieval period. The Donyatt kilns were operating until the early 20th century and the last kiln in Verwood closed in 1952. Verwood-type wares, however, are more likely to post-date the mid-18th century, the point at which production appears to have increased and these wares came to dominate the markets across much of Wessex; vessel forms are not particularly chronologically distinctive but there is one 18th century cylindrical tankard in a manganese-mottled Verwood variant of a type originally (and erroneously) termed 'Wiltshire Brown ware'. The red-firing slipwares in West Country style are 17th or 18th century. There may be plain redwares here dating earlier than this; one or two sherds have been recognised as having the appearance of 15th–16th century wares, which tend to be thinner-walled with more mottled glazes, but otherwise there is nothing that is clearly diagnostic of an earlier date. The repertoire of vessel forms is limited and does not change significantly through time. Nine sherds of redware are internally white-slipped and belong to large kitchen bowls dating to the 19th or early 20th century. Bowls and dishes predominate amongst the other diagnostic forms (largely in flared or flanged profiles), with smaller proportions of jars (some are definitely, and some probably, tripod pipkins) and jugs. There is also one costrel. A preponderance of open forms could indicate a more prevalent use in dairying (for example, for cream settling pans).

Other post-medieval/modern wares suggest that there is little or nothing here that is earlier than the 17th century. There are a few sherds of 17th–18th century German stonewares (Frechen and Westerwald) and one of late 17th–18th century Staffordshire-type yellow slipware (a handle from a cup or porringer). Other wares are 18th century or later, and include white saltglaze, creamware, pearlware, whiteware and buff/yellow ware, all providing a range of tea and tablewares, and yellow ware, with some stoneware household containers.

Post-medieval/modern sherds came largely from topsoil, clearance and rubble layers. Just over half (55% by sherd count) were found in topsoil, clearance and other unstratified layers. A further 26% were recovered from contexts in and around the stone-built structures, where a concentration in and around B1 suggests that post-medieval activity may have been focused here. Cobbled surface (15-111) appears to date to this phase.

Discussion

Chronology and sequence

In terms of chronology, and excluding the obviously residual prehistoric and Romano-British sherds, the earliest material in this assemblage belongs to the Saxo-Norman period (10th–12th centuries), although the main emphasis seems to lie between the 12th and 14th centuries. However, the fragmentary nature of the assemblage, and the fact that just over half (52.3% by sherd count) was recovered from unstratified or poorly stratified contexts (topsoil, subsoil etc), places limitations on the confidence with which the ceramic sequence can be defined. Moreover, mean sherd weights calculated for each phase are rarely greater than 10g and the highest is 12.2g. This degree of fragmentation is consistent with a high level of reworking and residuality. Bearing this in mind, Table 2.4 breaks down the stratified assemblage by phase (no pottery was associated with deposits in Phase 1). Apart from unstratified or poorly stratified contexts, a significant proportion (882 sherds; 17.0% of the total by sherd count) was recovered from rubble layers overlying the medieval buildings, and these have been assigned to Phase 5+.

Phase 2

Pottery from features stratified beneath the earliest buildings (B1, B4 and B5) amounted to 75 sherds. This small group includes two sherds of fabric E400, one of them a typical Saxo-Norman jar rim, and there is one other rim of similar profile in fabric F401. Otherwise there is nothing amongst the diagnostic sherds to confirm an early date. Perhaps of more significance is the absence or scarcity of fabric types which are assumed to be of 13th century date or later, such as West Dorset sandy ware (eight sherds only) and the finest variant of Wessex coarseware (two sherds only). A date range of 11th–12th century, with a possible extension into the early 13th century, can be suggested for this phase. Three of the sherds came from a pit (F84) which could either pre-date or be contemporary with B1. While the construction of the courtyard ditch F85 may belong to this stratigraphic phase, pottery from the fills suggests that it was not infilled until later.

Phase 3

Comparatively little pottery could be related directly to the construction of the earliest phase of buildings on the site (B1, B4 and B5), and none to the actual occupation of the buildings. A total of 302 sherds has been attributed to this phase, but about two-thirds of this total (204 sherds) is made up of sherds from a single vessel, the lower part of a jar in West Dorset sandy ware containing an infant burial, deliberately deposited in B1. The remaining 98 sherds include pottery from two post-pits (F82, F83) which either predate or have been tentatively linked to the construction of B1, the construction cut for W20 (B1), and deposits underneath B2 which presumably date somewhere prior to Phase 4. This group, as for Phase 2, is rather too small for definitive comment, but the presence of a higher proportion of West Dorset sandy ware (54.1% by sherd count, excluding the burial jar) confirms a date range no earlier than the 13th century, while the absence of Poole Harbour whiteware and Saintonge wares could limit the date range to the early part of the century. Almost all other fabrics present also occurred in Phase 2.

Phase 4

Of the 372 sherds assigned to this phase, in which B1 and B4 continued in use but B5 was replaced by B2, more than half (225 sherds) were recovered from the midden deposit in Area 2. Other groups of pottery came from the bedding trench for W6 in B2 (14-108), a rubble layer (12-137) representing the collapse of W18 in B5 (the only deposit firmly associated with the demolition phase); and the backfilling (and therefore disuse) of various field system ditches in Area 2. As in Phase 3, West Dorset sandy wares predominate (58.6% by sherd count), while Normandy Gritty ware, Poole Harbour whitewares and Saintonge wares make their first appearance. A date range of 13th century (perhaps from mid-century) to mid-14th century can be suggested. The midden deposit cannot be regarded as a particularly well stratified group, but generally reflects a 13th to mid-14th century date range; the only hint of any later material is a single sherd of fabric E425E, the later medieval variant of West Dorset sandy ware (14th–15th century).

The backfilling of the courtyard ditch F85 may also belong to this phase on ceramic grounds. The small assemblage of 107 sherds recovered from the ditch fills includes a lower proportion of West Dorset sandy wares (31.8% by sherd count) and a relatively high

Table 2.4 Medieval fabrics by phase.

Ware group	Fabric type	P2	P3	pre-P4	P4	P4+	P5+	P6+	pre-P7	P7+	alluv.	terrace	subsoil	topsoil	unstrat	Total
Saxo-Norman	E400	2				1	6								22	31
W Dorset sandy wares	E425A	8	212	5	218	94	323	72	34	126	269	7	248	82	708	2406
	E425B		45	4	40	20	56	2		45	4	1	53	13	56	339
	E425E				1	3	11				8		4		1	29
Wessex coarsewaes	E422A	2	1	1	3	4	15	1	3	54	3		6		8	101
	E422B		6	1	5	1	26	4	6	4	1	3	64	48	50	219
	E422C	2	1	6	6	2	26	1	27	11	3	3	22	8	69	187
Poole Harbour whitewares	E426A			3	1		8	1	1	4		1	3		27	49
	E426B						2									2
Imports	E515				1				1				1			3
	E520A				3	4	7				3		5	3	23	48
	E520B				2		1									3
	E520C				1						1				2	4
	E530				2		1						1		2	6
Other wares	C400	1	1			1	16			3				13	6	41
	C401				17	2	3						5		8	35
	C402	2					1								1	4
	F400	13	13	12	24	4	95	7	19	33	1		21	11	68	321
	F401	26	3		11	12	74	2	10	3	1	2	23	4	82	253
	Q400	10	6			2	9			4			2	1	22	56
	Q401	5	1		2		12			3			1	2	6	32
	Q402	1		1	7	2	3						3		21	38
	Q403	3	5	6	15	9	21	6		3	7	1	41	5	21	143
	Q404		8		8	3	51	1	4	43			33	33	100	284
	Q405				5								1			6
	Q407			1			5						1		2	9
	Q408							23					4			27
	Q409														1	1
	R400					2	4		2						2	10
	Total	75	302	40	372	166	776	120	107	336	301	18	542	223	1308	4687

proportion (25.2%) of the finest variant of Wessex coarseware (13th century or later). There is one sherd of Normandy Gritty ware and one of Poole Harbour whiteware.

PHASE 5 OR LATER

No pottery could be related specifically to the demolition of B1, B2 and B4. Pottery recovered from rubble layers over the walls of the medieval buildings could be associated with their use but could equally include later material. As well as a large quantity of medieval and earlier material (782 sherds), 100 post-medieval/modern sherds were found in these layers, mostly from B1 but also from B2 and B4. These sherds would appear to be contemporary with the occupation of B3, B6, B7 and B9 and could indicate some continued use of the demolished buildings, perhaps in some agricultural capacity (see below, Phase 7).

PHASE 6

B8 was thought to be a later medieval construction. Analysis of pottery from this building, however, encountered the same problem as for the earlier buildings in that pottery was recovered only from demolition/disuse layers rather than any associated with its occupation. The quantity overall is small (120 sherds) and the range of ware types is much the same as for B1, B2, B4 and B5, with a similar proportion of West Dorset sandy wares (59.5% of the total by sherd count). There is only one sherd of Poole Harbour whiteware and none of Saintonge; the scarcity of these 13th to early 14th century types could have a chronological explanation, but could equally well be functional, the assemblage being more utilitarian and containing little tableware. There are, however, a few sherds of Donyatt ware, including a sgraffito-decorated vessel, and one sherd of redware that has the appearance of an early post-medieval vessel (15th–16th century). The evidence is slight and poorly stratified but could support a later medieval date for this building.

PHASE 7

As for the medieval buildings, no pottery can be associated with the occupation of the post-medieval buildings (B3, B6, B7 and B9), but there are two areas of cobbled surface that appear to be contemporary with their use (context (15-111) in

the angle between B1 and B3, and F44 to the east of B1). Of the 79 sherds recovered from these layers, 29 are medieval and the remainder post-medieval/modern. The predominance in this group of redwares and Verwood-type earthenwares and the scarcity of sherds dating later than early to mid 18th century (i.e. white salt glaze and later refined wares) suggests that activity here was sporadic after that date.

GENERAL COMMENTS

The ceramic sequence outlined above is perhaps easier to define at the earlier end, where a start date in the 11th or 12th century can be relatively convincingly identified and includes well stratified sherds. After the mid-14th century, however, the evidence is not so clear. Later medieval wares (e.g. sgraffito slipwares in Donyatt style) and vessel forms (cisterns, candlestick) have been identified, and on this basis a late medieval date has been suggested for B8, but none of this pottery is well stratified. It seems evident now that West Dorset sandy wares continued in production and use into the late medieval period, but apart from these more diagnostic forms it is difficult to isolate the later products. Other late medieval consumer sites are scarce so there is little in the way of comparable data, and this in any case is not unambiguous.

The wider context

The pottery from the Lower Putton Lane settlement forms one of three significant assemblages from medieval manorial sites in the county, the others being the nearby manor at Sutton Poyntz (Rawlings 2007; Mepham 2007) and Stratton Old Manor (Maw and Mepham forthcoming). All three have produced assemblages covering a similar chronological period, focusing on the 13th–14th century. The assemblages from Chickerell and Stratton are similar in size (4687 medieval sherds from Chickerell, 5146 from Stratton), whilst Sutton Poyntz produced a somewhat smaller collection (1763 sherds from the area of one building in an apparently wider complex). Comparisons between the three have highlighted areas of similarity, but also interesting differences.

Looking at the proportions of the major ware groups represented at each site (Fig. 2.3, Fig. 2.4 and Fig. 2.5), all three appear to have had some sources

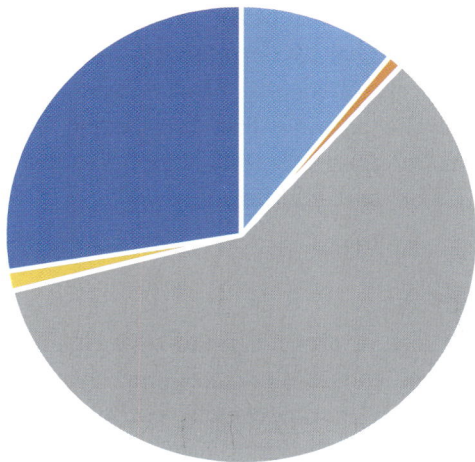

■ WC ■ PHW ■ WDS ■ IMP ■ Other

Fig. 2.3   Major ware groups, Chickerell.

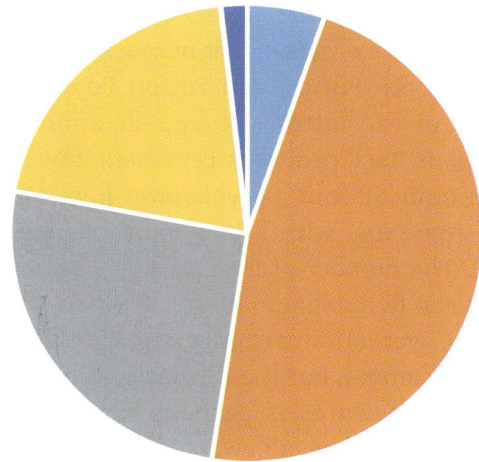

■ WC ■ PHW ■ WDS ■ Imports ■ Other

Fig. 2.5   Major ware groups, Sutton Poyntz.

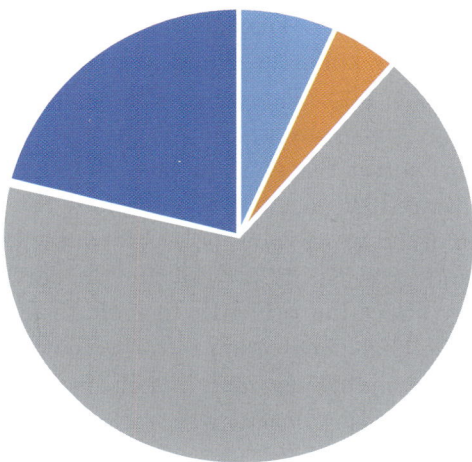

■ WC ■ PHW ■ WDS ■ Imports ■ Other

Fig. 2.4   Major ware groups, Stratton.

27 Poole Harbour jugs, as well as a number of sherds in other wares).

If differing chronology is ruled out, other factors affecting the proportions of the various ware types could include accessibility and site function. Looking at the broadly comparable assemblages from Chickerell and Stratton, the pattern accords with broad distribution areas outlined by Spoerry (1990, figs. 5 and 6); the slightly higher proportion of West Dorset sandy wares at Stratton almost certainly reflects a closer proximity to the known production centre at Hermitage.

The presence of imported wares is often taken as an indicator of a site's high social status, but this interpretation is by no means straightforward – the perceived value and desirability of imported vessels may have varied according to location. Along the south coast imports are primarily concentrated in major ports such as Poole and are rare occurrences on inland sites, where they do tend to be restricted to 'high status' sites such as castles and manorial settlements. Their scarce occurrence at Stratton would fit this interpretation, with Poole Harbour whitewares making up the tableware requirement instead. The picture is more complex for coastal sites, which could have accessed such wares through coastal redistribution, or through direct import – Weymouth is documented as one of a restricted number of south coast ports receiving wine imports

of supply in common: West Dorset sandy wares, Wessex coarsewares, Poole Harbour whitewares and imported wares (mainly Saintonge). However, while Putton compares well with Stratton, the Sutton Poyntz assemblage shows a different composition, with unusually high proportions of finewares (Poole Harbour and Saintonge wares). While the proportions in this case are undoubtedly skewed by the fact that several vessels were fragmentary and were each represented by a large number of sherds, the number of vessels still appears unusually high in comparison with the other two sites (it includes four Saintonge polychrome jugs and a minimum of from France (Allan 1983, 204). This could account for the presence of significant numbers of imported vessels at both Putton and Sutton Poyntz. Sherd numbers at the latter site appear anomalously high, but in fact probably represent few vessels (a minimum of four polychrome jugs and one monochrome jug, with a maximum of nine other vessels). The number of imported vessels at Lower Putton Lane (a maximum of 64, of which 60 are in Saintonge wares) is certainly high for Dorset (J. Allan pers.comm.), but the low proportion of Poole Harbour whitewares is perhaps surprising. The large quantity of fine tablewares (both locally made and imported) found at Sutton Poyntz is thought to reflect the use of the excavated area of the site as a chapel rather than as part of the domestic accommodation of the manorial complex. Sutton Poyntz is discussed further in Chapter 6.

THE CERAMIC BUILDING MATERIAL,
By Lorraine Mepham

Introduction

The assemblage of ceramic building material (CBM) amounts to 439 fragments, weighing 23,867 g. The assemblage is overwhelmingly of medieval date, with one or two possible Romano-British fragments, and a few post-medieval items.

The assemblage has been quantified (count and weight) by type within each context (e.g. ridge tile, floor tile, etc). Diagnostic features (such as crests on ridge tiles) have been noted. All these details can be found in the project archive. Table 2.5 gives the

Table 2.5 CBM quantification by type.

Period	CBM type	No. frags	Wt. (g)
?Romano-British	All types	2	202
	undiagnostic	1	63
Medieval	hearth tile	36	1474
	ridge tile	368	20,248
	roof furniture	6	514
Post-medieval/ modern	All types	27	1429
	Total	439	23,867

quantified breakdown of the assemblage (fragment count and weight) by chronological period and by type. Only the medieval CBM is discussed here; details of the possible Romano-British and post-medieval/modern material can be found in the assessment report for the site.

Ridge tile

With the exception of a small quantity of hearth tile, the medieval CBM consists entirely of roof tile. Flat (peg) tiles are apparently completely absent, and instead the tile largely comprises fragments of ridge tile. Their distribution shows a distinct concentration in the area of B2.

The ridge tiles are remarkably homogeneous in appearance. The more complete examples show that they were inverted V-shaped and crested, adorned with triangular knife-cut crests in a 'cock's comb' effect (Fig. 2.6, 1–2). Crest heights range from 25–35 mm but are generally in the range of 30–35 mm. Surviving mortar traces show that the ridge tiles were mortared in place end to end along the ridge. The sides of the crests were slashed, on one side only, at the junction with the body of the tile, partly as a decorative effect, but primarily to avoid firing faults by allowing heat penetration into the thicker parts of the tile. Only one example is not slashed at all, although otherwise identical to the rest in appearance.

The tiles were at least partially glazed; most examples show the survival of a thin, patchy, pale olive-green glaze over oxidised surfaces, but a smaller proportion carries a thicker, more even olive-green glaze on reduced surfaces; the significance of the distinction is uncertain, but the more evenly glazed tiles may be slightly later in date. It may be no coincidence that the only crested example with this thicker glaze has a crest height at the lower end of the range (25 mm), as there is a demonstrable chronological pattern of crest reduction into the early post-medieval period, although later examples do tend to be thumbed rather than knife-cut (see, for example, Coleman-Smith and Pearson 1988, fig. 168, 33/18–19).

The fabric of the ridge tiles is very similar throughout; a relatively fine sandy fabric with a powdery feel, oxidised to a pale brown-orange, although a

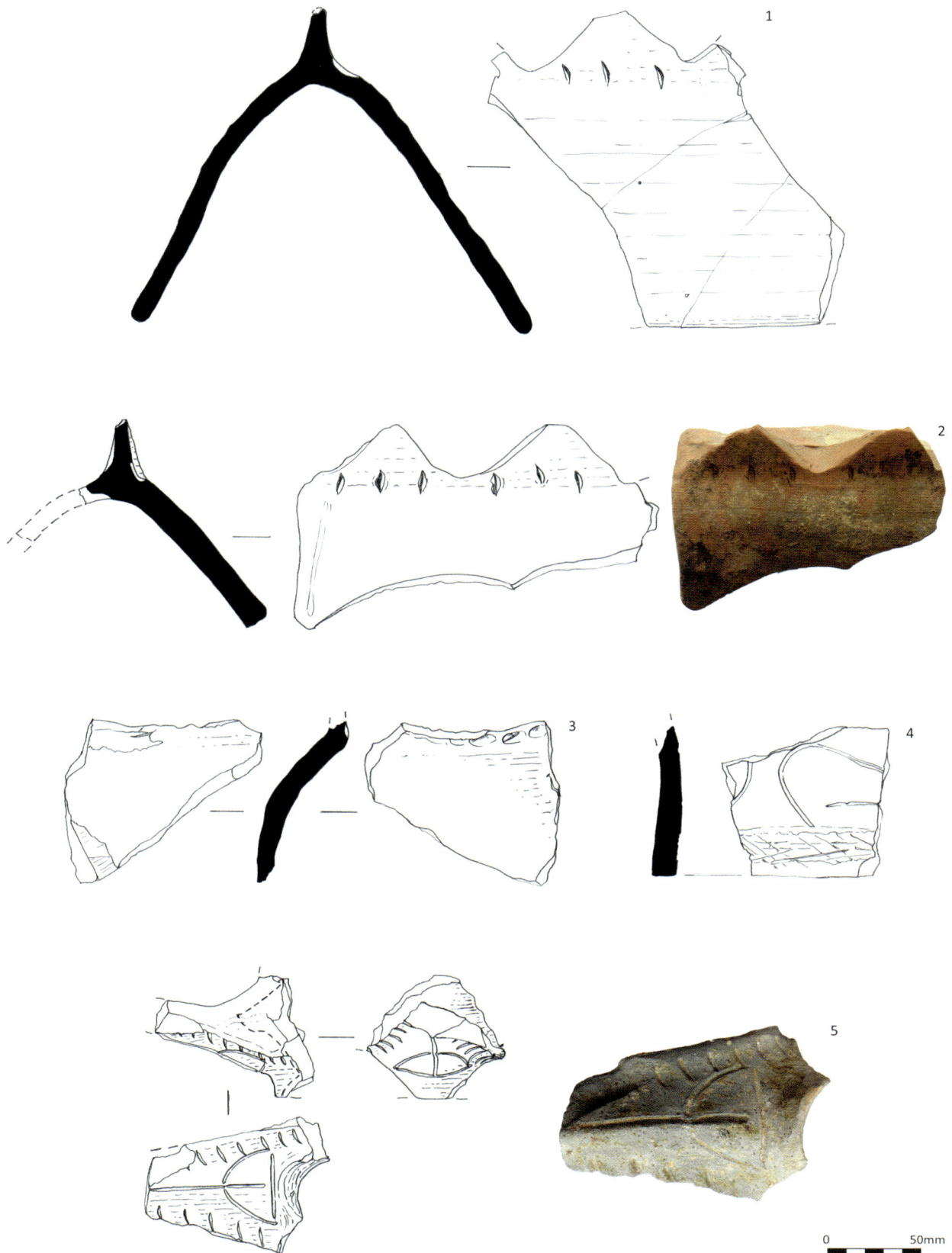

Fig. 2.6 Ridge tiles. 1. Crested ridge tile, full profile. Context (1601). 2. Crested ridge tile, part profile. W5. 3. Possible louver fragment, glazed. Unstratified. 4. Possible roof furniture, incised decoration and traces of glaze. Rubble west of W5. 5.Possible roof furniture; tooled decoration; unglazed band keyed for attachment of applied element; glazed. Context (1001), topsoil. Drawings © Liz James.

few examples are a brighter red-orange; there is generally a pale grey core. This is macroscopically comparable to the sandy pottery wares from West Dorset (see Pottery, this chapter). Examples were found at the pottery kiln at Hermitage and dated as late 13th century on the basis of the knife-cut crests – earlier examples were apparently thumbed (Field 1966, 172, fig. 9, 41).

In general, medieval ridge tiles elsewhere in Dorset appear to be confined to urban sites, such as Dorchester (Bellamy 1993), Wimborne (Woodward 1983, fig. 6; Graham 1984, fig. 5) and Poole (Jarvis 1992, fig. 77, 1–2; Jarvis 1994, fig. 44) and 'higher status' (e.g. manorial or castle) sites, such as Sutton Poyntz (Wells 2007a), Sherborne Old Castle (Wells 1993) and Corfe Castle (RCHME 1960, fig. 14; Mepham 2012). Where sufficient details of tile fabric are provided, it seems that most ridge tiles were made in fabrics which correspond to local pottery, as is the case at Chickerell. Ridge tiles from Sherborne Old Castle and Sutton Poyntz are also largely in fabrics equivalent to West Dorset sandy ware and are very similar in appearance to the Chickerell tiles. There is, however, also some evidence for longer distance movement, such as white-firing ridge tiles from Wareham being transported for use at Glastonbury Abbey (Coleman-Smith and Pearson 1988, 321). In areas with ready supplies of stone for roofing slabs, as over much of Dorset, the use of ceramic tiles was confined to the ridge.

Roof furniture

There are a few fragments of what appears to be more elaborate roof furniture. Two fragments found unstratified may be from a roof-finial, louver or chimney pot (Fig. 2.6, 3), although not enough survives to enable reconstruction of the form – a louver from Southampton gives one possible parallel, based on the curvature and possible edge of a curved opening (Platt and Coleman-Smith 1975, fig. 215, no. 1413), but there are many other possibilities. The fabric is similar, although not identical, to that of the ridge tiles, and the glaze is a more even, mottled green. One fragment from rubble west of W5 of B2 is a hollow tapering object with rhomboid cross-section, with incised decoration and traces of a thin glaze (Fig. 2.6, 5). This may belong to a finial, or to a very elaborate ridge tile crest. Finally, three fragments from topsoil context (1001), two of them conjoining, may belong to a ridge tile as above, but the object has random curvilinear tooled lines on the surface, a thick, mottled olive-green glaze, and a narrow unglazed band just above the lower edge which is scored, perhaps for the attachment of some other element (Fig. 2.6, 4).

Hearth tile

A small group of 36 fragments, of which 25 were found in one unstratified context (801) have been identified as hearth tiles, although few carry diagnostic features. These fragments are in coarse fabrics, with sparse flint or other coarse inclusions. The upper surface is flat, and one or two large fragments have multiple tapering circular perforations made from the rear, but not perforating the complete thickness of the tile.

THE ARCHITECTURAL STONE, By Cheryl Green

The buildings at Lower Putton Lane utilised stone quarried from the underlying cornbrash limestone bedrock, however the shaped blocks and ashlar used as facing material and the roofing tiles were derived from limestone quarries on the Isle of Portland, situated a few miles to the south-east. No architectural fragments were found in situ or amongst the vast quantities of building material present on the site however the local Portland beds were probably the source of the dressings. A single piece of ashlar stone was collected, and nine exemplar stone roofing tiles selected from amongst the extensive spreads of this material recorded close to and within the medieval buildings.

The roof tiles were derived from rubble layers (12-121) and (12-124) within B2, from within W4 and W15 also of B2, and from the walls of B4. All the samples from the walls had lime mortar adhering to them, suggesting the walls may have incorporated tiles from earlier buildings. One of these tiles had light sooting on one flat surface consistent with smoke residues from an interior hearth; clusters of tile within B2 were also heavily sooted and may have collapsed together during dismantling of the building (see Chapter 1, Phase 5).

The tiles were fabricated from the Portland limestone beds and retain at least one straight edge and with a maximum of two straight edges. Thickness varies between 5–20mm, consistent with handmade tiles, and where circular peg holes are present, these measure 8–10mm diameter. Some were lipped at the edges for overlapping with the next tile, helping to ensure a firm fixing. No complete tiles were observed on the site, the largest specimen measuring 200mm by 180mm. This is broadly consistent with the tiles found at Sutton Poyntz, where the Portland/Purbeck limestone tiles measured 180–240mm by 125–160mm (Wells 2007b, 55). The single small piece of dressed building stone (801) is a fine textured, shelly, oolitic limestone with a Portland provenance, a finer grained version of the Portland Roach and therefore more likely a shelly Portland Whit Bed (Leary 1983, 51).

The Putton manor is broadly contemporary with the chapel excavated at Sutton Poyntz, which is thought to date to the 13th–14th century (Rawlings 2007), therefore it would seem that both sites were tapping into the Portland resource. Documents record Portland stone being transported for use at prestigious buildings such as Exeter Cathedral and Westminster in the 14th century although the stone had long been appreciated (Salzman 1952, 133). High status exploitation was centred on the fine-grained oolitic limestones of the Portland Whit Bed (a fine grained oolitic limestone with broken shell debris) and Portland Base Bed (a pure, fine grained oolite with shell fragments). In the East Midlands it has been demonstrated that from the 13th and 14th centuries most quarries were under royal control as opposed to the jurisdiction of local lords within manorial holdings, ensuring the crown had adequate resources for the numerous building programmes that were underway (Alexander 1995, 110). Quarrying rights in England were often acquired through royal consent and then patronage, as demonstrated for the exploitation of Quarr stone from the Isle of Wight from the late 11th to 13th centuries (Bishop 2000, 27). As such, access to the Portland quarries likely reflects the wealth and connections of both Putton and Sutton Poyntz, although ease of transportation (in this case mostly by sea) would also have been a major consideration alongside other factors.

The absence of architectural stone, such as chamfered blocks for door surrounds or window tracery, indicates wholesale removal during careful and deliberate dismantling perhaps for re-use in the construction of new buildings. However, the tiles may not have been valued in quite the same way, with several dumps of broken stone slates being consistent with the roofs falling in on themselves and large swathes sliding to the ground. This seems to have been a preliminary step in the demolition process and might also explain why the lower courses of the walls survived as a consequence of being buried beneath this debris.

The building materials at Lower Putton Lane reflect access to local resources, both those immediately available and those from the Portland limestone beds a few miles distant. It is possible that Purbeck limestone and indeed Purbeck marble may have been utilised, however any such material must have fallen victim to the extensive robbing to which the site was subject. Both stones were being quarried in the 13th century (Leary 1983, 60), and Purbeck marble was employed at the 13th–14th century chapel at Sutton Poyntz and within numerous extant churches within Dorset.

3

THE SMALL FINDS, GLASS, STONE OBJECTS AND HUMAN REMAINS

THE SMALL FINDS, By Jörn Schuster

Methodology

The objects were examined visually and, where required, with hand lenses (×4, ×8 magnification). Basic type identifications such as 'pin' or 'nail' were recorded. Broad period dates attributed to the finds are based on the intrinsic dates established by comparison to known parallels and typologies. X-radiographies prepared of selected objects by Wessex Archaeology, Salisbury aided identification of further details where necessary. Object identification, measurements, including weight, and detailed descriptions as well as contextual details are available in the archive. Unillustrated objects are identified below by either an originally allocated small finds number (SF) or x-radiography group number (XR).

Quantification, Provenance and Chronological Range

The assemblage comprises approximately 1073 objects; due to the frequently very poor preservation condition of many items, and those made of iron in particular, the exact number of objects recovered from the site can only remain an approximation. In spite of this, the assemblage includes a number of exquisite and very rare objects, for instance a Salian oval gold filigree brooch with (probable) rock crystal setting or a very rare coin type minted in the last year of Emperor Gallienus' reign (AD 268). A breakdown by material is shown in Table 3.1. The

Table 3.1   Number of objects per material across all periods.

Material	Total
Gold/?rock crystal	1
Silver	23
?Silver	2
CuA/Gold	9
CuA	244
CuA/Iron	2
CuA/Leather	1
CuA/Stone	1
CuA?/Lead alloy?	1
Iron/CuA	1
Iron	692
Nickel-Silver (incl. EPNS)	2
Pewter	4
Lead	73
Lead/CuA	3
Lead/Glass	1
?Glass	1
Aluminium	2
Aluminium/CuA	4
Aluminium/Worked bone	1
Worked bone	3
Worked stone	1
Mortar	1
Grand Total	1073

small finds in this report are arranged in groups of functional categories following Crummy (1983, 5–6), with the addition of a category "commerce" covering

Table 3.2 Number of objects per functional catergory and site phase (after Crummy 1983, 5–6, with additions). U/S = Unstratified.

Site phase Function Group	2	3	3&4	4	5	7	8	U/S	Total
Personal			4			4	29	50	87
Toiletry/Medicine								2	2
Textile working							4	3	7
Household			4			2	23	7	36
Leisure								6	6
Metrology			1				3	2	6
Commerce			1	1			18	67	87
Writing							1	1	2
Transport	4		2		1	2	77	11	97
Building			1				5	4	10
Tool					3		13	3	19
Fitting	1	13	12		34	2	420	57	539
Agriculture			1				1	10	12
Weapon					1		7	23	31
Metalworking		1	1				3	3	8
Uncertain		3	3		14	4	82	18	124
Grand Total	5	17	30	1	53	14	686	267	1073

all coins (Table 3.2), and the subsequent period-based discussion will follow this sequence.

The assemblage ranges in date from the Roman period to the 20th century. A summary overview of finds assigned to broad periods is presented in Table 3.3. The wide range of materials listed in Table 3.1 is owed in part to this wide date range as it includes a considerable variety of modern and composite materials. Details of the modern finds were recorded in a database and are available in the archive, but they are not included in the discussion presented in this report.

The assemblage exhibits a high degree of residuality, with 267 objects either unstratified or from surface/topsoil contexts, predominantly recovered by metal detecting, while most of the remaining objects derive from demolition or clearance layers. However, almost 38% of the assemblage is intrinsically dateable, and this permits a reasonable degree of chronological analysis.

Discussion here will focus on the Roman, medieval and post-medieval periods, and to that end many of the objects with either no or very broad intrinsic dates have been combined into 'discussion phases'. Comparison between Table 3.3 and Table 3.4 demonstrates that this division is undoubtedly somewhat arbitrary; it is in large parts due to the decision to include most of the finds listed in the category 'fasteners and fittings', which is dominated by nails, in the medieval discussion even though many of the objects have date ranges that cover the subsequent and/or previous periods as well. The rationale behind this decision was that the contexts containing the majority of the finds in the younger phases are predominantly clearance-, demolition- and levelling deposits, but most of the intrinsically dateable finds they contained were demonstrably older, residual finds; for instance, almost 69% of all objects that were intrinsically dateable to the medieval period were recovered from Phase 8 contexts.

The Roman small finds

There are five objects of Roman date, a copper alloy needle and four coins of the same material; however, none was recovered from contemporary features,

Table 3.3   Intrinsically datable objects per site phase. U/S = Unstratified.

Site phase Intrinsic date	2	3	3&4	4	5	7	8	U/S	Total
Roman							3	2	5
Medieval	4		7		5	2	104	30	152
Post-medieval			2	1	1	6	47	73	130
Modern							15	104	119
?	1	17	21		47	6	517	58	667
Grand Total	5	17	30	1	53	14	686	267	1073

Table 3.4   Number of finds considered in discussion phase chapters per site phase. U/S = Unstratified.

Phase	2	3	3&4	4	5	7	8	U/S	Total
Roman							3	2	5
Medieval	5	17	30		53	6	550	82	743
Post-medieval				1		5	29	39	74
Modern						1	19	132	152
?						2	85	12	99
Grand Total	5	17	30	1	53	14	686	267	1073

and they merely attest to human occupation in the wider vicinity of the site.

The needle (Cat. No. 1; Fig. 3.1) with a round-sectioned shaft and missing tip has a lanceolate eye with bulging sides set in a groove slightly below a round-sectioned terminal. It was a residual find from a clearance layer assigned to Phase 8. The treatment of the head is unusual for Roman needles from Britain, where the best comparisons might be needles of Crummy's type 3 'with a groove above and below the eye', but in those needles the groove above the non-bulging eye continues to the end of the head (Crummy 1983, 66–7, fig. 70, 1991, 1993). The closest parallels for Cat. No. 1 can be found among Beckmann's Gruppe 1, Form 1 of needles from Roman Iron Age contexts in Germany and Denmark; the slight groove above and below the eye is a feature that leads onto Form 2 (Beckmann 1966, 14–16, Taf. 1,1.2; see e.g. Schuster 2006, 66, 263, Taf. 16, 127, 129). Although the closest morphological comparisons are found among the Roman Iron Age-needles mentioned above, the possibility of a later date should not be entirely discounted since there are forms of later needles with bulging eyes set in a groove, although their terminals are either flat and

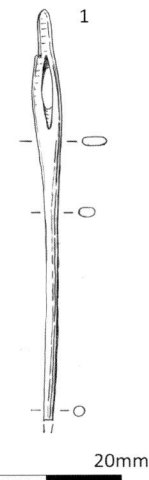

Fig. 3.1   Copper alloy: Cat. No. 1. © Liz James.

blunt (e.g. late 16th century Norwich. See Margeson 1993, 186, fig. 137, 1453) or split by the groove and soldered (e.g. late medieval Kloster Arnsburg, Germany. cf Austermann 1999, 313, Abb. 3, 13).

The four coins are all made of copper alloy. The earlier ones are probably all from the reign of Antoninus Pius (AD 138—161), including one *as* and two *dupondii*, while the later coin is an extremely rare

Fig. 3.2   Antoninianus of Gallienus (minted AD268), copper alloy.

example of an Antoninianus of Emperor Gallienus minted in Rome in the last year of his reign (AD 268) (Fig. 3.2), i.e. it is a coin of the central state at a time when the British provinces were part of the Gallic Empire under Posthumus. An overview of the coins is presented in the following (the format lists small finds number, weight and dimensions (in mm), issuer, description. Date range. Excavation event and context information; followed by site phase):

1. SF76, 2.8g, D20.9–23.9, T1.7, ?**Antoninus Pius**, As? Obv. Bust facing right, legend illegible. Rev. completely denuded (AD 138–161). EXC/16, (2005), Area 2; 8.
2. SF95, 11.2g, L28.9, W18.2, T3.7, **Antoninus Pius**, ?Dupondius. Broken in half across neck and chin missing, obv. [A]NTONINVS AVG [?..], radiate head right. Rev. [?..?], female draped figure standing left sacrificing at altar to her right? (AD 138–161). EXC/16; U/S.
3. 15.3g, D27.6–28.4, T3.9, ?**Antoninus Pius**, Dupondius Obv. Radiate bust facing right, legend illegible. Rev. completely denuded. ??RIC III Antoninus Pius 658? (?AD 140–144). AMR/13; U/S.
4. XR111, 1.8g, D19.7–21.2, **Gallienus** (253–268), Antoninianus. Obv. Radiate bust from front facing r., IMP GALLIENVS [AVG]. Rev. Centaur walking r aiming a bow and arrow held in both hands, [APOL] LINI CON[S] AVG // Z. Officina 7. Normanby 339. (AD 268). AMR/13, (501), Building 1; 8. Fig. 3.2.

The medieval small finds

Objects of dress and personal adornment

Brooches

The four brooches from the site cover the basic three different forms of brooch shapes, i.e. bow, plate and annular or penannular. All are residual finds, with Cat. Nos. 2 and 3 found by metal detector as part of the initial archaeological monitoring, while Cat. No. 4 and SF122 were recovered from the subsoil in Areas 2 and 3 of the excavation respectively.

The copper alloy ansate brooch (also known as caterpillar, equal-armed or gleicharmige Bügelfibel) Cat. No. 2 (Fig. 3.3) has a bow decorated with tri-lobed leaf-shaped terminals and a hemispherical element at the apex of the bow. Although the head terminal with the attachment lug for the spring and pin is missing, it will almost certainly have replicated the shape of the foot which has a strip-like, right-facing, catchplate. Ansate brooches are among the most widespread early medieval brooch forms in Northwest Europe and have been the subject of a major study by Thörle (2001; for a summary of previous research see also Schuster 2006, 56). The classification system has also been adopted and adapted by Weetch (2014, 140–2) for the English material, which has been substantially augmented since the inception of the Portable Antiquity Scheme (PAS). On this basis, the Chickerell brooch can be assigned to Weetch's type XII.Aiii (Weetch 2014, 169, 172–3), a subdivision of Thörle's Pommerœul type, type XII.A2, characterised by four outfacing C-shaped lobes. The pronounced hemispherical element on the bow could be a very worn example of the facetted treatment with flattened apex seen in brooches of Weetch type XII.Ai. (see e.g. Handringham, Norfolk, Weetch 2014, 171, fig. 3.81), but an only marginally less pronounced bow can also be seen on a type XII. Aiii-brooch from 16–22 Coppergate, York (Weetch 2014, 213, Cat. No. 1419; Mainman and Rogers 2000, 2570–1, fig. 1266, 10426). The date range of type XII.A brooches on the Continent covers the 9th and 10th centuries, while in England a type XII. Aii brooch was found in a 10th century male burial at Norwich Castle. The above-mentioned brooch from York came from a Period 4B context dated to AD c. 930/5–c. 975 (Weetch 2014, 170, 261). The Chickerell brooch is the first example of the type to have been found this far south and west, with most examples concentrated in East Anglia and a loose scatter around the edge of the fens and along the Thames (Weetch 2014, 262, fig. 5.10; 250, fig. 35). As a typological phenomenon, the general abundance of ansate brooches, especially in eastern and southern England, has been seen as an expression of a distinct cultural identity across the southern North Sea zone, based on trade and exchange (Weetch 2014, Ch. 5 with extensive discussion). Even though ansate brooches are generally assumed to be an element

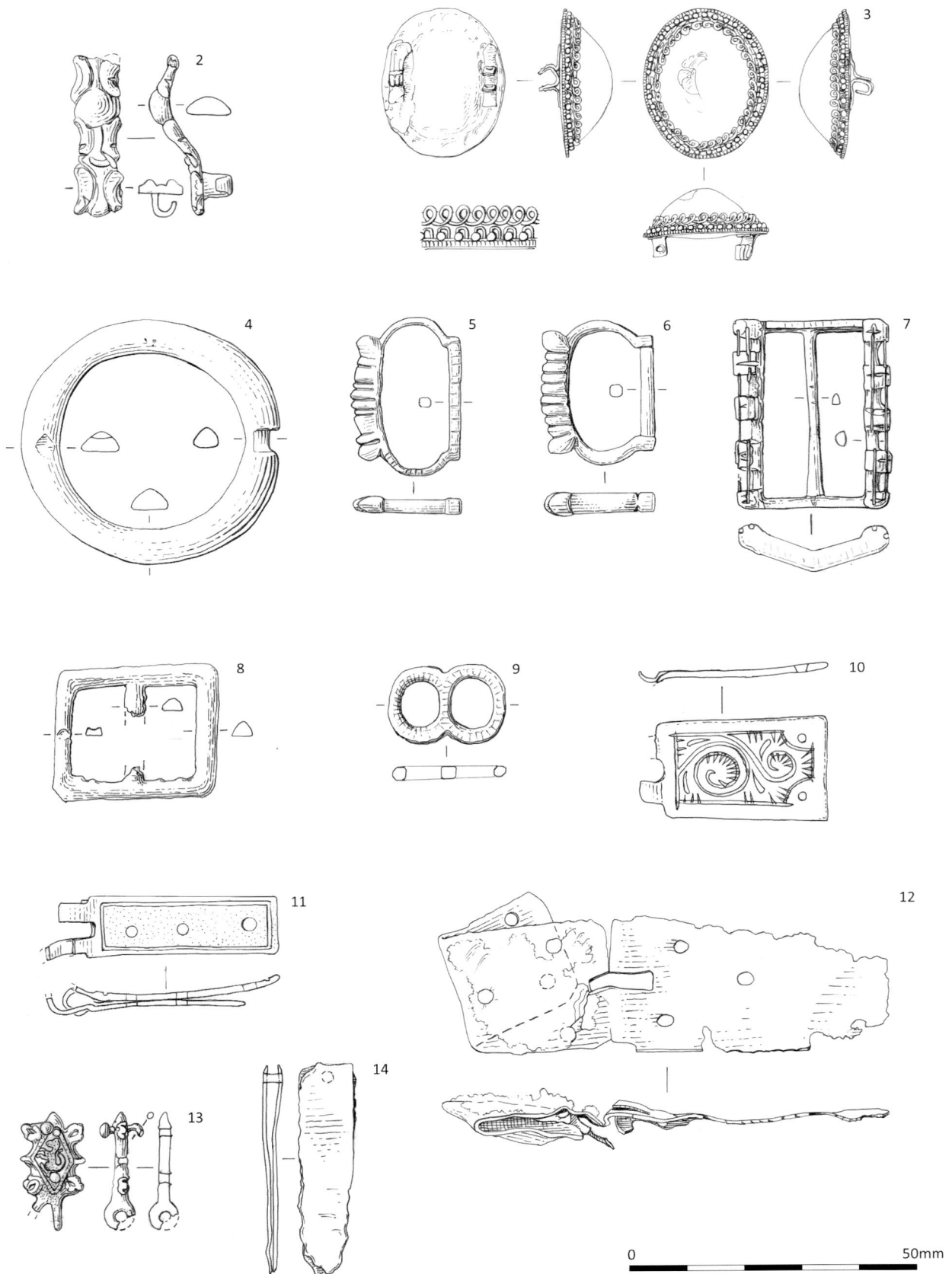

Fig. 3.3   Gold and rock crystal: Cat. No. 3; copper alloy: Cat. Nos 2, 4–7, 9, 11–12, 14; copper alloy and gilding: Cat. Nos 10–11, 13; pewter: Cat. No. 8. © Liz James.

Fig. 3.4   Oval plate brooch Cat. No. 3; gold and rock crystal.

of female dress, a small number have been found in male burials, like the above-mentioned example from Norwich Castle (Weetch 2014, 327), as well as on the eastern margin of the Continental distribution area (Truc 1997, 40–1; Hübener 1972, 215).

By far the richest object in the entire assemblage is an oval plate brooch, Cat. No. 3 (Figs. 3.3 and 3.4). It has a golden base plate with filigree setting for a polished stone, almost certainly a rock crystal (N.B. no gemmological analysis of the gemstone has been carried out). The intricate filigree setting is made of three concentric zones rising towards the stone. Set on an oval base plate with an outer rim of block-twisted gold wire ('Spiralspuldraht mit quadratischem Querschnitt', see Wolters 1985, 1073, Abb. 2, 1; Frick 1992, 259, Abb. 7, 11), the first zone is decorated with globular granules set at more or less regular intervals. The first and second zones are separated by a flange of flat sheet with crenellated edge/flattened corbeled wire (which at the time of analysis was still largely obscured by adhering soil). The second zone is filled by a plain wire set in undulating loops. The third zone is separated off by a block-twisted wire. The wire acts as the base for the inner collet, above the wire a second wire with continuous loops is soldered onto the collet so that the loop tops, which are bent inwards to hold the stone, extend above the collet edge. The base below the damaged stone is silver-coloured and now discoloured reddish-brown and grey in some places. It is assumed that this is due to post-depositional corrosion rather than deliberate colouration. However, it was not possible to ascertain whether the golden base would have been silvered or applied with a silver sheet in the area below the stone, although based on a distinct line visible on

lateral x-radiographs the latter would appear to be the more likely explanation. With the catchplate opening pointing upwards, the hinge sits on the left side of the backplate (as seen from the front) and the H-shaped pin-lug is folded out of one strip of sheet metal. The catchplate on the right consists of two double-grooved strips. When worn, this transverse pin construction would cause the top of the brooch to slant forwards across its long axis. Although the stone is now damaged its shape can be described as oval and probably plano-convex in section, but it has to be emphasised that it was not possible to ascertain the exact shape of its base, which is obscured by the setting (the potential relevance of the shape will be discussed below).

The construction details of Cat. No. 3 find a close comparison in another gold brooch, but set with an irregularly shaped garnet, which was found by metal detector in a field at Plashes Farm, Colliers End, near Ware, Hertfordshire (now in the British Museum, No. 1994,0516.1). Both brooches can be linked to Salian goldwork from the middle of the 11th to early 12th centuries. A close parallel is the looped wire setting of an oval gold filigree brooch set with an 'Alsengemme' (an intaglio in blue-black glass) from Lübeck, Germany; it was found below the floor of the first stone church, built around 1100/first third of the 12th century, within the Slavic hillfort Alt-Lübeck. It has been suggested that the – most likely redeposited – brooch derived from one of the princely tombs within the church from the period after 1100 (Schulze-Dörrlamm 1990, 217 Taf. 30,1; Schulze-Dörrlamm 1992, 438–9 Vitrine 8, 10 and Farbtaf.). The detail of the looped wire, soldered onto the top of the collet and extending above it, is found on many examples of exquisite late Salian German goldwork from the 11th and 12th centuries but for example never occurs on work associated with the Egbert workshop at Trier, working between AD 977 and 993 (Schulze-Dörrlamm 1990, 217–18 with notes 23 and 24). It is seen on numerous gem settings on the front faces of altar crosses like the 'Hezilokreuz' (third quarter 11th century) from the 'Heilig-Kreuz' church in Hildesheim (Schulze-Dörrlamm 1990 359–60, Vitrine 1) or the 'Heinrichskreuz' from the Dom at Fritzlar (Schulze-Dörrlamm 1990, 365–68, Vitrine 5; see also 217, Taf. 30, 3).

The same treatment of looped wire is also encountered on a crescent-shaped earring found in Mainz together with a – probably associated – monkey skull and a coin of the Byzantine emperor Romanos III Argyros (1028–1034), although it is likely that the treasure was buried much later, located within the treasure chamber in the compound of the Imperial Palas, where it might have become trapped during a riot in the year after Empress Matilda's wedding to Emperor Henry V at Mainz on 7 January 1114. Apart from the looped wire, the earring also features beaded wire around the rim of the base, followed by an undulating flat wire, but it also includes other, richer decoration like loops for the suspension of a string of pearls as well as filigree wire cones with granules. It belongs to a type of crescent earrings, like those from the treasure of the Empress Agnes, also from Mainz, that imitated Fatimid and Byzantine earrings and which were made during the middle third of the 11th century (Schulze-Dörrlamm 1992, 276–77 and Farbtaf. Vitrine 9, 7; 2020; 292, Abb. 3, 3, with new evidence and discussion of the circumstances of the treasure's deposition).

The Chickerell brooch represents the high-end version of an as yet relatively small group of oval plate brooches with rock crystal setting with a wide distribution across Scandinavia, northern Germany and southern England (for a distribution map lacking the English examples, see Sørensen 2005, 349, Abb. 9). An interesting find, linking the Chickerell brooch to this group, comes from Østergård, Denmark, where a very ornate gold brooch was found in the post-hole of a large house, possibly a wooden palas, dated to the 12th century. The brooch has broad filigree zones with a central rock crystal in a setting similar to the Chickerell brooch, but with a spirally wound wire where the Chickerell one has its undulating loops. The same spirally wound wire construction is seen in the second brooch found in the post-hole, made of silver and set with a large rock crystal (Sørensen 2005, 347, Abb. 6 [silver] and 7 [gold]). A lead alloy brooch from Vintry, London, has a comparable spirally wound wire surrounding a plain collet for a now missing stone or possibly glass setting (Weetch 2014, Vol. 1, 372, fig. 7.17B). While the Chickerell and Plashes Farm brooches are likely to have been manufactured by possibly Italian goldsmiths in a workshop with relations to the imperial court of the

Holy Roman Empire – as has been assumed for those from Østergård (Sørensen 2005, 382) – they could well be the high-end, precious metal brooches that could have served as the models for such lead alloy examples as that from Vintry, or a brass example missing its stone from Lund, Sweden (Schulze-Dörrlamm 1992, 151, Vitrine 3, B21); the latter could have been produced in Germany or northern Europe (Müller-Wille 2005, 382).

How such a high-end brooch could end up at Chickerell will of course remain unknown, although close links between the English and German courts in the early 12th century, and maybe Empress Matilda's temporary return to England in September 1126 (Poole 1955, 128) might provide the background for one of her retainers or their wives to receive such a piece as a gift.

One aspect of the Chickerell brooch deserves a short mention, although it was not possible to fully explore it as part of the analysis reported here. While some of the brooches discussed above have rock crystals with a central ridge, for instance those from Østergård, others have a smooth, apparently plano-convex shape. If the shape of the lower face was slightly more convex (which is usually not observable with the assembled object), there is a distinct possibility that the gem could have optical properties of an aspheric lens which could serve as a very effective magnification lens. A number of such rock crystal gems from Gotland have been examined for these properties. Some of them were found to be of optical quality with almost perfect elliptical shape and very low spherical aberration. This would have been much better than Roger Bacon's reading stones of the 13th century and was not explained scientifically until Descartes' calculation of the ideal shape of a focusing lens at least 500 years later. Mounted lenses with silver backplates would have reflected clear images of what was placed in front of them (Schmidt et al. 1999). Although beyond the scope of the present study, future analyses of such gems should include an investigation of their optical qualities as part of the examination of their manufacture and origin.

The first of the two copper alloy annular brooches is an example (SF122) with square/diamond-sectioned ring (diameter 25.5mm) and a recess for a sub-circular sectioned pin (still moving) which is attached to a recess in the ring, although the pin loop is not joined at the back. The ring appears undecorated, but the surface is too corroded to discern faint decoration like lines or dots. The brooch can be compared to similar examples from Salisbury (Goodall 2012, 92, 120, fig. 13, 7) and London (Egan and Pritchard 2002, 248–9, fig. 160, 1303–7) dated to the 13th to 14th centuries. The second annular brooch (Cat. No. 4; Fig. 3.3) has a plain triangular sectioned ring; although missing its pin it has a recess and a rest for the missing pin. While it is sufficiently substantial that a use as a buckle cannot be excluded, following Egan and Pritchard's definition of frames with restrictions for the pin it is here classed as a brooch (Egan and Pritchard 2002, 248). In Thuaudet's typology the object would fit in with rings and buckles of his Type B11, which ranges in date between the beginning of the 13th and the beginning of the 15th centuries (Thuaudet 2015, 322–24, fig. 141–42).

Belt and strap fittings

This section summarises 34 objects like belt buckles, buckle plates and pins, mounts, strap ends and chapes as well as a button and a bell.

BUCKLES

All of the 15 buckles are residual finds, recorded either in Phase 8 layers or during metal detecting. The two oval copper alloy buckle frames Cat. Nos. 5 and 6 (Fig. 3.3) both have ornate outside edges decorated by grooves set between lateral knops. Both belong to Thuaudet's type E4, variants b and c, respectively (Thuaudet 2015, 397–401). Although a widespread type, relatively close parallels come from Castle Rising Castle, Norfolk (Williams 1997, 86, fig. 53, 3), and Meols (Egan 2007a, 91, pl. 14, 527). An oval frame (SF16), of which only the decorated outside edge and beginning of the sides remains, is slightly less ornate, featuring a facetted/hexagonal outside edge decorated with transverse lines on its outer and upper sides. The form with all its variants was used between the late 12th and 14th centuries (Egan and Pritchard 2002, 76).

Cat. No. 7 (Fig. 3.3) has an intricately manufactured double-rectangular frame with four deep rabbets on the crenelated inside and outside edges, each with an inlay of two thin wires applied to transverse

grooves in the thicker areas. Based on the slight colour difference, the wires were made of a different copper alloy to that used for the frame. A parallel from Swan Lane in London was found in a context dated c. 1270–c. 1350 (Egan and Pritchard 2002, 97–98, fig. 62, 443), while the fragment of another example from Norwich was found in a, presumably residual, context dated 1550–1700 (Margeson 1993 ,29, fig. 15, 154). Another buckle with rectangular frame, Cat. No. 8 (Fig. 3.3), has a pewter frame with broken central bar, all of triangular cross-section. It compares best with an equally broken pewter example of Thuaudet's type P1c from the Castrum de Montpaon, Fontvieille, Dép. Bouches-du-Rhône, France, found in a mid–late 16th century context (Thuaudet 2015, 503, fig. 246, 10), although a copper alloy frame from Billingsgate lorry park, London, found in a context of the later 13th to earlier 14th century, provides a morphologically even closer comparison (Egan and Pritchard 2002, 97–98, fig. 62, 442).

Two double-oval copper alloy buckles, Cat. No. 9 (Fig. 3.3) and SF43, were found residually in the subsoil of Area 2 and a clearance layer in Area 3, respectively. Both can be classed as Thuaudet's type O1a (Thuaudet 2015, 482–4, fig. 234), which are longer than they are wide and can have copper alloy or iron pins; remnants of the latter were found on the central bar of SF43. Two from the *Mary Rose* (sunk in 1545) have copper alloy sheet plates attached to the bar (Klein 2005, 104, fig. 2.83, 80A0992/2 and 83A0197). The London comparisons mostly date from the mid-14th to mid-15th centuries (Egan and Pritchard 2002, 82–3, fig. 50, 333–3, 337 and 339); one from Victoria Road, Winchester is probably 15th century in date (Rees et al. 2008, 224–5, fig. 118, 1499). While the larger examples, like SF43, could have been used on shoes and other straps, a small buckle like Cat. No. 9 from a context of c. 1700 at Beeston Castle, Cheshire, demonstrates their use on a rowel spur as well as the longevity of the form (Ellis 1993, 169, fig. 115, 36).

A buckle (SF56) with forked spacer and an oval bevelled frame with lipped pin rest was collected from the subsoil in Area 2. Its pin, the cover plates and most of one of the spacers are missing. Like the series from London, this example was well-finished. The type was widespread in this country during the mid-14th and early 15th centuries, representing the best quality of mass-produced buckles (cf Egan and Pritchard 2002, 78–82, closest to 81, fig. 49, 330). The construction is also found on the corresponding strap ends like Cat No. 15 (see below).

Only one of the six D-shaped buckles (SF82) was made of copper alloy and showing remnants of surface gilding. The small buckle (L 16mm; W 20.7mm) has a wide, bevelled outside edge (W 4.5mm) and narrow, circular-sectioned bar. It could have been attached to a leather strap but would equally fit buckle plates like Cat. Nos. 10 or 11 (Fig. 3.3). The remaining five D-shaped frames were made of iron and include examples that are longer than wide, like SF110 from clearance layer 302 and one from PH II, as well as three examples that are wider than long. As all are residual finds, they add nothing to the dating of the long-lived form, which could be of medieval or younger date.

One metal-detected iron buckle has a rectangular frame of bevelled, sub-rectangular cross-section with groove-shaped pin-rest; its recessed, lower-set bar has frame ends that are rounded and extend further back than the bar. The latter detail is similar to copper alloy oval frames from London with curved projections on the inside edge (Egan and Pritchard 2002, 71–2, fig. 43), while on this iron specimen it is not impossible that the projections are all that is left from one side of a double rectangular frame.

A copper alloy pin (SF75) has a shallow transverse ridge indicated by a facet line below the loop of which only half remains. The 35.7mm-long pin is straight and wedge-shaped, tapering to the tip and might have been part of an annular buckle or brooch. It was found residually in a clearance layer between Buildings 1 and 4. An example attached to an annular buckle from 16–22 Coppergate, York, dates to the 14th or early 15th century (Ottaway and Rogers 2002, 2887, fig. 1465, 12880).

BUCKLE PLATES
Five copper alloy buckle plates were found, three of which by metal-detector (Cat. Nos. 10, 11 and 13; Fig. 3.3); apart from Cat. No. 12, all show remnants of surface gilding.

Cat. No. 10 is the front plate of a rectangular buckle plate with a decoration of floral spirals and twirls set within a void frame. A gilded rectangular buckle-plate with rocker-arm ornament on its border and a cast double-spiral in an enamelled, possibly white, field was found in Norwich in a pit fill dated to the 13th or 14th centuries (Margeson 1993, 26, fig. 13, 134). An even closer comparison for Cat. No. 10, even damaged in a comparable manner, was found by metal detector at Saltfleetby, East Lindsey, Lincolnshire (PAS: LIN-595303).

A rectangular folded buckle plate (Cat. No. 11; Fig. 3.3) has recessed loops and three holes in or below the centre line; the back plate is slightly narrower and shorter than the show side and only has two holes. It is undecorated apart from a line along three sides, but the surface was gilded. The present author is unaware of published parallels with three rivets aligned along the centre line, but the form is generally comparable with buckles and recessed plates like an example from Billingsgate lorry park, London, found in a mid-13th century context (Egan and Pritchard 2002, 74–5, fig. 45, 304); based on its general similarity to plates with more or fewer rivets the form can be expected to have a wider, at least high-medieval date range. Several examples with three rivets arranged like Cat. No. 11 have been reported to the PAS, for instance from Merstham, Surrey (PUBLIC-C4C3AF); Calbourne, Isle of Wight (IOW-26AB4A); White Waltham, Berkshire (SUR-BB4415); Goodnestone, Kent (KENT-F36950); Latton, Wiltshire (WILT-5C9E36); Langley with Hardley, Norfolk (NMS-216294, with rocker mark line); Baston, South Kesteven, Lincolnshire (LIN-B7E8C3, complete with D-shaped buckle).

Cat. No. 12 (Fig. 3.3) is a now much distorted folded rectangular sheet plate with rectangular slot for a pin and five rivet holes set 2-1-2. It has no discernible decoration. Parallels from London cover the 13th to 14th centuries (Egan and Pritchard 2002, 111, fig. 72, nos. 499, 502–3, esp. 505), and an example from King John's House, Tollard Royal, Wiltshire (Pitt-Rivers 1890, pl. 19, 23), could well expand this range even further.

A small plate (Cat. No. 13; Fig. 3.3) of gilded copper alloy with damaged suspension loops has a lozengiform field decorated with what looks like a lion rampant facing left (heraldically right). Its hind legs have been obliterated by a circular hole that was drilled from the front; burrs remaining on the back of the hole suggest the piece has seen little wear. If not used on a belt, the object could have been an attachment for a pendant harness fitting like a possibly 13th century example from Castle Rising Castle, Norfolk (Williams 1997, 88, fig. 60, 18), or a less ornate example, for instance from Salisbury (Cherry 1991a, 27, fig. 4, 23, 25); in that case it should be counted among the objects associated with transport (see below). Due to the popularity and widespread use of the lion as an armorial bearing on both sides of the Channel, exemplified by the well-known 12th century adage "qui n'a pas d'armes porte un lion" (Neubecker 1980, 90; Pastoureau 1984, 134 and map between pp. 140–1), the use of the lion in this decoration cannot be used to identify the person owning the belt which this fitting would have decorated.

A small buckle plate (SF64) was found residually in clearance layer (1004) between Buildings 1 and 4. It has a sub-rectangular plate with uneven edges and loops that are not recessed. Its short back plate, soldered onto the back of the front plate, has a punched sub-square hole near its inside edge. The front shows the remains of surface gilding, which appears out of place for this very rough-made object. It could be of medieval or later date.

STRAP ENDS

Of the seven medieval strap ends from the site, only one (Cat. No. 16) comes from a medieval context (10-108), a midden layer in Area 2 belonging to Phases 3 and 4; all others were either residual finds in later layers or metal detected. Apart from Cat. No. 16, probably made of pewter, all others are made of copper alloy.

Cat. No. 14 (Fig. 3.3) is most likely made of sheet metal rather than cast (the lateral x-radiograph is less conclusive than the illustration might suggest), possibly folded lengthways and secured with one rivet that was still visible in the x-radiograph, similar to a slightly longer, later 14th century example from London (Egan and Pritchard 2002, 130–1, fig. 85, 604) or undecorated examples of Thuaudet's type B1c

(Thuaudet 2015, 682–3, fig. 288, 5). A good comparison from a context in Norwich, dated c. 1275–1400, is said to be made of two separate plates joined by a single rivet in the same position as Cat. No. 14 (Margeson 1993, 35, fig. 20, 228). However, the metal-detected piece from Chickerell is much affected by corrosion, to the extent that any possible surface decoration or structure has been obliterated and, although unlikely, it could have been of a much earlier form of strap end of the later Anglo-Saxon period, possibly belonging to Thomas' Class A, although these have a split end for the strap and usually two rivets at the proximal end but do also occur with only one (Thomas 2000, 69).

As mentioned above, composite strap-end Cat. No. 15 (Fig. 3.5) would have been worn in combination with buckles like SF56. The strap end has a forked spacer with an acorn knop at the distal end. The longer of the two covering plates, which would have been soldered to the forked spacer, is decorated either with a pattern of various double lines or an (attempt at an) inscription, with possible letters including 'V', 'I', 'Λ' and possibly an inverted 'N'. The markings along the edges of a folded buckleplate from London displays a very similar sequence (Goodall 1981, 68, fig. 66,4; Museum of London, 4264). It is possible that the lettering was intended to spell 'AVE MARIA', similar to an attempt on a buckleplate from Wendover, Hampshire (PAS HAMP-02D831), bearing the letters 'AVM'. A good comparison for the decorated plate, but with two rivet holes, comes from Meols on the Wirral (Egan 2007a, 133, 135, pl. 23, 1503). The form presents the best of the mass produced belt fittings, introduced towards the end of the 13th/early 14th century and going out of fashion by the 15th (see e.g. Egan and Pritchard 2002, 144, fig. 94, esp. 682 for knop; Goodall 2012, 130, fig. 23, 121 for shape of plate with two rivets). Another cover plate (SF97) for this type of strap-end is slightly smaller (L 53.8mm; W 11mm) and has a rounded end, an inside edge with a slight concave curve and two round holes drilled from the outside (slight burrs still remaining on the inside). There are possible solder residues along one long side edge. A third, plain example (XR122) features a scalloped attachment edge with round aperture and a pointed groove on the front plate, as well as two rivets either side of the aperture. The spacer and both sheets end in a small, pointed

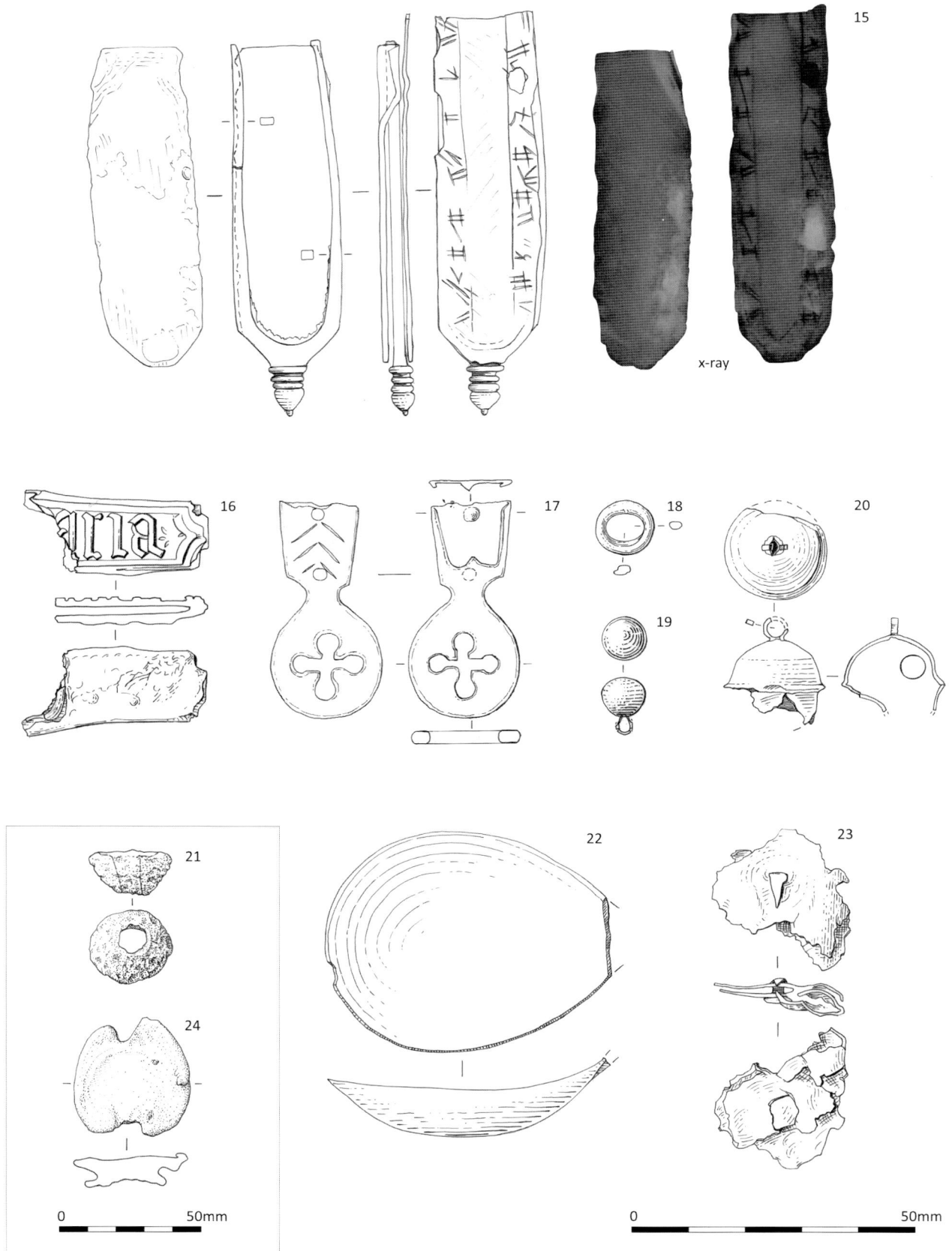

Fig. 3.5 Copper alloy: Cat. Nos 15, 17, 19, 22–23; copper alloy and gilding: Cat. No. 18; copper alloy and iron: Cat. No. 20; pewter: Cat. No. 16; lead: Cat. Nos 21, 24. © Liz James.

extension. An exact parallel was found in London in a context dating to the second half of the 14th century (Egan and Pritchard 2002, 140, 142 fig. 93, 654). The simpler form of composite strap ends of the later 13th to 14th centuries, with 'sheet spacers occupying the whole width' is represented by SF148, which has remains of white metal coating on its surface. An exact parallel comes from Billingsgate lorry park, London (Egan and Pritchard 2002, 147, fig. 96, 694).

Following on from the possible inscription on Cat. No. 15, the increase in Marian devotion in the later medieval period is likewise exemplified by Cat. No. 16 (Fig. 3.5), the only strap end found in a medieval layer (10-108; see above). The cast piece, damaged at its proximal end, features the inscription '[M]aria' on its obverse. A similar piece, but spelling 'Iōn·Bōn' (maybe 'John the Good') was found at Meols (Egan 2007a, 133, 135, pl. 23, 1501).

Cat. No. 17 (Fig. 3.5) is a strap-end with forked spacer and circular terminal with a quatrefoil opening. The form can be dated to the later 14th century based on comparisons from London; there, a similar decoration was used for a pewter one-piece strap-end, of which only the quatrefoil terminal survives (Egan and Pritchard 2002, 150, fig. 98, 706), as well as a more ornate openwork example with its plate still intact (Egan and Pritchard 2002, 152, fig. 99, MOL acc. no. 84.267/2).

MOUNTS AND LOOPS

A small ringlet/loop (Cat. No. 18; Fig. 3.5), made of gilded copper alloy, could have been part of a bar mount with pendent loop like an example from Salisbury (Goodall 2012, 129, fig. 22, 116). The loop's sub-oval cross section might have been caused by a misaligned two-part mould. It was found residually in a clearance layer (1004) between Buildings 1 and 4. The same layer also yielded a purse bag loop (SF77) with a biconvex-sectioned loop of ovoid shape and only the top of its circular-sectioned stem still present. Unfortunately, the loop alone is not sufficient to assign it to one of William's classes (Williams 2018), thus it can only be broadly dated between the second half of the 15th and early 17th centuries.

SF142 from midden layer 10-108 in Area 3, Phase 3&4, is a small mount (diam. 10.8–11.3mm) with a

circular, plain domed head and integral short stem rivet (L c. 4mm). It is comparable with such mounts from London found in contexts of the later 13th and 14th centuries (Egan and Pritchard 2002, 171, fig. 110, 824 CuA, 830-7 lead/tin). For his type A7a, which includes similar mounts, Thuaudet (2015, 779–81, fig. 345, 10–24) proposes a longer range, covering the 12th to at least the 14th centuries.

BUTTONS, LACE CHAPES AND BELLS

A small cast copper alloy button (Cat. No. 19; Fig. 3.5) was found in the same layer as Cat. No. 18. It has a copper alloy wire loop soldered or embedded into a hole in its base but shows no sign of white metal covering. Examples from London were found in contexts of ceramic phases 8 and 9, dating to c. 1230–c. 1350 (Egan and Pritchard 2002, 274–5, fig. 178, nos. 1384–95; cf also Read 2010, 26–7, nos. 78–87).

Two lace chapes were identified in the assemblage; one (SF130) comes from the same midden layer as mount SF142 (above). The plain chape is of long conical shape (L 60.3mm; diam. 1.7mm), its end overlap appears to have been trimmed or maybe broken (the area is corroded); the seam is slightly open, which may have been caused by bending through distortion either while wearing or following deposition. A good comparison from London was found in a later 13th to mid-14th century context (Egan and Pritchard 2002, 288, fig. 188, esp. 1439). The second example was a metal-detector find of a plain chape of long conical shape with overlapping seam edges. It measures 32.2mm long, 4.1–7.3mm wide and has a sub-circular hole (diam. 0.9mm) near its wide end. Dimensionally, it would fit among Thuaudet's type A1, but this is defined as plain and without rivet (cf Thuaudet 2015, fig. 444, especially 2–4). Maybe the hole in this case is the result of a later repair because the chape came loose from its lace and needed a more permanent fix.

Found residually in a service trench in area 2, the copper alloy rumbler bell Cat. No. 20 (Fig. 3.5) is made of two halves soldered together. Surprisingly, the iron pea is still present even though the lower half is damaged. The piece belongs to a widespread form during the 13th to 15th centuries, and although the use of bells on human dress is shown on numerous medieval images, the same forms were also worn by pets, hunting dogs or horses (see e.g. Egan and Pritchard 2002, 336–7 figs 219–20; 339, fig. 221, 1645, 1666; Margeson 1993, 214, fig. 162, 1759; Rees et al. 2008, 233, fig. 122, 1586).

Objects used in the manufacture or working of textiles

With only two items, the quantity of this category is surprisingly small, and the identification and purpose of the lead objects can at best be described as likely but not definite. Both were found residually in Phase 8 contexts.

Cat. No. 21 (Fig. 3.5) could be a conical spindle whorl with a conical hole. Its weight of 48.3g is towards the heavier end of Anglo-Saxon whorls (Walton Rogers 2007, 24), whereas medieval lead whorls appear to cover a wider range than their equivalents in other less dense materials. Two plano-convex whorls from later 14th and earlier 15th century contexts from London weigh 77.5g and 38.5g respectively (Egan 2010, 260–1, fig. 203, 803–4), and the 34 listed from Meols, including at least 14 plano-convex lead whorls, range between 9.9g and 55.9g (Egan 2007a). A rather lop-sided lead whorl from a 13th–14th century property boundary ditch at Winchester is a close parallel for Cat. No. 21 (Rees et al. 2008, 247, fig. 133, 1682).

What might have been a cloth seal was collected from the subsoil between Buildings 1 and 4. It has no discernible marking, and the reverse has a rectangular flap along its centre line. If it was indeed a cloth seal, it could belong to either the medieval or post-medieval periods.

Household utensils and furniture

Of the 18 objects assigned to this category, the vast majority belongs to utensils in the wider sense. Only one metal-detected lead vent with a flat rectangular frame with two struts at right angles and floral twirls near its base might belong to either a piece of furniture or even a vent (in which case it would belong in the category buildings and services).

Cat. No. 22 (Fig. 3.5) is a metal-detected deep bowl of a fig-shaped spoon, probably made of brass. The fig-shaped bowl is generally assumed to be the main shape of English spoons between the 14th and the middle of the 17th centuries (Jackson 1892, 129), whereas during that period the use of copper alloy for spoons was less common than lead/tin (Egan 2010, 249), but by the 17th century brass had become the predominant copper alloy used for small or portable objects (Dungworth 2002, 9, fig. 6; Ströbele and Schuster 2019, 15).

Nine fragments of metal vessels were recovered, mainly from clearance features in Areas 2 and 3. Apart from three sub-rectangular pieces of cast iron, all others are copper alloy, including two thin rim strip fragments that are slightly swollen along their outer halves. Three copper alloy fragments might derive from some form of cast vessel, two of which have rounded wire moulding running across their surfaces; the lack of obvious curvature suggests that they are more likely to come from larger cauldrons rather than posnets or skillets (cf Butler et al. 2009, 3–4). Additionally, there are four fragments of thin copper alloy sheet which might be part of wrought metal dishes. However, the lack of detail does not permit any of the vessel fragments to be more precisely dated than broadly late medieval or post-medieval.

Rather than simply being discarded when damaged, three vessel patches are testament of the value such metal vessels represented to their owner. Cat. No. 23 (Fig. 3.5) is a fragment of a repair with a folded rivet. SF92 is a bent piece of sheet metal with folded rivet (8.7×5.5mm) and a further slot on the opposite edge, possibly for another rivet. A third, sub-rectangular piece of sheet metal was found by metal-detector and consists of two sheets riveted together by eight tubular sheet rivets, arranged in two rows of four (one now missing, leaving 3.9mm-wide sub-circular hole); it also has a folded rivet (11.1×7.9mm) attached to the top sheet only. A damaged rim fragment from London shows a repair with eight folded rivets (Egan 2010, 176, fig. 144).

Cat. No. 24 (Fig. 3.5) is a lead repair plug, and although no pottery fragment was found to have survived in the groove between the two discs, the dimensions of the groove indicate that it was intended for a ceramic vessel (cf Egan 2010, 240–2, fig. 188), but similar repairs were also carried out on pewter vessels (e.g. Egan 2010, 189, fig. 153).

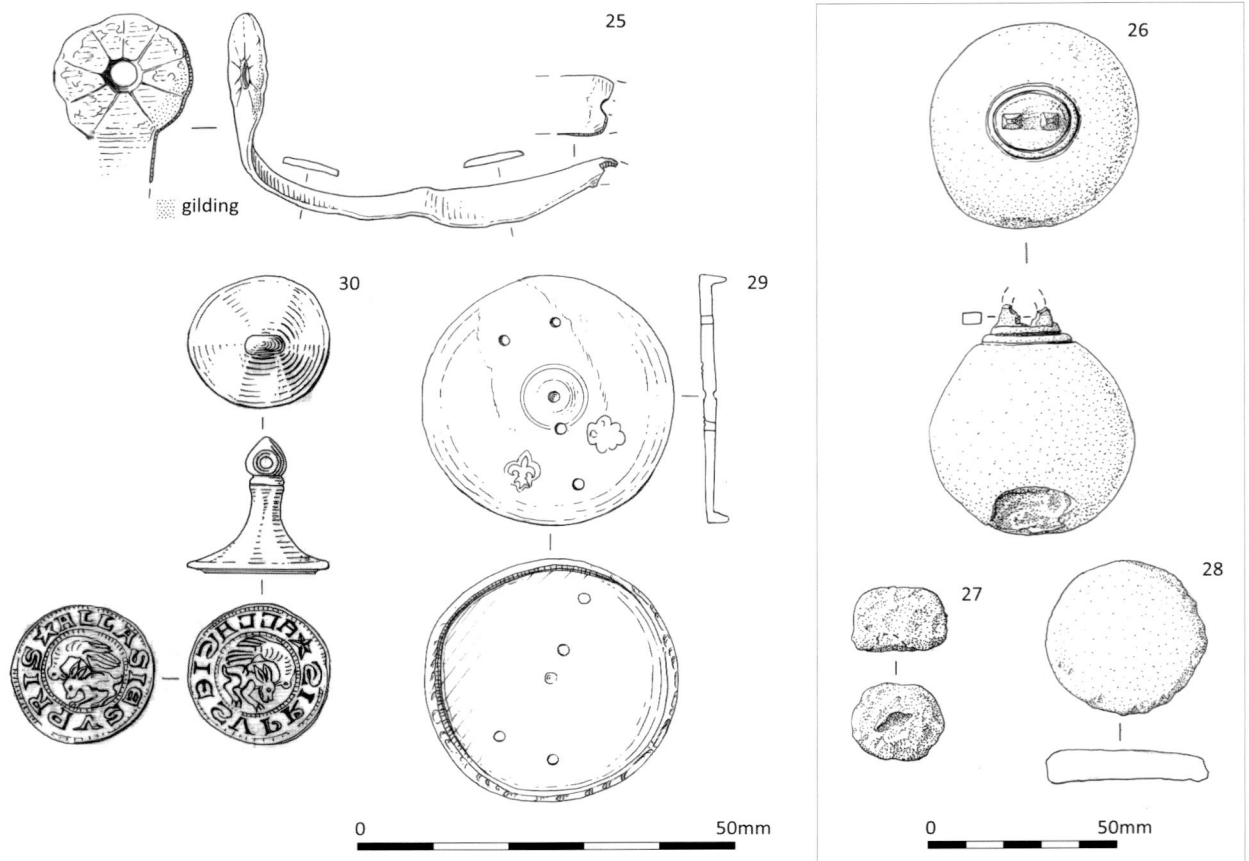

Fig. 3.6   Copper alloy and gilding: Cat. No. 25; lead and copper alloy: Cat. No. 26; lead: Cat. Nos 27–28; copper alloy: Cat. Nos 29–30. © Liz James.

A chest mount or casket binding (Cat. No. 25; Fig. 3.6) was found residually in a Phase 8 clearance layer. It has a floral terminal with a central hole and its surface shows remnants of gilding on the terminal as well as the broken end. Comparisons come from London, including one with tinning at the terminal (Brennan 2010, 76, fig, 53, 181, 183); Norwich (Margeson 1993, 76, fig. 41, 462); and a morphological particularly close comparison made of iron was found at Barentin's Manor, Chalgrove, Oxfordshire (Goodall, I. H. 2005b, 97, fig. 3.20, 76).

Objects employed in weighing and measuring

The six objects recorded in this category are all weights, including one copper alloy coin weight (Cat. No. 29) and one steelyard weight (Cat. No. 26) with copper alloy mantle and lead filling; all others are made of lead. All are residual finds, found in Phase 8 layers or during metal-detecting, only SF125 was found in a midden layer of Phase 3&4 in Area 3. The

use of the terms *probably* (within 2% of the standard), *possible* (between 2% and 5%), *almost precise* (less than 1% deviation) and *perhaps* (>5%) follow the definition by Egan (2010, 307).

The pear-shaped steelyard weight Cat. No. 26 (Fig. 3.6) weighs 890g and has a large irregular-shaped scar near its base. Among the weight systems in use during the high medieval period, its mass is closest to two pounds in the avoirdupois system of a pound made up of 16 ounces or 28.4g. The obvious damage appears to be the reason for it being slightly underweight, by 1.9%, for two pounds which should weigh 907.2g. The lack of obvious assay marks suggests that it is probably an unofficial copy of weights issued during the reign of Edward I (AD 1272–1307) when it is assumed the avoirdupois system was introduced (Egan 2010, 302, table 14). Alison Goodall (1981, 64; including references) reports that 'lead-filled pear-shaped steelyard weights have been found at Writtle, Essex (Rahtz 1969a, 91, fig. 51, 121) and Castell-y-Bere, Gwynedd (Butler 1974, 93, fig. 6, 1), the latter in a 13th century context: neither has the heraldic shields characteristic of the type (Renn 1959, 148–9).' Regional comparisons of similar weights lacking assay marks reported to the PAS include examples from Edmondsham, Dorset (DOR-9B08D5, which at 904g is only 0.035% underweight for two pounds); Cricket St Thomas, Somerset (SOM-4A51E5, substantially damaged but weighing 601g) and Micheldever, Hampshire (HAMP-82F1C1, weighing 614g). When used on a steelyard, the mass of the poise was not necessarily of importance as long as the beam used with the poise had marked graduations displaying the weight with the poise in that position (Crawforth-Hitchins 2005, 330). A nice reconstruction of a poise and weight is based on an assemblage from Huish, Wiltshire (Shortt 1982).

The following two lead weights (Cat. Nos. 27 and 28; Fig. 3.6) are likely to belong to more or less the same period as the aforementioned. The small ovoid piece Cat. No. 27 weighs 58.1g, which is equivalent to two ounces in the Mercantile system with one pound of 16 ounces or the Tower system with one pound of 12 ounces. In both systems this would equate to 58.3g, making this an *almost precise* weight which is only slightly lighter than the standard, by <0.2g=0.3% (Egan 2010, 302, table 14). The discoid weight Cat. No. 28 has a mass of 104.8g which suggests it was *probably* a quarter pound weight in the avoirdupois system of 1lb of 15oz weighing 28.4g. According to that standard, the weight should be 106.325g, and it is thus under-weight by <1.5g=1.43% (see Egan 2010).

SF28 is a cast lead cone segment, with an uneven surface. It weighs 31.9g and is thus *possibly* intended to be 1oz in the English troy or Apothecaries' systems (31.1g, overweight by>0.8g=2.6%; see Egan 2010, 302, table 14). Morphologically, it is not dissimilar to a fairly pure lead weight of 58.6g from 16–22 Coppergate, York, found in a context dated *c.* 930/5–*c.* 975 (Mainman and Rogers 2000, 2562, fig. 12569, 10586).

SF125 is a block of sub-ovoid cross section with a flat base and flattish ends, the smaller end face has a hole/cavity (diam. 4.2–5.7mm) with rust-coloured residue, and rusty corrosion products also adhere to

its rounded top. Its weight of 71.5g might relate it to a morphologically totally different weight from London, featuring two opposed fleur-de-lis on a discoid weight, *possibly* intended to weigh 48 pennies or four shillings, although bulk coin was usually weighed in five-shilling batches (Egan 2010, 312–3 fig. 233, 993).

The only copper alloy weight, Cat. No. 29 (Fig. 3.6), weighs 11.7g. It shows two marks, a fleur-de-lis and what is likely to be a crown either side of two holes drilled along a radial alignment from the central lathe pin scar. Two further holes were drilled on a tangential alignment on the opposite side. The presence of the crown and fleur-de-lis would suggest that it would be for the noble or its half and quarter pieces, but its mass, which is the equivalent of 180.56 grains (gr), is one-and-a-half times the standard noble or three half nobles. The standard of 120 gr for the noble was in use from 1351 to 1412, and again for a ryal (rose noble) from 1465 (Biggs 1990, 72, pl. 15, 10–15). A good comparison for the shape of the crown comes from a weight found in a cellar in Norwich dating to 1507 (Margeson 1993, 210, fig. 158, 1750). Whatever denomination this weight was intended for, it was certainly the case that coin weights were frequently retained well beyond the currency of the piece they were intended for, as 'weights for obsolete coins were often included in boxes of weights in case the coins ever came into a merchant's hands' (Bell and Knight 2004 , 362).

Commerce

The 15 medieval coins are all of silver. Fourteen coins cover almost the entire period between the reigns of Henry II and Henry VI or Edward IV, i.e. the late 12th to 15th centuries. Additionally, a hacksilver coin fragment represents less than a quarter of a 'Longcross' Silver Penny for Aethelred II (the Unready, AD 978—1016), minted in Oxford by the moneyer Aelfwine. The only non-English coin is a Venetian soldino (galley halfpenny) of the Doge Michele Steno (1400–1413).

An overview is presented in the following (the format lists small finds number, weight and dimensions (in mm), issuer, description. Date range. Excavation event and context information; followed by site phase):

1. **SF150**, 0.2g, L9.7, W8.4, T0.5, **Aethelred II** 'Longcross' silver penny. Oxford mint, Aelfwine; less than upper left quarter. Obv. [ÆÐ]ELRÆ[D REX ANGLO]. Bare head bust l. Rev. [+ ælf pine m'o·o] xna. Voided longcross only half of arms present (terminating in three crescents, pellet to centre). Spink 1151; North 774. 978–1016. EXC/16; U/S.

2. **SF135**, 0.6g, L19.0, W9.0, T0.5, **Henry II**? Hammered short cross penny, cut in half. Obv. Only top of crown central cross and pellet-like curls on to right, legend: ENRICV. Rev. Open cross with pellets at end and 4 in each quarter, legend: [RAV]/?-?/?-?/NDE. Spink 1344? 1180–1189? EXC/16, Area 3; 8.

3. **SF149**, 0.4g, D15.9, T0.5, **Henry III**? Hammered short cross penny, cut in half. Obv. Worn bust, legend: only base of letters on flan. Rev. Open cross with pellets at end and 4 in each quarter, legend, see obv. 1216–1247. EXC/16; U/S.

4. **SF24**, 0.3g, L10.5, W9.9, T0.4, Hammered long-cross coin, York mint, cut down to quarter, probably along lines of cross on reverse. Obv. With centre and right side of crown with fleur de lis, legend beyond edge only base of letters visible. Rev. lower left quarter of coin with left arm of cross potent and 3 pellets; legend: EBO. 1247–15th C. EXC/16, F24, Area 3; 8.

5. **SF7**, 0.4g, L8.7, W16.5, T0.7, **Henry III**, Long cross penny cut in half across head, lower half present. Obv. Long narrow bust [...]RICUS REX, curly X; Rev. [?]OHL¦[?]AC?? Spink1361A. 1248–50. EXC/16, (2001), Area 2; 8.

6. **SF74**, 1.3g, D18.4–19.4, T0.6, **Edward I**, Hammered long cross penny, London mint. Obv. Bust with drapery of two wedges, no star on breast, EDWRANGLDNShYB, mintmark worn cross. Rev. long cross potent, 3 pellets in each quarter, CIVI/TAS/LON/DON. Spink 1407 (?). 1279–1307. EXC/16, (1004), between Building 1 and 4; 8.

7. **SF128**, 1g, D17.3–18.4, T0.6, **Edward III**, Penny, (reigned 1327–1377), London mint. Third (Florin coinage). + EDW R [ANGL] DNS HYB, crowned bust facing / CIVITAS LONDON, long cross with three pellets in each angle. North 1115 or 1116. Seaby 1544 or 1545. Spink 1545? 1344–1351. EXC/16, (10-108), Area 3; 3 & 4.

8. **SF65**, 0.9g, D16.5–17.8, T0.5, **Edward III**? Hammered long-cross penny, Durham mint. Obv. bust almost completely worn away, faint locks and crown visible, Mintmark plain cross EDW[ARD ?[R]ANGLI[?.]. Rev. cross potent and 3 pellets in each quarter, second quarter with additional subround pellets at top; legend: CIVI/TAS/DV[R]/E[ME]. Mintmark Spink 7a would suggest post-treaty period 1369–1377. 1351–1377? EXC/16, (1004), between Building 1 and 4; 8.

9. **SF136**, 1g, D15.6–16.7, T0.4–0.6, **Edward III** penny, post-treaty issue, York mint, Spink 1648 (variant). Obv. -EDWA[RDVS REX] ANGL Z FR. Rev. [CIV]I TAS [EBO R]ACI long cross with quatrefoil at centre and three pellets in each quarter. Post Treaty period, Archbishop Thoresby Issue, 1369–1377. Seaby 1648; North 1293. 1369–1377. EXC/16; U/S.

10. **SF121**, 0.8g, D16.6–17.4, T0.3–0.5, **Richard II**, York Mint. Obv. Bust nearly all worn away, Type II local dies with cross on breast (and pellets above shoulders; not visible), legend [?-?]xR[E? -?]. Rev. Cross potent with quatrefoil centre and 3 pellets in each quarter, [?-?]/[E]BOR/A[CI?]. Spink 1692. 1377–1399. EXC/16, (10-115), Area 3; 8.

11. **XR130**, 0.4g, **Doge Michele Steno** (1400–1413), Venetian soldino of ?Type 5, mint of Venice. Obv. Doge Michele Steno kneeling left holding a banner with mint control mark, star over D, to right; legend: +MIChA[EL] [S]TEN.DVX. Rev. Winged and nimbate lion of St Mark facing within a circle, holding a book of gospels; legend: .+.S.MARC[V]S VENETI. 1400–1413. AMR/13; U/S.

12. **SF115**, 1.8g, , D21.0, T0.6, **Henry VI**, Hammered halfgroat, Calais mint. Obv. Bust with annulets either side of neck, legend hEnRICDIGRAxREXANGL&FR. Rev. cross potent, 3 pellets in each quarter, 2&3 with additional annulet in centre; legend: POSVUI °/ DEV[M]/ADIVT/[O]RExMx; inner circle: VIL/LA[2× above one another]/CAL/IS[2× above one another]. Spink 1840, mm. 18 (pierced cross). North 1429. 1422–1427. EXC/16, (2005), Area 2; 8.

13. **XR129**, 1g, D16.9–18.4, T0.6, possibly **Henry VI** or **Edward IV**, York Mint. Penny, hammered. Obv: Facing crowned bust in pelleted circle, no marks; legend: on upper left before illegible mintmark [...NRI?...]. Rev. Long cross potent with quatrefoil with cross in centre, 3 pellets in each quadrant; legend: [...]I TAS [EBO ...]. Orientation: 10 o'clock. 2nd half 15th c. AMR/13; U/S.

14. **SF113**, 0.3g, L15.0, W10.4, T1.1, Hacksilber coin; c. 1/4 of flan preserved, cut from obv. (angled cutting edge); might have been perforated for suspension. Obv. Edges of 2 arms of cross potent; legend: [...]TRES×D[...]. Rev. [...]MONET[...], field:?. Both legends set between reeded circles. 12th–14th C.? AMR/13, (801), Building 4; 8.

15. **SF10**, 0.2g, L9.8, W8.0, T0.6, Hammered coin, cut down to quarter, probably along lines of cross on reverse, but too worn now to identify details. Medieval. EXC/16, (2002), Area 2; 8.

Objects used for, or associated with, written communications

The only object in this category is a seal matrix, Cat. No. 30 (Fig. 3.6), found residually in a Phase 8 clearance layer. It has a hexagonally facetted trumpet-shaped handle with a rounded-diamond loop. This is a common form, but morphologically close examples come, for instance, from Salisbury, on a seal with an oval face (Cherry 1991b, 37, fig. 7, 17). The circular seal shows the image of a hare with a bird of prey (probably an eagle) above. The legend in Lombardic letters reads: *ALLAS IE SV PRIS, middle-French for 'alas, I am caught/taken'. Stylistically, the object dates to the 13th and especially the 14th century (see below), but the prolonged use of one seal of a similar form, albeit with trefoil loop, is demonstrated by Holbein the Younger's 1532 portrait of the Hanseatic trader Georg Gisze (Goodall 1981, 64; portrait in the Gemäldegalerie, Berlin). The spelling of the legend exists in a number of variations; a seal matrix with the same legend comes from Newark Priory, Ripley, Surrey (Hicks and English n.d., 50, AG 24706). The PAS database lists several examples with ALAS, i.e. one 'L' instead of two in the legend, for instance from South Somercotes, East Lindey (PUBLIC-BA1836, with same image) and Minting (LIN-BAE37A), both Lincolnshire, or Cuddesdon and Denton, Oxfordshire (BERK-AD4DD6). Examples of yet another variation of the legend (*ALLAS : IE : SV : PRIYS) have been recorded, e.g. from Burton (LIN-4CED36), Lincolnshire, and Broughton, Hampshire (HAMP-DAE905), the latter on a matrix with ridge and loop. The legend with one 'L' also occurs with variations of the image, depicting a bird instead of a hare being caught (e.g. Huntingfield, Suffolk, SF-A47BE8) and on the seal attached to a deed conveying land in the marsh of Megham, in Hailsham, Sussex, dated 22 May 1373, in the East Sussex Record Office (ref: ESRO AMS 5592/42) with yet another example of the legend: ALAS IE SV PRIST.

With all its permutations, it is evident that this is a common legend, and, unfortunately, neither the image nor the legend are person-specific but are found instead on a number of 'off-the-shelf' matrices which became common during the later medieval period when the use of seals spread to include land-owning farmers (see e.g. Harvey and McGuinness 1996, 88–9; ref. 82).

Objects associated with transport
The 79 objects classed in this category comprise items like bridle cheek pieces, harness buckles as well as horseshoes and the nails to attach them to the hooves of equids and bovids. A further ten iron objects, all residual finds from Phase 8 layers, include two buckles, one with a trapezoidal and one with a D-shaped frame; two possible iron buckle pins, one

of which might have fitted the latter buckle; the left and right branches of two fragmented horseshoes as well as three nails with swollen or expanding sub-square heads and double clenched tips. These objects will not be considered in the following discussion as they are not chronologically distinctive, but all could belong to the medieval and/or post-medieval phases at Putton Lane. The small buckle plate Cat. No. 13, discussed under personal items (see above), might also belong in this category if it was a harness pendant mount rather than a belt mount.

Two copper alloy loops (Cat. Nos. 31 and 32; Fig. 3.7) for horse harness cheek pieces belong to a type dated to the first half of the 11th century: Williams type 1 (Williams 2007, 3, fig. 3a). Although the pieces are similar, it is likely that they belonged to two separate sets. Both pieces could alternatively have been part of four-way strap distributors similar to examples from, for example, Winchester (Goodall 1990, 1043–5, fig. 334, 3885A and 3886) or Glastonbury (Courtney et al. 2015, 306. fig. 8.46, 73).

Based on their size and shape, two iron buckles have been included in this category rather than under objects of dress and personal adornment. A buckle with a T-shaped frame and separate revolving outer bar at the narrower end (Cat. No. 33; Fig. 3.7) can broadly be dated to the 12th to 16th century (cf Clark 2004, 59–61, fig. 45, 40, 47; Goodall 2011, 355, fig. 12.8, K197-203). This form would be useful to attach a wider strap to a narrower one, an arrangement that is – still – frequently used for the girth that passes under the horse's belly and attaches to the girth straps coming from the saddle. Another rectangular frame with sheet roller (Clark 2004, 56, fig. 42, 35) would equally fit a medieval or post-medieval date.

The majority of the 18 horseshoes or fragments thereof belong to identifiably medieval types, although all are residual finds, mainly from Phase 8 layers. Three wavy edged shoes (Cat. Nos. 35–7; Fig. 3.7) belong to Clark type 2B, i.e. all have rectangular countersunk holes. The series illustrated here shows different treatments of the heel end, with slightly upset end, as well as right-angled calkin and feathered heel, respectively (Clark 2004, 81, fig. 59a–c). Although there are some early examples of the wavy-edged type, from contexts of the 10th and

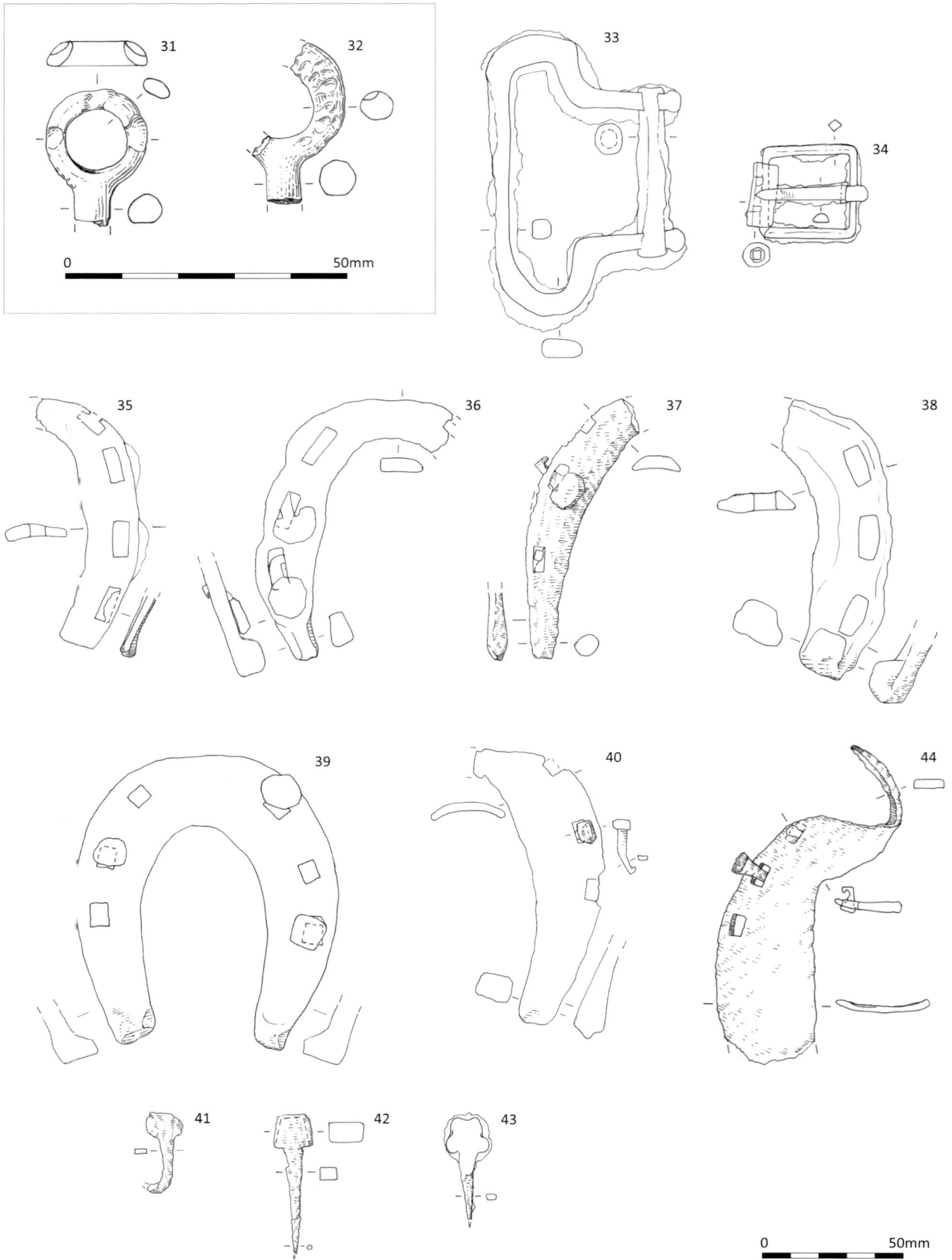

Fig. 3.7   Copper alloy: Cat. Nos 31–32; iron: Cat. Nos 33–44. © Liz James.

earlier 11th centuries, the floruit of type 2B in this country lies in the later 12th century, continuing into the 13th century. By that time, it was replaced by the heavier type 3 with rectangular countersunk holes as on the previous type (Clark 2004, 95–6). Four examples of type 3 were found at Chickerell; Cat. No. 38 (Fig. 3.7) is an example with a folded calkin of type C, while of the other three two have feathered heels and one straight heels. None of the type 3 shoes has retained any nails, but the type is found with the fiddle-key type nails (see Cat. No. 41) as well as the type with expanding heads with 'ears' that would have sat in the countersunk holes (see Cat. Nos. 42–3). The shoes belong to the 13th and 14th centuries (Clark 2004, 96; Goodall 2011, 369, fig. 13.3, L10–14). In contrast to the preceding types, the following type 4 has square or rectangular holes that taper inwards but no longer sit in a separate countersunk slot. With nine specimens this type is the most numerous at Chickerell (Cat. No. 39–40; Fig. 3.7). Cat. No. 39 is one of only two complete examples and its V-shaped outline suggests it might be a shoe for a rear hoof, while the other complete example (XR94) is more U-shaped, and thus likely intended for a front hoof (Clark 2004, 100, fig. 78). Type 4 was introduced towards the end of the 13th/early 14th century, very widespread during the 15th century and probably continuing into the early post-medieval period (Clark 2004, 96–7; Goodall 2011, 371, fig. 13.4, L15–28). Two further fragments both have right-angle calkins and could be medieval or later forms.

The assemblage in this category is dominated by 56 iron horseshoe nails and, in turn, 39 of these are so-called fiddle-key nails (Cat. No. 41; Fig. 3.7) (Clark 2004, 86, fig. 64), used on horseshoes with wavy outside edges and the subsequent heavier, smooth-edged shoes of the mid-11th to mid-14th centuries, Clark types 2 and 3, respectively. Examples for their use on these two types of shoes can be seen on Cat. No. 36 and 38 where some holes still had fiddle key nails in them. The remaining 17 nails are also predominantly of medieval date, including at least eight nails with expanded trapezoidal heads and 'ears' (Clark 2004, 87, fig. 66), at least two of which are clearly unused (Cat. Nos. 42–3; Fig. 3.7). Of the remaining nine nails, one from the topsoil in the area of Building 6 (Phase 8) has a flat expanding rectangular head similar to a nail still attached to a

Clark type 1 horseshoe – the type dates from the 10th to 12th centuries (Clark 2004 114, fig. 80; MoL 16248; 93–5). Another nail with a rectangular club-shaped head and rectangular-sectioned shaft can best be compared to an example from a type 3 shoe (Clark 2004, 118, fig. 84, 152). As those two nails do not look very different from one another, the possibility that one or both are in fact much worn fiddle-key nails should not be discounted. Seven further nails have expanding club-shaped heads of Goodall type D, probably predominantly dating to the 15th–16th century; some of the smaller examples measuring between 20.9mm and 25.7mm could well have been used on oxshoes like Cat. No. 44 (Goodall 2011, 364).

Although – in common with the vast majority of the Chickerell assemblage – most of the horseshoe nails (47) were residual finds in Phase 8 layers and four more were metal-detected, three fiddle-key nails and one with expanded trapezoidal head and 'ears' were found in Phase 2 deposits under Building 5, and a further example of the latter type comes from a demolition feature in Building 1 of Phase 5.

Neither the quantities of horseshoes nor that of the nails will permit commenting upon the number of horses kept at Chickerell at any one time, other than the fact that shod horses were present and presumably also kept at the site. The numbers of nails required to keep a horse shod per year will vary somewhere between 200 to 400 nails, the number being dependent on the frequency of changing the shoes (for example, 20th century military manuals suggest every four to six weeks) and the number of nails per shoe, which for all the examples from the site appears to have been six (Buora 2018, 28, table).

An oxshoe (Cat. No. 44; Fig. 3.7) attests to the use of oxen as traction animals during the medieval or post-medieval period (Goodall 2011, 363, 371, fig. 13.4, L29–32); its middle hole still retains a nail of Goodall type D, which were used with later medieval horseshoes as well as oxshoes (Goodall 2011, 364, fig. 13.1).

Buildings and services
Of particular note among the six objects in this category is a metal-detected fragment of what is likely to be a lead window- or vent grille (Cat. No.

45; Fig. 3.8). Such grilles usually imitate architectural tracery of Gothic windows. An association with high-status high-/late-medieval and early post-medieval buildings – both ecclesiastical as well as seigneurial or royal – is indicated by architectural lead grilles from sites like Bardney Abbey, Lincolnshire; Stanley Abbey, Wiltshire; Battle Abbey, East Sussex; Hampton Court or Clarendon Palace (Anon, 1911, 367–9, figs 1–5; Geddes 1985, 155, fig. 48, 1a–b; James and Knight 1988, 225, fig. 85, 1, pl. 59a and c; Egan 2001, 107, 118, fig. 39, 188). An example from an episcopal manor house (palace) of the Bishops of Wells was found at Court Farm, Wookey, Somerset (Schuster 2014, 6, fig. 3).

Cat. No. 45 consists of a lozenge-shaped plaque with an integral oval-sectioned bar. The arms on the plaque can be blazoned as follows: a saltire of two transverse hatched bends, the sinister above the dexter, between four fleurs-de-lis. Although theoretically the object has the potential to provide some information as to the identity of one/some of the occupants of the manor house, unfortunately there are no indications of tinctures or residues of colours, which would have helped to exclude similar bearings in other tinctures and narrow the search for bearers of this coat of arms. The lozenge shape might have been chosen to represent a female member of a family, although an exclusively female use of the lozenge was not yet established in the medieval period, and the term 'lozenge' has even been described as interchangeable with shield (Ashley 2002, 16). An enamelled horse harness pendant of similar shape from Hockering, Norfolk (PAS NMS-BFA9FE) has a red field and silver fleurs-de-lis. A similar shaped pendant with this charge comes from Horsham St Faith, Norfolk (Ashley 2002, 51 s.v. Saltire Between). A shield-shaped pendant from Thame, Oxfordshire (PAS BH-6E3387) has been described as having a red field and golden fleur-de-lis which would match the armorial crests of the Brittaine family (of Farlington, Hampshire) as well as that of Tywardreath Priory, Cornwall (Pascoe 1979, 139). If the transverse hatched bends were not intended to denote a tincture, which according to Fox-Davies was only introduced around 1623, then it is not impossible that the intention might have been to show ermine; the addition of the three spots above the tail are a modern variant, which

in turn would provide another indirect argument for an earlier date for this piece (Fox-Davies 1949, 75–6, 78; Anthony Camp *pers. comm.*). One prominent bearer of arms that include a saltire ermine between four fleur-de-lis is St Hugh of Avalon; he was made the first prior of the Carthusian house of Witham Charterhouse in Somerset in 1179 before becoming Bishop of Lincoln in 1186 (Poole 1955, 229; Butler 1910). A use of the arms of St Hugh, if representing him as an individual, would put this object into the very earliest period of personalised arms, which developed in the early to mid-12th century (Oswald 1984, 9–10), whereas if representing him as a saint, it could be of considerably later date.

Other objects include an iron window bar (Cat. No. 46; Fig. 3.8), two wall anchors (L243mm and 70mm, respectively) as well as a fragment of molten glass which had run onto molten lead. These pieces can only summarily be assigned a medieval or post-medieval date, although good comparisons for the larger of the wall anchors, which was found in a Phase 3&4 midden layer in area 3, are illustrated by Goodall (2011, 189, fig. 9.11, H233–5).

Tools

Sixteen objects have been included in this category, and apart from three (Cat. No. 47–8 and XR14) of the nine knives found in Phase 5 demolition layers of Buildings 1 and 2, respectively, the remainder was found residually in Phase 8 layers.

Knives

The nine knives include at least six of whittle tang and only two of scale tang construction; one might be an unfinished workpiece, probably intended to be finished with a whittle tang. Most medieval knives were made with whittle tangs, while the use of scale tangs saw a hiatus of almost a millennium since the end of the Roman period (see e.g. Manning 1985, 109, fig. 28). They were, for instance, lacking from the assemblage of knives from 16–22 Coppergate in York with its substantial deposits from the 13th to 14th centuries (Ottaway and Rogers 2002, 2751, 2762). Scale tangs are found again in increasing numbers from the 14th century onwards, with some of the earliest medieval examples recorded from mid-13th century contexts in Winchester (Goodall 1990, 838–9; cf. also Goodall 1993, 128; Schuster et al. 2012, 146).

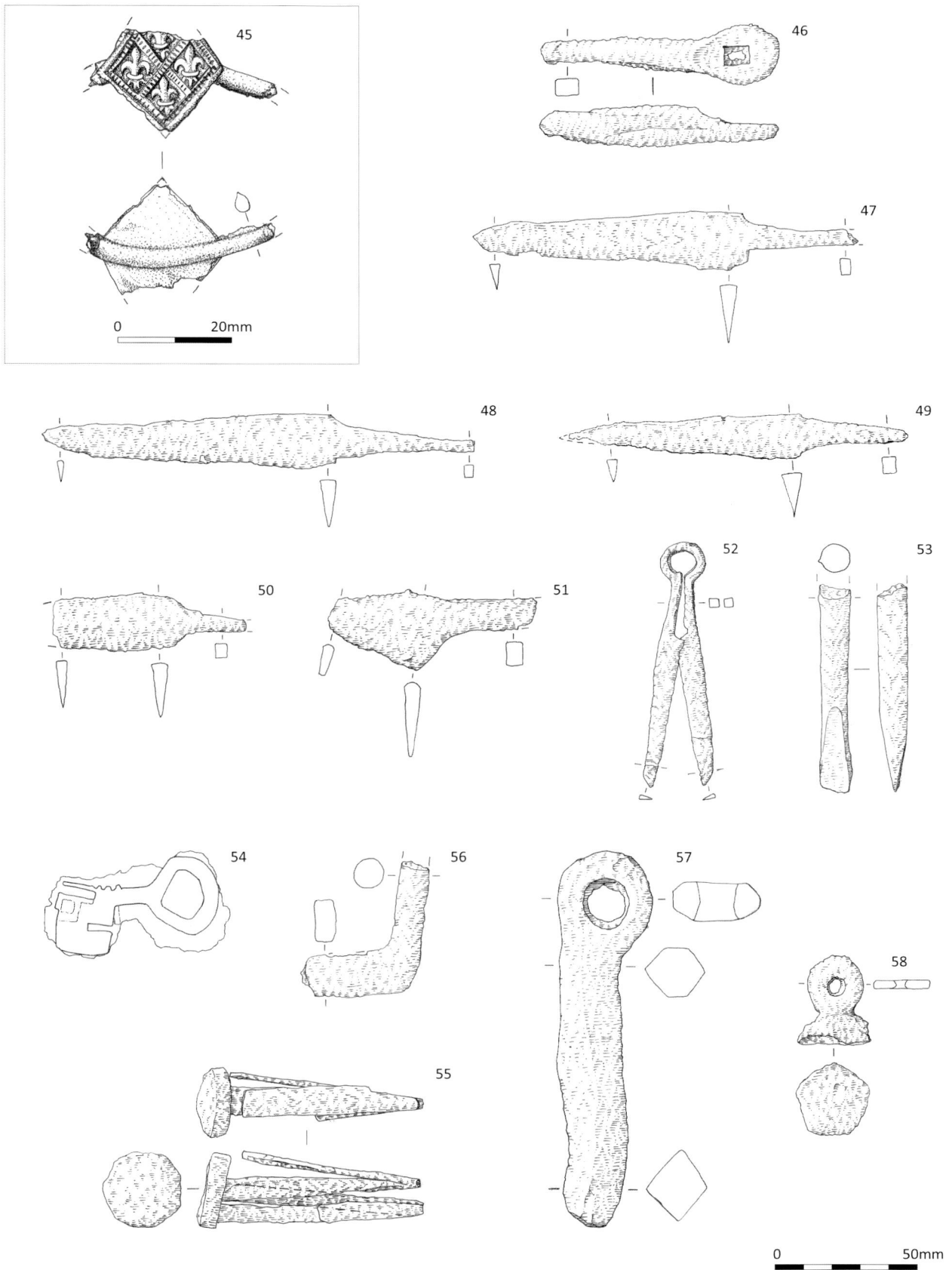

Fig. 3.8 Lead: Cat. No. 45; iron: Cat. Nos 46–58. © Liz James.

At least four different types of both constructions can be distinguished in the assemblage.

The most frequent whittle tang type in the assemblage belongs to Goodall's type E, which has a more or less triangular blade with the tang set in the middle of the blade in line with the tip. Cat. Nos. 47–50 (Fig. 3.8) and SF127 belong to this type, which is found throughout the medieval period with a floruit in the 13th and 14th centuries (Goodall 2011, 106–7, fig. 8.2). The fragmented knife Cat. No. 50 with its narrow whittle tang and triangular blade has a good comparison in a knife that was found during road construction in the east suburb of Old Sarum (Schuster et al. 2012, 147; 180, fig. 40, 29). Cat. No. 48 demonstrates the difficulty in being too specific with knife typologies as the damage and wear of this piece could well have affected both back and cutting edge to such an extent that it is not impossible it might originally have had a straight back and a cutting edge curving up to the tip in line with the back. If that were the case it would be more like Goodall's type D, which is again generally medieval but with a slightly earlier peak during the 12th and 13th centuries (Goodall 2011, 106–7). A seriously fragmented whittle tang knife from a demolition feature in Building 2, Phase 5, is too fragmented for closer typological analysis.

A metal-detected knife hilt plate (XR123), probably for a whittle tang knife, has a sub-oval outline with rectangular/trapezoidal opening (L10.8mm; W5.8–6.4mm), similar to copper alloy examples from Meols, London (Egan 2007a, 171–2, pl. 32, 2141) and from deposits dating to the 11th–14th century in York (Ottaway and Rogers 2002, 2759, fig. 1364).

Of the two scale tang knives, only SF35 is complete enough to attempt typological determination. Although the knife has a fragmented tang, it is still the longest knife in the assemblage, measuring 174mm in length and 25mm wide just before the shoulder. It has one circular hole near the base of the tang, a curved shoulder to the straight back sloping slightly downwards to the last quarter of the blade before tapering to the tip. It has a straight, albeit worn cutting edge with a straight choil inclining at an angle of c. 35° to the tang. Although featuring slightly straighter lines, it would fit best into Goodall's type M which is one of the less common types, but comparisons come

from 13th/14th century contexts at Winchester and Raleigh Castle, Essex (Goodall 2011, 107, 137, fig, 8.18, 261–2). The other example is a possible scale tang knife (SF54) featuring a strip with one end possibly a scale tang with two rectangular rivets and a parallel-sided blade missing its tip.

One blade (XR15), found in a Phase 8 clearance layer associated with WA18 in Building 5, has a straight back, its last third curving down to the missing tip; the long sloping shoulder continues into the bent tang without break and there is no choil to the unfinished edge. This unfinished blade could date from the medieval or subsequent periods of occupation.

CREASER
A blade (Cat. No. 51; Fig. 3.8) with a triangular blade and a sturdy but broken tang could be a creaser for leatherwork, similar to examples from Netherton and Winchester, both Hampshire, from contexts of the late 13th/early 14th and 15th centuries, respectively (Goodall 2011, 73, fig. 6.2, E20–21). One from Norwich, dated to c. 1400–1625, has a more curved blade (Goodall 1993, 190, fig. 141, 1476). Rather than being the tool of a tanner, whose workshop and pits would most likely not be located in the vicinity of a manor house, such a tool could, amongst others, be used to create tooled and creased edges on the leather straps and harnesses required, for instance, for riding and cart equipment (Moreland and Hadley 2020, 199–200; see also Goodall I.H. 2005a, 395). A morphologically very similar, but at 155mm much longer, knife is listed among the medieval kitchen utensils from a disturbed context in Hulst, Netherlands (Grimm and Hoss 2017, 331, Cat. No. 474).

SHEARS
The pair of shears Cat. No. 52 (Fig. 3.8) with omega-shaped bow and narrow blades can be classed among the smaller examples of Goodall's type 2a for which he cites comparisons from generally later medieval contexts in Oxfordshire, Warwickshire and Hampshire (Goodall 2011, 111–2, 155, fig. 8.27, G461–3); another good parallel comes from the Salisbury Drainage Collection (Schuster et al. 2012, 184, fig. 44, 76).

CHISELS
Of the two chisels, which could be of medieval or later date, Cat. No. 53 (Fig. 3.8) has a sturdy, sub-

Table 3.5 Quantity of 'fasteners and fittings' per site phase. U/S = Unstratified

Phase	2	3	3&4	5	7	8	U/S	Total
Qty.	1	13	12	34	2	412	36	510

circular sectioned shaft whose head is broken. Given its carefully sharpened edge, it could be a cold chisel, although the examples illustrated by Goodall from medieval context all have square or sub-rectangular stems (Goodall 2011, 15, fig. 2.5, A38–42). A cold chisel with faceted/sub-circular shaft was found in a Roman-period context at Bloomberg Place in London (Humphreys 2018, COL10).

A possible hot chisel was found in context (301), a Phase 8 clearance layer. The wedge-shaped object is 58.7m long, 10.1–15.4mm wide and 3.6–10.5mm thick. Its head is slightly burred, but most of its surface is lost. Similar objects from Winchester were found in contexts dating from the 16th–17th century as well as the early 12th century (Goodall 2011, 16–7, fig. 2.6, A50–1). The date range of the example from Chickerell could be similar or even continue into the modern period since the shape of such tools is dependent more on the purpose to which it is put rather than any fashion.

DRILL BIT
A drill bit (SF83), with a lozenge-shaped tapering top and a circular-sectioned stem with its tip missing, was found in a Phase 8 clearance layer of Building 7. Although more commonly made with square or sub-rectangular stems, drill bits like this have a long currency from at least the Roman to the post-medieval period (e.g. Manning 1985, pl. 12, B64; Halbout et al. 1987, 131, no. 278; Scott 2011, 18, Cat. No. 14; Goodall 2011, 35–7, fig. 3.6, B41; 3.7, B82; Heindel 2019, 21, Abb. 22c and 23a).

Fasteners and fittings
Due to the wide-ranging scope of this category, it is frequently among the most numerous in assemblages of small, due to the fact that it is only rarely possible to identify the exact purpose for which a given fastener or fitting was used. Apart from horseshoe nails or hobnails, for instance, it is difficult or impossible to identify the purpose of a nail, unless it was found *in situ*, for example

attaching a door hinge strap, in which case it would be classed in the category 'buildings and services'; attached to a hinge strap of a chest it would be part of 'household utensils and furniture'. In this assemblage the quantification of the 510 objects or fragments discussed in the section on medieval small finds is rather random, given that 420 come from Phase 8 layers, and a further 57 are unstratified; a breakdown is presented in Table 3.5. This is amplified by the circumstance that most (487) of the items in this category are intrinsically un-dateable or can only be assigned the broadest date ranges, like the hinge pivot Cat. No. 56, which could date from at least as far back as the Roman period onwards (Manning 1985, 125, fig. 31, 1b). The finds have been included here because it is possible that they had been used at the site as early as the medieval period, but they could equally well relate to the dumping of debris from demolition events at the site or its immediate vicinity. If no material is mentioned, the objects in question were made of iron.

KEYS
All of the four keys are made of iron. No rolled, brazed stems were observed on any of the keys, but this may be due to their generally poor preservation. Cat. No. 54 (Fig. 3.8) can be ascribed to Goodall's type E keys which have 'solid stems with tips which end in line with the bit'. The bows can have a variety of shapes, including ring-, D-, oval- or thistle-shaped; this example appears to have been made less carefully. Although moulded and/or grooved stems are not uncommon in the type, the small notches shown on the illustration might never have been visible at the surface of the stem, although they are in the area that is commonly treated in this way. The type was probably introduced in the 13th century and continued to the end of the medieval period (Goodall 2011, 241). A smaller (L35mm) but otherwise similar key from a 14th century context at the Franciscan Friary in Salisbury has a channelled bit (Schuster et al. 2012, 192, fig. 52, 193), a detail which could not be observed here due to the preservation condition. A

larger example (XR16; L100.8mm, W29.6mm) of the type was found in WA7 of Building 2, Phase 8; it has a rectangular bit with four wards but no rear cleft.

A key bit (XR13) with clefts (trapezoidal, square, rectangular) on three sides could be from a key of Goodall's rare type C which has hollow stems with bits that were welded or brazed into position. Examples come from contexts dating between the 12th and 16th centuries (Goodall 2011, 241). An example from the Salisbury Drainage Collection, thus post-1220, has a very similar bit (Schuster et al. 2012, 160–1, pl 13, 167). Alternatively, on account of its asymmetrical wards, it could be the bit of a Type F key, found throughout the medieval period but with a floruit during the 12th to 14th centuries.

SF144 is the only key from a medieval context (a midden cf Phase 3&4 in Area 3). Missing its bow, it has a solid circular-sectioned stem with a square bit and one cleft cut parallel at an oblique angle from each of the front and back edges. A small hollow, drilled into the tip, might be visible on the x-radiograph. Only one of the keys illustrated by Goodall has an oblique cleft in its front, an example of the rolled type B from Thuxton, Norfolk, dated to the 12th–14th century (Goodall 2011, 275, fig. 10.21, 338), but there are several of that type from the Salisbury Drainage Collection (Schuster et al. 2012, 161, pl. 13, 164–5 and esp.172; see also Penny 1911, 11, pl. 1, 1–2). However, the solid stem with the hollow tip would suggest that SF144 might well be of Goodall's type H, the iron examples of which he suggests are post-medieval (Goodall 2011, 242).

Cat. No. 55 (Fig. 3.8) is the T-shaped bolt for a barrel padlock with shackles. The outer face of the circular closing plate is now too corroded to show how the spines were riveted into the plate. The piece belongs to Goodall's type E, the most popular type and in use throughout the medieval period. Such padlocks were intended for restraining animals as well as humans, but they were also used more widely, e.g. as gate locks (Goodall 2011, 233, 255, figs. 10.10–12). Human burials found with shackles or manacles still *in situ* have been interpreted as either belonging to executed criminals or denoting a penitent or someone suspected of demonic possession (Gilchrist and Sloane 2005, 105, fig. 66). The shackles found

with human remains in the cathedral of Old Sarum (Schuster et al. 2012, 167, 194 fig. 54, 238), for instance, are an especially severe form of shackle – and therefore perhaps more suited for a penitent? – as they had been locked with sturdy bolts riveted shut which could not have been taken off as easily as padlock Cat. No. 55.

LATCHES, HINGES, LOOPS

Doors, window shutters or lids of box or chests are represented by a latch rest, a door hook (cf Goodall 2011, 227, fig. 9.31, H685), seven hinge pivots (including Cat. No. 56; Fig. 3.8), at least two hinge straps, a stapled hasp (Goodall 2011, 215–219, figs. 9.25–9.27) and possibly many of the 16 roves and clench bolts as well as the 15 strips and straps. One of the latter could be a hinge strap with a flaring terminal and central hole (cf Goodall 2011, 209 fig. 9.22, e.g. H477–482); it was found in a Phase 5 demolition layer of Building 1. The ring-ended bar Cat. No. 57 (Fig. 3.8) with its thick stem of lozenge-shaped cross-section was most likely fixed in a wall to receive an inverted hinge pivot, although no traces of mortar were observed on the stem. Cat. No. 58 (Fig. 3.8) might be another example of such a bar for a smaller pivot, although no exact parallel is known to the author, and as it was collected from the subsoil in Area 2 it is a residual find that could date from the medieval period onwards. A 38.7mm-long flat rectangular strip (XR74) with a tapering end bent to form a U-shaped loop was found in Phase 8 clearance deposits of WA9, Building 1; it could be a simpler form of a looped strap hinge like an example with three holes from Flixborough, Lincolnshire (Ottaway 2009, 169–70, fig. 5.3, 1678) or the broken end of a stapled hasp like an example from the Ailey Hill cemetery at Ripon, North Yorkshire; stapled hasp appear not to have been used in Britain or elsewhere in Northern Europe before the 8th century (Ottaway 1996, 103–4, fig. 23, 575).

STAPLES, TIES, CLIPS AND SWIVEL RINGS

Ten of the 12 staples, ranging in length between 31.0mm and 66.7mm, come from Phase 8 clearance deposits, the smallest was found in a Phase 5 demolition deposit of Building 1. Two are rectangular staples, including the largest, which could have been used as timber dogs or bolt keepers on door jambs (Ottaway 1996, 173, fig. 9.3, H47&49), the rest

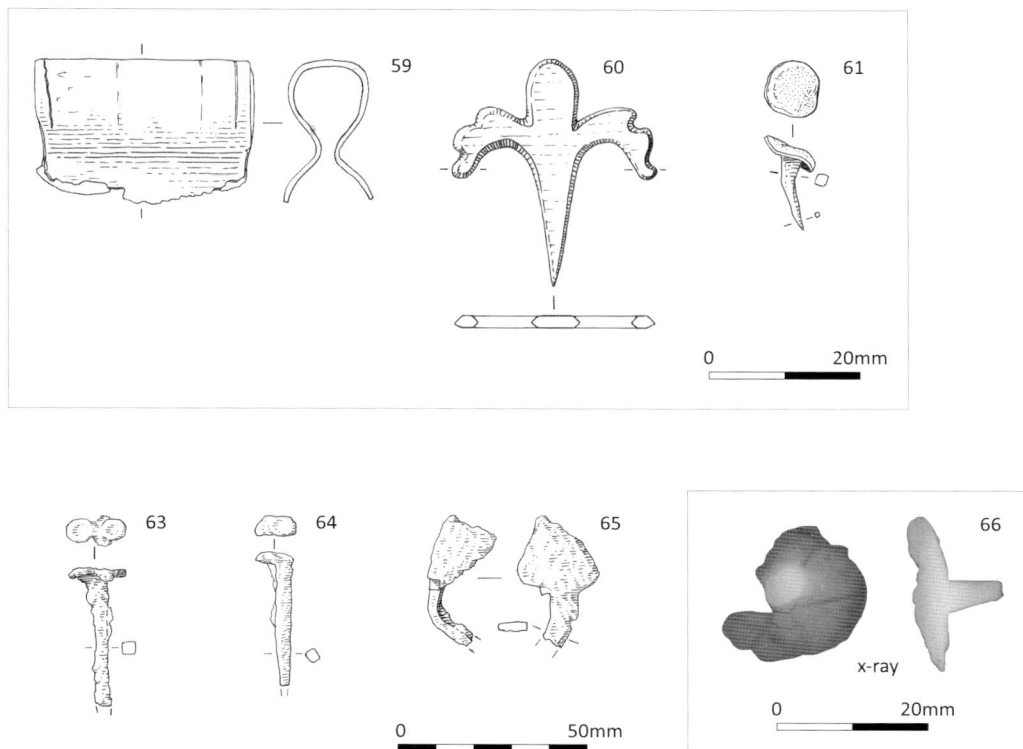

Fig. 3.9 Copper alloy: Cat. Nos 59–60, 66; copper alloy and gilding: Cat. No. 61; iron: Cat. Nos 62–65. © Liz James.

are U-shaped and could have served a multitude of purposes, such as holding chains and hasps on doors or gates, tethering rings as well as handles. An L-shaped hook/timber dog with high-rectangular cross-section, 61.4mm long, was found in the rubble of WA18, Building 5, Phase 3. A broken and bent tie with one end bent at right angles, the other at oblique angle is 155mm long. Such objects were used to bind timbers together, similar to timber dogs and stirrups (Ottaway 1996, 163).

Cat. No. 59 (Fig. 3.9) is a copper alloy clip of unknown purpose, found residually in a Phase 8 layer. An equally unexplained clip, but with a waisted area just above cylindrical part, was found at Norwich in a context dated 1275–1400 (Margeson 1993, 139, fig. 104, 940).

Four swivel rings, three with hooks or open loops similar to later medieval examples from Somerby and Goltho in Lincolnshire (Margeson 1993, 333, fig. 11.16, J245–6); a ring, a ring and chain and a chain link could have varied uses, including possibly on horse gear, or lifting gear to move farm material. A similar

range of uses could apply to a hooked strap or hinge with spiked U-shaped eye and expanding strap with rivet heads on one side. A morphologically similar piece, but twice as long and dating c. 1150–c. 1600, from North Elmham Park, Norfolk (Margeson 1993, 207, fig. 9.21, H453, was clearly a hinge, whereas a later 14th century strap hook of similar dimensions from London was listed among harness fittings (Clark 2004, 60, fig. 45, 52).

Again, none of these objects are chronologically distinct and they could date from the medieval to the early modern periods, but one of the swivel hooks and rings (XR96) was found in a medieval layer, the spread of a midden in Area 1, Phase 3&4.

ORNAMENTAL FITTING

The purpose of the metal-detected fitting Cat. No. 60 (Fig. 3.9), in the shape of a heraldic fleur-de-lis fitchy, is equally unexplained. Maybe it was a wall or ceiling ornament like gilded lead/tin alloy stars and a crescent from Clarendon Palace, Wiltshire (Egan 2001, 118, fig. 39, 190–2); however, Cat. No. 60 has no discernible mode of attachment, whereas those from

Table 3.6   Quantity of nails and studs per phase. U/S = Unstratified.

Phase	2	3	3&4	5	7	8	U/S	Total
Qty.	1	11	9	30	1	348	25	425

Table 3.7   Quantity of nail and stud types (after Goodall, I. H. 2011, 164, fig. 9.1).GRL=greatest recorded length in mm.

Type	1	2	3	4	5	6	7	8	10	11	12
Qty.	109	30	4	4	12	15	2	2	3	16	1
GRL	82.9	92.2	50.2	151.4	38.5	71.2	38.4	62.9	53.4	>90	49.0

Clarendon had small loops. As a heraldic charge the fleur-de-lis fitchy is very rare, Rietstap lists its use in the arms of the Provençal family Mandon (Rietstap 1884, s.v. Mandon), but the present author was not able to find any other mention.

SHEET CONUS

A rolled copper alloy sheet conus (SF48; L21.9mm, D9.6–12.5mm) might have been a late medieval or early post-medieval dagger sheath chape or a ferrule. Its overlapping join has no visible traces of solder, and its top and end is damaged. It might be comparable to a dagger sheath (Ottaway and Rogers 2002, 2904, fig. 1478) or a ferrule (Ottaway and Rogers 2002, 2853–4, fig. 1431, 9161) from York, dated to the late medieval- or early post-medieval periods.

RIVETS AND TACKS

A 30mm-long copper alloy rivet, SF138, with conical head (base diameter 9.3–10.5mm) and a globular top (diameter 5.5mm), sub-circular-sectioned shaft and upset end was metal-detected. It has small flecks of gilding on the head. If not used on a box, it could be similar to the fittings of a non-ferrous coated iron purse frame from Norwich, found in a context dated to 1507 (Margeson 1993, 44, fig. 25).

A metal-detected small copper alloy tack or mount (Cat. No. 61; Fig. 3.9) has a gold-plated flat circular head. A similar piece from an early–mid 17th century context comes from Acton Court, South Gloucestershire, (Courtney 2004, 390, fig. 9.53, 189) but lacks the gold plating. Both pieces could have been used on wood or leather (for lead/tin examples on spur straps, cf Clark 2004, 156, fig. 112, 397–8).

NAILS AND STUDS

Nails are frequently the most numerous object type in an assemblage of metal small finds. From the quantification in Table 3.6 it is obvious that most of the 397 nails and 28 studs discussed in the medieval chapter are residual finds in demolition and clearance layers. It is therefore impossible to reach any reasonable level of certainty as to the actual date of most of the simple hand-wrought forms of nails with flat rectangular or sub-circular heads, which can be faceted or domed, as these can range in date from at least the Roman period (Manning 1985, type 1; Wastling 2009, 144, Fig. 4.1, type A; Goodall, 2011, 164, fig. 9.1, type 1 and 2), and these forms are also the most frequent from Chickerell (see Table 3.7).

Only three nails, which are most likely of post-medieval or younger date, will be considered in the chapter on post-medieval small finds, but a fair number of the examples discussed here, could also have been used in the subsequent period.

More than half the nails and studs considered in Table 3.6 were too damaged or corroded to attempt any meaningful typological identification (Table 3.7), while Cat. No. 65 (Fig. 3.9) does not fit into any of the typologies mentioned above; it was found in the clearance of WA20, Building 1, Phase 8. Other types, like Goodall type 4 (Cat. No. 62), type 5 (Cat. No. 63) or type 7 (Cat. No. 64) were no doubt more numerous, but their distinctive traits (type 4 = faceted rectangular head; 5 = flat head of figure-of-eight shape; 7 = flat L-shaped head) could all be stages in the deterioration of a type 1 nail. Similarly, nails of type 6 with flat rectangular heads formed

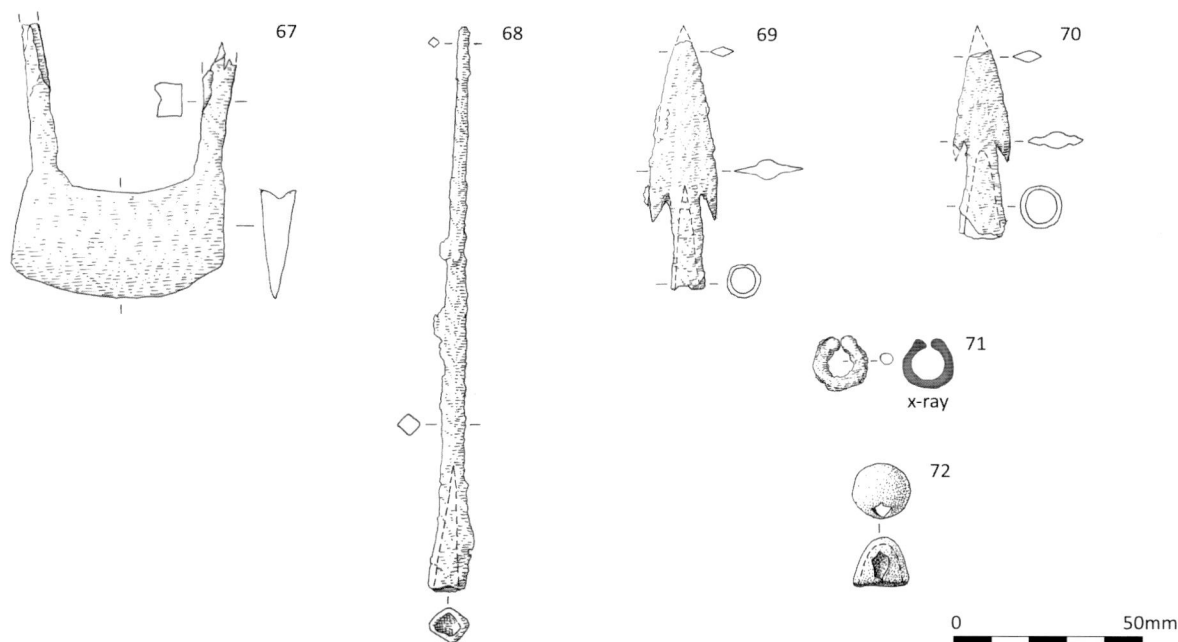

Fig. 3.10   Iron: Cat. Nos 67–71; lead: Cat. No. 72. © Liz James.

by a flaring, wedge-shaped shank and headless nails of type 8 are virtually indistinguishable among the larger number of shank fragments. Types 10 to 12 are sturdier studs with rectangular/rounded flat or faceted heads, rectangular pyramidal heads, or circular domed heads, respectively, which could have served both structural as well as more decorative purposes, e.g. on a door (cf Schuster et al. 2012, 155–6,187, fig. 47, 111). The decorative aspect is certainly emphasised in copper alloy stud Cat. No. 66 (Fig. 3.9). A comparable stud from Barentin's Manor, Chalgrove, Oxfordshire, dates from the mid- to later 15th century (Goodall, A. 2005, 81, fig. 3.9, 36–37).

Objects associated with agriculture, horticulture and animal husbandry

Of the 12 objects that have been assigned to this category, only a fragmented iron spade shoe (XR89) was found in a context assigned to medieval Phase 3&4 ((1005), an alluvium spread from a midden in Area 1). The nearly 80mm-long fragment of the spade iron has a grooved edge with a rectangular mouth and blade, similar to a fragment from the construction pit of a 13th–early 14th century well in Lyveden, Northamptonshire (Goodall 2011, 89 fig. 7.4, F16). Spade irons are associated with Romanisation in Britain but might be an Iron Age idea (Rees 2011,

100), and both rectangular- as well as round-mouthed spade shoes also existed during the Roman period and continued well into the post-medieval period (Rees et al. 2008, 346); with the exception of the medieval triangular types, a distinction between these and later types, especially when fragmented and from undated contexts, is – in the opinion of this author – not convincing (cf Manning 1985, 45–6, figs. 10–11; Humphreys 2018, 587–91). However, it is interesting to note that medieval documentary evidence for rectangular-shaped spade irons points to their dating from the 14th century and later (Goodall 2011, 79).

The small iron shoe Cat. No. 67 (Fig. 3.10) is only 57mm wide and could perhaps have been intended for a small weeding spade. No similarly small implement is known to the author.

Among the metal-detected objects from the site are ten lead net-weights. Two main forms can be distinguished. Three simply consist of a rolled tubular strip, between 18.6mm and 52.8mm long and weighing between 4.5g and 54.6g (cf Steane and Foreman 1988, 163, fig. 15, 1–20). Four are sub-cones or cylinders of sub-oval section with large sub-circular holes, their surfaces marked with several cut marks (Steane and Foreman 1988, fig. 15, 39); they are 29.2–33.2mm long and weigh between 46.3g and 95.7g. The remaining three are of cone, sub-spherical and annular shapes. Their presence at the site could attest to exploitation of the marine resource in the vicinity or they could simply have been collected for recycling. Given the otherwise low quantities of Roman material from the site, it is unlikely that these weights date from that period, but it should be remembered that they also had been widespread during the Hellenistic (in the Mediterranean) and Roman periods (Dütting and Hoss 2014).

Weapons and military equipment

Only four items belong in this category, three arrowheads and one chain mail ring, and although all are from demolition or clearance layers, all are intrinsically dateable to the medieval period.

Cat. No. 68 (Fig. 3.10) is a 153.8mm-long socketed arrowhead of Jessup type M7 for which he cites examples from dated contexts from the 11th–14th centuries (Jessup 1996, 198). An example from Barentin's Manor, Chalgrove, Oxfordshire, could extend this into the early 15th century (Goodall, I. H. 2005b, 102, fig. 3.25, 162). The effectiveness of long, narrow-bladed bodkin-type arrowheads against different types of chain mail was experimentally shown to be much greater than for shorter types of bodkin or even leaf-shaped heads, achieving lethal penetration in rings of 8mm diameter even without breaking any ring (Jones 2014).

The two arrowheads Cat. No. 69–70 (Fig. 3.10) both have triangular, flat oval-sectioned blades and barbs curving down from the shoulders. Although they are 68.3mm and 57.9mm long, respectively, and thus exceed the range of 25–40mm for Jessup's type M4, morphologically they clearly belong to this military form of arrowhead (Jessup 1996, 198). A 60mm-long close parallel for the Chickerell heads from Salisbury (Borg 1991, 86, fig. 22, 31) is even listed by Jessup as type M4, although two closely comparable examples from York, c. 50mm and 70mm long, are referred to as multipurpose forms (Ottaway and Rogers 2002, 2968, fig. 1532, 14158 & 14160), and given their size, this might also apply to the Chickerell examples.

Both the terminals of the single ring of chain mail (Cat. No. 71; Fig. 3.10) are unfortunately missing, as

the shape of the rivets are chronologically sensitive. Mail rings up to the 11th century were usually closed with round-sectioned rivets passed through punched holes. By the 14th century, this was achieved with small triangular rivets cut from sheet iron and pressed through a slit that was punched through the overlapping terminals. The earlier construction did, however, not disappear entirely (Jones 2014).

The weapon-related equipment from the site could relate to episodes of conflict or simply the storage and/or maintenance of such equipment; given the small number of items, the latter might be the more likely explanation.

Objects and waste material associated with metalworking

The categorisation of the eight objects associated with metalworking is rather tentative, for instance in the cases of the fragments of run-off copper alloy metal, which might have occurred accidentally as the result of one (or more) fires on sites (as might be more likely in case of the 20 fragments of lead spillage recorded as uncertain), rather than during the process of casting metal. Three strips of iron, however, are clearly exhibiting evidence of smithing, with the splaying/widening of an end or the probable welding of two bars onto each other. Two of these were found in a rubble deposit of B5, Phase 3, and a midden in Area 3, Phase 3&4, respectively. Whether this, as well as the presence of a fragment of copper alloy bar/ingot (SF57; L37.3mm, W11mm), is evidence of on-site metalworking or simply the collection of scrap metal for later use on site or elsewhere has to remain uncertain. However, neither traces of pyrotechnical installations of any kind nor scatters of hammerscale, which might have indicated the location of a blacksmith's anvil, have been recorded.

Objects of unknown or uncertain function

Across the entire date range of the assemblage this category comprises 125 items (Table 3.2). Of the 42 pieces of lead, most are fragments of spillage or cut-offs. Most of the 33 pieces of copper alloy are sheet or plate fragments of uncertain use. The 42 iron objects in this category comprise various unidentifiable strip, strap and sheet fragments as well as rods and wires. The records are available in the archive. A small selection of objects which might be of medieval date is discussed in the following.

Two objects possibly made of silver include a possible strap-end (SF133) made of folded sheeting (cf Egan and Pritchard 2002, 159, fig. 104, 744) and a flat circular disc with no discernible motif or decoration.

Found in Phase 7 clearance layers of Building 3, a curved rectangular-sectioned iron rod with one straight and one broken end might be a fragment of an oval purse frame (cf Goodall 2011, 361, fig. 12.11, K294).

Cat. No. 72 (Fig. 3.10) is a small lead cone found residually in the subsoil in Area 2. It is possibly the filling for a sheet-metal cover of a decorative boss, stud or pin (cf Egan and Pritchard 2002, 174, nos. 873–888; 194–5, fig. 122, 1045).

A thin, turned bone disc (diam. 30.9mm) with a large circular hole in its centre (diam. *c.* 8.3mm) was found residually in a clearance layer of Building 1, Phase 8. Less than half of the disc remains. No suggestions of the purpose of such discs was found for comparisons from Marlowe Car Park, Canterbury (Greep 1995, 1149–50, fig. 506, 1051), from a medieval well, but intrinsically undateable, as well as an example from Norwich from an 18th century context (Margeson 1993, 230, fig. 177, 1871).

The fragment of a tubular bone of plano-convex section, broken at both ends, has a sub-circular hole in the flatter side near its wider end. Most of its surface appears polished, and there are facets from polishing on the convex side. A broken bird-bone flute from London, made from the ulna of a large bird, has a blow hole and, now missing, finger holes which were cut into the flat, posterior side of the bone (Pritchard 1991, 207, fig. 3.88). Maybe this piece, found in the demolition debris of Building 3, Phase 7, was a – quickly abandoned – attempt at making such a flute.

The post-medieval small finds

This section provides a brief overview of 74 objects which can intrinsically be dated to the post-medieval period. Only five objects were found in two post-

medieval structures assigned to Period 7, a path in Area 3 and a demolition layer of Building 3; the remainder came from Period 8 contexts (27), or were recovered unstratified or during metal detecting (44). As mentioned previously, it is likely that an unknown number of objects with wider date ranges, especially undecorated or non-decorative objects like tools or fittings, could well belong in this period, but since the majority of occupational activity occurred during the medieval period it is considered more likely that most objects were manufactured during the medieval period.

Objects of dress and personal adornment

Apart from two heel irons, the remainder of the 16 objects in this category are made of copper alloy. Ten objects are buckles or fragments thereof. Among the earliest is a figure-of-eight double loop buckle (XR126) with a cast rosette on each loop, although in this example one loop has broken off near the central bar. The type, used on belts, shoes and probably also sword belts, is widespread during the 16th and early 17th centuries, exemplified by examples from the Mary Rose (Klein 2005, 104, fig. 2. 83, 82A5069); Camber Castle, East Sussex (Biddle et al. 2001, 260–1, fig. 7.2, 27); Canterbury (Blockley et al. 1995, fig. 455, 616), Norwich (Margeson 1993, 31, fig. 17, 174) West Thurrock, Essex (Schuster 2010, 60, fig. 20,3) and from a possibly residual late 17th/early 18th century context in Portsmouth (Pearce 2016, 206–7, fig. 22, 74). Two individually bagged fragments of rectangular, double-looped buckle frames with incised double line along outer edges, followed on the inside by a floral pattern of long zig-zag lines, the other with a wavy line on the inside and a transverse hatched ridge between lateral lines, can broadly be dated to the 16th–17th century; the pieces could potentially belong to the same frame but do not join. Cat. No. 73 (Fig. 3.11) is a double-oval frame decorated much like a comparison from Norwich dated between 1625 and 1700 (Margeson 1993, 28, 31, fig. 17, 175). A slightly smaller buckle with profiled frame and separate iron bar with openwork tongue is stamped with a maker's mark TP or IP. The form dates to the later 17th and earlier 18th centuries, and a comparison for a TP stamp was found at Meols on the Wirral (Egan 2007b, 217, 219, no. 3082). A similar data range applies to a slightly less ornate rectangular-ovoid buckle with iron bar (now broken, but present) and strap with a

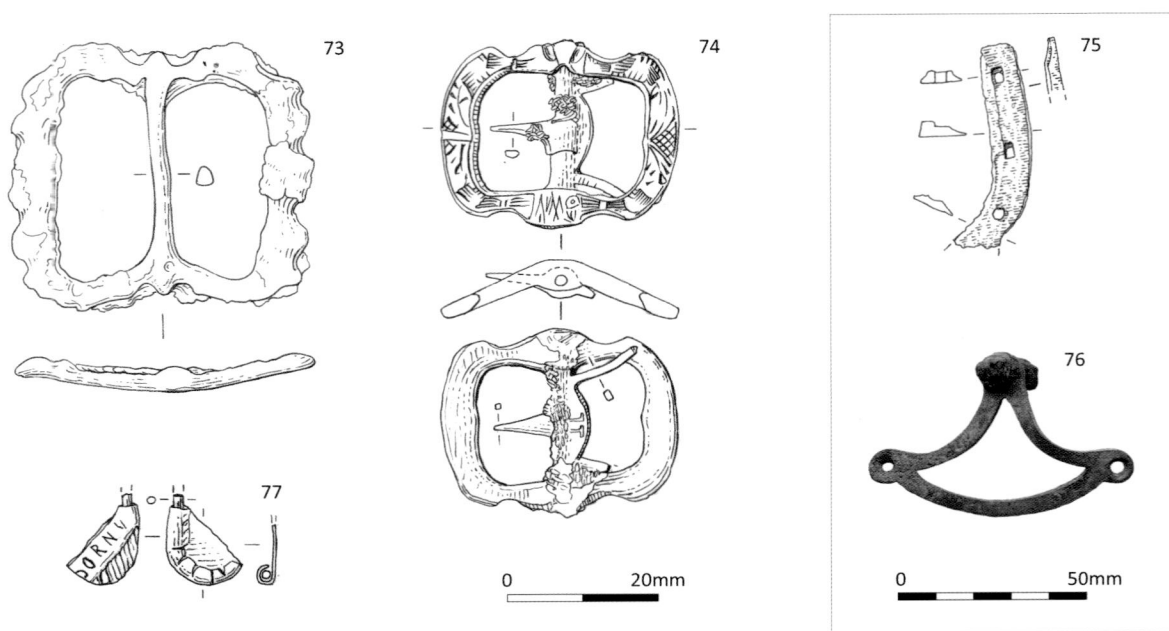

Fig 3.11   Copper alloy: Cat. Nos: Cat. Nos 73–74, 77; iron: Cat. No. 75; copper alloy and iron: Cat. No. 76. © Liz James.

double-lugged hinge plate, stamped with the maker's mark 'COOK'; the rounded strap end has a mushroom-shaped button rivet. Additionally, a second, similar strap end with the same mark was also found. This is a widespread type, see e.g. examples from King John's House, Tollard Royal, Wiltshire (Pitt-Rivers 1890, pl. 19, 25) or Chadlington, Oxfordshire (PAS SUR-A5CAD9). A further two rectangular frames, originally with separate iron bars, as well as a separate buckle pin can also broadly be dated to the post-medieval period, the frames possibly to the 18th century.

Three 18th century buttons were found. SF96 is made of gilded copper alloy and has a flat circular head with oval-sectioned loop soldered onto its back. The front appears polished and might have been decorated with an armorial bearing, but this is now too faint to be certain. The back has a raised mark 'GILT' and remains of gilding all over, including the loop. Two tombak buttons include the dished base of a composite button (SF32) as well as a plain, flat button (SF13) with noticeably bevelled edge and central cone soldered onto its back for the attachment of a soldered loop made of an oval-sectioned copper alloy shank. A similar button was among the six buttons found in association with a non-cemetery burial at Taunton, Somerset (Schuster 2015, 4 esp. SF no H; cf Bailey 2004 ,40).

Two heel irons were found, Cat. No. 75 (Fig. 3.11) in a demolition deposit of Building 3, Phase 7, and SF106 in a Phase 8 clearance layer. It has been claimed that '...there is little certain evidence of the use of the heel and toe irons before the 19th century' (Margeson 1993, 63). One from a Phase 5 context (1682–88) at Nonsuch Palace was even dismissed as 'probably intrusive in its context since there is no reliable evidence for other examples at such an early date' (Goodall, I.H. 2005a, 407); but there are examples, for instance from a Civil War context at Beeston Castle, Cheshire (Courtney 1993, 142, fig. 97, 99) or a late 17th–early 18th century context at Tilbury Fort, Essex (Moore 2000,70, fig. 49, 222). However, whether Cat. No. 75 is of such an early date cannot be decided with the contextual evidence for Chickerell.

Toilet, surgical or pharmaceutical instruments
The profiled copper alloy nozzle for an enema syringe could be of 18th century date or younger.

Household utensils and furniture
The nine records in this category belong to eight individual objects, including two spoons and six knives or fragments thereof. The spoon stem fragments SF84 and SF85 were found in F38, a path in the south-east corner of Area 3, Phase 7; they comprise the top and knop as well as part of the

stem of a seal-top knop spoon. The terminal is a flat disc below which is a baluster with moulded decoration of longitudinal ribs. Below this collar is a section of moulded decoration in relief, but it is too worn to identify clearly. A final narrow collar runs below this motif, and from this collar the sub-rectangular stem extends to a worn break. The spoon belongs to the developed series of the later 16th/early 17th century when the decoration occupied a greater length of the stem than on earlier examples (Jackson 1892, 133). A stem top from a context dated 1590–1630 at Moulsham St, Chelmsford, is an example of this (Goodall 1985, 44 fig. 28, 40), and the PAS lists other close morphological parallels, including from Whimple, Devon (DEV-C3EDA2) and East Hendred, Oxfordshire (WMID-12BC66). Spoon SF84/SF85 was made of copper alloy, probably brass, which by the 17th century had become the predominant copper alloy used for small or portable objects (cf Dungworth 2002,9, fig. 6; Ströbele and Schuster 2019, 15).

The fragment of a probably silver spoon stem terminal was found in the topsoil in Area 1, Phase 8. It consists of a slightly cupped oval sheet with raised floral scroll motif on its convex side, but there is no trace of the motif on the back, suggesting that it was cast rather than stamped. The floral decoration would be commensurate with a date in the 18th century or later.

Six iron knives in different stages of repair, mostly of later 16th/early 17th century date, were collected from topsoil and clearance layers of Phase 8. The most complete one (SF105) has a short bone handle (c. 38mm), with 26mm-long whittle tang and 43mm-long octagonal-sectioned bolster; the parallel-sided blade has no shoulder, a sloping choil and is missing its tip. Of the fragment of a second example only the square-sectioned whittle tang, octagonal bolster and top of the blade survive. A comparison from Beeston Castle, Cheshire, was found in a Civil War-period context (Courtney 1993, 135, fig. 93, 4), others come e.g. from Basing House, Hampshire (Moorhouse and Goodall 1971, 36–7, fig. 17, 4 & 8), and a very ornately decorated example from King John's House, Tollard Royal, Wiltshire (Pitt-Rivers 1890, pl. 18, 11). A very corroded whittle tang knife (XR102), with a rectangular sectioned bolster and an angled choil to the cutting edge which rises slightly to its missing tip, can be compared to a knife from Castle Rising Castle, Norfolk, that additionally has four sets of decorative copper alloy collars on the tang (Williams 1997, 94, fig. 66, 6). Two further knife fragments include part of a blade and a bolster or collar for a knife with a circular socket with a flattened top and a high-triangular (blade-shaped) socket at the other end. The only scale tang knife has a circular bolster, a flat choil and shoulder and a flat-triangular angled back.

Objects used for recreational/leisure purposes

A Jew's harp or trump was found during the initial archaeological monitoring work. In plan, the 63.2mm-long instrument consists of a sub-circular head and two tapering arms, both with the characteristic lozenge-shaped cross-section. The rectangular rabbet is located at the apex of the 28.8mm-wide head, where no traces of the iron tongue remain. It has the larger and wider mouth common of the post-medieval forms (cf Egan 2010, 284–5). An example of similar dimensions was found at Bearwardcote, Derbyshire (PAS DENO-912BB4, and at least a further 12 similar examples recorded on the database).

Commerce

The 14 post-medieval coins cover the period between the reigns of Elizabeth I and George I. Many are badly affected by corrosion, thus in those instances only a very cursory description is given. Of note are No. 23, a French liard for Louis XIV, and two trade tokens (Fig. 3.12): No. 28 is a Weymouth farthing token of 1669, the issuing of which was agreed at a hall held on Friday, 5th November 1669 for the sum of £10 in farthings (Williamson 1889, 194–5, No. 194, pl. 3, 7). The other (No. 29) is probably a half penny draper's token which was

Fig. 3.12   Draper's token, No. 29; Farthing token, No. 28; both copper alloy.

most likely issued by one John Swetman (sic) who was mayor of Weymouth and Melcombe Regis in 1652, and the name "Mr. Swetnam" also appears as present at a hall held on Monday, 23rd January 1662 (cf Williamson 1889, 183 with entry under farthing tokens Nos. 104–5). The farthing of George I (No. 27) recorded as coming from F39 in Building 2, Phase 4, was a later intrusion in rubble overlying the floor area.

An overview of the post-medieval coins and tokens is presented in the following (N.B. the coin numbers continue the sequence from the previous chapter). The format lists small finds number, coin material, weight and dimensions (in mm), issuer, description. Date range. Excavation event and context information; followed by site phase:

16. XR131, Silver, 0.3g, D9.5–10.5, T0.65, Elizabeth I, Halfpenny. Obv. Portcullis. Rev. Cross fleury with 3 pellets in each quarter. Hole punched through from top of obv. above portcullis (obliterating mint mark if it had been present, but that would suggest Spink 2588). Good preservation: circles on joins of portcullis bars all visible and hardly worn. Spink 2581. 1582–1600. AMR/13, U/S.

17. XR128, Silver, 1.3g, D22.1–23.1, T0.6, Elizabeth I, Groat hammered (?first issue). Spink ?2551. ?1559–60. AMR/13, U/S.

18. XR116, CuA, 0.3g, D13–15, Charles I, Farthing. Obv. Traces of crown, see No. 21. 1625–1649. AMR/13, U/S.

19. XR117, CuA, 0.3g, D15.9–16.4, T0.3, Charles I, Farthing. Obv. Traces of crown, see No. 21. 1625–1649. AMR/13, U/S.

20. XR118, CuA, 0.3g, D15.7–16.3, T0.3, Charles I, Farthing. Obv. Traces of crown, see No. 21. 1625–1649. AMR/13, U/S.

21. XR119, CuA, 0.5g, D16.5–16.9, T0.4, Charles I, Farthing. Obv. Crown and two sceptres crossed CAROLVS DG MAG BRI. 1625–1649. AMR/13, U/S.

22. SF15, CuA, 5.2g, D28–29.1, 1.9–2.1, ??Oliver Cromwell, or Charles I, ?Farthing token? Arms appear to show George cross in 1st and 4th with additional crosses in 3rd (but could also be very worn leopards) and lettering below shield [?.?AR_._]. ?17th C. EXC/16, F23, Area 2; 8.

23. CuA, 3.6g, D20.8–21.2, T1.4, Louis XIV, Liard de France, Obv. [?..?]XIIII ROI DE[-?], faint bust facing right. Rev. LIAR[D]/D[E]/[-----]/I (or ?crowned L for Lille?), Fleur-de-lis below. Most of both surfaces completely blank. 1643–1715, AMR/13, U/S.

24. Silver, 2.6g, Charles II, Sixpence; ?Spink 3382. 1674–1684, AMR/13, U/S.

25. XR7, CuA, 8.1g, D27.9–28.4, T2.0–2.2, Possibly William III halfpenny. Almost completely defaced, portrait discernible in x-radiograph. ?1695–1701, EXC/16, U/S.

26. SF104, CuA, 9.1g, D27.8–28.6, 1.9, Milled coin, possibly halfpenny of William III, both surfaces almost completely worn away., Late 17th C. AMR/13, 101; 8.

27. SF104, CuA, 3.9g, D22.0–22.2, T1.5, George I, farthing. Probably Spink 3662. 1719–1724. EXC/16, F39, Building 2; 4.

28. XR120, CuA, 1.6g, D20.6–21.2, T0.8, Farthing. Obv. ¨A¨ / WEYMOVTH / FARTHING / FOR ·THE / · POOR · / 1669 Rev. Arms of Weymouth; an antique three-masted ship, on the hull an escutcheon, per fess in chief three chevrons, in base three lions passant gardant. Williamson 1889, 194 No. 194. Fig. 3.12b.

29. SF151, CuA, 0.5g, D15.9–16.6, T0.5, Token. Draper's ?half penny token. Obv. *IOHN [SW]ETNA[M]/ *S*/ I A. Rev.: *OF.MELTON DRAPER / *S*/ I A. Mid-Late 17th C. EXC/16, U/S. Fig. 3.12a.

Objects associated with transport

Of the six objects, four are horseshoes and two shoe nails with expanded club-shaped heads and rectangular-sectioned tapering shafts; the latter had become the common form of nail on Clark type 4 horseshoes and continued into the post-medieval period and beyond (cf Clark 2004, 120, fig. 86, 212 & 214). Apart from horseshoe SF89, all other examples as well as the nails were from Phase 8 layers. The right branch of horseshoe SF89 was found in the path in the southeast corner of Area 3, Phase 7, and features two rectangular holes in a wide fuller. Fullered shoes were probably not introduced before the second quarter of the 17th century (Clark 2004, 82), as exemplified by examples found at Camber Castle, East Sussex, in post-1637 demolition deposits (Biddle et al. 2001, 209–10, nos. 177, 179, 181), and at Nonsuch Palace in a Phase 5-deposit (Goodall, I.H. 2005a, 407, 409, fig. 203, 225). One left branch of a shoe with three rectangular straight holes has rectangular-headed nails still remaining in the lower two holes. One fragment of a right heel, possibly with a double-folded calkin, is rather wide (29.6mm), and could be from a Clark type 4 or later types, although the presence of a calkin might suggest an earlier date; the frequency of calkins decreases during the course of the medieval period (Clark 2004, 82, tab. 6).

Buildings and services

The three items in this category could be of post-medieval or younger date. Of particular note is a copper alloy, probably brass, wire crank (Cat.

No. 76; Fig. 3.11) for a door or servants bell. The wire would have been attached to two hourglass-shaped holes on the sides of its anchor-shaped triangular frame, while the top hole still has an iron attachment spike in place. The installation of such a device in a house is an expression of the increasing importance placed upon the separation between servants and masters within a household. The earliest mention of such a bell system was found in a 1727 inventory of Kiveton Hall at Kiveton Park, near Rotherham, South Yorkshire, the seat of the Marquess of Carmarthen (Murdoch 2006). Although Cat. No. 76 is likely to be slightly younger, its presence at Chickerell is, nevertheless, testament to the presence of a dwelling of elevated social status either on the site itself or its immediate vicinity during the 18th century.

The other two items are a fragment of a lead piping junction (SF110) and what might be an iron window stay (XR102), both from Phase 8 clearance layers. The latter is a length of circular-sectioned wire with looped end (L 182mm) attached to a looped attachment plate (31.7×7.5mm) with a flat-rectangular plate extending into a rectangular-sectioned wire loop. Alternatively, it could be an eyed spike with attachment plate like an example from a 17th–18th century context at Winchester (Goodall 2011, 189, fig. 9.11, H228).

Fasteners and fittings

Only eight items are considered in this section, all either from phase 8 layers or found during metal-detecting. However, it has to be remembered that an unknown number of the intrinsically un-dateable finds discussed under this category in the medieval chapter could equally well have been deposited during the post-medieval period.

A 133.4mm long key with and oval bow, has a circular-sectioned solid stem and a double ridge before its square bit which is separated into two parts by a cruciform cleft. It can be classed among Goodall's type G2, which could be used from both sides of a lock as the key was prevented from pushing in too far by the ridge or thickening of the stem half-way across the bit. The form has a long currency from the medieval period until well into the post-medieval period. Particularly close comparisons come e.g. from 16th century contexts at Winchester,

Hampshire, and demolition layers at Ospringe, Kent (Goodall 2011, 242, 295 fig. 10.38, I556, I559).

A fragmented oval copper alloy base plate (L 32.6mm), with two bevelled circular holes either side of a larger central hole, could have been a fitting for a locker or window latch.

An oval copper alloy plaque (61.4×48.5mm), with bevelled edge and six spikes for attachment on its back, might have been a decorative fitting for a harness strap. A flat-headed copper alloy rivet (diam. 15.6mm; L12.3mm) was possibly also part of a harness; it has a thick stem and counter rivet holding a washer of similar diameter to the head. Leather remains adhering to the top and base of the stem indicate that it had been attached to a leather strap. A chain with six figure-of-eight links (each *c.* 32mm long) and two rings with open, rectangular-sectioned hoops (diameter 25.2–27mm) was found in the topsoil in the area of Building 6.

Of the three nails considered here, one from topsoil context 2001 in Area 2 is the longest nail found during the investigations, measuring 199.5mm. It has a T-shaped head with slightly expanding arms and a square-sectioned shaft tapering to a chisel tip. A similar, French made nail, although almost twice as long, is illustrated by Richard Jones. It has barbs cut into its corners to prevent it coming back out of the wood (https://www.historicnails.com/board-3-pg-1; accessed 28.10.2020; Board 3, no. 86). Another, metal-detected nail with triangular head is 93.5mm long, with a shaft cross-section tapering from square to rectangular at the tip (cf ibid., Board 4, nos. 132 & 134 the latter also French and with barbed corners). The last nail (XR102) has a flat, sub-square head swelling out of a rectangular-sectioned, bent shaft. Comparable nails were found at Basing House, Hampshire, but like the Chickerell example, they were individual examples of this shape rather than a recognisable type with numerous specimen (Moorhouse and Goodall 1971, 50, fig. 22, 98–100)

Military or weapon equipment

Eleven bullets of lead shot were collected from the site, including one 12 bore ball for a musket and three 15 bore balls for a bastard musket. Four balls weighing between 17.4g and 11.9g are pistol shot of

26-, 27-, 29 and 38 bore. Three small balls weighing between 2.3g and 3.5g can be described as hail shot. Although of slightly uneven circumference, they are not teardrop-shaped, which would have been the case had they been produced with the Rupert method, whereby molten lead was poured through a colander-like dish into water. This method was created in 1665, while the mass production with the shot tower, producing perfect spherical balls, was only developed in 1769 (Foard 2008, 126; 2009, 12). All balls show more or less pronounced facets and dimples, suggesting that they had at least been rammed into a barrel, four are uneven enough to suggest they might have been fired. Although there is of course no possibility of confirming the notion, one may wonder whether these balls of lead shot are related to one or other of the skirmishes and attacks on Weymouth and Melcombe Regis in February 1645 in the course of the Civil War (Bowles Barret 1910).

Objects of unknown or uncertain function

A possible fitting made of sheet metal (Cat. No. 77; Fig. 3.11) is shield-shaped with the sheet crimped over a wire running around the edge. It shows a possibly heraldic decoration of five horizontal bars (or paly of ten), bend sinister with the motto [?S ORN[?O]. No comparison has yet been found, and it remains uncertain whether the object represents a late medieval or post-medieval fitting, perhaps part of horse gear, or maybe some form of device, badge or lapel pin.

A folded, 53mm-long piece of sheet metal (SF116) with unevenly broken edges is now bent into a sub-pentagonal shape. Although its purpose could not be determined, one possibility could be that it is a fragment of a powder flask nozzles (cf Grimm and Hoss 2017, 312-5). It was found in the subsoil in Area 2.

The fragment of a 2.4mm-thick cast sheet or metal object wall (XR10) has an irregular trapezoidal shape (29.2×27.5mm); all its edges are still sharp and it has the remnant of a rounded ridge near one point. It was found in a Phase 8 clearance layer of Building 3. Although it is not impossible that it is a piece of shrapnel, the rounded ridge might suggest that it could have been a fragment of a cauldron or similar cast vessel.

Discussion

The archaeological investigations at Putton Lane have produced a sizable assemblage of archaeological small finds (see Table 3.1 and Table 3.2). However, the large proportion of finds from unstratified or widespread demolition and clearance layers limits the possibility of meaningful spatial analysis in interpreting the function of individual features. Building 5 might serve as an example: of the 61 horseshoe nails recorded across all periods, for instance, only four were recovered from Phase 2 contexts located below Building 5, which was constructed in the subsequent phase (N.B. these are the only horseshoe nails from Phase 2). It is thus questionable whether this might provide a tentative hint at the purpose of this area before the construction of Building 5. All the 17 small finds assigned to Phase 3 across the entire site were recovered from this building, but they were all found in rubble deposits and, apart from one possibly half-worked iron bar fragment with flared end, only comprised nails and fittings like an L-shaped hook, which were most likely part of the structure of the building rather than what it was used for. The 20 finds from the building assigned to Phase 8 are again dominated by fasteners and fittings like nails, but they also include three further fiddle-key nails as well as a probable unfinished knife. From the perspective of the small finds it therefore appears that the assemblage in the area of that building did not change to a significant degree during the three periods from which small finds were recorded from it.

It might thus be more interesting to compare the assemblage with that from another medieval manor house. Barentin's Manor at Chalgrove in Oxfordshire was a moated manor with evidence of occupation from the first half of the 13th century, which may not have been seigneurial at this stage. In the mid-13th century a moated manor house was constructed. Documentary evidence shows that it belonged to the Barentin family who held the manor until shortly before its demolition in the late 15th century (Page et al. 2005).

An overview of the assemblages from Chickerell and Barentin's Manor is shown in Table 3.8. Some of the categories occur at both sites in similar quantities and

Table 3.8 Comparison of finds categories from Chickerell and Barentin's Manor, Chalgrove, Oxfordshire. Both assemblages are listed without nails and studs.

	Chickerell medieval		Barentin's Manor	
Personal	40	12.5%	189	38.3%
Toiletry/Medicine		0.0%	1	0.2%
Textile working	2	0.6%	5	1.0%
Household	23	7.2%	23	4.7%
Leisure		0.0%	3	0.6%
Metrology	6	1.9%	6	1.2%
Commerce	15	4.7%	21	4.3%
Writing	1	0.3%	0	0.0%
Transport	79	24.8%	31	6.3%
Building	6	1.9%	10	2.0%
Tool	16	5.0%	33	6.7%
Fitting	85	26.6%	146	29.6%
Agriculture	12	3.8%	3	0.6%
Weapon	4	1.3%	7	1.4%
Metalworking	2	0.6%	0	0.0%
Uncertain	28	8.8%	16	3.2%
Grand Total	319	100.0%	494	100.0%

proportions, e.g. textile working, household utensils or objects associated with weighing and measuring, while some like toiletry utensils or leisure articles are not represented at Chickerell but likewise only occur at Barentin's Manor in very small numbers. An interesting discrepancy exists with objects of dress and personal adornments. This is due to the large number of pins from the Oxfordshire site, whereas no pins at all were recorded from Chickerell. It is tempting to associate this lacuna with a change in the occupation of the site before the use of wire drawn sewing pins increased during the course of the 14th century before becoming more widespread in the post-medieval period, although evidence from Winchester and Southampton shows that they were available from the 13th century (Biddle and Barclay 1990, 560–5). The quantities of such pins from a single site can extend into the thousands, such as at Acton Court, South Gloucestershire, where almost 5000 were recorded, with 3946 from beneath the former wooden floor of Room 30 in the west range, dating to the late 16th to mid-17th century (Courtney 2004, 396–7, tab. 53).

In contrast to the situation at Barentin's Manor, the find of the gold and rock crystal brooch Cat. No. 3 suggests that some of the individuals at Putton Lane during the earlier stages of the medieval occupation were of an elevated social echelon. A link to one of these individuals, from a slightly later date than the brooch, might be represented by the lead window grille fragment with armorial bearing, although it has not been possible to establish a connection with any of the families known to have been involved with the site.

The slight difference in the figures for items related to agricultural activities is due to the recording of ten lead weights from Chickerell, probably indicative of the exploitation of the marine resource, but since they were all metal-detected and the chronological depth of the assemblage remains unknown, it is impossible to decide whether they relate to the one-time use of a casting net, an activity which requires some skill (Dütting and Hoss 2014), or whether they were used as line sinkers, possibly over an extended period. The small number of weapon-related finds from both sites suggests that neither saw any military conflict, and it is possible that the arrowheads were simply part of the equipment of the occupants for use elsewhere, both for hunting as well as armed conflict.

The post-medieval assemblage is of significantly reduced size, and nothing in the finds from the early part of the period would suggest any particularly elevated status of the occupants at that time. The presence of the bell wire crank dating from the end of the period is, however, indicative of a certain level of sophistication displayed in a building at the site or its immediate vicinity. Given the local events during the civil war, the assemblage of 11 lead bullets could well be interpreted as evidence of military action during the battles of Weymouth in February 1645, but like so many of the suggestions in this chapter, the largely residual nature of the assemblage only provides glimpses of possible scenarios without providing final proof of their plausibility.

CATALOGUE OF ILLUSTRATED FINDS

The format lists small finds (SF) or x-radiography group (XR) number, material, weight, description.

Excavation event and context information; followed by site phase.

1. SF102 CuA, 1.3g. Needle with lanceolate eye set in groove and bulging in area of eye, round shaft, tip missing. AMR/13, 201; 8.

2. XR125, CuA, 3.6g. Ansatae brooch with tri-lobed leaf shaped terminal, head with spring attachment missing. Right-facing strip-like catchplate. AMR/13; U/S.

3. XR132, Gold/?rock crystal, 8.1g. Oval plate brooch with rock crystal setting. The oval base plate has a stepped setting consisting of 3 concentric zones. The outer rim is created by a block-twisted gold wire soldered onto the edge of the base plate, which in most areas has slightly been flanged upwards. The ends of the wire meet above the inner end/base of the catchplate; a tiny triangular sheet fragment is attached across the join area. The first zone is decorated with globular granules; two granules above the triangular sheet there are 2 joined granules, exactly above the catchplate loop. The first and second zones are separated by a flange of flat sheet with crenellated edge/flattened corbeled wire. The second zone is filled by a plain wire set in undulating loops. The third zone is separated off by a block-twisted wire. Its ends meet in the area above the hinge, but are set at different levels: with the hinge seen from the back, held on the left, the lower wire is higher than the upper one, which meets at the level of the base plate. The wire acts as the base for the inner collet, above the wire a second wire with continuous loops is soldered onto the collet so that the loop tops, which are bent inwards, extend above the collet edge. The central gem stone, a ?rock crystal, is set on a silver-coloured base which is in places discoloured by reddish-brown and grey ?corrosion. The top of the stone is damaged at its apex, with two tiny flakes missing and further cracks extending in the area around the apex. With the catchplate opening pointing upwards the hinge sits on the left side of the backplate. The H-shaped pin-lug is folded out of one strip of sheet metal; the perforations have distinct burs on the outer sides of the lugs' arms, suggesting they were either perforated from the inside, or the burrs on the inside were worn away by the missing pin. The catchplate consists of two double-grooved strips; one longer, folded double and forming the pin rest, the other shorter and supporting the side opposite the opening. The catchplate is set on a base of at least two amorphous strips of sheet metal soldered onto the edge of the base plate which is moulded to show an outer rim and the inner area commensurate with the shape of the gemstone at the front. AMR/13; U/S.

4. SF68, CuA, 19.3g. Annular brooch (or buckle??), plain circular, triangular-sectioned frame with recess and pin-rest for the missing pin. EXC/16, 2005, Area 2; 8.

5. SF106, CuA, 2.4g. Buckle. Oval frame with ornate outside edge decorated by 2 double-groove elements, a plain element each side set between two knops, bar recessed; pin and probable plate missing. EXC/16, 1004, Between Building 1 and 4; 8.

6. XR127, CuA, 4.4g. Buckle. Oval frame with ornate outside edge decorated by 2 quadruple-groove elements between two knops, bar recessed; pin and probable plate missing. AMR/13; U/S.

7. SF58, CuA, 10.5g. Buckle, rectangular frame, out- and inside edges hemispherical with four deep rabbets with one transverse and two lengthways grooves each, the latter each hold a thin wire (in a different alloy to the frame) running the width of the frame. Frame curved downwards, circular-sectioned bar lower than edges; pin missing. EXC/16, 2005, Area 2; 8.

8. SF45, Pewter, 5.8g. Buckle with rectangular frame and central bar, all with triangular cross section, with small notch as pin rest on outer edge; bar is broken and pin missing, but remains of iron corrosion at break and inside frame edge suggest pin was of iron. EXC/16, 2005, Area 2; 8.

9. SF102, CuA, 2.4g. Buckle, small double-oval frame with cross section of flat inside and convex-triangular outer edges; pin missing. EXC/16, 2005, Area 2; 8.

10. SF152.2, CuA/Gold, 5.4g. Buckle plate; rectangular (trapezoidal, slightly wider at base) plate with (?chip carved) decoration of floral spirals in field, surrounded by lateral void frame including two holes in corners of inner edge; recessed outer edge with two loops, only one remaining fragmented. Remains of surface gilding of obverse visible in area near loop bases. EXC/16; U/S

11. SF152.3, CuA/Gold, 3.6g. Folded buckle plate, rectangular plate with recessed loops and 3 holes in or below centre line, the hole nearest outside edge only in front plate, the other two with corresponding holes in back plate, show side, slightly and with convex curve, is wider than back part (8–9mm), the latter tapering to inside edge and broken across third hole. No decoration apart from lateral line along three side apart from inside edge, but surface gilding. EXC/16; U/S.

12. XR5, CuA, 9.1g. Folded sheet plate for (missing) buckle. Plate with rectangular slot for pin and 5 rivet holes set 2-1-2, narrow inside edge due to corrosion with breaks across rivet holes, other side's inside edge present with original width 22.8mm. No discernible decoration. EXC/16, 10-108, Area 3; 3 & 4.

13. SF152.1, CuA/Gold, 2.4g. Buckle plate; lozengiform field decorated with ?lion rampant facing left (heraldically right), his hind legs which would have been in the lower quarter, obliterated by a circular hole, drilled from the front with burrs remaining on the back, another similar hole above head with spherical-headed rivet still in situ and free moving; sub round lobes extend either side of the upper and lower point of the lozenge, smaller ones from the tips

of the centre points, fragmented double hinge lobes extend from the lower point. Most of obverse with surface gilding still intact. EXC/16; U/S.

14. XR3, CuA, 2.1g. Strap-end, tongue-shaped with top split for insertion of leather strap, fixed by rivet (still in situ (see x-radiograph), no discernible decoration on tongue, but too worn/corroded to be certain. EXC/16; U/S.

15. SF109, CuA, 12.9g. Strap-end. Composite strap-end with forked spacer with acorn knop decorated with two collars and ending in small point. The two covering plates are of different length (L 59.1mm and 64.4mm), the longer with a line 5mm from long edges decorated either with pattern of various double lines or ?inscription? Inside surface of both plates with mineral preserved organic remains (?leather) and remains of solder around all edges apart from upper edge. AMR/13, 302; 8.

16. SF143, Pewter, 7.8g. Strap end or chape, cast in one piece, with ogee-shaped end, obverse with inscription in Gothic letters: [M]aria. EXC/16, 10-108, Area 3; 3 & 4.

17. SF100, CuA, 6.8g. Strap-end with forked spacer (W11.8–13.9mm) and circular terminal (diam. 20mm) with quatrefoil opening. The integral cover of the attachment plate has a wavy edge with 3 chevrons (visible in x-radiograph) and rivet above point of uppermost chevron, further rivet in base of spacer above terminal base; back of plate open. EXC/16, F35, Area 1; 7.

18. SF80, CuA/Gold, 0.7g. Ringlet/loop, possibly part of bar mount with pendent loop; slightly oval loop sub-oval cross-section (giving the impression of two D-shaped rings being put on top of each other slightly askew, possibly due to a misaligned two-part mould). EXC/16, 1004, Between Building 1 and 4; 8.

19. SF107, CuA, 2.4g. Button with cast round biconvex top with overworked equator, thin plano-convex CuA wire loop (L 3.3mm) soldered into hole in base. EXC/16, 1004, Between Building 1 and 4; 8.

20. SF93, CuA/Iron, 2.4g. Open rumbler bell with thin strip loop (W 1.8mm) holding iron pea on inside, top hemisphere slightly bent, lower hemisphere broken and less than a third preserved; solder visible along join. EXC/16, F27, Area 2; 8.

21. SF112, Lead, 48.3g. Spindle whorl, conical whorl with sub-circular conical hole (diam. bottom 8.5–9mm; top 10mm). AMR/13, 304; 8.

22. SF146, CuA, 15g. Spoon bowl, deep, fig-shaped, stem broken off probably slightly before junction between bowl and stem. EXC/16; U/S.

23. SF51, CuA, 1.4g. Bent piece of sheet metal with folded rivet (7.1×5.8mm, top now unattached), unevenly broken edges. EXC/16, 2005, Area 2; 8.

24. SF41, Lead, 65.3g. Repair plug, large face with sub-circular outline and two notches on opposing sides, smooth surface with some undulations, a dimple and a hole. Smaller side (diam. 27.6–29.1mm) with uneven surface (from pouring onto soil). No fragment of ?ceramic vessel surviving in groove between the two discs. EXC/16, 2005, Area 2; 8.

25. SF108, CuA, 5.2g. Chest mount with circular end with central round hole and flat parallel-sided strap, bent at c120° to terminal and slightly twisted. Surface of end and strap near end with flecks of surface gilding. X-radiograph shows lines at end creating radial pattern around hole. AMR/13, 304; 8.

26. SF17, Lead/CuA, 890g. Steelyard weight, piriform (pear-shaped) weight with integrally cast loop of which only rectangular-sectioned stumps remain at narrow top, two concentric grooves below top, large irregular-shaped scar near base (reason for weight being slightly underweight for 2 pound). Copper alloy mantle with faint, reworked seam (from two part mould), filled with lead, visible in scar. No obvious assay mark (thus probably unofficial copy of weights issued during Edward I (AD 1272–1307) reign). EXC/16, F24, Area 3; 8.

27. SF109, Lead, 58.1g. ?Weight. Ovoid piece with flattish base with concave cavity of irregular outline. EXC/16, 1004, Between building 1 and 4; 8.

28. SF145, Lead, 104.8g. ?Weight. Discoid piece with flat base and slightly convex face. The base has several crescentic marks near one side and possibly very faint markings of 2 letters (?H or ?R and ?E) and an equal-armed cross or ?X (but uncertain!). EXC/16; U/S.

29. SF153, CuA, 11.7g. Coin weight, ?top face with double-lined border, central dimple (centre mark from turning to weight) and concentric line (diam. 9.3mm), 4 holes drilled through disc (probably from back, as hole' edges are less well defined), 2 arranged in a radial line with fleur de lis on left and possible ?crown on the right an slightly higher than lis, 2 holes in tangential line on opposing side. ?Reverse also with central dimple and raised rim (H 2.1mm), otherwise plain surface with some scuff marks. AMR/13; U/S.

30. SF25, CuA, 5.8g. Seal matrix, hexagonally facetted trumpet-shaped handle with rounded-diamond loop. Circular seal showing in centre, surrounded by beaded circle, mirrored image of hare walking right with bird of prey (eagle) above, lowering head to right with beak at eye level of hare; legend (Lombardic letters): ALLAS IE SV PRIS followed by six-armed star. EXC/16, F24, Area 3; 8.

31. SF123, CuA, 5g. Horse harness cheek piece, loop for cheek piece strap, possibly decorated with (now very worn) wide dimples at 9, 12 and 3 o'clock (with stem at bottom) of outer frame; oval-sectioned stem. See Cat. No. 32. EXC/16, 10-115, Area 3; 8.

32. XR11, CuA, 6.7g. Horse harness cheek piece, fragment of loop for cheek piece strap, possibly decorated with (now very worn) radial grooves on upper inner face of loop frame. See Cat. No. 31. EXC/16, 2002, Area 2; 8.

33. SF124, Iron, 108.4g. Buckle with T-shaped frame, the narrower end has a separate revolving bar, held by looped ends on the narrower side, pin (which would have been attached to the wider bar) missing. EXC/16, 10-10ε, Area 3; 3 & 4.

34. XR96, Iron, 18.7g. Buckle with rectangular frame and sheet roller on outside edge, sturdy, plano-convex pin. EXC/16, 1006, F35, Area 1; 3 & 4.

35. XR100, Iron, 43.7g. Horseshoe with wavy outside edge, left branch broken across toe; 3 countersunk rectangular holes in web and continuing into heel (third hole nearly at end of heel), the lower hole filled by remains of nail head; no obvious calkin, but end might have been upset (denser end in x-radiograph). AMR/13, Building 200, Area 3; 8.

36. XR107, Iron, 85.4g. Horseshoe with wavy outside edge, right branch broken across toe at inside edge of top left hole; 3 countersunk rectangular holes in web and continuing into heel, the lower two holes with double-clenched heads with large fiddle-key type nails; square calkin (probably double-folded. AMR/13, 501, Building 1; 8.

37. XR85, Iron, 46.3g. Horseshoe with slightly wavy outside edge, right branch broken across right side of toe; 3 countersunk rectangular/sub-oval holes in web and beginning of long heel, the middle hole filled by remains of fiddle-key nail, beginning of clenched tip remains; feathered heel. AMR/13, 301; 8.

38. XR85, Iron, 86.7g. Horseshoe, right branch with wide web and 3 sub-rectangular, countersunk nail-holes, the lowest ending in line with the folded calkin. AMR/13, 301; 8.

39. SF72, Iron, 260g. Horseshoe, wide web and three square holes in each branch, left heel with ?upset or thickened heel calkin, right heel with ?right angle calkin Kink on inside edge of toe area (?i.e. V-shaped shoe for rear hoof). EXC/16, 1004, Between building 1 and 4; 8.

40. XR103, Iron, 58.1g. Horseshoe, left branch with wide web and two countersunk rectangular holes, feathered heel, broken across very worn mid toe; there is a possible third hole on the left of the toe, now outside edge due to wear. Both preserved holes with nails, the upper with swollen rectangular head. AMR/13, 601, Building 3; 7.

41. XR100, Iron, 2.7g. Fiddle-key nail, with wide flat upright semi-circular head, end bent at right angles but tip missing. AMR/13, Building 200, Area 3; 8.

42. XR46, Iron, 6.2g. Horseshoe nail with expanded trapezoidal head and "ears". Rectangular-sectioned tapering shaft. Complete and unused!, AMR/13, Building 500, Building 1; 8.

43. XR37, Iron, 5.4g. Horseshoe nail with expanded trapezoidal head and "ears". Rectangular-sectioned tapering shaft. Complete and unused!, EXC/16, 13–131, Building 5; 2.

44. SF117, Iron, 70.4g. Oxshoe, for right part of hoof, clip curved to right at toe, 3 rectangular nail holes near out edge of quarter, nails with square, swollen heads in upper two holes present; widening to heel. EXC/16, Area 3; 8.

45. SF147, Lead, 3.5g. Window- or air vent grille fragment; lozenge-shaped plaque, top broken obliquely, with integral oval-sectioned bar (continues in curved line as raised bar on back of plaque). Armorial bearing on obv., set in reeded groove: a saltire of two transverse hatched bends, the sinister above the dexter, between 4 fleur de lis. EXC/16; U/S.

46. SF100, Iron, 53.6g. Window bar. Sub-oval, flattish end with rectangular hole attached to a thick-set bar (W 14.9mm, Th. 11.5mm), tapering to blunt, rounded end. AMR/13, 201; 8.

47. XR108, Iron, 31.2g. Knife; triangular whittle tang set slightly nearer back of triangular blade with angled shoulder and choil, broad back and cutting edge tapering to tip set in centre line. AMR/13, 507, Building 1; 5.

48. XR108, Iron, 31.5g. Knife; triangular whittle tang set in middle of triangular blade with curved shoulder and rectangular choil, broad back and cutting edge tapering to tip set in centre line, cutting edge curving up to tip. AMR/13, 507, Building 1; 5.

49. XR85, Iron, 24.7g. Knife; wide triangular whittle tang set in middle of triangular blade with curved shoulder and choil, broad back and cutting edge tapering to tip set in centre line. AMR/13, 301; 8.

50. SF119, Iron, 21.2g. Knife with whittle tang set in middle of blade, sloping shoulder and choil wide, straight back, possibly sloping but tip missing. AMR/13, 502, Building 1; 8.

51. SF111, Iron, 20.1g. Leatherworking creaser. Sub-triangular blade with part of tang continuing line of back, set at angle of *c.* 30° to cutting edge. AMR/13, 302; 8.

52. SF107, Iron. Shears with omega-shaped bow and narrow blades with slanted, plain tops at junction between handle and thin narrow blades which are tapering to tips. AMR/13, 301; 8.

53. XR100, Iron, 41.8g. Chisel with sturdy sub-circular-sectioned shaft, tapering on two sides to 11.4mm-wide cutting edge. Head ?broken at a slightly oblique angle, some burring on one side only. AMR/13, Building 200, Area 3; 8.

54. XR80, Iron, 41.1g. Key with lozenge-shaped bow, channelled bit, one ward in rear edge. EXC/16, F53, Building 5; 8.

55. XR108, Iron, 62.1g. Padlock bolt. T-shaped padlock bolt with two spines, the upper horizontal spine with one spring ?brazed/soldered? onto the upper tip, the lower, vertical spine with two lateral springs. Circular closing plate (diam. 28.1–28.6mm; Th. 7.2mm). AMR/13, 507, Building 1; 5.

56. XR81, Iron, 33.4g. Hinge pivot, sub-circular-sectioned guide arm, high-rectangular-sectioned shank, mostly broken off. EXC/16, Wall 32/35, Building 4; 8.

57. SF105, Iron, 322g. Bar with ring end, thick stem of diamond-shaped cross-section, end ring with sub-hexagonal cross section (int. diam. 12.8mm). EXC/16, 3002, Area 1; 8.

58. XR82, Iron, 37.3g. Looped fitting with circular-sectioned hoop and conical base. EXC/16, 2002, Area 2; 8.

59. SF86, CuA, 6.1g. Clip? Sheet, with sub-cylindrical fold and flared ends with irregularly broken sides. The cylindrical part has lateral line along either opening. EXC/16, 3001, Area 1; 8.

60. SF78, CuA, 3.5g. ?Fitting, pointed-oval shape with, near rounded end, two arched extensions with two rounded recesses. Flat-rectangular cross-section with bilaterally bevelled edges (cast in two-piece mould and worked over/filed from two sides), sharp point slightly bent. EXC/16; U/S.

61. SF94, CuA/Gold, 0.5g. Tack or mount with flat circular head plated with gold sheet; short tapering, square-sectioned stem (L 9.9mm), tip slightly bent. EXC/16; U/S.

62. XR25, Iron, 1.5g. Nail with facetted rectangular head and square-sectioned shaft. EXC/16, Wall 22, Building 6; 8.

63. XR22, Iron, 3.7g. Nail with flat head of figure-of-eight shape, square-sectioned shaft. EXC/16, 16–105, Building 1; 5.

64. XR34, Iron, 2.7g. Nail, flat L-shaped head, square-sectioned tapering shaft. EXC/16, Wall 20, Building 1; 8.

65. XR44, Iron, 13.7g. Nail with thick triangular head and flat-rectangular-sectioned shaft, slightly curved, tip missing. EXC/16, Wall 20, Building 1; 8.

66. SF119, CuA, 3.5g. Stud with flat discoid head (diam. >21.6mm) square-sectioned shaft tapering to missing tip. Head decorated with pattern of crossing lines creating pattern of large rectangles (see x-radiograph). AMR/13, 907, Building 6; 8.

67. SF29, Iron, 61g. Small shoe for a ?weeding spade. U-shaped blade with rounded corners and sub-rectangular-sectioned side arms. , EXC/16 Area 2; 8.

68. SF117, Iron, 19.3g. Socketed arrowhead with square/sub-circular socket and square blade tapering to (now) blunt tip. AMR/13, 901, Building 6; 8.

69. SF116, Iron, 10.2g. Arrowhead with triangular, flat oval-sectioned blade and barbs curving down from the shoulders, tubular socket (L 25mm). AMR/13, 902, Building 6; 8.

70. SF120, Iron, 10.7g. Arrowhead (warhead) with triangular, flat oval-sectioned blade with slightly convex cutting edges and short close-fitting barbs curving down from the shoulders, tubular socket (L 25.9mm). AMR/13, 507, Building 1; 5.

71. SF101, Iron, 1.5g. Chain mail ring. Open ring with slightly expanding ends, but terminals with holes for rivet missing. AMR/13, 201; 8.

72. SF154, Lead, 8.1g. Cone with large irregular hole in base (diam. 9.1–11mm) and pointed-oval opening in the mantle (4.7×6.9mm). EXC/16, 2002, Area 2; 8.

73. XR124, CuA, 8.7g. Double oval buckle-frame with lobes at junctions of bar and frame, and at four symmetrical points on frame. AMR/13; U/S.

74. SF4, CuA, 6.6g. Shoe (or knee, or hat?) buckle. Profiled oval buckle with floral decoration and remains of white metal coating, arched frame, separate iron bar with separate triangular tongue and hook of which only one outer side and the beginning of the opposite side survive. Makers mark ?TP or ?IP. EXC/16, 2001, Area 2; 8.

75. XR40, Iron, 8.3g. Heel iron, left branch with three evenly spaced sub-square holes. Broken at heel end (toe of a horseshoe). AMR/13, 605, Building 3; 7.

76. CuA/Iron, 26.1g. Wire crank for doorbell or servants bell. Anchor-shaped triangular frame of trapezoidal cross section, extensions at the ends with hourglass-shaped holes (for the attachment of wire), top hole still has iron attachment spike in place. AMR/13; U/S.

77. SF152.4, CuA, 0.4g. Fitting made of sheet metal, shield-shaped with sheet crimped over a wire running around the edge; obv. ?Heraldic decoration of five horizontal bars (or paly of ten), bend sinister with motto [?S]ORN[?O], top part of shield above bend missing. EXC/16; U/S.

THE GLASS, By Cheryl Green

A large quantity of 19th and early 20th century glass was recovered during site clearance, mostly comprising broken wine bottles and various other common vessel types. Amongst this topsoil material, six shards of earlier glass were retained which appear medieval or early post-medieval in date. This includes three thin-bodied shards from drinking vessels, one a mossy green colour and the other two of clear glass. The remaining three shards are window glass, very pale green in colour and possibly with some etched lines. A further shard of window glass, also unstratified, was dark green with numerous large air bubbles, also indicating a late medieval or early post-medieval date.

Three further medieval or early post-medieval glass shards were retrieved from excavated contexts. One was associated with W16 from B2, a very

Fig. 3.13   Objects of stone.

small fragment of mossy green window glass. The presence of a couple of air bubbles in the window glass indicates a medieval to early post-medieval date. Given the small size of the shard it is likely to be intrusive as opposed to having been a residual object incorporated during construction. A single rim shard of very pale bluey green vessel glass was found in W22 of B6, the presence of two slightly diagonal depressions, regularly spaced and running towards the rim, suggesting some decoration. The glass contains abundant bubbles and therefore has a slightly rough surface texture. A medieval to early post-medieval date is suggested.

THE STONE OBJECTS, By Cheryl Green

Fragments of a quern, two mortars, an additional mortar or storage vessel, a whetstone, and four other items were recovered during the excavations. These all represent either household or leisure activities.

A small sub-cuboid piece of Mayen Basalt Lava appears to have been re-worked but the use of lava identifies it as a quern fragment, with the two opposing sides polished or worn. Basalt lava from the area of Mayen in the Eifel region of Germany has a long tradition of exploitation for quern manufacture, the properties being almost unrivalled throughout North-Western Europe. Blanks for the manufacturing of querns were imported into Britain from the early medieval period until well into the post-medieval period (Parkhouse 1997), although this trade had origins in the Romano-

British period (e.g. Crummy 1983, 75–6) and possibly the Iron Age (Fitzpatrick 2017). Increasing evidence for commercial trade in so-called low value or bulk goods during the 8th and 9th centuries, indicates that a largescale trade of unfinished Mayen lava quern stone was widespread in coastal settlements, where these 'blanks' would be finished off (Verhulst 2002, 103; Parkhouse 1997; Pohl 2010; refs after Weetch 2014, 241). The fragment at Lower Putton Lane was recovered from the uppermost fill (9–129) of Phase 2 ditch F98 which ran beneath B4. It is suggested that this building may have served as the manorial kitchen where the processing of grain might be expected. It is possible that the quern was associated with this activity, however given the small size it is more likely to be either intrusive or residual, the latter supported by the Romano-British pottery also recovered from this area.

Pieces of two stone mortars were recovered from the area of B1. A Portland Whit Bed stone rim (35mm thick) from rubble layer (501) had a square profile to the rim, the external surface pecked, and the internal wall worn smooth (Fig. 3.13.1). A Purbeck marble body fragment (28mm thick) from clearance layer (301) retained a band of wide vertical chisel marks on the external surface below a further band of finer vertical chiselling, possibly a decorative feature, and the internal wall is also worn smooth. This material is more commonly known for its widespread architectural and decorative use however it was also exploited for hand-held objects from the Romano-British period onwards (Drury 1949; Palmer 2014).

Mortars in the medieval period were a by-product of the industry, but they represented a higher quality utensil, demonstrated by their occurrence at generally higher status sites (Hinton 2002, 99). A further large fragment of Portland Base Bed was recovered from within W12 of B8 (18mm thick to 30mm for the rim). This appears to be part of a mortar or large stone storage vessel, although both sides are quite smooth and perhaps more akin to architectural decoration. However, the smooth edges may be associated with post-depositional processes and on balance it seems more likely to have formed part of a mortar or storage vessel.

Two objects appear to have been associated with sharpening or honing. A hand-held rectangular whetstone was recovered to the east of B9; both ends were broken but the width is 33mm wide and the depth 20mm. All the sides are worn smooth and the edges rounded-off from use. The fabric is a micaceous reddish grey very fine-grained siltstone and not a local material, however these sharpeners could form part of an individual's 'tool kit' and therefore travelled with the owner. A small fragment of Kimmeridge shale from Purbeck may represent a honing tool, measuring 15mm wide and tapering from 5mm to 7mm thick. Although fashioned from a more local material, this may also have been a personal item, indeed it appeared to have been deliberately pecked with a number of small dots on both surfaces although a pattern could not be discerned. This was recovered from deposits associated with W18 of B5 dated to the 13th century and may relate to activity pre-dating the construction of this building.

A chalk bi-conical spindle whorl (SF12-5) was also retrieved from deposits associated with W18 of B5. It measured 34mm in diameter and 22mm deep, with the central perforation measuring 10mm at the top and widening to 12mm at the base (Fig. 3.13.2). Similar objects span the late Iron Age to medieval periods and are associated with spinning wool. The nature of its deposition prevents any meaningful comment regards where this spinning activity was taking place, however it is possible that it took place at the north end of B5, either inside the house or outside.

A circular piece of worked chert was recovered from context (12-137), situated on the north side of W18 of B5 (Fig. 3.13.3). It measured 35mm diameter and a maximum depth of 6mm, with a domed upper surface (the pebble exterior) and a flat lower surface and appears to have been fashioned from the side of a beach pebble. The small size means it was unsuitable as a hand-held tool, and the absence of any sharp edges or abrasions would support this. Given the perfectly spherical shape and symmetry of the domed surface, it is possible that this was a games counter.

The tiny number of objects recovered during the excavations accord with the exploitation of local resources; Portland limestone, Kimmeridge shale, chalk and a beach pebble. However, the whetstone is derived from a non-local source while the small fragment of Mayen Basalt Lava quern provides evidence of longer distance trade, and no doubt a much-valued item within the household. The objects mostly reflect a small proportion of activities that would have taken place on a daily basis; grinding and pounding of food stuffs, sharpening of tools, and spinning of wool, with the chert disc perhaps providing a tantalising glimpse of a fun activity, perhaps as part of a game.

THE PERINATAL HUMAN REMAINS, BY CLARE RANDALL

A single set of perinatal remains was recovered from the floor of B1. They were contained within the lower half of a 13th century pottery cooking vessel which was embedded in the underlying deposits. Within the fill of the pot was an oyster shell, which may have been incidental or a deliberate inclusion (Fig. 3.14).

Methods

The material was examined to determine where possible age and skeletal pathology, in line with BABAO/CIfA guidance (Brickley and McKinley 2004). Bone condition was assessed utilising scores following Behrensmeyer (McKinley 2004). Estimation of age was carried out by considering dental development and eruption and skeletal development and fusion (Scheuer and Black 2000). Measurements were taken where appropriate and utilised in assessing age (Fazekas and Kósa 1978), in order to compare to the

Fig. 3.14   Infant within pottery vessel, inside B1, looking south (0.2m scale).

general perinatal (36 weeks in utero-4 weeks post-partum) age range suggested by morphological and developmental criteria. It should be noted that due to its relation with stature, use of diaphyseal lengths for determination of age at death in infants is the least reliable method, especially as individuals may only vary by a few weeks gestation/post-partum, and ages expressed in weeks should be seen in the light of this. Pathological conditions were considered by reference to a variety of sources (e.g. Brickley 2000; Lewis 2000; Ortner 2000; Rogers 2000).

The individual

The material from context (14-101) was relatively well preserved, and almost complete with about 90% of the skeleton of a single individual present and preservation scores of 2 or less frequently 3. The state of preservation and particularly its completeness

probably relates to having been recovered from within a vessel and wet sieved. Considering fusion states, tooth formation and eruption and metrical analyses, the individual was clearly perinatal, that is aged around the time of birth, although that may have been slightly pre-term or a couple of weeks post-partum. It is not possible in this case to determine whether the individual survived for any time after birth. There were no obvious pathological changes or developmental defects. It is not possible to state whether the individual was male or female.

Discussion

The inclusion of the burial of a late term foetus or newborn within a building at Putton is clearly a departure from the norm for medieval England. Burial for the majority was within cemeteries associated with churches. Perinatal individuals are often seen within settlements and buildings in Dorset and beyond during the Romano-British period (e.g. Randall 2018; Randall in prep) but are considerably less frequent in a medieval context. To date there is none which appear to have been identified in Dorset. This may purely be related to the number of buildings of medieval date which have been excavated within the county. It is not possible to discuss the rate of infant mortality without a better understanding of the population as a whole and we do not have the burial area for the rest of the community. High infant mortality is to be expected, but this declined during the 12th–13th centuries (Roberts and Cox 2003, 225). There is no evidence of any congenital abnormality or disease in this individual, but childbirth was a high-risk exercise for both mother and child as obstetric assistance was limited (Roberts and Cox 2003, 253).

Burials of this type, of foetal, perinatal or infant remains are not common in medieval England, although they are not unknown, for example a neonate buried in the corner of a later 12th century manorial building at West Cotton, Northamptonshire (Chapman 2010, 102; fig. 5.18). Infant burials within or close to domestic structures have been identified in urban and more frequently rural settings (Gilchrist 2012, 284–5). The rural examples are exclusively associated with crofts and tenements or occasionally buildings identified as barns. Several examples were interred with objects which appear to be deliberate inclusions. Whilst of limited number, these burials are interesting as they demonstrate a motivation to carry out an action which was contrary to religious and social practice, although there may have been issues with the burial of unbaptised individuals in consecrated places (cf Craig-Atkins 2014, 106). They also have ritualistic elements, positioned in some cases in ways which suggest a foundation deposit (Crawford 2014, 34). An infant of 3–6 months of age, dating to the mid-late 13th century, was buried within a longhouse at Upton, Gloucestershire. Included in the burial was a limestone spindle whorl and a whelk shell (Rahtz 1969b). The spindle whorl may have been a toy, or it may signify a domestic link. The whelk shell is perhaps paralleled in the Putton example by the oyster shell positioned immediately over the centre of the body.

The choice of container, a West Dorset sandy ware jar (Mepham, Chapter 2) and the location, situated beside the door jamb of the chamber block, invites consideration of the context of the burial. Firstly, no other burials within a vessel have been identified for southern England. There may have been an element of serendipity or convenience about the nature of the container. However, it should be noted that the use of a cooking vessel may have carried a particular domestic connotation. Whilst a wide range of tasks which occurred within the manorial context could be carried out by men or women, it is clear from documentary sources that many activities, such as cooking, were gendered (Crawford 2014). Also, akin to examples in Romano-British contexts, there may be a link between interment of infants in a domestic space and the fertility of the household or land (Gilchrist 2012, 222). The use of the vessel might support the interpretation of the building itself as having an intimate domestic nature. The desire to retain the child within the confines of this building may then sit within a feminine framework. Whilst infanticide was not unknown in the medieval period, and a motivation in concealing a birth (which would attract 'childwite' a fee payment by serfs for children born out of wedlock [Bailey 2002, 33]), or avoidance of the cost of a funeral (Gilchrist 2012, 221), the treatment of the remains might suggest a desire to keep close a longed for child, perhaps stillborn, within the domestic sphere.

The shell included within the burial may be incidental. Oyster shell did occur in overlying deposits. However, this example was clearly within the vessel, and centrally situated over the body in contact with it. Scallops were occasionally incorporated in graves as amulets, reminiscent or souvenirs of pilgrimage to Santiago de Compostela (Gilchrist 2008, 130). Dorset had a strong connection with this particular pilgrim route, with the port of Poole heavily involved in transport of pilgrims from the 14th–15th centuries (Ecchevarría Aruaga 2007). It is possible that an association with a marine shell was misunderstood and translated to a protective symbol in the infant burial. Shells had a general apotropaic use in protecting children and women in childbirth (Hildburgh 1942).

Gilchrist (2008, 122–3) notes the earlier medieval connection between women, charms, magic and the dead. The utilisation of often domestic objects within graves, particularly of children, not only marked them out in need of special protection or treatment but underlines the domestic context of practices (Gilchrist 2008, 152). The situation may have acted in some mnemonic fashion. However, there may also be an apotropaic element to this burial. The location close to the southern wall of B1, beside the jamb of the main door may have been regarded as a prominent location, even if the space operated as an undercroft (see Green, Chapter 1). This placing may also have been intended as a protective charm for the house.

A range of magical or apotropaic practices are known in funerary contexts. Young children were regarded as special, as they were by their nature less guilty of sin (Gilchrist 2008, 148), and therefore potentially a pure conduit of prayer and protection. An unbaptised infant might be regarded as a potential revenant (Craig-Atkins 2014, 103), but how often this occurred is debateable, given that in extremis anyone could baptise an infant as long as the correct formula was followed (Gilchrist 2012, 138–9). On the other hand, stillborn infants or unborn foetuses appear to have been regarded as things rather than people, which may render their remains more acceptable as a component within a charm or magical practice. Accounts of medieval women tried for utilising infant corpses in witchcraft indicate that the body of a newborn could constitute 'occult material' (Gilchrist 2012, 219, 222).

It has been suggested that practices for protecting houses from evil entities in the early modern period, involving incorporation of various objects and materials within the building structure, may be a development of medieval belief (Merrifield 1987, 129). These practices were certainly widespread in Dorset from at least the 18th and 19th centuries and

included concealment in roofs, walls and chimneys of shoes, mummified cats, bottles and livestock hearts (Harte 2020). Concern to protect the household from the revenant dead was widespread during the medieval period, and thresholds were regarded as a particular point of danger (Gordon 2015). At Upton, Gloucestershire a clear foundation or warding deposit involving the burial of a dog and a knife buried upright in the ground occurred in the threshold (Hilton and Rahtz 1966). Another house at Upton contained the 13th century infant burial with a whelk (Rahtz 1969b) mentioned above, and it is therefore possible that the Putton infant burial served a similar function. The ambiguity of other occurrences of infant remains in houses is recognised by Gordon (2015, 80) but it is rightly suggested that they need to be seen within this milieu.

In the case of Putton, the likelihood of this interment being a deliberate ritual action is increased by the containment of the body within a pot buried in the floor. Containers buried into the floors of houses, particularly beside notable features such as hearths has been recognised in a number of places. A large cooking pot dating to the 13th to 14th centuries was located beside the hearth in the house at Dinna Clerks, Dartmoor (Beresford 1979). At Shapwick, Somerset a medieval cistern was found in a similar location (Gilchrist 2012, 232). Pots also feature as what appeared to be structured or 'special' deposits in houses (Hinton 1968), and there are references in medieval recipes to using buried pots for preparation of medicines (Moorhouse 1978). The combined ritual and practical purpose of buried pots, and their likely use by midwives and female healers has been noted (Gilchrist 2012, 233). In the Putton example, a range of elements, the location, the vessel, the child and the shell come together in a powerful unity of protective intentions.

4

THE ECONOMY AND ENVIRONMENT

INTRODUCTION, By Clare Randall

The economic basis for the Putton manor was clearly rooted in its agricultural regime and the natural resources which its surroundings afforded. This was primarily arable and livestock husbandry, but the evidence of fish bones and marine molluscs indicate a degree of coastal exploitation. The assemblages have their limitations. With very few cut features or well-sealed deposits a clear chronological spread of soil samples was not available for recovery of plant remains. In the event there was so little identifiable charcoal that it was not used in analysis. Hand recovered molluscs and faunal material occurred largely within the overlying deposits and most were highly fragmentary. However, with these caveats there is still a considerable amount which can be reconstructed with respect to the plant and animal economy during the main phases of occupation of the manorial centre.

NB Some features and deposits which produced remains straddled Phase 3 and Phase 4 but could only be assigned broadly to the periods of creation and use of the main manorial buildings. These were assigned their own 'phase' for the purposes of discussing the material and are referred to throughout this chapter as 'Phase 3&4'.

THE PLANT REMAINS, By Wendy Carruthers

Introduction

Fourteen soil samples were taken from ditches, pits, a deposit under B2 and test pits through a midden. The aims of the environmental sampling were to recover information about the environment and economy of the medieval settlement of Putton. The samples were processed by Context One Heritage and Archaeology staff using standard methods of floatation with a 500 micron mesh being used to catch the flots and a 1mm mesh used to hold the residues.

Methods

The fourteen flots, two sub-samples of residues (sample TP1 lower and TP2 middle) and charred plant remains sorted from the residues by C1 staff were sent to the author. The flots were dry-sieved through a stack of sieves (3mm, 1mm and 350 microns) to facilitate sorting. An Olympus SZX7 stereomicroscope (×8 to ×56) was used for sorting and identification.

Uncharred seeds were common in most of the samples, in particular elderberry (*Sambucus nigra*) and bramble (*Rubus* sp.). These tough-coated seeds are often found in archaeobotanical samples. While they are often modern contaminants, they are known to be able to survive for centuries under the right conditions. Although it is possible that these are medieval in date, the analysis of these remains would require a radiocarbon date to determine this, and the information recovered would not be particularly useful because of the differential survival of thick-coated remains.

Results and notes on cereal quantification

Table 4.1 presents the results of the analysis, using the traditional nomenclature system from Zohary et al. (2013) for cereals and Stace (2010) for nomenclature and habitat information for other taxa. Ellenberg (1988) and Hill et al. (1999) were also consulted for ecological information. Pulses were only identified to species level where hila were present, except for field/Celtic beans that were complete enough to be morphologically unmistakable.

Most of the flots contained frequent to abundant charred plant remains but the preservation of cereal grains was poor in many cases due to vacuolation and fragmentation. When cereal grains are charred in hearths and ovens under oxidising conditions they often become puffed-up and fragile. Constant re-heating and physical damage due to the cleaning out of these structures can lead to large numbers of broken, vacuolated grains being present. All of the deposits analysed for this report appear to have contained this type of waste material, in particular the Phase 2 pit fills. The two poorest-preserved assemblages came from the primary fills of pits F110 and F108. In these cases the numbers of broken unidentified grains outnumbered those of identified grains. Because very little information can be extracted from unidentified, hard to quantify grain fragments the remains were not fully extracted or quantified. In Table 4.1, wherever possible, unidentified grains are quantified as minimum numbers of grains, with fragments being roughly grouped together as whole grains.

Some notes on identification

Free-threshing wheat *(Triticum aestivum/turgidum-type)*
The grains of hexaploid (bread wheat) and tetraploid (includes rivet wheat) free-threshing wheats cannot be differentiated to species level as their morphologies are too variable. Well-preserved rachis fragments can be separated into bread wheat *(T. aestivum)* and rivet/durum wheat *(T. turgidum/durum)* on the basis of characters described in Jacomet (Jacomet 2006). Between rivet and durum, rivet is more likely to have been grown in the British Isles, being better suited to the climate. The use of rivet wheat (or 'cone' or 'pollard') in the past has also been confirmed by writers such as Thomas Tusser (1573), who recommends growing it on heavy soils. Moffett published a review of the evidence for free-threshing tetraploid wheat in the British Isles in 1991, showing that (at that time) it was being grown from the medieval period onwards from Taunton in the south west to Chester and Ipswich in the north and east. Many more sites have been added to the list since then, the earliest being late Saxon in date (Carruthers and Hunter Dowse 2019, 214) though none is located in the north of the British Isles. In the medieval period many sites appear to have grown both types of wheat, perhaps as a maslin (mixed crop) to 'hedge one's bets' against damage from due to adverse weather or pests and diseases, or maybe as separate crops. Growth characteristics and cooking qualities vary between the two wheats; bread wheat produces a well-raised loaf due to higher levels of gluten while rivet wheat is better suited to making biscuits. Rivet matures later in the field, grows on a longer straw and is awned, making it better protected from bird predation. However, it is less hardy than bread wheat so may fail in very cold winters. The recording of rivet-type wheat at Putton adds a useful south-western record to the distribution map.

Hulled wheats, emmer *(T. dicoccum)* and spelt *(T. spelta)*
A total of 55 wheat grains morphologically resembling emmer/spelt were recovered from the samples, spread across eight samples (all phases). Sample 13-5, from a Phase 2 pit F108, contained 42 caryopses but most samples only produced one or two grains. A few deposits of hulled wheat have been radiocarbon dated to the Saxon period (Pelling and Robinson 2000), but in general hulled wheats were not grown in the British Isles after the end of the Roman period. If frequent chaff fragments had also been recovered it would have been considered

Table 4.1   Charred plant remains.

sample	9-2	9-3	13-1	13-3	13-4	13-5	12-1	13-2	TP1	TP1	TP1	TP2	TP2	TP2
context	9-131	9-133	13-105	13-110	13-137	13-131	12-144	13-112	lower	middle	top	lower	middle	top
feature type & number	D F98	D F99	P F76	P F78	P F110	P F108	deposit under B2	bedding trench	midden	midden	midden	midden	midden	midden
Phase	2	2	2	2	2	2	3	3	3 & 4	3 & 4	3 & 4	3 & 4	3 & 4	3 & 4
CEREAL GRAINS														
Triticum aestivum/turgidum -type (free-threshing wheat-type grain)	40	55	336	269	195	183	216	80	135	69	11	27	56	45
Triticum dicoccum/spelta (emmer/spelt grain)	1	1		3		42	1			2			3	2
Triticum sp. (poorly preserved indeterminate wheat grain)														3
Hordeum vulgare sens. lat. (hulled barley grain)	1	1	2	1	5				1	2				
Hordeum vulgare sens. lat. (twisted hulled barley grain)					1									
Hordeum sp. (poorly preserved barley grain)	9	1	11	25	12	89	2	3	4	5	2	2	13	
Avena cf. sativa -type (>6mm cf. cultivated oat grain)			2	9	1	5	9	1	2	3	3	2		2
Avena sp. (wild/cultivated oat grain)	6		23	4	9		21	4		3	3		1	3
Secale cereale L. (rye grain)	cf.5		cf.5	cf.3		3				cf.1f			cf.2	
Indeterminate cereal (fragments=whole grain)	114	71	700	299	226+	158+	277	48	315	106	1		91	111
CEREAL CHAFF														
Triticum aestivum L. (bread wheat rachis fragment)	1		1				1							1
Triticum turgidum - type (rivet-type rachis fragment)	1	1			1									
Triticum aestivum/turgidum -type (free-threshing wheat rachis fragment)	17	22	6	30	10	3	29	3	11	5		1	5	8
Triticum spelta L. (spelt glume base)	1							1		1				
Triticum dicoccum Schübl. (emmer glume base)										cf.1				
Triticum dicoccum/spelta (emmer/spelt glume base)									1	1			2	
Triticum dicoccum/spelta (emmer/spelt spikelet fork)							2		1	1			1	1
Hordeum sp. (barley rachis fragment)	1							1	1				1	
Avena sp. (oat awn fragment)	+		++	+			+	+	++	+				
Secale cereale L. (rye rachis frag.)			1	1		2		1						
Cereal-sized culm node			1	2				1						3
Cereal-sized culm base			1											
OTHER FOOD, FLAVOURINGS AND FIBRE CROPS														
Corylus avellana L. (hazelnut shell fragment) HSW			3	8		3			5	3			1	4
Pisum sativum L. (pea with hilum, 5 mm)	2					1								
Pisum sativum/Vicia sativa L. (pea or cultivated vetch, no hilum, >4mm)			2	2	1	4	2f		1	2	1		1	3
Vicia sativa (cultivated vetch seed with hilum, 5mm)									1	1		2f		
Vicia faba L. (field/Celtic bean)	1		1	1	3	3	1		1	cf.5f	cf.1f		1f	1
Vicia faba/V.sativa/Pisum sativum (large pulse fragment)	4f		4f	1f	3f	3f	2f						4	3f
Brassica nigra L. (black mustard seed)							2		4	2	1		1	3
Linum usitatissimum L. (flax seed)						1	1	1				1		
Daucus carota L. (wild/cultivated carrot mericarp) GDc				2				3						
WEEDS AND WILD PLANTS														
Papaver sp. (poppy stigmatic disc) AD					1									
Ranunculus acris/bulbosus/repens (buttercup achene) CDG								1	1					
Hippocrepis comosa L. (horseshoe vetch seed) Gdc														
Vicia/Lathyrus sp. (<2mm vetch/tare)	7		7	10		3	9	3	19	9	1	1	1	3
Vicia/Lathyrus sp. (2-3 mm vetch/tare seed) CDGH	7	1	4	4	4	3	6	2	20	22	1	1	15	12
Vicia/Lathyrus sp./Pisum sativum (3-4mm vetch/tare/pea)	6		6	13	2	8	3	4	9	10			6	5
pea/bean/vetch/tare funicle (stalk attaching seed to pod)														
Trifolium/Lotus/Medicago sp. (clover/trefoil/medick seed) CGH	2	1	1	1	15	4	3	22	44	37	14	13	39	36
Malva sp. (mallow nutlet) DG			1	1										
Brassica cf. rapa/napus (cf. rape/turnip seed, faint reticulum)	1		1	1	2	2	2	1	1				2	
Brassica/Sinapis sp. (turnip, mustard, charlock etc. seed without seed coat) CD	3		3	2									2	

Habitat key: C=cultivated; D=disturbed; F=fens; G=grassland; H=hedgerow; P=ponds, rivers; S=scrub; W=woods; Y=wayside; SOILS: a=acid; c=base-rich; d=dry; h=heavy; n=nutrient-rich; o=open; w=wet

sample	9-2	9-3	13-1	13-3	13-4	13-5	12-1	13-2	TP1 lower	TP1 middle	TP1 top	TP2 lower	TP2 middle	TP2 top
context	9-131	9-133	13-105	13-110	13-137	13-131	12-144	13-112	midden	midden	midden	midden	midden	midden
feature type & number	D F98	D F99	P F76	P F78	P F110	P F108	deposit under B2	bedding trench	midden	midden	midden	midden	midden	midden
Phase	2	2	2	2	2	2	3	3	3 & 4	3 & 4	3 & 4	3 & 4	3 & 4	3 & 4
Raphanus raphanistrum L. (wild radish capsule) CD			4f			1		1f						
Fallopia convolvulus (L.) Á.Löve (black bindweed achene) CD	1									1				
Polygonum aviculare L. (knotgrass achene) Cdon			1	7										
Rumex acetosella (sheep's sorrel achene) Ga					1					3		1		
Rumex sp. (dock achene) CDG	2	1	30	7		6	3	8	4	10		1	8	5
Stellaria media L. (common chickweed seed) CDn														1
Stellaria graminea L. (lesser stitchwort seed) Gd														
Scleranthus anuus L. (annual knawel fruit) CDdo								1	1					
Agrostemma githago L. (corn cockle seed) AD							4					1		1
Agrostemma githago L. (corn cockle capsule valve) CD			11	4									1	
Silene cf. vulgaris L. (bladder campion seed) Dgo			cf.1											
Chenopodium rubrum L. (red goosefoot seed) CDn					2		2							
Atriplex patula/prostrata (orache seed) CDn				1			2				1			
Chenopodiaceae (seed without seed coat) CD							1	1		1	1			
Ericaceae (indeterminate heather fruit) Ea									1					
Sherardia arvensis L. (field madder nutlet) AD										1				
Galium aparine L. (cleavers nutlet) CDHn		2	3				1	2	3	2				1
Hyoscyamus niger L. (henbane achene) Dn				2	1			2	1f				2	
Plantago major L. (greater plantain seed) CG			1			1			1					
Plantago lanceolata L. (ribwort plantain seed) G										1				
Odontites vernus/Euphrasia sp. (red bartsia/eyebright seed) AD	1		3	1	1	4	34	1			1		1	
Rhinanthus sp. (yellow-rattle achene) G								1						
Centaurea cf. nigra -type (cf. knapweed achene) DGY							1	1		1				
Cirsium/Carduus sp. (thistle achene) CDG								1						
Helminthotheca echioides (L.) Holub (bristly oxtongue achene) D														1
Glebionis segetum (L.)Fourr. (corn marigold achene) AD			1					2	1					1
Anthemis cotula L. (stinking chamomile achene) CDwh	20	5	44	77	37	16	76	9	31	18	2	17	21	6
Tripleurospermum inodorum (L.) Sch.Bip. (scentless mayweed achene) CD	1		1	4	3	3	1	3	1	1			3	
Sambucus nigra L. (elder seed) DHSWn										1				
Valerianella dentata (L.)Pollich (narrow-fruited corn salad achene) CD								1			1			
Scandix pecten-veneris L. (sheherd's needle mericarp) AD	1f		1f											
Indeterminate Apiaceae, cf. Apium sp.									2					
Cladium mariscus (L.)Pohl (great fen sedge nutlet) Fw				3										
Carex sp. (trigonous sedge nutlet) Pw									3					
Lolium temulentum L. (darnel caryopsis) AD			40	5	6	9	27	5	cf.1	6			cf.3	5
Bromus secalinus -type (rye-brome-type caryopsis) AD			4	10	4	2				1				
Bromus hordaceus -type (soft-brome-type caryopsis) DG										4				
Bromus sp. (brome grass caryopsis) CDG	4	7	19	14	3	13		3		1	1			4
Anisthantha sp. (barren brome caryopsis) ADGo			2								6			cf.1f
Avena sp./Bromus sp. (oat/brome caryopsis) CD			15								2		5	2
Poaceae (small Poa -type, 1mm) CG	12	1	118	25	12	2	3	10	17	10		3	3	7
Poaceae (indeterminate c. 2-3 mm long caryopsis) CDG	4	1	10	2	9	2	6	5	13	21	2	5	9	2
Unidentified whole berry							1							
Arrhenatherum elatius var. bulbosum (Willd.) St-Amans CDG			2					1						
Anguina tritici (wheat nematode gall)	1		3	cf.1										
grass-stem frags			++					+						
TOTAL	264	116	1434	855	566+	594+	750	234	657	377	52	78	306	287
volume of soil processed (litres)	40	20	20	20	20	20	30	20	20	20	20	20	20	20
charred plant remains per litre	6.6	5.8	71.7	42.8	28.3	29.7	25	11.7	32.9	18.9	2.6	3.9	15.3	14.4

Habitat key: C=cultivated; D=disturbed; F=fens; G=grassland; H=hedgerow; P=ponds, rivers; S=scrub; W=woods; Y=wayside; SOILS: a=acid; c=base-rich; d=dry; h=heavy; n=nutrient-rich; o=open; w=wet worthwhile radiocarbon dating some of the material to see whether the remains were medieval in date. However, only three spelt glume bases, one possible emmer glume base and seven emmer/spelt chaff fragments were recovered. It is more likely, therefore, that the remains were residual, probably dating to the Roman period since a few sherds of Roman pot were recovered from the site.

Barley (*Hordeum vulgare* s.l.)
Barley grains were present in all of the samples but were never dominant. Most of the grains were poorly preserved (eroded) but a few twisted grains and some well-preserved grains demonstrated that six-row hulled barley was present. The cultivation of some two-rowed barley, however, cannot be ruled out. Barley prefers free-draining calcareous soils but can grow on a wide variety of soils.

Oats (*Avena* sp.)
Wild or cultivated oat grains were present in all except two samples. Most of the grains were too poorly preserved or too small to consider them to have been a cultivated species, but eight of the samples produced large, plump grains with their widest point being below midway down the grain. Where grains were over 6mm long and of this morphological type they were tentatively identified as cultivated oat (*Avena* cf. *sativa*). However, identifications of oats cannot be confirmed without the preservation of chaff (floret bases) and none survived in the samples. Oats are an important fodder crop, providing higher amounts of energy for draught animals. They also grow well on poor soils and in damp climates.

Rye (*Secale cereale*)
Rye grains can be difficult to differentiate from long-grained wheat unless they are well-preserved,

though their bullet-shaped form is quite distinctive where lots of grains are present. A few grains were tentatively identified as rye in five samples and a single rachis fragment confirmed the presence of this cereal. Since rye was present in very small amounts it was likely to have been growing as a contaminant rather than a crop at this site. Rye is a useful crop on free-draining sandy soils.

Sample descriptions by phase
Phase 2: 11th–12th to 13th centuries
DITCH F98, CONTEXT (9-131), SAMPLE 9-2
This sample came from the basal fill of a west-east ditch located beneath an early building, B4, in the southern part of Area 3. The large soil sample (40 litres) produced a modest concentration of charred plant remains (6.6 fragments per litre (fpl)). The assemblage contained frequent vacuolated and fragmented charred cereal grains with unidentified grains outnumbering identified cereals. The presence of primarily grain with some poorly preserved chaff fragments, a few pulses and a range of weed/wild plant remains is very similar to all of the samples analysed from the site, the ratio being roughly 9 : 1 : 3 grain to chaff to weeds in this sample. As with all of the samples, free-threshing wheat dominated the cereal grains and chaff fragments, with smaller numbers of hulled barley grains (*Hordeum vulgare* s.l.) and cultivated or wild oat grains (*Avena* sp.) (see Table 4.2 below for summarised cereal data by phase). In addition, a single emmer/spelt wheat grain was recorded (*Triticum dicoccum/spelta*) and a spelt glume base (*T. spelta*), most likely representing residual material dating to the Roman period. Free-threshing wheat rachis fragments were poorly preserved but unusually frequent (18 rachis nodes), with one fragment retaining enough of the node

Table 4.2 Arable crops cultivated by phase.

% identifiable grain	Phase 2 (ditches and pits)	Phase 3 (deposit & bedding trench)	Phase 3 & 4 (midden)
Free-threshing wheat	80%	88%	85%
Hulled wheat (probably residual)	3%	<1%	2%
Barley	12%	1%	7%
Oats (including some cultivated)	4%	10%	4%
Possible rye	1%	0%	<1%
Total cereal grains	1353	337	396

characteristics to indicate that tetraploid wheat, most likely rivet wheat (*Triticum turgidum*-type), was represented. A single small fragment of barley rachis was also recovered. One well preserved field bean (*Vicia faba*), two probable pea or cultivated vetch seeds and four fragments of large pulse provide evidence for other crop plants being cultivated. At least twelve weed taxa were represented amongst the remaining items, all of which are commonly found growing as crop weeds, on other types of disturbed ground and sometimes in grassy places. The most frequent remains (in descending order of frequency) were stinking chamomile achenes (*Anthemis cotula*), small grass seeds (Poaceae) and small vetch/tare seeds (*Vicia/Lathyrus* sp.). Ecological information recovered from the weed assemblages is discussed below. One additional important item was a single wheat nematode gall (*Anguina tritici*), a parasitized grain of wheat that can provide useful information about crop husbandry (Carruthers and Hunter-Dowse 2019, 221), as described below. The assemblage has the character of mixed domestic waste, perhaps burnt processing waste mixed in with accidentally burnt grain. It is likely to derive from domestic hearths and ovens where processing waste or hand-picked crop cleanings were used as fuel and spoilt or spilt grains came from cereals being prepared for cooking.

DITCH F99, CONTEXT (9-133), SAMPLE 9-3
The sample came from the single fill of this ditch, located adjacent to F98 beneath B4. A similarly moderate concentration of charred plant remains (5.8 fpl) was recovered from the sample with a ratio of *c.* 6 : 1 : 1 grain to chaff to weed seeds. Free-threshing wheat was dominant (55 grains) and a single residual emmer/spelt grain was recovered. No cultivated pulses were present and no oat grains, though a rivet-wheat type rachis fragment was recovered in addition to 22 indeterminate free-threshing wheat rachis fragments. None of the few weed taxa were frequent, though five stinking chamomile achenes and seven brome grass caryopses (*Bromus* sp.) were recorded. As with sample 9-2, the assemblage represents mixed domestic waste.

PIT F76, CONTEXT (13-105), SAMPLE 13-1
This sample came from the primary fill of a shallow pit that lay within, but pre-dated, one of the main

medieval buildings on the site, B5. The sample produced the highest concentration of charred plant remains (71.7 fpl) and one of the most diverse assemblages. Free-threshing wheat dominated the assemblage (336 grains), with lower numbers of hulled barley, oats (including some probable cultivated oat grains (*Avena* cf. *sativa*-type), and possible rye grains (cf. *Secale cereale*). The presence of bread wheat (*Triticum aestivum*) was confirmed by the recovery of a reasonably well-preserved rachis fragment. The overall ratio of grain to chaff to weed seeds was 120 : 1 : 38. The assemblage probably contains a deposit of accidentally or deliberately burnt grain (perhaps grain being dried prior to milling or infested grain being disposed of), in addition to some crop cleaning waste or possibly animal fodder/bedding burnt as fuel. A straw-sized culm node and culm base were present, as well as two onion couch tubers (*Arrhenatherum elatius* var. *bulbosum*), frequent small grass seeds (128 caryopses) and some thin, grass-sized culm (stem) fragments. These items, and possibly some of the weed seeds (e.g. greater plantain (*Plantago major*) and barren brome (*Anisantha* sp.)) could have been burnt amongst hay, though all of these taxa will also grow as crop weeds, including onion couch tubers which can be harvested with the crop if uprooting is the method used. Amongst the wide range of weed taxa in this sample the most frequent (besides grasses) were stinking chamomile, darnel (*Lolium temulentum*) and dock (Rumex sp.). Other notable typically medieval weeds were corn cockle (*Agrostemma githago*) and shepherd's needle (*Scandix pecten-veneris*). The significance of finding these sometimes noxious, dark-coloured contaminants amongst burnt waste is discussed below. In addition, three wheat nematode galls were recovered from the sample. It would have been important to hand-pick these black grain-sized items from seed-corn, before the grain was dried prior to storage, so as to reduce contamination in the following years crop. Three fragments of hazelnut shell (*Corylus avellana*) and four fragments of large pulse (peas, vetches or beans) were the only other food items recovered from the sample.

PIT F110, CONTEXT (13-137), SAMPLE 13-4
This feature, within B5 but pre-dating it, was similar to the other three pits in this group; F76, F78 and F108. Like F108, it contained a higher proportion of

indeterminate cereal grain fragments which were not fully quantified as they were too abundant, which is probably why the concentrations of charred items in these features were lower than features 76 and 78 (28.3 fpl in F110). The ratio of grain to chaff and weed seeds was >41 : 1 : 10. One pea or large vetch/tare was the only pulse present. The most frequent weed taxa were stinking chamomile (37 achenes), small grass caryopses (21) and clover-type seeds (*Trifolium/Lotus/Medicago* sp.; 15). The only other notable weed/wild plant seeds present were two henbane seeds (*Hyoscyamus niger*), two carrot mericarps (*Daucus carota*) and three great fen sedge nutlets (*Cladium mariscus*). These three taxa represent three very different habitats, the first being nutrient-rich habitats such as farmyards or middens. It is a poisonous plant that nevertheless was used for medicinal reasons (described below) so might have been grown in herb gardens in the settlement. Wild carrot is commonly found growing in coastal locations on well-drained soils but can also grow on rough ground in chalky locations. The cultivated subspecies *D. carota* ssp. *sativus* is grown as a root crop and the mericarps (fruits) can be used for medicinal purposes (see below). Since the settlement is close to the coast but is also likely to have contained gardens and herb beds it is impossible to determine which interpretation is most likely. The final notable taxon, great fen sedge, was likely to have been growing on the lime-rich loamy and clayey soils with impeded drainage to the north of the site. The fruits were either brought to the site amongst vegetation used for fodder, tinder or building materials, or they were growing as weeds in ditches alongside crops brought in from this area. This is discussed further below.

PIT F108, CONTEXT (13-131), SAMPLE 13-5
The sample came from the primary fill of pit F108, a feature located below B5. A moderate concentration of charred plant remains was recovered (29.7 fpl) consisting primarily of free threshing wheat grains but also containing the largest number of barley grains (89) and the highest number of (probably residual) emmer/spelt grains (42). A few large oat and rye grains were also recovered. Indeterminate grains were too fragmented and abundant to fully quantify. The ratio of grain to chaff and weed seeds from this sample was >96 : 1 : 19. Chaff was infrequent (a few free-threshing wheat rachis fragments and

two cereal-sized culm nodes) but pulses were common, including a confirmed pea (*Pisum sativum*) with an intact hilum, four peas or cultivated vetch seeds, three field/Celtic beans and three large pulse fragments. Three small fragments of hazelnut shell were also recovered. None of the weed seeds were particularly abundant, the most frequent being stinking chamomile (16 achenes) and brome grass (15 caryopses).

PIT F78, CONTEXT 13-110, SAMPLE 13-3
This pit was located close to F76 (described above), within B5. Context (13-110) was the upper fill of the feature and contained pottery with date ranges that extended into the early 13th century. However, since the feature pre-dated B5 it was still considered to be in Phase 2 (see Chapter 1). A large and diverse assemblage of charred cereal remains was recovered from the sample (42.8 fpl) which closely resembled those of pits F76 and F110 on either side. The ratio of grain to chaff to weed seeds was 19 : 1 : 5 due to free-threshing wheat rachis fragments being common in the sample (30 rachis fragments). This was the only sample to produce rye chaff (*Secale cereale* a single rachis fragment), as well as three possible rye grains. Free-threshing wheat grains were dominant, with smaller numbers of barley grains and several large oat grains suggesting that cultivated oat was present (*Avena* cf. *sativa*). Other food/fodder items represented were hazelnuts (8 fragments of nutshell), two possible peas or cultivated vetch, a field bean and a large indeterminate pulse fragment. The most frequent weed taxa recovered were stinking chamomile achenes (77), brome grass (24 caryopses) and small grass caryopses (27). Corn cockle and darnel were also present and weedy vetch/tares were common. A single possible wheat nematode gall was recovered from this sample.

Phase 3: 13th century
DEPOSIT BENEATH CROSS-PASSAGE HOUSE B2, CONTEXT (12-114), SAMPLE 12-1
A charcoal-rich deposit located beneath the cross-passage house, B2, was sampled. It produced a high concentration of cereal remains (25 fpl) in addition to a field bean, two fragments of pea or cultivated vetch and two large pulse fragments. A cultivated flax seed (*Linum usitatissimum*) was also recovered. The cereals were dominated by free-threshing wheat

grains and the recovery of an identifiable rachis fragment confirmed that bread wheat was present. Barley was less frequent than oat grains, some of which were large enough to indicate a cultivated crop. A grain of emmer/spelt was probably residual. The ratio of grain to chaff and weed seeds was 16 : 1 : 6. The most frequent weed taxa were stinking chamomile (76 achenes), red bartsia/eyebright (*Odontites vernus/Euphrasia* sp.; 34 seeds) and darnel (27 caryopses). Although the seeds of red bartsia and eyebright cannot be differentiated it is most likely that red bartsia was the species present, as it grows as an arable weed whilst eyebright primarily grows in grasslands on very poor soils. Two seeds of probable black mustard (*Brassica* cf. *nigra*) probably represent a crop plant which only appears in Phase 3 but was present in all of the midden samples. Its use is discussed further below.

DITCH F80, CONTEXT (13-112), SAMPLE 13-2
This sample was taken from the fill of the ditch F80, possibly a part of the manorial enclosure ditch. It may have been cut during Phase 2, but the fills were of Phase 3. A moderate concentration of charred plant remains was recovered (11.7 fpl), as cereal remains were less frequent in this sample than in most or the others. The ratio of cereal grains to chaff and weed seeds was 19 : 1 : 13, demonstrating that cereal grains and weed seeds were still very much more frequent than chaff, and that the source of charred remains was likely to have been a similar type of domestic waste to the other samples. This sample and the one from Ditch F99 were the only samples to contain no remains of pulses. A seed of cultivated flax was recovered, however. The most frequent weed taxa were clover-type seeds (22) and small grass seeds (15). An onion couch tuber was also present, perhaps having been uprooted with crops such as flax which are typically harvested in this way so as to recover the maximum length of fibre.

Phase 3&4: 13th to 14th centuries
MIDDEN, CONTEXT (10-108), SAMPLES FROM TEST PITS 1 AND 2, LOWER, MIDDLE AND TOP
Six samples were taken from two test pits dug into the midden, with samples being taken from the top, middle and bottom of the pits in both cases. The midden reached c. 70cm deep in places and extended over the eastern part of Area 2 and into the south-

eastern part of Area 1. The overall character of the six midden samples was very similar to earlier samples from pits, ditches and layers in that free-threshing wheat was dominant, with small amounts of barley, oats and a trace of possible rye, and chaff and weed seeds were relatively common. Field beans, probable peas and/or cultivated vetch, flax and hazelnut shell fragments were present in low numbers. The identification of one cultivated vetch seed was confirmed (*Vicia sativa*) in the sample from the middle of TP1 due to the presence of a hilum. The dominant weed taxa in the midden as a whole were clover-type seeds (183), small-seeded vetches/tares (2–4mm, 137 seeds) and stinking chamomile (95 achenes). The dominance of leguminous weed seeds is discussed further below. Because all of this material was charred it most likely had the same origins as ashy deposits being dumped in the pits and ditches, i.e. waste cleaned out of domestic hearths and ovens. There is little to suggest that vegetation growing on the midden had been burnt on a regular basis, since very few nitrophilous plants were represented (one Chenopodiaceae embryo, a common chickweed seed (*Stellaria media*) and a fragment of henbane seed). Concentrations of charred plant remains ranged from 2.6 fpl to 32.9 fpl, reflecting the patchy dumping of different types of waste across the midden. The top of TP1 and lowest sample in TP2 produced much lower concentrations of charred plant remains than the other samples, perhaps relating to where the source of burnt waste was coming from at different times. Figures 4.1 and 4.2 show the compositions of the six midden samples and are discussed below.

Discussion
Almost all of the fourteen samples from Lower Putton Lane produced charred plant assemblages that were rich in cereal remains but also contained significant numbers of weed seeds and some chaff. On the face of it most of the samples produced very similar results, with free-threshing wheat the dominant cereal through all three periods. Both bread wheat and rivet-type wheat were confirmed as being present on the site from the identification of three rachis nodes from each cereal-type. Although this is not very substantial evidence out of a total of 156 free-threshing wheat rachis nodes recovered from the

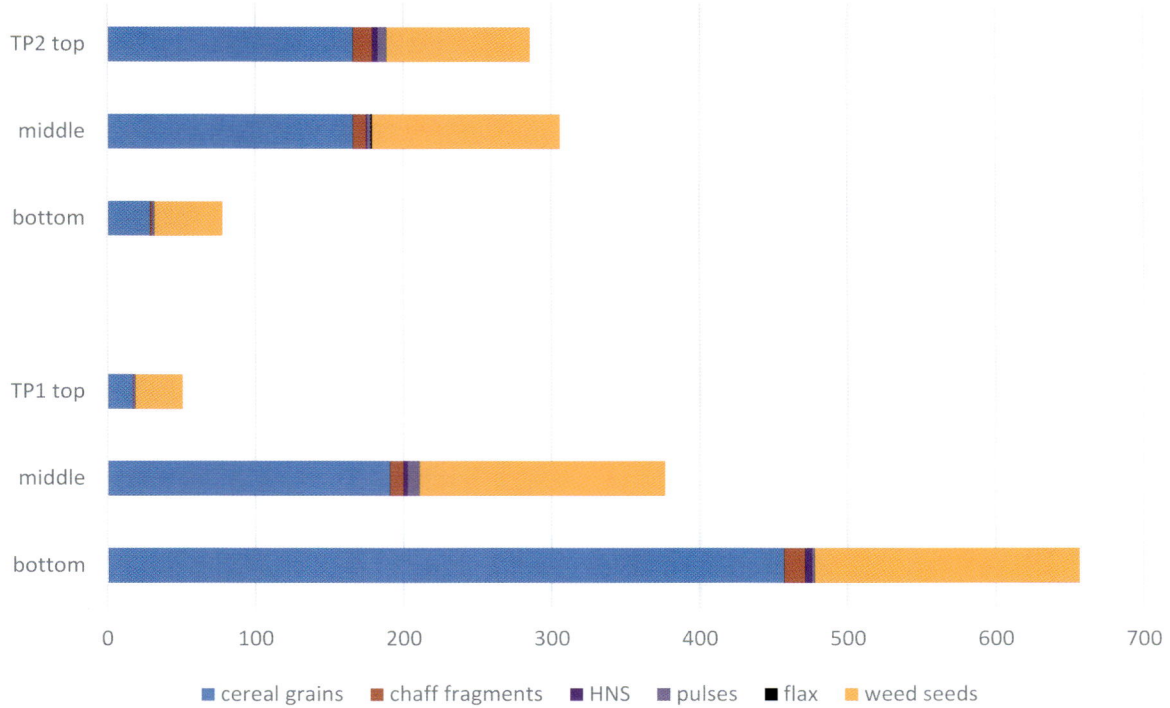

Fig. 4.1   Composition of midden samples using number of items (all 20 litres volume).

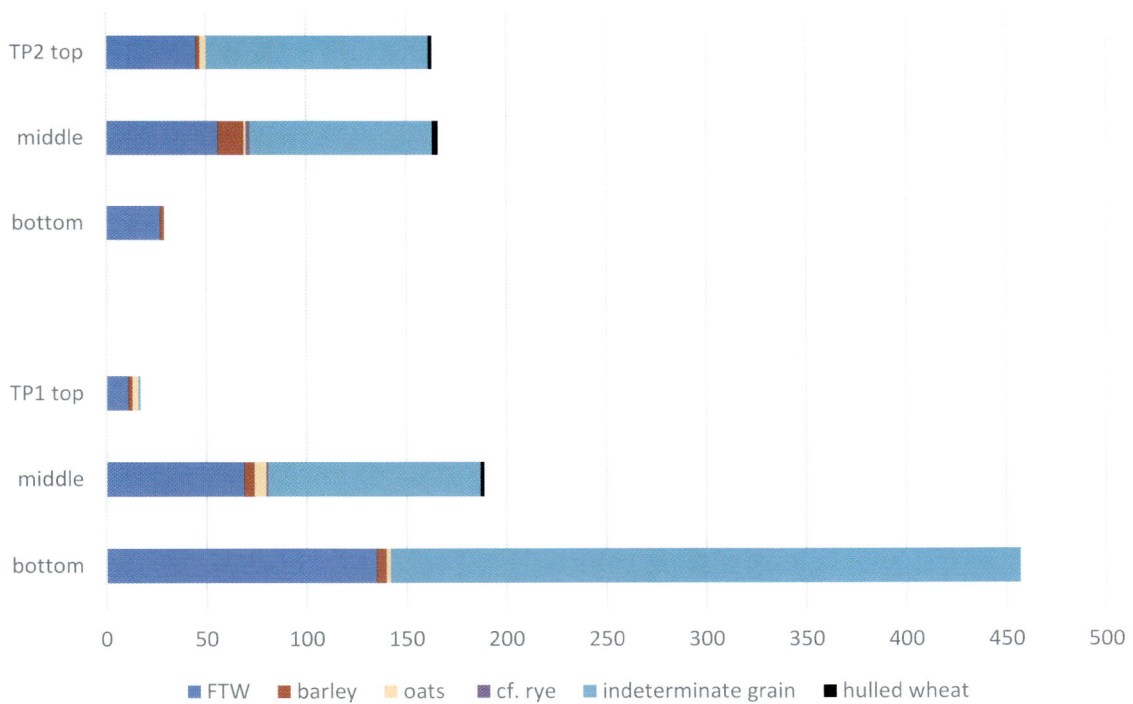

Fig. 4.2   Cereal composition of the midden samples using number of items.

samples, medieval sites rarely produce large amounts of wheat chaff since cereal processing was carried out in barns, some distance from habitation. Most of the material preserved as charred remains, therefore, is likely to consist of either accidentally burnt grain or contaminants cleaned from the processed grain

Table 4.3 Changes in weed taxa and CPR concentration by period.

	Phase 2 (pits and ditches)	Phase 3 (layer and bedding trench)	Phases 3 & 4 (midden)
Small-seeded leguminous weeds (Vicia/Lathyrus sp.; <2-4mm) per 10 litre soil sample	8	11	27
Weeds of nutrient-rich soils (Chenopodiaceae, knotgrass, cleavers) per 10 l sample	1.6	1.4	0.9
Stinking chamomile (per 10 l sample)	14	17	8
Darnel (per 10 l sample)	4	6	1
Wheat nematode galls (total number)	5	0	0
Black mustard seeds (total number)	0	2	15
Charred plant remains per 10 litres soil	96+	68	34

prior to cooking, thrown into domestic heaths and ovens as waste. Some of the grain may have been accidentally burnt during parching prior to milling into flour, or grain might be deliberately burnt if infested or mouldy. No sprouted grains were recovered, so there was no evidence of spoilage due to storage in damp conditions or evidence for malting. There was also no evidence for large quantities of hay, animal bedding or other types of vegetation being burnt and charcoal fragments were generally small and infrequent.

The removal of specific contaminants from the crop would have been particularly important where they may be toxic, taint the food or reduce yields where grain was being retained as seed-corn. Items in this category include corn cockle seeds, darnel caryopses and wheat nematode galls from the crop, all of which would have been relatively easy to pick out by hand being fairly large (3–4mm) and brown or black in colour. High numbers of corn cockle seeds, or darnel infected with ergot can have serious effects on the health of humans and animals. Darnel is particularly susceptible to ergot infection so it would have been removed from grain being cleaned for human or animal consumption, as well as seed-corn to prevent infecting vulnerable crops like rye. The removal of wheat nematode gall (or 'ear cockle') from seed corn would have been important since an infection in the crop can greatly reduce yields. It was also probably removed from grain being prepared for cooking because the dark colour of the gall looks very similar to grain infected with ergot.

Wheat nematode gall was a serious agricultural problem in the medieval period and is still found in countries that have not adopted modern methods of seed-screening. In damp climates crop rotations of 1–2 years can control infections, but where rotation cannot be practiced, as in the medieval village at Wharram Percy, infection rates can build up to damaging levels. At Wharram a 16th century barn burnt down, preserving entire crops of wheat, cultivated vetch, peas and barley (Carruthers 2010). Among the abundant charred grains 275 wheat nematode galls were recovered. On examination of documentary evidence legal disputes revealed that the tenant's ability to practice crop rotation had been reduced due to increases in land used for sheep being reared for wool production (Harding et al. 2010). Lower numbers of galls have also been recovered from other medieval settlement sites, for example at Furnell's Manor (9 galls) and Langham Road (1 gall) (11th century to high medieval; Raunds Project; Carruthers and Hunter-Dowse 2019). At Lower Putton Lane five galls were recovered from three Phase 2 samples only (Table 4.3), suggesting that crop rotation may have been increased in later periods, helping to control nematode activity.

Other typically medieval weeds present in the sample were corn cockle, shepherd's needle and darnel (*Lolium temulentum*). The presence of these items as burnt remains in a rubbish pit may indicate that effort was put into hand-picking these items from the crop prior to cooking, particularly as the seeds of both corn cockle and darnel are of a similar size to cereal grains so cannot be removed by winnowing and sieving.

Looking at the wide range of weed species present in the samples and the variety of soils on which they are most commonly found it is possible that grain was being brought in from a range of properties in the area, perhaps in the form of tithes. While weed/wild plants such as annual knawel and sheep's sorrel mainly grow on acidic soils, weeds and crops of *Brassica* species prefer more basic soils. Several weeds show preference for soils that are low in nutrients (annual knawel, field madder, narrow-fruited corn-salad, clover and vetches) and others are mostly found on fertile, nitrogen-rich soils (red goosefoot, orache, knotgrass, henbane, cleavers). Annual knawel, field madder and narrow-fruited corn-salad prefer dry soils whereas sedges and great fen sedge grow on damp to wet soils, with great fen sedge specifically growing in base-rich fenland. A few of these taxa may not have been growing as crop weeds, particularly the sedges which could have been growing along field margins in wet ditches or may derive from burnt marsh hay. Henbane is not typically found as a crop weed as it prefers very rich soils, typical of middens. The presence of hazelnut shell, charcoal and pulses demonstrates that the assemblages contain some mixed domestic waste, though they were very much dominated by cereal grains and cleaning waste.

The midden
The analysis of six samples from the two test pits through the midden provided useful comparative information by phase but did not provide clear evidence to demonstrate how the deposit built up. The compositions of the samples (using numbers of items) have been plotted in Figures 4.1 and 4.2 in order to find some sort of trends through the deposit. However, no clear patterns have emerged and the two poorest samples at the top of TP1 and bottom of TP2 give the impression that some sort of inversion of material could have taken place. However, charred material was only part of the waste being deposited so it is possible that deposition was too patchy to reveal any sort of definite pattern. In addition, reworking of the midden and the extraction of material to manure the fields over the decades may have destroyed any minor changes within the deposit.

Changes through time
CROP HUSBANDRY
Comparisons can be made between the three groups of samples assigned to Phases 2, 3 and 3&4. This is not straight forward as the types of deposits sampled in each group vary significantly and so in theory the assemblages could represent different types of waste or accidentally burnt deposits. However, on this site the characters of the assemblages were very similar in all three periods, with cereal grains dominating eleven of the fourteen assemblages, free-threshing wheat dominating all fourteen samples, chaff fragments being present in low numbers in thirteen of the samples and weed taxa being very similar in all fourteen samples. It is likely that the charred assemblages in each type of feature derived primarily from the same source, i.e. the bulk of the charred material coming from the cleaning out of domestic ovens and hearths. Small amounts of waste from other sources, such as floor sweepings, were probably too insignificant to affect the data. Charred waste was being deposited in pits, ditches, layers and in the midden over several centuries of occupation. During this time no major changes in the crops being grown or crop processing methods appears to have taken place.

However, a closer inspection reveals small differences which could be significant in terms of crop yields and crop husbandry methods. Looking at the more statistically and ecologically significant weed taxa and correcting for differences in litres of soil processed, some suggestions as to changes through time can be made.

The most notable change was the increase in small-seeded weedy leguminous weeds (vetches and tares) over time. Because many of the weeds in the Fabaceae family (previously 'Leguminosae') are able to fix atmospheric nitrogen with the help of nitrogen-fixing bacteria in nodes in their roots they can out-compete other plants on nutrient-poor soils (Moss 2004). This ability is what makes crops such as peas, cultivated vetch and beans valuable additions to crop rotation systems or within mixed cropping regimes. The increase in vetch- and clover-type weeds suggests that centuries of growing primarily nutrient-demanding crops, bread and rivet-type wheats without adequately replenishing the soils with manure had caused reductions in yields. Seeds from weeds of nutrient-rich soils were not as common in the samples so the data is less convincing, but a small reduction in these taxa over time can be seen, providing some support to the interpretation. It is not possible to directly relate this to the reduction of concentrations of charred plant remains, because as noted earlier, very different types of deposit were used for the comparisons. For example, middens will be composed of a range of types of waste with charred material perhaps only making up a small proportion and having a patchy distribution. This is not comparable to a sample from an ashy layer in a pit. In addition, behavioural changes such as changes in waste disposal methods could affect the data. Nevertheless, it is a useful statistic to bear in mind and could relate to other factors, such as decreases in population.

Possible increases in the use of crop rotation relating to the recovery of wheat nematode galls has been discussed above. Large pulses, including peas and cultivated vetch (one of each confirmed due to presence of hila) and field/Celtic bean were common in all phases and no doubt these crops would have been important as part of the crop rotation system. There was no evidence to suggest changes in pulse frequency over time. Increases in small vetch/tare/clover seeds are sometimes linked to a greater use of fallow, as many species in this group are primarily grassland plants. However, there were no significant changes in the numbers of small grass caryopses across the phases at Lower Putton Lane so reduced fertility of the land is the most likely interpretation.

The slight rise and fall of both stinking chamomile (a weed of damp, clayey soils) and darnel (a weed of alkaline soils), two persistent arable weeds, could relate to the rise and fall of percentages of free-threshing wheats as a proportion of arable crops grown, as seen in Table 4.2. In Phase 3 there was a slight increase in free-threshing wheat and oats but a small decrease in barley. These trends are reversed to some extent in Phase 3&4. Stinking chamomile is most likely to have been growing as a weed of wheat, since this most-valuable crop would have been grown on the most fertile soils. At Lower Putton Lane soils to the north of the site

are highly fertile lime-rich, loamy and clayey soils with impeded drainage (Chapter 1) and stinking chamomile is a weed of damp, clay soils. Soils in the immediate vicinity of the site would have also suited this weed, being base-rich, seasonally wet and loamy/clayey but of moderate fertility so manuring would have been essential to maintain fertility if demanding crops like bread and rivet wheat were grown over several centuries. Darnel is primarily found on the base-rich soils so would have thrived in crops growing in the area.

Because all of the samples studied for this report appear to have contained mixed waste from several crops it has not been possible to use weed ecology to determine the time of sowing for each crop. It is likely, however, that sowing would have been spread between autumn and winter as far as possible to spread the workload, with bread wheat and rye being hardy enough for winter sowing and the remaining crops (rivet wheat, barley, oats) being spring-sown (Woodward and Luff 1983).

ADDITIONAL CROPS, GARDEN PLANTS AND MEDICINAL PLANTS
Flax (*Linum usitatissimum*) – Three flax seeds were recovered, one from each of the Phase 3 samples and one from the middle of the midden in TP2. Flax was cultivated for a variety of purposes, including for oil from the seeds, fibre from the stems to spin and weave into linen and the seeds were also used in foods and as a medicinal plant (emollient, demulcent, pectoral and in poultices [Grieve 1931]). Flax prefers a well-drained, light soil.

Black mustard (*Brassica nigra*) – This species produces the most pungent mustard of the various species of *Brassica* and *Sinapis* species now used. It was used as a condiment from the Iron Age and Roman periods onwards (Carruthers 2009). On this site seven of the eight samples in Phases 3 and 3&4 contained a few probable black mustard seeds but a different species of *Brassica* was present in the Phase 2 samples (probably *B. rapa* or *B. napus*; fine, smooth reticulum on seed coat, includes rape and turnip). Mustards have also been used since classical times for medicinal purposes, internally for digestive and pulmonary disorders and externally as poultices placed near sources of internal inflammation so as to draw the blood to the surface (Grieve 1931, 569).

Cultivated vetch (*Vicia sativa*) – Because most of the large round pulses could not be identified beyond pea/vetch (due to loss of their hila) it is not possible to be sure whether vetches were grown throughout the phases represented. The only identified cultivated vetch came from the Phase 3&4 midden. The frequency of seeds in this category, however, suggests that it had been present in earlier phases, as pulses are likely to be under-represented in the charred plant record, having no need to be parched when being processed. Vetches may have been grown as maslins (mixed crops) with cereals in order to improve soil fertility and to help reduce lodging. At the Wharram Percy barn (described above) they appear to have been growing as a maslin with wheat. They are less palatable than peas so were primarily used for fodder but may have been consumed by people in times of famine (Wilson 1973, 202).

Wild carrot (*Daucus carota*) – It is uncertain whether the five fruits of this plant recovered from a Phase 2 and a Phase 3 sample represent wild plants growing along the coast, as crop weeds or grown in gardens as a vegetable. Carrots have been cultivated since classical times (de Rougemont 1989), probably originating from wild plants growing on free-draining coastal soils. Even if they had been growing as wild or weedy plants the seeds may have been collected for medicinal purposes, being useful as a carminative, stimulant and for digestive complaints (Grieve 1931).

Henbane (*Hyoscyamus niger*) – Although all parts of this plant are poisonous their value as medicinal plants was high enough for it to have been cultivated in the past (Grieve 1931, 400). Grieve notes that the seeds were a 'favourite remedy for toothache in the Middle Ages', though they did cause 'convulsions and even insanity in some instances.' A large deposit of seeds was thought to have demonstrated use for medicinal purposes at Waltham Abbey (Moffat 1987). At Lower Putton Lane six seeds were recovered from all phases.

COMPARISONS WITH OTHER RURAL MEDIEVAL SITES

Few other medieval settlements in the area have been excavated and sampled for plant remains, but the following two sites provide some useful comparative information.

A 12th to 13th century monastic grange in the deserted medieval village of Cawston, Dunchurch, Rugby (Warwickshire), was investigated (Monckton 2002). Ditch and floor deposits produced some rich charred plant assemblages containing frequent free-threshing wheat and rye chaff, large pulses and hazelnut shell. The small number of weed seeds suggested that the crops had been efficiently weeded. Occasional fruits/seeds of corn cockle, stinking chamomile and cornflower were present. Two ditch fills contained cereal processing waste containing roughly equal amounts of wheat and rye chaff, with both rivet and bread wheat present. Smaller amounts of barley and cultivated oats were also recovered, as well as pulse and hazelnut shell. A 13th to 14th century floor deposit and an enclosure ditch fill produced the waste from processing rye and mixed processing waste containing bread wheat, rivet wheat and some rye. Documentary evidence showed that Cawston produced bread for nine other settlements and had two ovens in the 13th century, accounting for the large amounts of processing waste present at the site. It was thought that the relatively high incidence of rye may have been in order to produce a low-cost mixed-flour bread for poorer people. There was very little evidence for oats and barley at the site (Monckton 2002). The results from Lower Putton Lane are comparable in the range of arable crops being grown though larger numbers of weed seeds appear to have been present and the scale of production of crop processing waste was clearly lower. Differences in the cultivation of rye are interesting if it was specifically being grown for economic reasons at Cawston.

Many of the elements of the deserted medieval shrunken hamlet at Eckweek, Peasedown St John (Somerset) were closely comparable to the late Lower Putton Lane samples. A sequence of medieval occupation dating from the 10th to 14th centuries was uncovered at Eckweek and a large number of samples were taken (Carruthers 2020). As at Putton, free-threshing wheat was dominant in all of the 53 samples analysed (92% of the identified grain on average in all five phases) and both bread and rivet-type wheats were confirmed as being cultivated. Barley (4%), oats (4%) and rye (<1%) were all present in low amounts and pulses were present in 75% of the samples, with peas, field beans and common vetch occurring in many samples. Despite the large number of samples analysed and the nature of the site (primarily a farmstead), only 505 free-threshing wheat rachis fragments were recovered, most coming from only four moderately rich samples. This is similar to the frequency of rachis fragments from the fourteen Putton samples; 9.5 rachis fragments per sample at Eckweek and 11.1 at Putton. Very few remains from other food plants were identified, with plum being the only cultivated fruit and the few other items (which included carrot) being in very low numbers. Weed taxa included darnel (42 caryopses), corn cockle (8 seeds), onion couch (1 tuber), and the same two wet ground taxa, great fen sedge and sedge, were present in very low numbers.

These similarities are most likely due to the rural, agriculture-based nature of the sites and their locations on base-rich soils in the Midlands and southern England. At Eckweek, *Anguina tritici* was not found to be a problem and numbers of darnel caryopses were lower (42 caryopses from 53 samples compared with 109 recovered from the 14 samples at Lower Putton Lane). Documentary information from 14th century title deeds at Eckweek revealed that a two-field system of rotation was used (Shorrocks 1974). This level of rotation appears to have been sufficient to have maintained soil fertility and kept pests (including the nematode, *Anguina tritici*) and diseases at manageable levels. Since the same range of crops was being grown at Lower Putton Lane and soils in the locality were of a similar level of fertility to those at Eckweek the limiting factors at Lower Putton Lane were likely to have been access to sufficient land by tenant farmers so that crop rotation could be used, and the imposition of restrictions by the land owner that might affect management of the land. By the late 13th century surviving court records from elsewhere provide details of a wide range of bylaw enactments which were served on villagers across Britain, including constraints on ploughing, planting, harvesting, gleaning and carrying (Gies and Gies 1989, 132). Of particular importance were regulations concerning grazing rights since fertility of the land would be dependent on having sufficient livestock to produce manure. At Lower Putton Lane the balance between grazing and ploughing may have begun to be lost by the end of the 14th

century. This theory needs to be tested on a larger scale on similar sites in the area.

MICROARTEFACTS AND ECOFACTS FROM BULK SAMPLES, By Clare Randall

The heavy residues from the soil samples were utilised for recovery of microartefacts and ecofacts. This was made possible as most of the deposits sampled had a minimal stone component. Material was sorted by eye under light and where necessary magnification. A variety of materials were recovered using this method. The identifiable component of the animal bone, the fish and marine molluscs will be discussed in detail below. In addition to this there were small amounts of metal fragments, mortar, glass and slag, but considerably more of pottery and other ceramic/fired clay (Table 4.4).

Most of this material, from all contexts, was highly fragmented and largely unidentifiable beyond material type. No diagnostic sherds of pottery were recovered; some were tiny fragments representing de-laminated surfaces. Nevertheless, no fabric was noted which was inconsistent with the range of medieval ceramics (described by Mepham, Chapter 2). The quantity of ceramic material which could not be identified as pottery was generally greater. It may include very badly degraded pottery, but also a range of ceramic building materials and fired clays which are too abraded to allow differentiation. There was a considerable quantity of mammalian bone which also could not be identified. The ceramic material and bone, as well as most of the metal, occurred mainly in fragments of 1–5mm, with fewer larger pieces. There was minimal variation in this between contexts.

By looking at the weight and number of fragments in relation to the volume sampled it is possible to make some broad comments. This is of particular use in understanding the formation of the midden (10-108). There are some differences in the proportions of abundance of materials (by weight and fragment numbers) between the four Phase 2 pits sampled. For instance, there is much less in the way of pottery, ceramic and bone in pit F110. Pit F76 had a minimal amount of pottery, but a significant amount of

Table 4.4 Microartefacts and ecofacts from heavy residues.

Context	Phase	Feature type	Vol (l)	Pottery g	Pottery No	Other ceramic g	Other ceramic No	Bone g	Bone No	Marine shell g	Marine shell No	Fe g	Fe No	Cu g	Cu No	Mortar g	Mortar No	Glass g	Glass No	Slag g	Slag No
(13-105)	2	Pit fill	20	1	1	160	1320	67	657	2	29	5	6	-	-	-	-	-	-	-	-
(13-110)	2	Pit fill	20	16	3	45	370	39	232	11	16	<1	7	-	-	-	-	-	-	-	-
(13-131)	2	Pit fill	20	11	18	59	490	27	606	8	123	1	18	-	-	-	-	<1	1	1	<1
(13-137)	2	Pit fill	20	-	-	1	22	2	42	1	1	1	8	-	-	-	-	-	-	-	-
(9-131)	2	Ditch fill	40	23	13	7	65	9	416	1	26	<1	4	-	-	-	-	-	-	-	-
(9-133)	2	Ditch fill	20	17	8	21	162	2	191	3	50	-	-	-	-	-	-	-	-	-	-
(12-114)	3	Deposit	30	6	8	14	115	3	165	5	11	<1	1	-	-	-	-	-	-	1	1
(13-112)	3	Ditch fill	20	7	3	5	41	3	133	6	32	-	-	-	-	-	5	-	-	-	-
TP1 – Top	3&4	Deposit	20	-	-	55	462	10	451	<1	2	<1	10	-	2	<1	-	-	-	<1	2
TP1 – Middle	3&4	Deposit	20	3	6	21	173	11	1096	-	-	3	7	-	-	-	-	-	-	-	-
Tp1 – Lower	3&4	Deposit	20	39	20	87	736	11	1252	-	-	<1	16	-	-	-	-	-	-	-	-
TP2 – Top	3&4	Deposit	20	36	28	49	395	14	549	-	-	2	14	-	-	-	-	-	-	-	-
TP2 – Middle	3&4	Deposit	20	38	36	65	518	12	785	1	4	3	8	-	-	-	-	-	-	-	-

ceramic. Both pits F78 and F108 had larger amounts of all materials. This is not surprising in this series of discrete features where one might expect individual fills to be created in similarly discrete disposal events. However, what is interesting is that variations in the abundance of materials also appear to have occurred within the midden dump (10-108). Material was recovered from two randomly located test pits, and samples taken from c. 20cm thick spits in the top, middle and lower portions. One sample had to be discarded, but the others indicated that the midden had, as was suspected from the spread at its edges, been reworked. This was probably caused by later agricultural action and may have occurred later in the medieval or early modern period. The bone within these deposits was noticeably more fragmented, which can be seen in the number of fragments versus the weight in the midden samples in comparison to those from the Phase 2 pits. Fewer marine mollusc fragments in the midden material may indicate that it was a biologically hostile environment. There also appeared to be variation between the two test pits by depth. In TP2 there was a degree of similarity between the upper and middle spits in respect of the pottery, ceramics and bone. However, in TP1 there was a difference in the amount of pottery in the top and middle portions compared with its lower spit. There were also differences between it and TP2. This supports the midden having formed through episodic dumping of household refuse.

THE FAUNAL REMAINS, By Clare Randall

Introduction

The majority of the faunal remains from Lower Putton Lane were hand collected. Bulk soil samples were also taken from several cut features and the Phase 3&4 midden deposit and bone recovered from the heavy residues. Most of the material from wet sieving comprised small fragments of unidentifiable mammal bone, but it complemented the hand collected assemblage providing small mammal, herpetofauna and fish remains which are dealt with in separate sections below.

The hand collected faunal remains assemblage from Lower Putton Lane consisted of a total of 2,239 fragments of which 2,143 were mammalian. These have been assigned to seven individual site phases and one combined phase (Phase 3&4). Most of the material came from contexts which had been redeposited. The site provided a limited number of cut features which yielded animal bone. A number of these were sealed beneath the earliest buildings on the site (Phase 2). A small range of deposits and features were more clearly associated with the construction and occupation of the main buildings dating to the 13th–14th centuries (Phase 3 and Phase 4). This included cut features and pre- building deposits in Area 3. The contents of field boundaries in Area 2 and the midden (10-108) span this entire period, but as explained in Chapter 1 cannot be individually assigned to either phase. These have been treated as a separate, but parallel unit Phase 3&4. The majority of the material was derived from demolition deposits (Phase 5) and later deposits derived from them (Phase 8). Phase 5 deposits mainly contained material culture recovered from the 13th–14th century period of site use and can be understood as deriving from the latter part of occupation. A very small amount of bone from a discrete part of Area 2 could be assigned to the Late medieval (Phase 6) whilst some deposits associated with the post-medieval buildings in Area 3 and parts of Area 1 were assigned to Phase 7, although much of the material is likely to be residual. Phase 8 comprised the most stratigraphically recent material. However, the majority of the material is almost certainly derived from the underlying medieval demolition deposits. As a consequence it is subject to detailed consideration, and also because it comprises most of the animal bone recovered from the site. For clarity, the data has been separated in tables into material which came from clearance layers overlying walls and medieval demolition layers (Phase 8.1) and clearly very recent and disturbed contexts such as service trenches (Phase 8.2).

The hand collected assemblage is summarised in Table 4 5. The majority was disarticulated and co-mingled bone from a total of 62 Phase 2-7 contexts, and overlying clearance layers (Table 4.6). Each bone fragment was identified to element and species, and where this was not possible cattle sized, sheep sized, and unidentified mammal categories. Indicators of age and sex were recorded along with metrical data, taphonomic and pathological changes as well as butchery marks and other modification. A full description of the methods and further data tables are included in the site archive.

Preservation and condition

The condition of the bone was largely poor-average and average (Table 4.7). No associated bone groups (ABGs) were noted, possibly a function of the lack of cut features and indicative of the movement of material around the site. In total, 45% of the mammalian bone was identified to species, of which 23% comprised loose teeth, which highlights the degree of fragmentation. Butchery, and/or breakage of the bone when fresh (which may indicate deliberate fragmentation), were noted in all periods. This probably contributed to the original fragmentary nature of the assemblage. A total of 140 fragments (7% of the assemblage, excluding material from the topsoil) demonstrated taphonomic changes (Table 4.8). Canid gnawing was the most common and was present in all periods. Weathering was generally rare with weathered fragments only occurring in five periods and represented by less than 2% of the material excluding topsoil contexts. This suggests that material was incorporated into deposits reasonably rapidly even if it was subsequently redeposited. Burnt material also occurred in four periods, albeit at low levels.

While the assemblage originated from all phases, 68% of the material came from the clearance layers overlying the site. There is some post-medieval cultural material within these clearance layers, particularly overlying the deposits around and within the post-medieval buildings in Area 3 and topsoil in Area 1. However, the proportion of medieval pottery in these clearance contexts suggests strongly that the majority of the animal bone most likely derived from the underlying medieval material. The material therefore needs to be regarded with some caution but given the paucity of animal bone assemblages of this date within Dorset it is still of value.

Table 4.5 Faunal remains. The hand collected assemblage by phase. NISP = Number of Identified Specimens, MNI = Minimum Number of Individuals.

Species	Period 2		Period 3.1		Period 3.2		Period 3 & 4		Period 4		Period 5		Period 6		Period 7		Period 8.1		Period 8.2		Total
	NISP/No	MNI	NISP/No	MNI	NISP/No	MNI	NISP/No	MNI	NISP/No	MNI	NISP/No	MNI	NISP/No	MNI	NISP/No	MNI	NISP/No	MNI	NISP/No	MNI	
Cattle	9	2	5	1	12	1	18	1	6	1+1	41	2+1	-	-	10	2	184	NA	25	NA	-
Sheep/Goat	9	2	5	1	6	1	13	2	4	1	48	5	6	1	10	1	285	NA	24	NA	-
Sheep	-	-	-	-	3	1	3	1	-	-	3	2	-	-	2	1	23	NA	-	-	-
Pig	1	1	1	1	2	1	5	1	1	1	18	3	-	-	9	1+1	95	NA	7	NA	-
Dog	-	-	-	-	-	-	2	1	-	-	1	1	-	-	3	1	11	NA	1	NA	-
Horse	5	1	-	-	-	-	3	1	-	-	8	1	-	-	3	1	19	NA	6	NA	-
Cat	-	-	-	-	-	-	3	1	-	-	1	1	-	-	1	1	6	NA	-	NA	-
Domestic Total	*24*	*-*	*11*	*-*	*23*	*-*	*47*	*-*	*11*	*-*	*120*	*-*	*6*	*-*	*38*	*-*	*623*	*-*	*63*	*-*	*966*
Deer	-	-	-	-	-	-	-	-	-	-	-	-	-	-	-	-	1	-	-	-	-
Rabbit	-	-	-	-	-	-	-	-	-	-	-	-	-	-	-	-	1	-	-	-	-
Hare	-	-	-	-	-	-	-	-	-	-	-	-	-	-	-	-	1	-	-	-	-
Rat	-	-	-	-	-	-	-	-	-	-	-	-	-	-	-	-	1	-	-	-	-
Mole	-	-	-	-	-	-	-	-	-	-	-	-	-	-	-	-	3	-	-	-	-
Small mammal	-	-	-	-	-	-	-	-	-	-	-	-	1	-	-	-	-	-	-	-	-
Wild Total	*-*	*-*	*-*	*-*	*-*	*-*	*-*	*-*	*-*	*-*	*-*	*-*	*1*	*-*	*-*	*-*	*7*	*-*	*-*	*-*	*8*
Domestic fowl	-	-	-	-	-	-	-	-	-	-	3	1	-	-	-	-	14	NA	-	-	-
Domestic Goose	-	-	1	1	-	-	-	-	-	-	2	1	-	-	-	-	-	-	-	-	-
Goose	-	-	-	-	-	-	1	1	-	-	-	-	-	-	-	-	1	NA	-	-	-
Duck (mallard)	-	-	-	-	-	-	-	-	-	-	-	-	-	-	-	-	2	NA	-	-	-
Duck (teal)	-	-	-	-	-	-	-	-	-	-	-	-	-	-	-	-	1	NA	-	-	-
Crow (*Corvus* spp.)	-	-	-	-	-	-	-	-	-	-	-	-	-	-	-	-	1	NA	-	-	-
Godwit (*Limosa* spp.)	-	-	-	-	-	-	-	-	-	-	-	-	-	-	-	-	1	NA	-	-	-
Unidentified bird	-	-	2	-	-	-	1	-	-	-	1	-	-	-	-	-	8	NA	-	-	-
Bird total	*-*	*-*	*3*	*-*	*-*	*-*	*2*	*-*	*-*	*-*	*6*	*-*	*-*	*-*	*-*	*-*	*28*	*-*	*1*	*-*	*40*
Fish total	*-*	*-*	*-*	*-*	*-*	*-*	*-*	*-*	*-*	*-*	*-*	*-*	*-*	*-*	*-*	*-*	*56*	*-*	*-*	*-*	*56*
Large mammal	16	-	5	-	23	-	28	-	5	-	42	-	8	-	5	-	498	NA	26	-	-
Medium mammal	5	-	5	-	7	-	8	-	3	-	22	-	1	-	8	-	84	NA	7	-	-
Unidentified	18	-	13	-	4	-	15	-	10	-	22	-	2	-	-	-	230	NA	49	-	-
Unidentified Total	*39*	*-*	*23*	*-*	*34*	*-*	*51*	*-*	*18*	*-*	*86*	*-*	*11*	*-*	*13*	*-*	*812*	*-*	*82*	*-*	*1169*
Main total	*63*	*-*	*37*	*-*	*57*	*-*	*100*	*-*	*29*	*-*	*212*	*-*	*18*	*-*	*51*	*-*	*1526*	*-*	*146*	*-*	*2239*

Table 4.6 Animal bone fragments by context type Phases 2–7, number of fragments and number of contexts.

Feature	Phase 2		Phase 3		Phase 4		Phase 3&4		Phase 5		Phase 6		Phase 7	
	No.	No Cont.	No.	No Cont.	No.	No Cont.	No.	No Cont.	No.	No Cont.	No.	No Cont.	No.	No Cont.
Pit	31	9	4	1	-	-	-	-	-	-	-	-	-	-
Bedding trench	-	-	12	3	-	-	-	-	-	-	-	-	-	-
Ditch	6	2	-	-	-	-	11	5	-	-	-	-	-	-
Enclosure Ditch	-	-	-	-	-	-	10	4	-	-	-	-	-	-
Surface	-	-	-	-	29	2	-	-	-	-	-	-	-	-
Deposit	1	1	21	3	-	-	-	-	-	-	-	-	-	-
Layer	22	2	-	-	-	-	-	-	-	-	-	-	4	2
Rubble	-	-	57	2	-	-	-	-	212	12	18	3	47	4
Alluvial deposit	-	-	-	-	-	-	56	2	-	-	-	-	-	-
Midden	-	-	-	-	-	-	13	2	-	-	-	-	-	-
Terrace	-	-	-	-	-	-	6	1	-	-	-	-	-	-
Holloway	-	-	-	-	-	-	4	1	-	-	-	-	-	-

Table 4.7 Animal bone preservation summary by phase (% of total fragments).

	2	3.1	3.2	3 & 4	4	5	6	7	8.1
Poor	-	-	-	1	-	-	-	-	0.5
Poor-Average	52	59	63	73	83	48	67	27	63
Average	37	36	33	21	10	45	33	61	27
Average-Good	11	5	4	5	7	7	-	12	9
Good	-	-	-	-	-	-	-	-	0.5

Table 4.8 Summary of gnawed weathered and burnt animal bone fragments by phase.

Period	Total Frags.	Gnawed No	Gnawed %	Weathered No	Weathered %	Burnt No	Burnt %
2	63	3	5	3	5	-	-
3.1	37	1	3	-	-	2	5
3.2	90	5	6	-	-	6	7
4	29	-	-	-	-	1	3
3&4	100	3	3	1	1	1	1
5	212	17	8	7	3	-	-
6	18	2	11	-	-	-	-
7	51	4	8	6	12	-	-
8.1	1526	55	3	17	1	6	<1

Phase 2 – Initial medieval phase – pre-building features (c. 10th–12th centuries AD)

This small assemblage of 63 fragments came from a small group of pits and deposits which predated the construction of B5, pits under B1 and ditches deposits beneath B4. The assemblage is too small to make many observations about the distribution of material other than that the greatest proportion (37 fragments) came from the B5 area, the second greatest amount (23 fragments) from B4, and the least number of fragments from the area of B1 itself (6 fragments).

The 63 fragments of disarticulated and co-mingled bone were recovered from 15 Phase 2 contexts (Table 4.5), spread across pits, ditches, layers and deposits. Analysis did not indicate the presence of any concentrations of material or readily identifiable patterning in the deposition of species, limiting consideration of this type.

A total of 38% of the mammalian bone could be identified to species. 52% of the material scored as poor-average on bone condition, with 37% average, and 11% good. The material was generally fragmentary, and 21% of identified mammal bone comprised loose teeth. The species identified were cattle, sheep/goat, pig, and horse. Sheep/goat and cattle were the best represented, with only a single pig fragment. Both cattle and sheep/goat were derived from a minimum of two adult individuals (MNI 2). There was, however, a greater abundance of unidentified fragments which could be assigned to cattle-sized animals rather than sheep-sized animals. However, this may not indicate under-representation of cattle, rather that, larger bones suffered greater fragmentation. The handful of horse elements present only included a single metapodial fragment, so it is difficult to say whether it received similar treatment to cattle.

The assemblage was highly fragmented, with virtually all elements, where more than 80% of the bone was present, relating to a handful of tarsals and phalanges. There was no porous bone. No butchery was noted. In five examples there was indication of breakage of the bone when fresh, which may relate

to processing. This involved one cattle and four cattle-sized fragments. A total of six fragments had taphonomic changes, spread across five contexts in four locations. Three fragments were weathered and three gnawed; there were no burned fragments.

Phase 3 – The initial building phase (c. 13th century AD)

A total of 94 fragments of disarticulated and co-mingled bone were recovered from nine Phase 3 contexts. In Table 4.5 this has been divided into contexts directly associated with the construction and use of the initial suite of buildings (B1, B4 and B5), and contexts associated with the demolition of B5, and are referred to in tables as Phases 3.1 and 3.2 respectively. However, they are discussed below as one unified phase, given the chronological span over which the material is likely to have been derived and the small dataset. There was some variability in the amount of material represented between contexts, but this is largely associated with the volume of the original deposit. For example, the largest number of fragments was recovered from the rubble deposits related to the demolition of B5.

A total of 39% of Phase 3 material could be identified to species. 62% of the material scored as poor-average on bone condition, with 34% average and 4% average-good. This probably relates to the nature of the contexts themselves, where much of the material is likely to be re-deposited. Whilst the material was generally fragmentary, only 9% of identified mammal bone comprised loose teeth. The species identified were cattle, sheep/goat, sheep, and pig.

Butchery was noted on a total of four sheep/goat, cattle-sized, and sheep-sized fragments (3% of the total assemblage). A total of 12 fragments had taphonomic changes. Gnawing occurred at a rate of 5% of the assemblage, while there was no evidence of weathering. Burnt fragments accounted for 6% of the assemblage. There was a greater representation of fragments not identified to species amongst the burnt material, this most likely being a function of the burning process.

Phase 4 – The re-building phase (c. Late 13th–14th centuries AD)

A total of 29 fragments of disarticulated and co-mingled bone were recovered from two contexts directly associated with the construction of B2 (Table 4.5). Both of these were internal floors within the building. Eleven fragments could be identified to species. 24 out of 29 fragments scored as poor-average on bone condition, probably reflecting the type of context it was recovered from. Four out of 11 fragments identified to species were loose teeth. The species identified were cattle, sheep/goat, and pig. No butchery or evidence of breakage of the bone when fresh was noted. One unidentified mammal fragment was calcined.

Phase 3&4 – The use of the buildings (13th–14th centuries AD)

A total of 100 fragments of disarticulated and co-mingled bone were recovered from 15 Phase 3&4 contexts in Area 1 and 2 (the midden and field ditches), and from the upper fills of the enclosure ditch F85 in Area 3 (Table 4.5). The upper fills of F85 have been included as, although the ditch may have been excavated earlier, it was filling during the use of the site in Phase 3 and Phase 4. Many contexts (e.g. ditches, terrace etc) contained only a small number of fragments, whilst the majority of fragments came from the midden deposits.

A total of 48% of the material could be identified to species. 73% of the material scored as poor-average on bone condition, with 21% average. The material was generally fragmentary, with 15% of identified mammal bone comprising loose teeth. The species identified were cattle, sheep/goat, sheep, pig, dog, horse, and cat. Cattle were the most abundant livestock mammal by NISP with a lesser representation of sheep/goat and pig, although sheep/goat may be under-represented, having an MNI of two. The abundance of cattle is also reflected in the number of cattle-sized mammal fragments. Butchery was noted on a single cattle scapula, and there were no examples of breakage of the bone when fresh. A total of four fragments had taphonomic changes. Three fragments were gnawed, one weathered and one burnt.

Phase 5 – The demolition of the manorial buildings (c. 14th century AD)

A total of 212 fragments of disarticulated and co-mingled bone were recovered from 12 Period 5 contexts, all of which were rubble or deposits within these spreads (Table 4.5).

A total of 58% of the material could be identified to species. 47% of the material scored as poor-average on bone condition, with 45% average, and 8% average-good. The material was generally fragmentary, and 19% of identified mammal bone comprised loose teeth. The species identified were cattle (34% of NISP), sheep/goat (40%), sheep (2%), pig (15%), dog (1%), horse (7%), and cat (1%). Six bird bones were also identified including domestic fowl (NISP 3) and domestic goose (NISP 2). Sheep/goat were the most numerous livestock mammal by NISP (46% of the three main livestock species), with a lesser representation of cattle (37%) and pig (17%). The greater relative abundance of sheep/goat is also reflected in the minimum number of individuals, with sheep/goat originating from at least five animals, cattle from at least three animals and pig from at least three animals, suggesting under-representation of the latter in the NISP, which is not uncommon.

Butchery was noted on a total of five cattle, pig and cattle-sized fragments (2% of the whole assemblage). In eight examples breakage of the bone when fresh had taken place (4% of the total assemblage), with cattle, sheep/goat, and cattle-sized fragments involved. A total of 25 fragments had taphonomic changes (in one case more than one). Gnawing occurred at a rate of 8% of the assemblage, while weathering was rare (3%). There were no burnt fragments.

Phase 6 – Late medieval (c. 14th–16th centuries AD)

Only 18 fragments of disarticulated and co-mingled bone were recovered from three Period 6 contexts, all rubble deposits (Table 4.5). Six fragments could be identified to species, all of it sheep/goat, of which two were loose teeth, and which could have been contributed by a single individual. Two thirds of the material scored as poor-average on bone condition, with one third average. No butchery or deliberate fragmentation was noted. Two fragments, one of sheep/goat, one of cattle-sized mammal had been gnawed.

Phase 7 – Post-medieval (*c.* 17th–19th centuries AD)

A total of 51 fragments of disarticulated and co-mingled bone were recovered from six Period 7 contexts, all layers or rubble deposits overlying B3 and its surroundings (Table 4.5). Whilst these deposits were associated with what is most likely a post-medieval building, it is highly likely that the material is residual and probably derives from the earlier deposits over and surrounding B1. A total of 74% of the material could be identified to species. 27% of the material scored as poor-average on bone condition, with 60% average and 13% average-good. This may be a function of the small sample size or indicate that there was less residuality than assumed. Whilst the material was generally fragmentary, only 16% of identified mammal bone comprised loose teeth. The species identified were cattle, sheep/goat, sheep, pig, dog, horse, and cat. The assemblage was fragmented. Butchery was noted on a single sheep-sized mammal bone and there was a single example of breakage of the bone when fresh in a cattle-sized fragment. A total of nine fragments had taphonomic changes (in some cases more than one). Four fragments were gnawed and six fragments weathered, with no burned material. No pathological changes were noted.

Phase 8 – Clearance layers and modern deposits

Phase 8 encompasses material which was included in topsoil, clearance layers (Phase 8.1) and modern features (Phase 8.2). These have been separated out in Table 4.5. Material assigned to Phase 8.2 accounted for 146 fragments of animal bone which has been included in the quantification table, but not considered further. A total of 1526 fragments of disarticulated and co-mingled bone were recovered from 12 Period 8.1 clearance layers which covered Areas 1, 2 and 3.

A total of 41% of the material could be identified to species. 63% of the material scored as poor-average on bone condition, with 27% average, and 9% average-good which is similar to the material from more secure deposits discussed above. The material was generally fragmentary, and 28% of identified mammal bone comprised loose teeth. The species identified were cattle (29% of NISP excluding birds and fish), sheep/goat (45%), sheep (4%), pig (15%), dog (2%), horse (3%), and cat (1%), deer (<1%), hare (<1%), rabbit (<1%) and mole (<1%). Twenty-eight bird bones were also identified including domestic fowl (NISP 14), domestic goose (NISP 1), duck (NISP 3), godwit (NISP 1) and crow (NISP 1). In addition, there were 56 fragments of fish which are dealt with separately below. The majority of the identified mammal bone related to the three main livestock species (93%). Sheep/goat were the most numerous livestock mammal by NISP (53% of the three main livestock species), with a lesser representation of cattle (31%) and pig (16%). The greater relative abundance of sheep/goat is also reflected in the minimum number of individuals, with sheep/goat originating from at least 16 animals, and cattle and pig from at least seven animals each suggesting under-representation of the latter in the NISP, which is not uncommon.

The representation of elements between the three main livestock species is quite different, and whilst there may be some taphonomic reasons for this, it does appear that there may be some differences in the treatment of the three species which are discussed below. Butchery was noted on a total of 20 cattle, sheep/goat, pig and cattle-sized, sheep-sized and unidentified mammalian fragments (1% of the whole assemblage). In 26 examples breakage of the bone when fresh had taken place (2% of the total assemblage), which may relate to processing, with cattle, sheep/goat, and cattle-sized and sheep-sized fragments involved. A total of 74 fragments had taphonomic changes (in four cases more than one). Gnawing occurred at a rate of 4% of the assemblage, while weathering was rarer (1%) and burnt fragments infrequent (<1%). All but one of the burnt fragments were not identified to species, most likely a function of the burning process.

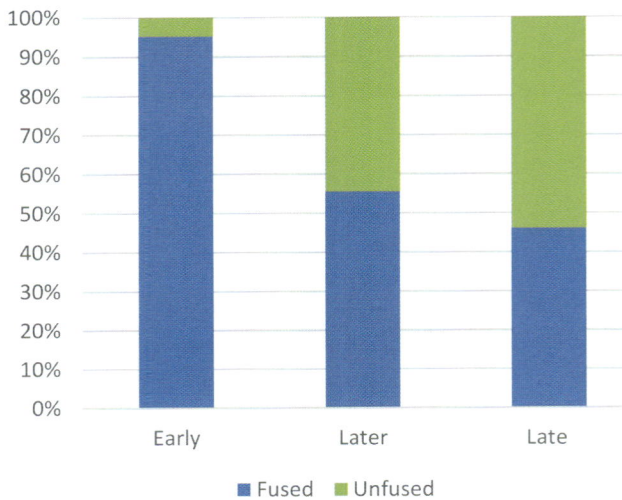

Fig. 4.3   Cattle fusion, Phase 8, N= 43.

Cattle

Cattle bone was present in all phases. Because of the fragmentary nature of the material only one withers height could be calculated, which came from the Phase 8 material. At 1.17m this was a modest sized animal, typical of the medieval period. Cattle bone displayed various taphonomic markers throughout the phases but the numbers are too small to make much comment.

Herd structure

There was very little porous bone present, only occurring in very small amounts in Phase 3&4, 4, 5 and 8. Aging information was limited throughout the phases with only four partial mandibles present, one in Phase 3&4 and three in Phase 8. The former had well-worn first and second molars. The three partial toothrows from Phase 8 all indicate adult animals, two of which were probably in the older category. Five loose third molars were also well worn. Two well-worn permanent fourth premolars were present, but no deciduous premolars suggesting that younger animals were not present in any number. The limited fusion data appears to support this. Only in the Phase 8 material could this be analysed but it also favoured older animals (Fig. 4.3). Almost half of assessable elements were fused in the early fusing category. However, animals of under 3 years of age are indicated by a number of unfused later fusing elements, and there are also unfused elements in the late fusing

category, suggesting that animals under four years may have been under-represented in the very limited toothwear data. The presence of porous bone suggests that young animals were present, but clearly the depositional and preservational conditions affected the assemblage. The presence of older animals conversely may indicate use of cattle as multi-purpose animals, including for traction. The lack of evidence of very young individuals under these depositional circumstances might not preclude dairying. No elements were complete enough to carry out an assessment of sex, which might have elucidated this.

Element representation and disposal

Consideration of element representation was similarly limited by small numbers of fragments in the better sealed and earlier phases; all that can be said is that all areas of the body were represented including the head, axial skeleton, limbs and feet. Phase 8 again provided the only opportunity to consider this but given the nature of the deposits from which the material came there was no benefit to comparing the contents of different contexts. Again, all areas of the body were represented (Fig. 4.4). There is some emphasis on the scapula and mandible, but these are robust and readily identifiable elements, so this is likely to be an artefact of the degree of fragmentation of the assemblage. However, there is no evidence that animals were not being slaughtered and processed on or near the site.

Butchery and carcase processing

Butchery marks and other indications of carcase processing were not common, but cattle and cattle-sized fragments displayed them most frequently in the assemblage. A range of cuts included light cuts, heavy and very heavy cuts (into or through the bone) and several examples of sawing. Only three examples occurred between Phases 2 and 7. Heavier cuts predominated, but the degree to which this observation relates to other taphonomic factors is hard to tell. In Phase 8 there were only two examples of butchery on cattle bone. A single heavy cut across the ascending ramus of a mandible, was probably associated with removing the head. A scapula had 13 closely spaced heavy cuts across the margin of the blade on the ventral aspect which clearly relates to portioning the carcase. Thirteen

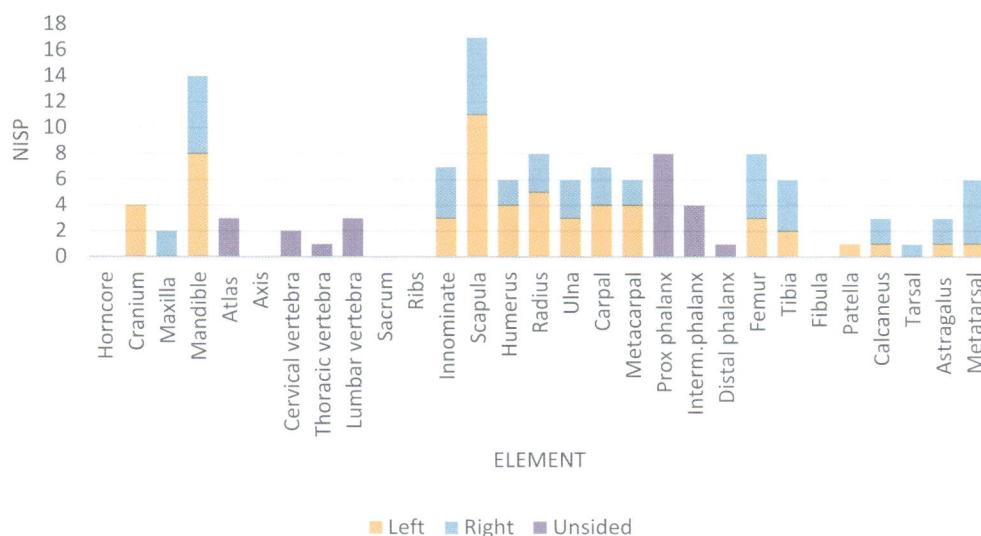

Fig. 4.4   Cattle element representation by NISP, Phase 8.

fragments of cattle-sized bone had butchery, eight of which were ribs. These displayed a range of cuts, from light and heavy cuts to three sawn examples. Whilst the former may indicate a more careful skinning and gutting of the animals, the latter may be post-medieval derived material. Fragmentation of bones when fresh was also only noted in a limited number of cases, although taphonomic explanations aside, this did seem to affect the larger animals to a greater degree and mainly involved limb bones.

Pathological changes

Only a handful of pathological changes were noted in cattle. In Phase 5 there was an example of surface roughening on the anterior distal shaft of a metatarsal. This potentially related to use for traction. In the Phase 8 material osteophytes had formed on the margin of the cranial border of a thoracic vertebral body. This was indicative of degenerative change but there was no indication of osteoarthritis. The infrequency of cattle vertebrae being recovered has resulted, in contrast to horses, in less understanding of how use in traction may have affected cattle (Bartosiewicz 2013), 142). It is possible that this change was related to use as a draught animal. However, where pathology in the spine has been related to traction, it is generally the lumbar spine which is involved (e.g. Fabiš 2005). It is therefore possible that this was a draught animal,

but also that the degeneration in the spine was the result of an accident. It may have been purely age related, given that there are indications of older animals in this assemblage.

Sheep/goat

Sheep/goat were identified in all phases and a total of 34 fragments, in Phases 2, 3&4, 5, 7 and 8 were positively identified as sheep. No goats were positively identified. No withers heights could be calculated.

Taphonomic factors

A scatter of sheep/goat fragments in Phase 2, Phase 3&4 and Phase 8 had been subjected to gnawing and weathering, whilst one example each, of gnawing and weathering occurred on sheep-sized mammal fragments only occurred in Phase 8.

Flock structure

Sexing information was only present in two cases. One Phase 5 innominate, was probably from a male. In Phase 8 a single innominate was probably from a female. Ageing information for sheep/goat was, like the other species, limited, particularly for the well-sealed and earlier phases. Porous bone was only identified in Phase 8. There were very few mandibles to provide information.

The wear data from one mandible in Phase 3&4 provided a Grant mandible wear stage and Payne stages of 45 and H (6–10 years of age). In Phase 5 two mandibles provided Grant mandible wear stage of 41 and Payne stages of E and G. Six loose mandibular teeth were all from the permanent dentition and worn, including a 3rd molar possibly at Payne stage G or greater. In Phase 7 one mandible was of an adult of 6–10 years. The wear data from two mandibles in Phase 8 provided a Grant mandible wear stage of 25 and Payne stages of D and estimated G/H. Loose 3rd mandibular molars were also assessed from Phase 8 (Fig. 4.5) and whilst this suggests a wider range of ages there is still a fair emphasis on older animals. The representation of younger animals appears to be genuinely low as only three deciduous fourth molars were recorded. There were only four fragments of porous sheep/goat bone.

The fusion data from the earlier phases was also limited, with no unfused elements present. In the Phase 8 material there was however an emphasis on older animals (Fig. 4.6). Virtually all of the early fusing elements were fused, more than 80% of later fusing and 70% of the latest fusing. The lack of loose deciduous teeth does seem to imply that this is a genuine pattern, and older sheep were more frequent. Whilst some animals were apparently dying or being culled at an age where they had achieved a meat weight, the suspicion has to be that the motivation for maintenance of older animals was secondary products, most likely wool.

Element representation and disposal

In the earlier phases only a limited range of body parts were represented, with good representation of loose teeth and limb bones, probably because these are robust. The smaller selections of elements in these phases represented most parts of the body. Considering the Phase 8 material, most parts of the body were represented (Fig. 4.7) but, many elements, particularly those of the axial skeleton and extremities, only occurred in small numbers. There was an emphasis on limb bones. These are more robust, but there was an absence of other similarly robust elements, for example mandibles. There was however a fair representation of loose teeth. These inconsistencies may suggest that some sheep/goat were being slaughtered and processed elsewhere.

Butchery and carcass processing

Evidence of butchery and fragmentation was very limited in sheep/goat fragments. This is often the case as a smaller carcase requires less dividing than a larger animal. However, out of the handful of elements from four phases, the majority of these were heavy cuts which occurred across limb bone shafts in Phases 2 and 3 and a Phase 7 sheep-sized rib. These appear to relate to portioning the carcases, and there is no evidence that the approach changed over time. There was limited evidence of fragmentation of fresh bone, as in cattle suggesting that full utilisation of the carcase was as important in the smaller livestock.

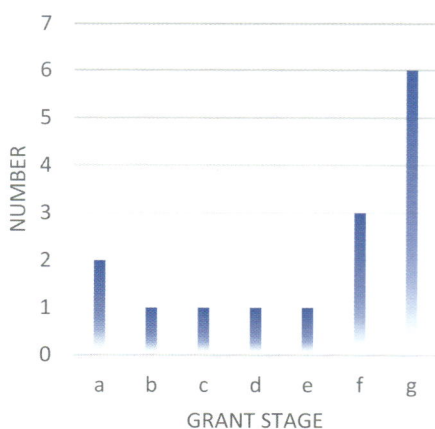

Fig. 4.5   Sheep/goat mandibular 3rd molar wear, Phase 8, N= 15.

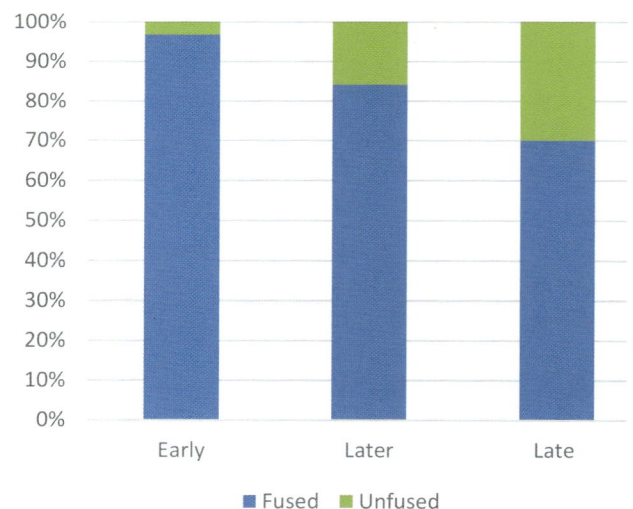

Fig. 4.6   Sheep/goat fusion, Phase 8, N=70.

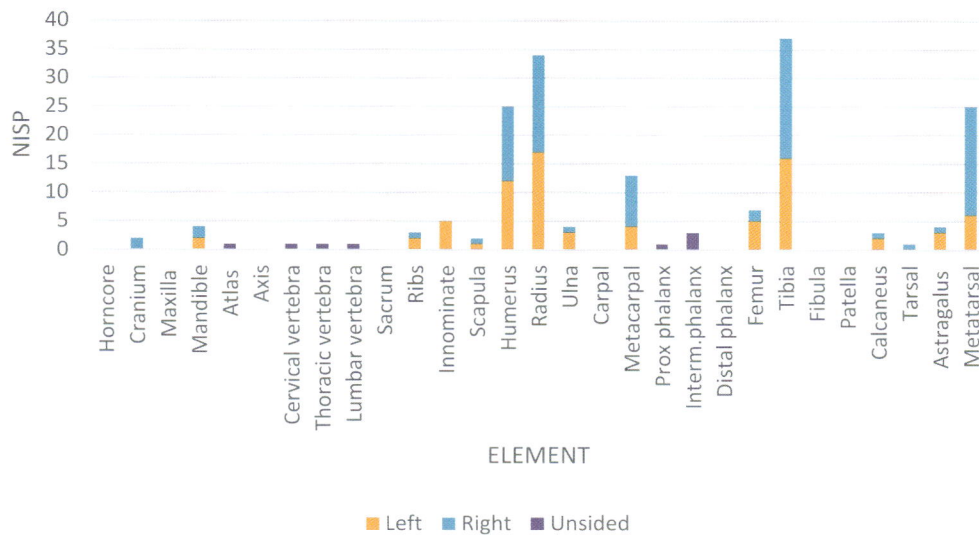

Fig. 4.7 Sheep/goat element representation, Phase 8.

Pathological changes

A handful of elements displayed pathological changes all from the Phase 8 material. One metacarpal had changes indicative of osteitis in the shaft representing a non-specific infection. Two humeri showed changes to the distal articulation normally referred to as penning elbow. This is a degenerative change possibly associated with walking or standing on hard surfaces (Baker and Brothwell 1980) but may also be age related and is not surprising in relation to the flock profile outlined above.

Pig

Pig only contributed a very small number of fragments in many of the Phases which has seriously limited what can be said about their husbandry or consumption. Pig bone was available to dogs in Phases 3, 5 and 8 with gnawed fragments present. There were a handful of weathered fragments

Herd structure

Information on the age of pigs is minimal throughout all phases, with very few toothwear data. There was little porous bone, which included two fragments each in Phases 7 and 8. For the earlier periods there was a scattering of fused and unfused elements. Phase 8 again provides the most complete information. There were few mandibles which could provide age information, but those which could be assessed or

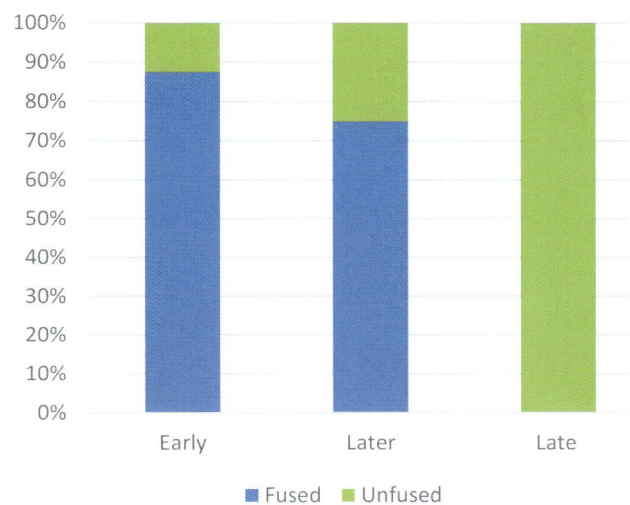

Fig. 4.8 Pig fusion, Phase 8, N=22.

estimated included one sub-adult and three young adults. However, the fusion data (Fig. 4.8), with no fused examples of the latest fusing elements supports a typical profile for pigs where the majority of individuals are culled for meat before full skeletal maturity is achieved. Of the four Phase 8 lower canines which could be considered in relation to the sex of the animals, three out of four were female and one male.

Element representation and disposal

Where pig was present in the earlier phases,

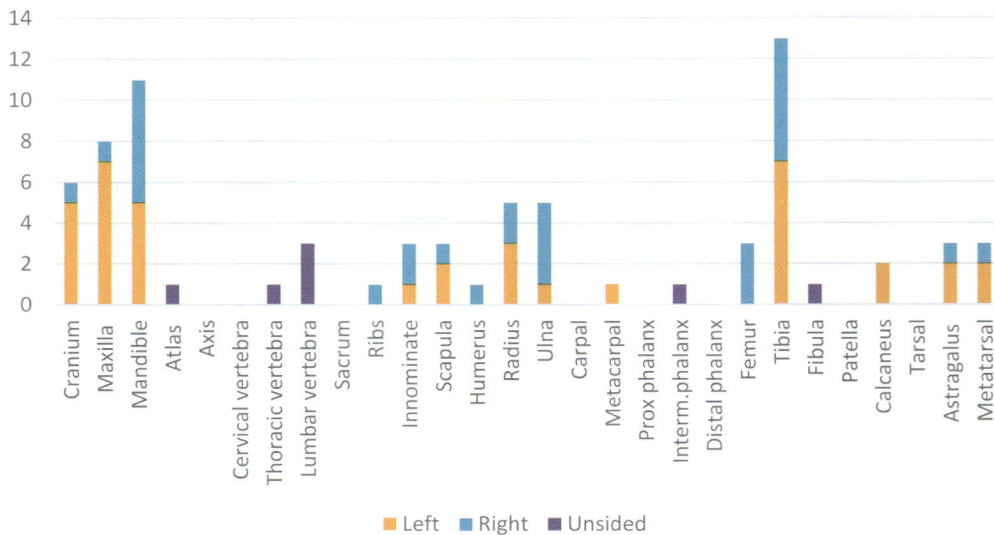

Fig. 4.9   Pig element representation, Phase 8.

the elements were limited to the head, the axial skeleton, and limbs. Lack of some peripheral elements is likely to be related to recovery bias. These elements are similar in size to those in sheep/goat which had similar representation of phalanges and other small elements. All parts of the pig carcase were represented in Phase 8 (Fig. 4.9). The tibia was particularly well represented, and this may be a function of the robustness of this bone. However, unlike sheep/goat, there was good representation of head and other peripheral elements. This evidence may be an indication that pigs were slaughtered and processed on or near the site.

Butchery and carcase processing
Related to its limited general representation, very few pig bones showed signs of butchery. Two fragments were affected in Phase 5 which consisted of heavy cuts to the ventral surface of a scapula related to jointing, and a very heavy cut through the distal joint of a tibia indicative of initial trimming of the carcase. In Phase 8 a single pig bone showed a single very heavy cut across the iliac ramus, presumably related to disarticulation and jointing. No pig elements showed evidence of fragmentation when fresh.

Pathological changes
Pathological changes were only seen in three Phase

8 pig elements. One tibia displayed a cushion of new bone which united the distal tibia shaft with a fragment of fibula. This possibly represented a non-specific infection consequent to a fracture. These types of injuries are not uncommon in pig populations and can be caused by tethering or methods of handling involving holding the hind limb (Bartosiewicz 2013, 77–78). The unfused distal growth plate of a tibia and a radius from context (301) displayed periostitis and changes to the morphology of the bone indicative of a non-specific infection. This may also have been concomitant to injury or resulted from a systemic infection, but it seems likely that these two elements came from the same individual.

Horse
Five fragments of horse bone were recovered from Phase 2 contexts, distributed across three pits (F77, F78 and F108) and a deposit (13-120). A large portion of left innominate and an astragalus came from pit F78. Other elements were a fragment of metapodial, a first phalanx and mandibular tooth. All of these fragments were consistent with at least one adult animal. Given the concentration in one location and intercutting between features, these fragments may have been originally related but re-deposited. Of eight horse bones in Phase 5, six came from the same context (601) within B1. The axial skeleton was

represented by two elements; there was a single loose tooth. The rest of the elements related to the lower limb and foot. A fused acetabulum represented an animal of more than 18–24 months of age. A fused distal metacarpal came from an animal of at least 20–24 months and a fused calcaneus an animal of more than 36 months. These could all relate to one animal. Another younger animal is suggested by an unfused vertebral body. There was no evidence for butchery or processing of horse for consumption.

Dog

Dog was represented by a handful of fragments in four phases, Phase 3&4, 5, 7 and 8. In most cases only adult individuals were suggested, although in Phase 5 dog was represented by a single element from a juvenile individual. Eleven Phase 8 dog bones were recovered from a minimum of two dogs, an adult and a juvenile. In this case one bone was porous, a mandible with the first molar erupting. Dogs are more widely represented in the assemblage by evidence of gnawing on other bones.

Cat

A few cat bones were recovered in four phases. In Phase 3&4 three cat elements came from one context. In Phase 5 cat was represented by a single element. These were all from adults but the one cat bone from Phase 7 was a tibia which was unfused proximally. Six cat bones in Phase 8 were contributed by at least one adult and one juvenile individual.

Wild species

A very limited selection of wild mammals was recovered, with all of the identified examples coming from Phase 8 contexts. A single fragment of deer tibia and one hare radius came from deposits over B1 whilst single rabbit, rat and three mole bones came from context (801) over B4. All of the latter could be intrusive as a result of burrowing, whilst the former suggest a minimal number of hunted animals reaching the site.

The birds

Both domestic and wild birds were identified in four

phases, Phase 3, 3&4, 5 and 8. Three bird bones were recovered from Phase 3 deposits (12-114) and (12-116) contemporary with B5 and from F79. One was the ulna of a goose, of a size consistent with a domestic bird. A juvenile tarsometarsus was not identified to species but was feasibly from a domestic fowl. A right tarsometatarsus of a juvenile goose occurred in Phase 3&4. As the bone was not fully formed it was not possible to determine if this was likely to be a wild or domestic bird. Of the six Phase 5 bird bones three were domestic fowl, one of which was male and two goose, of domestic size. Twenty-eight bird bones were also recovered from Phase 8 which seem to confirm the dependence on domestic species. Fourteen bones were contributed by domestic fowl, three of which were juveniles. Seven were of similar size to, or just slightly larger than, a bantam. No indication of the sex of birds such as spurs or medullary bone was noted. There was also one domestic goose bone. Of the three duck bones, one was similar in size to teal, one mallard, and one of a size between the two. There was no indication of domestic ducks. Wild species were poorly represented with a single godwit and single crow bone. The godwit (*Limosa limosa*) is a large wading bird, and it is possible that this wetland bird was exploited rather than incidental. The crow (*Corvus* spp.) is probably an incidental inclusion. No butchery or taphonomic changes were noted on the bird bone.

Material from sieved samples

Animal bone was recovered from samples from nine contexts from Phase 2, Phase 3 and contexts treated as Phase 3&4 (as described above). The taphonomic information provided by this material (including a discussion of the incidence of the unidentifiable material) is detailed above, and unidentifiable material excluded here.

A total of 2,142 fragments were identified as domestic mammal (and mammal bone of either cattle-sized or sheep-sized animals), small wild mammals, domestic and wild birds, amphibians, and fish (Table 4.9). Three of the sampled contexts produced bone where none had been recovered in the hand collected assemblage. However, these three contexts only produced a total of 14 fragments which might reasonably have been expected to be collected by hand (e.g. sheep-sized mammal rib

Table 4.9 Wet sieved assemblage.

Species	Pit F76 (13-105) NISP/No	Pit F78 (13-110) NISP/No	Pit F107 (13-131) NISP/No	Pit F110 (13-137) NISP/No	Ditch F98 (9-131) NISP/No	Ditch F99 (9-133) NISP/No	Total NISP/No	Deposit (12-114) NISP/No	Ditch F80 (13-112) NISP/No	Total NISP/No	Midden (10-108) NISP/No
Cattle	-	1	1	-	-	-	2	-	-	-	1
Sheep/Goat	4	4	1	-	3	-	12	-	-	-	11
Pig	1	-	-	-	-	-	1	-	-	-	-
Dog	-	-	-	1	-	-	1	-	-	-	-
Domestic total	*5*	*5*	*2*	*1*	*3*	*-*	*17*	*-*	*-*	*-*	*12*
Rat	-	-	-	-	-	-	-	-	-	-	1
Mouse	-	-	-	-	-	-	-	-	-	-	1
Mouse (*Apodemus* spp.)	-	-	-	-	1	-	1	-	-	-	2
Vole	-	1	1	-	-	-	2	-	-	-	7
Bank vole (*Myodes glareolus*)	-	-	-	-	-	-	-	-	-	-	1
Field Vole (*Microtus agrestis*)	-	-	-	-	1	-	1	-	-	-	5
Unidentified small mammal	4	4	1	6	18	3	36	8	3	11	70
Wild Total	*4*	*5*	*2*	*6*	*20*	*3*	*40*	*8*	*3*	*11*	*87*
Domestic fowl	1	1	-	-	-	-	2	-	-	-	2
Thrush (*Turdus* spp.)	-	-	2	-	-	-	2	-	-	-	3
Redwing (*Turdus iliacus*)	-	-	-	-	-	-	-	1	-	1	-
Tit or finch	-	-	1	-	-	-	1	-	-	-	3
Unidentified bird	-	-	8	-	1	-	9	-	1	1	3
Bird total	*1*	*1*	*11*	*-*	*1*	*-*	*13*	*1*	*1*	*2*	*11*
Frog (*Rana temporaria*)	19	-	-	-	1	1	21	-	-	-	-
Unidentified Amphibian	392	5	2	1	6	2	408	-	-	-	3
Amphibian Total	*411*	*5*	*2*	*1*	*7*	*3*	*429*	*-*	*-*	*-*	*3*
Fish total	*4*	*13*	*131*	*3*	*16*	*13*	*180*	*47*	*19*	*66*	*452*
Large mammal	-	2	-	-	-	-	2	-	-	-	1
Medium mammal	4	9	-	-	1	-	14	3	1	4	20
Unidentified Total	*4*	*11*	*-*	*-*	*1*	*-*	*16*	*3*	*1*	*4*	*21*
Main total	*429*	*40*	*148*	*11*	*48*	*19*	*695*	*59*	*24*	*83*	*586*

fragments). In general, the larger fragments reflect the species in the hand collected assemblage, and includes smaller elements and teeth, suggesting that the general recovery rate of the hand collected material was good. There was some variation in the species represented between periods and contexts, although the variation is more likely to depend on context type than date. Most positively identified species occurred in very small numbers which will not support a great deal of analysis. The fish are discussed separately.

Phase 2

695 fragments came from six Phase 2 contexts, in four pits under B5 and two in ditch contexts beneath B4. The species represented were cattle, sheep/goat, pig and dog; mouse (*Apodemus* spp.) and field vole (*Microtis agrestis*); domestic fowl, songbirds (*Turdus* spp.) and a single tit or finch bone; frog and fish. The ditches contained a selection of domestic mammal, small mammal, bird, fish and amphibian bones, but there were clear concentrations of material in two of the pits. Pit F76 contained 411 amphibian bones in is basal context (13-105). Pit F107 contained 131 fish bones and scales.

Phase 3

Two contexts associated with the construction and use of B5 produced 83 fragments of small mammals, bird and fish. Few species were positively identified; small mammals, redwing (*Turdus iliacus*) and fish were represented.

Phase 3&4

All of the material came from a series of samples from the extensive midden deposit (10-108). The species represented were cattle and sheep/goat; rat, mouse (*Apodemus* spp.), bank vole (*Clethrionomys glareolus*), field vole (*Microtis agrestis*); domestic fowl, songbirds (*Turdus* spp.) and three of either tit or finch; amphibian and fish.

Discussion of the small vertebrates and birds from sieved material

The small vertebrates are represented by a selection of rodents and frog. A single rat molar was recovered from the midden deposits but could not be speciated. Considerable amounts of post-cranial bone from all deposits were of mouse or vole size. A single example from Phase 2 contexts and two fragments from the midden could be identified as wood/field mouse (*Apodemus* spp.). Several voles were also identified, but only two could be speciated. A field vole (*Microtus agrestis*) tooth came from one of the Phase 2 ditches and five from the midden, whilst a single bank vole (*Myodes glareolus*) tooth came from the Phase 3&4 midden.

As these species burrow, there is potential for these elements to be intrusive, although this seems less likely in the Phase 2 deposits. If contemporary with the medieval deposits, these are all species which would be present in an agricultural landscape, but they are not present in the numbers needed to infer anything about the environment. The amphibian bone which has been identified to species was all frog (*Rana temporaria*). In pit F76, there were numerous juvenile amphibian bones, and it seems likely that this material related to frogs in some number, implying a consistently damp, if not waterlogged base to this feature.

The birds represented in these samples included a few additional domestic fowl bones, adding this species to the list of domesticates present on the site in Phase 2. A number of elements of the blackbird/thrush family (*Turdus* spp.) came from both the Phase 2 pits and the Phase 3&4 midden. A redwing (*Turdus iliacus*) carpometacarpus in context (12-114) represents the smallest of the thrush family, being a winter visitor to Britain. There were also a handful of tit or finch sized bird elements from the two periods. These are most likely incidental inclusions.

Discussion

The Putton assemblage clearly has some considerable limitations, not only in identified numbers per phase but in the way that the contexts which the material was contained within derived. However, in the absence of any other assemblage of this type and date within Dorset, it has a degree of significance. As a large proportion of the Phase 5 demolition deposits and the majority of the Phase 8 material were likely derived from the main phase of habitation, we can consider it as a broad indicator of the local animal economy. Clearly the main livestock species were the most significant contributors to the assemblage and most likely the manorial economy and household diet. This was predominantly cattle and sheep, with pigs as a limited meat supply. Whilst the taphonomic issues with the assemblage have been well rehearsed above, it does appear that older cattle were more common, though less so than for sheep. In the former case it may be related to milk production and use as draught animals, whilst in the latter case, wool production is the most likely explanation. Pigs had a typically 'younger' profile reflecting their sole use for meat. They tend to be more problematic to keep but are useful at a household level, fed scraps.

There is a difference in the element distribution visible in the Phase 8 material between cattle and pig, where all parts of the carcase were represented, and sheep/goat where there is an emphasis on limb bones. It might be cautiously suggested that whereas cattle and pig were culled and butchered (and presumably kept) close to the point of consumption and disposal, there is a possibility that a proportion of sheep/goat were not, and sheep meat may have been brought to the manorial centre from elsewhere in the hinterland. The lack of wild species is striking. The only examples of hare and red deer occurred in Phase 8 material, but were clearly a minor element, possibly reflecting the middling status of the site. The lack of wild species was also seen within the bird assemblage. This was dominated by chicken and to a lesser extent goose, both commonly kept food birds from the early medieval period onward (Yalden and Albarella 2009, 130). Some of the geese may be wild, but it was unclear. The only wild probable food bird is represented by a single godwit bone. This wading bird would have been readily available in wetlands around the fringes of the Fleet. Greater proportions of domestic birds and pigs have been associated with higher status medieval sites, as have larger numbers of wild species. Whereas chicken and geese are relatively well attested, pig was clearly the least abundant livestock and hunted wild species almost non-existent. This might imply a relatively well provisioned settlement, but one without high pretensions.

Detailed comparison with other sites is limited by the number of medieval assemblages recovered within the county. Limited material at Melbury Abbas included cattle, sheep and pig bone with some dog and horse, but this was not quantified (Serjeantson

1993). Records of the 12th century for Melbury mention pigs, a cow or draught animal and a heifer. Sheep are not mentioned, but there was a shepherd, and the demesne staff included a dairyman (Ross 1993, 113). Excavation at Hooke Court only produced a handful of bones from the medieval deposits, but included cattle, sheep/goat, pig and dog (Wessex Archaeology 2006). At Ower Farm on the southern side of Poole Harbour the 12th to early 13th century midden contained cattle and sheep (Hamilton-Dyer 1991). Close to Putton, the very small assemblage from 13th–14th century deposits at Curtis Fields, Weymouth included cattle, sheep/goat, pig, horse and dog (Randall 2019, 95). Faunal remains of the medieval phase at Manor Farm, Portesham were limited to a few cattle and sheep/goat fragments and most material contributed by the remains of a juvenile pig (Sykes 2003). There are some similarities between Putton and the 12th–14th century midden at the Museum of Jurassic Marine Life at Kimmeridge, which may have related to a manor. There, cattle were the most abundant species with sheep/goat the next most abundant. Pig was poorly represented, with a few horse, dog and domestic fowl bones. The cattle were generally adult with few young animals, as were the sheep/goat. At Kimmeridge the butchery appeared to involve the systematic use of cleavers, whilst the sheep/goat were of similar sizes to animals of a similar period in Somerset (Coles 2018).

The relative status of manors can be considered by looking at Sutton Poyntz. Bone included cattle, sheep, pig and horse, but interestingly, there was more pig than sheep or cattle (Hamilton-Dyer 2007, 83-4). Pig has been regarded elsewhere as an elite food during this period. A high relative abundance of pig occurred at the moated manor of Mount House, Witney, Oxfordshire, related to the high status of the site (Ayres and Serjeantson 2002, 178). The assemblage at Sutton Poyntz also had cat, dog, hare and rat, but also a high proportion of domestic fowl as well as goose and ducks and a fragment of guillemot (Hamilton-Dyer 2007, 83). This emphasis on domestic birds may indicate the status of the inhabitants. At Kingston Lacy the small assemblage was very diverse. The assemblage included the main livestock species and chicken, a single example of fallow deer, hare and rabbit, goose, duck, pigeon and moorhen as well as probably incidental inclusions of

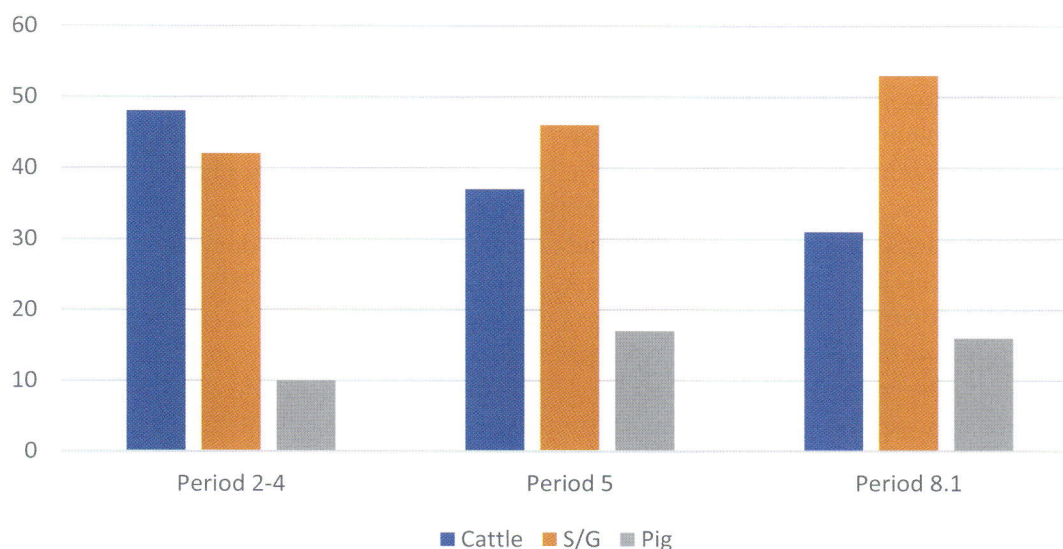

Fig. 4.10 Comparison of main three species, Phase 2–4 (N=103), 5 (N=110) and 8 (N=587).

jackdaw and crow (Locker 1998). Kingston Lacy was a higher status manor, with regular royal connections. However, the proportion of birds at Sutton Poyntz was also in keeping with a site of higher status (Hamilton-Dyer 2007, 83-4). It was a manor of some importance in the local hierarchy, which may explain the proportion of pig and bird bones there. Putton seems to have the domestic birds, and not the pigs, so we may be beginning to glimpse some subtle gradations within the status of individual manors.

It is worth comparing these rural sites with urban assemblages. Faunal remains from 12th–14th century deposits at Greyhound Yard, Dorchester, were dominated by domestic livestock, although cattle and sheep were the most abundant, and pig particularly poorly represented (Maltby 1993, 339). The sheep/goat remains in the Greyhound Yard medieval assemblage were from older animals than in the Romano-British deposits probably reflecting the greater importance of wool production in this period (Maltby 1993, 339). Material from the 15th century boat building site at The Foundry, Poole (Watkins 1994) produced an animal bone assemblage dominated by the three main livestock species, of which cattle were the most abundantly represented, followed by sheep and pig, and which had a negligible wild component of a handful of examples of roe and fallow deer, rabbit bone and domestic fowl (Bourdillon 1994, 76). Whilst calves were present, with older cattle, there were

few young sheep suggesting that they originated in a wool producing economy, whilst typically pigs were young adults having reached a meat weight (Bourdillon 1994, 82). Combined data for a number of medieval sites in Poole confirm the dominance of the main three livestock species, with cattle the most abundant by NISP followed by sheep/goat and narrowly pig. There was a significant number of rabbit bones, whilst bird bone was dominated by domestic fowl and goose, then wild ducks and a small number of mainly wetland species (Coy 1992, 187-8) as might be expected in that location. Comparison between rural and urban assemblages currently shows limited differences between them. There is clearly more to understand about the nature of supply from country to town.

Taking the limitations of the Putton assemblage into account, there is a potential alteration in the relative abundance of livestock over time, although it is not so clear at what point the change may have occurred. By aggregating the data of Phases 2 through to 4, which together represent the construction of the original manorial plan, its rebuilding and use, comparison can be made with the larger assemblage from Phase 5, the demolition deposits, and Phase 8 which probably derives from them. These presumably related to the later period of use of the site. There appears to be some contrast between Phases 2–4 and the other two assemblages (Fig. 4.10). Pig remained a minority in all three cases, but there does appear to be a shift from a greater relative abundance of cattle in Phases 2–4, to sheep/goat in Period 5 and Period 8. If we regard the earlier phases as having formed in the 12th–13th centuries, whilst the other material relates to the 13th–14th centuries, this would coincide with an increasing trend towards sheep husbandry in Dorset and more widely during this period. This shift to a more sheep-based economy is of no surprise against the backdrop of what we know about general changes in Dorset's agricultural economy during the medieval period. However, the possible emphasis on cattle in the earlier phases may have a bearing on the interpretation of certain land division features (see Chapter 1) and is discussed in Chapter 6.

THE FISH, By Clare Randall

Introduction

No fish bones were hand collected from any of the sealed features or deposits. A total of 56 hand collected fish bones (Table 4.10) came from Phase 8 context (801) overlying the north side of B4. A cod vertebra came from context (301) overlying Area 3 and a ballan wrasse vertebra from the area near B6. Of the hand collected fish bones, 42 were unidentified to species, the majority being rays, spine and rib fragments. The identified elements came from seabream, john dory, sea scorpion, brill, mackerel, sole and a ray. These are all coastal species which are well documented nearby.

In addition, 698 fragments of fish bone or scales were recovered from sieved samples from nine contexts relating to Phase 2, Phase 3 and Phase 3&4. The fact that fish remains occurred in all sampled contexts indicates that they were probably originally ubiquitous and most likely made a significant contribution to the diet. However, most of the material came from ribs and rays whilst other bones and scales were fragmentary, which has limited identification to species. It is therefore unclear as to whether there was targeting of particular species.

In Phase 2 eight fragments were identified to species. The species represented were seabream, wrasse, plaice and herring. As well as the limited numbers

of head elements and vertebra there were 100 scales or partial scales and 45 ribs or rays. This suggests that the fish may have been reaching the site already cleaned and filleted, explaining the remnants of skin and ribcage and fins. In Phase 3 eight fragments were identified to species. The species represented were seabream and john dory. The elements included some scales and ribs/rays, but not with the same emphasis as in Phase 2. A total of 34 elements were identified to species from the various samples of the Phase 3&4 midden. The greater number reflects the greater volume sampled, but there was a total of 452 fragments, with 155 ribs/rays and 182 scales or partial scales, which may indicate similar practices as reflected in Phase 2. The species represented were similar, including seabream (10 examples), wrasse (9 examples), john dory, plaice, sole, scad, cod, and ray or skate. The increased range of species is highly likely to be related to the increased number of fragments recovered. There does however seem to be a degree of emphasis on wrasse and seabream in this phase.

Species represented

Seabream

Seabream or probable seabream were represented in all sampled phases. These could be narrowed down to species in a limited number of cases. Probable black bream was identified in Phase 2 and the Phase 3&4 midden. Probable gilthead seabream (*Sparus aurata*) came from the latter. This is a generally sedentary and solitary fish, which lives on shellfish, and whilst normally found at *c.* 30m, occurs in deeper water and also in brackish coastal lagoons when feeding. Black Bream (*Spondyliosoma cantharu*) is a fish which prefers warmer conditions and is distributed around the south coast, retreating to deeper water in the winter. It feeds on small crustaceans, shellfish, other invertebrates and marine vegetation.

Wrasse

Wrasse or probable wrasse were represented in Phase 2, Phase 3&4 and Phase 8. Two species of wrasse are the most significant in British waters, ballan wrasse and cuckoo wrasse. Both live in rocky areas and are adapted to feed on shellfish and crustaceans. They also tend to live in relatively shallow water and are rarely found offshore. Examples were identified as

Table 4.10 Fish, wet sieved and hand collected.

Species	Phase 2 (Sieved) NISP/No	Contexts	Phase 3 (Sieved) NISP/No	Contexts	Phase 3&4 Midden (Sieved) NISP/No	Contexts	Phase 8.1 Clearance (Hand collected) NISP/No	Contexts
?Seabream	1	1	-	-	1	1	-	-
cf Seabream	1	1	7	1	6	1	2	1
cf ?Black seabream	1	1	-	-	2	1	-	-
cf ?Gilthead seabream	-	-	-	-	1	1	-	-
?Wrasse	2	1	-	-	2	1	-	-
cf Wrasse	1	1	-	-	5	1	-	-
cf ?Ballan wrasse	1	1	-	-	2	1	1	1
cf Plaice	1	1	-	-	4	1	-	-
cf Sole	-	-	-	-	1	1	1	1
cf Brill	-	-	-	-	-	-	1	1
?Herring	1	1	-	-	-	-	-	-
? John dory	-	-	-	-	1	1	-	-
cf John dory	-	-	1	1	2	1	5	1
cf Sea scorpion	-	-	-	-	-	-	1	1
cf mackerel	-	-	-	-	-	-	1	1
?Scad	-	-	-	-	1	1	-	-
?Cod	-	-	-	-	1	1	1	1
Ray or skate	-	-	-	-	2	1	1	1
ID total	*8*	-	*8*	-	*31*	-	*14*	-
Otolith	5	-	1	-	1	-	-	-
Scales	100	-	9	-	182	-	-	-
Rib/rays	45	-	26	-	155	-	15	-
Other unidentified	21	-	22	-	83	-	27	-
Total	*180*		*66*		*452*		*56*	

probable ballan wrasse in Phase 2, Phase 3&4 and Phase 8. The ballan wrasse (*Labrus bergylta*) are the biggest and most common wrasse around the British coast, although they are in modern times most common along the south and south west coasts. They can grow up to 9lbs in weight.

Flatfish

Plaice were identified in Phase 2 and Phase 3&4. Sole was identified in Phase 3&4 and Phase 8. Brill was identified in Phase 8. These flatfish all occur widely as coastal species. Plaice (*Pleuronectes platessa*) is found from spring to early autumn on muddy, sandy and shingle seabeds, feeding on marine worms, crustaceans and shellfish. It spends the winter months in deeper waters. The sole could not be identified to species and could be either Dover sole (*Solea solea*) or Lemon sole (*Microstomus kitt*). However, whilst both live on stony, mixed and sandy seabeds, lemon sole are less frequently available from the shore, preferring colder, deeper waters. Dover sole are common on sand and shingle beds along the Channel coast, feeding on marine worms, prawns and invertebrates, as well as molluscs and crustaceans. Brill (*Scophthalmus rhombus*) is a large flatfish, often found on the south coast and around the south west preferring sandy, muddy or shingle seabeds. It feeds on prawns, marine worms, crustaceans and occasionally other fish. It prefers to avoid very shallow waters, except when spawning in spring, generally living just offshore in water at least 10m deep.

Herring

A single example of herring was seen in the Phase 2 deposits. Herring (*Clupea harengus*) is a pelagic species found around the British Isles, although it generally prefers colder waters where it filter feeds on plankton and minute sea creatures, as well as the fry of other fish. It is infrequently caught from the shore but is a useful bait species due to its oiliness (britishseafishing.co.uk). Herring was often preserved and shipped long distances from the 11th century onward (Kowaleski 2016).

John dory

John dory or probable john dory was seen in Phases 3, the Phase 3&4 midden, and Phase 8. John dory (*Zeus faber*) is a generally solitary demersal fish which prefers warmer waters at depths ranging from a few metres to several hundred metres and feeds on small fish.

Sea scorpion (or Bullrout)

An example of sea scorpion (*Myoxocephalus scorpius*) was recovered from Phase 8. It is common around the British Isles, generally living in deep water and feeding on other fish. They are generally around 1lb in weight, and feed on the sea bottom.

Mackerel

A single mackerel element was recovered from Phase 8. The mackerel (*Scomber scombrus*) is common throughout British waters in the summer. It is a pelagic fish which feeds on small fish and sandeels. It can be caught easily from the shore and is a good bait fish due to its oily flesh (britishseafishing.co.uk).

Scad (or Horse mackerel)

One element from a probable scad came from the Phase 3&4 midden. The scad (*Rachurus trachurus*) is common in the south and west of Britain during the summer months and will feed on a wide range of prey focussing on small fish, sandeels and squid. They occur at all levels of the water, moving into shallow water in the summer months.

Cod

A single cod vertebra came from the midden material (Phase 3&4) and from a Phase 8 deposit. Cod (*Gadus morhua*) are common around Britain, although they move into cooler waters during the summer months. They are almost omnivorous, consuming worms, prawns, shellfish, crabs, lobsters, octopus and smaller fish. They can be caught from shingle beaches (britishseafishing.co.uk).

Ray/skate

Dermal denticles of ray or skate were recovered from the midden (Phase 3&4) and Phase 8. There are a number of rays which are common in British waters on sandy, muddy and shingle seabed, but not particularly close to shores. This includes the common skate (*Dipturus batis*), and thornback ray (*Raja clavata*) and on the south coast the common stingray (*Dasyatis pastinaca*). They will eat crustaceans and crabs as well as small fish, especially flatfish. As they are cartilaginous the dermal denticles are the only element generally recovered.

Discussion

The species represented indicate a clear emphasis on the exploitation of coastal species. Many of these could have been obtained from the Fleet which borders the southern part of the Putton manor (see Chapter 5). The Fleet is a narrow lagoon, which lies between the shingle ridge of Chesil Beach and the mainland shore. It is 13 km long and opens to the sea at a narrow marine gap into what is now Portland Harbour, within Wyke Regis at Smallmouth. Its other extremity is at Abbotsbury. Wrasse prefer rocky shores, but many of the other species prefer the relatively shallow waters common around this part of the Dorset coast. Some of the species represented in small numbers (e.g. cod, herring) are generally thought of as pelagic coldwater fish, but these will all venture into local waters on a seasonal basis. There is therefore no evidence of fish being brought in from further afield. The species are all easily available and abundant locally and could be obtained from the shore or from inshore boats. The numbers of identified fragments are not great enough to identify any specific target species. Some of the least abundant species are seasonally present, so there may have been greater exploitation of fish during the summer months.

It is possible to speculate further as to the degree to which species would have been obtainable directly from the manorial shoreline (Fig. 4.11). In the later 20th century, a wide range of species occurred within the Fleet. Many were regularly associated with the weed and rocks present within its lower reaches, to which Putton had direct access. This included several species of wrasse (including ballan wrasse), and sea scorpion. Seabream (both black bream and gilthead seabream) and herring seem to have probably entered the mouth of the Fleet as larvae. Flatfish such as flounder occurred throughout the Fleet's length (Bass 1986). However, mackerel, scad, cod, ray and john dory do not appear to have been recorded. This potentially suggests that during the medieval period these came from beyond the confines of the Fleet lagoon. If this was the case, fishing beyond the Chesil Bank is likely. This may have taken place by line or nets from the shore or by boats accessing Weymouth Bay through the mouth of the Fleet at Wyke Regis.

There are few medieval fish bone assemblages from the local area to which Lower Putton Lane can be compared, but there are some suggestions of highly localised differences. The 15th century deposits at The Foundry, Poole contained almost 30 species of fish, all of which could have been obtained locally within Poole Harbour. However, it included a significant representation of pelagic fish. Some of the gadids (cod family) were of considerable size indicating that they had been obtained from deeper, colder waters (Bullock 1994). Bones from a large ling also came from Thames Street, Poole (Coy 1992, 189). These large fish relate to the documented involvement in deep sea fishing and the fish trade. This is not at all surprising given Poole's role by the 15th century as a major trading port (Horsey 1992). By contrast, the 12th to 13th century midden at Ower Farm on the southern shores of Poole Harbour contained eel, herring, flatfish, whiting, conger, scad, ray and bass, all species available from within the Harbour area. There was however an absence of the large gadids (Hamilton-Dyer 1991). The small 14th–15th century assemblage from the manor house at Kingston Lacy was all sea fish, including conger eel, seabream, herring and plaice. These presumably came from Poole Harbour (Locker 1998). It seems that exploitation and trade in fish was operating at multiple scales within Dorset.

At Sutton Poyntz, the fish bone assemblage included sharks and rays, eel, conger eel, herring, hooknose and flatfish, which were probably obtained from the nearby coast (Hamilton-Dyer 2007, 82–4). It is possible in this case that the differences in species composition between Putton and these other sites relates to highly localised differences in coastal conditions. Sutton Poyntz could have obtained its fish within Weymouth Bay which provided a subtly different marine environment. Further assemblages from a variety of sites could further elucidate what appears to be a clear contrast between the species represented in assemblages in south coast ports and small coastal sites exploiting inshore species for their own consumption.

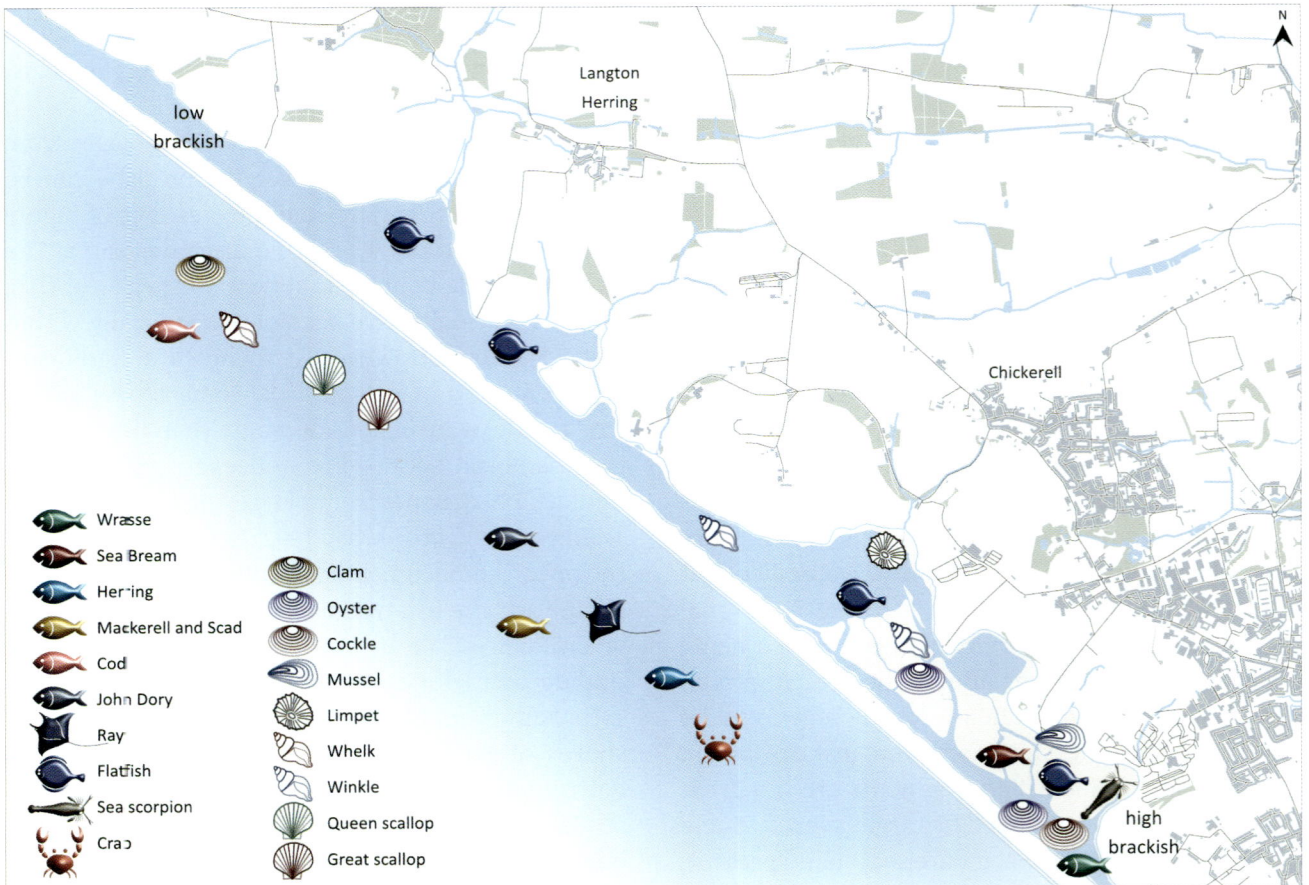

Fig. 4.11 Possible location of marine resources.

THE MARINE MOLLUSCS, By Clare Randall

Introduction

A total of 446 fragments of marine molluscs were hand recovered from all phases. Most were oysters, 225 of which represented a complete or near-complete valve. This is likely to reflect a combination of fragmentation and collecting bias, as a large amount of fragmentary shell was noted throughout the site as part of context descriptions. In addition, 144 shells or part shells of scallops, cockles, whelks, limpets, and periwinkles were recovered (Table 4.11). A single fragment of a large claw of the edible crab *Cancer pagurus* was recovered from context (8-117) the primary fill of the Ditch F85 and assigned to Phase 2.

As well as the hand collected assemblage, nine bulk samples produced marine shell, including oyster, limpet, periwinkle, cockle, clam and mussel (Table 4.12). Some whole examples of the smaller species (e.g. periwinkle) were present but were generally very small fragments (5–10mm). All six species occurred in the Phase 2 contexts, oyster, cockle periwinkle and limpet in Phase 3 samples and oyster, periwinkle and cockle in the Phase 3&4 midden material. This suggests that shellfish may have been exploited to a greater extent during the initial phases of activity on the site than the hand collected assemblage suggests. It is notable that clams and mussels were not recovered in the hand collected assemblage but did occur in the wet sieved samples. This may be a function of the relative fragility of the shells. The number of fragments recovered from Phase 3&4 was fewer than the other contexts, and it is likely that this related to the conditions in the midden deposit. It may have been more hostile to shell preservation, both due to mechanical reworking of the soil and chemical processes.

Table 4.11 Marine shell by phase. Hand collected.

Phase	Ostrea edulis Oyster Left	Right	Pecten maximus Great Scallop	Aequipecten opercularis Queen scallop	Cerastoderma edule Common Cockle	Glycymeris glycymeris Dog cockle	Buccinum undatum Whelk	Littorina littorea Common Periwinkle	Patella vulgata Common limpet	Cancer pagurus Edible Crab
2	-	2	1	-	-	-	-	4	-	1
3	24	14	2	1	1	-	-	5	2	-
4	-	-	-	-	1	-	-	-	-	-
3&4	1	1	-	1	-	2	1	1	-	-
5	6	5	-	-	-	-	2	-	2	-
7	3	2	-	-	-	-	-	1	-	-
8	80	87	4	-	-	3	94	6	10	-

Table 4.12 Marine shell fragments from sieved samples by phase. NB some entire smaller species (e.g. periwinkle), mainly fragments of <10mm.

Phase	Total weight (g)	Ostrea Oyster	Spisula spp. Clam	Mytilus spp. Mussel	Cerastoderma edule Common Cockle	Littorina littorea Common Periwinkle	Patella vulgata Common limpet	Unidentified small shell fragments
2	26	27	1	12	14	14	5	-
3	89	6	-	-	6	3	1	5
3&4	2	1	-	-	1	3	-	1

The species represented

Oyster (Ostrea spp.)
Oysters generally grow sub-littorally on firm substrates. They are able to tolerate reduced salinity and can therefore live in intertidal locations and be exposed at low spring tides (Winder 1991, 214).

Great Scallop (Pecten maximus)
Great scallops are generally found in shallow depressions on the seabed. They prefer clean firm sand, or fine/sandy gravel, although may occasionally be found on muddy sand between 10–110m deep.

Queen Scallop (Aequipecten opercularis)
The queen scallop is a modest sized mollusc, which is found all around the British coast. It lives between the tidemarks but down to depths of 100m on sand and gravel substrates.

Clam (Spisula spp.)
Clams occur around the British coast. They are a burrowing bivalve occasionally found at low water but more commonly in the sublittoral zone. They prefer sandy beds with continually moving water generally avoiding muddy substrates.

Mussel (Mytilus spp.)
Mussels are extremely common all around the British coastline. They occur from high up in the intertidal zone to the shallow subtidal zone. They attach themselves by fibrous byssus threads to suitable substrata. They are often found on rocky shores of open coasts attached to the rock surface and in crevices, and on rocks and piers in sheltered harbours and estuaries. In these situations they often occur in dense masses.

Common Cockle (Cerastoderma edule)
A filter-feeding bivalve, cockles occur all around the British coast. They bury themselves up to 50mm deep in a range of substrates ranging from soft mud to gravel. They are however most abundant in intertidal mud flats within estuaries (Winder 1991, 214).

Dog cockle (Glycymeris glycymeris)
Currently found widely around the shores of southern

and western Britain, the dog cockle creates shallow burrows in fine gravels or sandy/muddy gravels. It occurs offshore to depths of approximately 100m.

Periwinkle (*Littorina* spp.)

Winkles occur commonly around the British coast and can be found on a wide variety of surfaces from rocks, between stones, on gravels as well as on muds in the intertidal zone. They can cope with high energy wave environments as well as favouring sheltered estuaries. They can cope with fluctuations in salinity (Winder 1991, 214).

Common limpet (*Patella vulgate*)

Limpets are found all around the British coast wherever there is something firm enough for them to attach to including rocks, stones and in rock pools, from the high shore to the sublittoral fringe. Abundant on all rocky shores of all degrees of wave exposure the highest densities occur in high wave energy conditions. However, they also occur in estuaries, and can survive lower salinity.

Whelk (*Buccinum undatum*)

Whelk occur around the entire British coast. They live occasionally in the intertidal zone but mainly prefer the subtidal down to considerable depths. They are found on a range of substrates including muddy sand, gravel and rock. They can also tolerate a degree of low salinity.

Discussion

The contexts from which most the hand collected assemblage came suffered from the same issues as the animal bone assemblage. The majority of the material was recovered from deposits associated with the demolition of buildings rather than included in sealed contexts. Consequently, the same caveats apply to these data, although it seems reasonable to conclude that most of the material is derived from the main period of occupation of the manorial complex. What is clear is that a range of shellfish was being exploited from Phase 2 onward. Prior to the main building phase oysters, great scallop, clam, common cockles, mussels, periwinkles, and limpets were used, with the addition of edible crab. The species list is similar in Phase 3 with the addition of queen scallop. Dog cockles and whelks began to

be used during the lifetime of the buildings (Phase 3&4). Most of the species were recovered from the overlying demolition and associated deposits (Phases 5 and 8).

The clear candidate for the source of these shells is the Fleet, the southern end of which marked the southern limit of the Putton manor (see Chapter 5). Most of the species found at Lower Putton Lane are tolerant of both the type of shoreline and the substrate as well as the fluctuations in salinity that occur within the south-eastern end of the Fleet. Conditions for mollusca are good, with abundant marine molluscs present in recent times. It provides a range of slightly different habitats (Seaward 1986).

In the Lower Fleet there are fine sand floors for the first 2 km from Smallmouth. For the next 1 km the Fleet constricts to less than 0.1 km wide in the Narrows. This channel, with a floor of shingle, clay, limestone outcrops and rocks is scoured by a strong tidal flow. The salinity, flora and fauna in the lower Fleet are typically marine. In the 9 km long middle section there is very shallow water, with a few deep and meandering channels. The substrate is soft, organic silt which supports meadows of weed. The lower 3 km of this area forms mud flats at low tide, but the next 6 km experiences little tidal effect. The salinity is 'high brackish', and there is much lower species diversity Within the upper part of the Fleet the landward side at Abbotsbury is fringed with phragmites marsh (now occupied by the Swannery). At this point the salinity is generally 'low brackish'. The exposed Lyme Bay side of Chesil Beach is a high energy environment, but on the Fleet side it is sheltered with undisturbed shingle (Seaward 1986).

Most of the species seen at Lower Putton Lane could have originated in the Fleet (Fig. 4.11). Limpets and periwinkles occur in the middle, but particularly the lower Fleet. Mussels, oysters and cockles only occur in the lower part of the Fleet, but whelks, great scallops, queen scallops and clams have not been recently recorded (Seaward 1986). Winkles were recorded in the late 19th century as far up the Fleet as Chickerell (Sykes 1892), and at Tidmoor Point in the 1970s (Seaward 1978). Oysters were abundant in the mouth of the Fleet in beds in the 1890s (Mansell-Pleydell 1898) but extinct by the 1970s (Seaward

1978). The oyster beds have now been re-established. It can therefore be suggested that most of the species in the Putton assemblage could have originated near the area of the Fleet bordered by the southern extent of the manor (see Chapter 5).

Clearly oysters provided the greatest proportion of the diet. Oyster shell was present in every phase in both the hand collected and sieved material, and there were numerous additional contexts in which flakes and traces of degraded shell were noted but not collected. Upper and lower shells appear to occur relatively evenly, which suggests that the oysters were not prepared to a great extent before being transported to the site. Aside from the limited proportion of the assemblage which could be securely assigned to a phase, the condition of the oyster shell has limited its analysis. Most shells were incomplete; delamination was common, and shells were generally chalky and, in some cases clearly abraded. This is probably a function of the process of re-deposition within rubble spreads. The result is that consideration of shape, dimensions, and presence/absence of epibiont organisms is considerably limited. In a number of cases indications of infestation by worms (probably *Polydora ciliata* and *Polydora hoplura*) and bore holes possibly associated with sponges (*Cilona celata*) were noted, as were a few calcareous tubes. Nevertheless, from the measurable portion of the assemblage, it seems that a wide range of sizes were present, varying for the top (right) shell from less than 60mm maximum height through to *c.* 130mm. As regularity of size (with other indicators) may suggest, as well as selectivity in harvesting, farmed oysters (Winder 2017, 246), lack of regularity in this case may be more indicative of opportunistic exploitation of a local resource. A single example of an adherence of two shells is suggestive of clumping of the oysters, something which occurs more frequently in wild unmanaged populations (Winder 2017, 247).

The wide range of species which was used from Phase 2 onward, and the suspicion that the smaller species with more delicate shells are under-represented in the main assemblage, suggests that shellfish was both an important component of the diet but was also enjoyed in some variety. However, as with the oysters, there is no evidence of systematic

exploitation of particular species or a propensity to being particularly selective in their harvesting, given the range of species and the sizes of shells. This is particularly clear with respect to whelks. The earliest instance of whelks in the assemblage occurred in Phase 3&4, but they were numerous in the clearance deposits which probably derived from the building collapse deposits. A wide range of sizes is represented, with numerous very small examples of less than 40mm total length, through small and medium shells up to the largest at 81mm in length. Rather than representing only a food item, it seems likely that some of these shells represent use as bait.

There are few assemblages of marine shell of medieval date from Dorset with which to compare. Marine molluscs from 15th century shoreline deposits at The Foundry, Poole were dominated by oyster, but included all of the species seen at Lower Putton Lane with a few additions (Winder 1994). The 10th–13th century deposits excavated adjacent to Paradise Street, Poole and other sites in the old town have been argued to represent systematic and almost commercial level oyster exploitation, which may even have influenced the location of the later town (Winder 1992, 194). Other species present in much smaller quantities included whelk, cockles and winkles indictive of small-scale foraging (Winder 1992, 199–200).

On the southern shore of Poole Harbour, the substantial marine mollusc assemblage from the 12th to 13th century midden at Ower Farm, displayed different relative abundance of species from the Poole shell deposits. Here, winkles and cockles were the most common species, with oysters, mussels and carpet shells accounting for less than 5% of the assemblage. Whilst the winkles were probably collected from adjacent to the site at Ower Farm, the cockles probably came from somewhere nearer the Harbour mouth, with higher salinity and less mud. Whilst it appears that the shellfish were probably for local domestic consumption (Winder 1991, 215–6), access to a wider area seems to have been possible and a degree of preference in species selection was exercised. Lack of oyster at this site may imply that in contrast to the other species they were traded inland rather than being consumed at Ower. Over a hundred oyster shells, two cockles and a whelk were recovered from excavation on the manor house site at Kingston Lacy. These were assumed to have been transported from Poole Harbour (Locker 1998, 60).

The geographically closest site to Putton is the 13th–14th century manorial site at Sutton Poyntz. There 95% of the marine mollusc assemblage was composed of oysters. The rest was made up of small numbers of scallops, cockles, winkles, limpets and mussels (Wyles 2007), which is very similar to the representation at Putton. At Sutton Poyntz, the oyster had similarities in shape and infestations as oysters from Poole Bay, and it was suggested that they originated there (Wyles 2007). However, the soft substrate and fluctuating salinity indicated for these species would also be provided by the Fleet, and given the proximity across Weymouth Bay, that would seem to be a better source for Sutton Poyntz. The preservation of the Putton oysters was not good enough to assess the rate of infestations or shape of the oysters but the conditions in the Fleet may have been similar to Poole Harbour. If so, there may have been contact between the two manors in relation to shellfish exploitation which is interesting in the light of the tenurial relationships between the two manors (see Chapter 5).

DISCUSSION OF ECONOMIC AND ENVIRONMENTAL RESOURCES,
By Clare Randall

The limitations of the material available from the site at Lower Putton Lane have been well described above. However, it provides a significant contribution to the data available for Dorset and indicates some important areas which future research could explore. The evidence of the plant resources suggests that there were localised adaptations to circumstance, not only in matching crops to the general soil types of the locale, but also in response to changing conditions, land pressure and ownership. There are suggestions of production of oil/fibre plants which may relate to household level or more substantial engagement with textile production. The presence of potential garden plants suggests questions around food and medicine production in the county. There are also questions of land management and farming practices to be addressed. Diachronic exploration of these issues would be valuable if pursued elsewhere.

Similarly, the resolution of the animal bone assemblage is poor, but hints at the generally recognised pattern of a shift to sheep production over time. There may well be nuances in this process which could be further elucidated by the retrieval of suitable assemblages. There are further questions around the degree to which the relative status between rural manors can be understood from their food resourcing and consumption. The relationships of these sites to urban supply is clearly in need of additional consideration. The marine resources seen at Lower Putton Lane are interesting in their similarities and differences with other coastal Dorset sites, more of which need to be investigated. The Putton material is clearly related to exploitation purely for household consumption, whereas elsewhere exploitation appears to have been more systematic and probably related to provisioning religious houses or trade. Further examination of the environmental agricultural data from these types of sites has much to contribute to better understanding of urban/rural relationships. The nature of any agricultural surplus and the mechanism of provisioning of towns should be explored. There is much to do in understanding the pattern of coastal resource exploitation, and how this related to coastal trade and long-distance links. Both issues could inform on how rural estates obtained other elements of their diet and material culture from towns.

'RENT OF ONE PAIR OF GILT SPURS, ONE POUND OF CUMIN, AND ONE SPARROWHAWK' – DOCUMENTARY EVIDENCE, MANOR AND LANDSCAPE

By Clare Randall

The modern civil parish of Chickerell is large, but its current extent includes what were separate entities in the past, including the church and village of Buckland Ripers to the north, and parts of Upwey and Radipole to the east. To the south are peripheral areas of the large coastal parish of Wyke Regis. The original core of what is now Chickerell parish was a series of three settlements and their associated land, West Chickerell (the current village centre), Podington (Putton) located in the centre and East Chickerell (now beneath an electricity sub-station), arranged in sequence from west to east along the Chickerell brook. The northern part of this area occupied slopes, whilst East Chickerell bordered the low lying and marshy areas of Radipole parish, and to the south was a boundary with Wyke Regis allowing access to the Fleet. The three holdings of West Chickerell, Putton and East Chickerell are repeatedly mentioned in relation to each other in medieval and later documents.

The farmhouse of Putton Farm remains as a residential property to the north side of Lower Putton Lane, immediately north of the site. There is a longstanding identification of this area with the medieval manor of Pod(d)ington (Podinton, Podyngton etc). Hutchins (1863, 495) describes Putton as 'anciently a manor', from which the title of this book derives. The regular identification of Putton with Podington endured throughout the post-medieval period. For example, a release and assignment dated 1799 referred to 'Lands in Putton, otherwise Puddington' (Dorset History Centre D1/MC/93), whilst in 1845, Lewis's *Topographical Dictionary of England* described it as 'Putton or Podington, a tything in the parish of West Chickerell, union of Weymouth, Hundred of Culliford Tree.'

Therefore, the archaeological evidence of the substantial manorial centre described in this volume can be placed within a contemporary documentary context. That context includes being an element in a network of medieval land holding relationships as well as the nexus of a productive system. Understanding the structure of the landholding involves postulating the location of its boundaries to consider what resources the area had within its control, and against which the archaeological material can be considered. This chapter will therefore consider the aetiology of the manor and holdings of Putton as indicated in place name evidence and charters; descriptions of the nature of the manor (the land unit) in medieval sources and the evidence for familial and other relationships in which it sat; its re-establishment as Putton Farm in the early modern period; and clues to the earlier extent of the manor.

GLIMPSING THE EARLIER MEDIEVAL LANDSCAPE – NAMES AND PLACES

Putton and Chickerell

The place name 'Podington' has an Old English origin, which implies some degree of settlement or defined land holding in the area during the last centuries before the conquest. The root of the place name is an Anglo-Saxon personal name, referring to a man called Pod or Poda, combined with an -ingtun suffix, making it the 'farm or settlement of the people of Poda', or possibly 'on the stream of Poda' (Mills 1998, 124) or 'farm of Podda's descendants'. The earliest form in which it appears in 1237 is Podinton, with Pudington by 1288, and Podington by 1293. Putton appears in 1430 (Fägerstern 1978, 154), with a range of variants which are used throughout this chapter.

Chickerell is referred to as a single place in Domesday Book (discussed further below). Intriguingly the place name 'Chickerell' (Cicherelle in Domesday, Chikerel by 1227) remains one of a few local place names which have not yet achieved satisfactory explanation (Mills 1998, 56). Fägerstern (1978, 153) suggests that it was originally the name of the Chickerell brook, and that it may have a similar root to Chicklade, Wiltshire, or Chideock, Dorset. The first element of these names has a British origin root, – cēd meaning 'wood'. Cēd as the origin for Chicklade has been documented as passing through cēd – chet –chick. Eagles (2018, xviii–xix) includes both Chicklade and Chideock in his map of ancient or Brittonic place names in Wessex. With respect to the second half of the name, Buckerell in Devon is similarly unexplained (Fägerstern 1978). It may be worth considering a comparison to Deverill place names in Dorset and Wiltshire which it is suggested is derived from British Dubro-ial (Gover et al. 1939, 6–7) where -ial has the meaning 'fertile or cultivated upland region', and which might be applicable to parts of the Chickerell area. Therefore, whilst Chickerell remains unexplained, it is not Old English in origin, implying an earlier root. There are some other potentially early name elements within the area. South-west of Chickerell village, Crook Hill has a British root in *crūg a hill or mound, with the addition in English of hyll (Mills 1986, 205), evidently after appreciation of the original meaning was lost. Tidmoor Point on the shore of the Fleet is similarly descriptive of a landscape feature, albeit with an Old English root, being 'marshy ground reached by the flood-tide' (Mills 1986, 205).

The wider landscape

More widely, most of the surrounding pre-18th century settlements carry Old English names and many of them have references at least as early as Domesday, if not in late Anglo-Saxon sources (Fig. 5.1). To the west, the monastery at Abbotsbury was an early church foundation, occurring as Abbedesburie in a later copy of a charter of 946, and referring to the defended settlement of the abbot; the land was held by Glastonbury Abbey. The Abbotsbury monastery itself was founded (or re-founded) in 1026 (Mills 1998, 25). The second element may be derived from burh in a similar fashion to several other early monastic foundations such as Glastonbury or Malmesbury (Michael Costen pers. comm, cf. Blair 2005, 250), and which would be supportive of an earlier foundation. It has been suggested as an early minster site (Hall 2000). The location of a church at Portesham was also apparently early, and Porteshamme in a charter of 1024 was mentioned as 'the enclosure attached to the port/town' (Mills 1998, 122). This probably refers to Abbotsbury with which it had an enduring relationship. Port is an Old English borrowing from Latin (cf. Portland) and is also an early name (Eagles 2018); it implies a town-like function or trading activity. A number of chapels came into existence within Portesham parish, but their origins and the relationships between the monastery at Abbotsbury and potential ecclesiastical centre at Portesham are not clear. The small settlements of Shilvinghampton and Coryates in Portesham parish also have Old English name origins as does Rodden near Abbotsbury. The Fleet (and the manor of Fleet, mentioned in Domesday) is also derived from Old English fleot. The original centre of Fleet was also in possession of an early church site (Hall 2000). It can be suggested that the appearance of both these places and chapels in the pre-Conquest landscape relate to the distribution of land to, and subsequent demonstration of status of the late Anglo-Saxon warrior-gentry class (Michael Costen pers. comm.). In the case of Fleet, the parish boundary is interestingly contrary to the prevailing

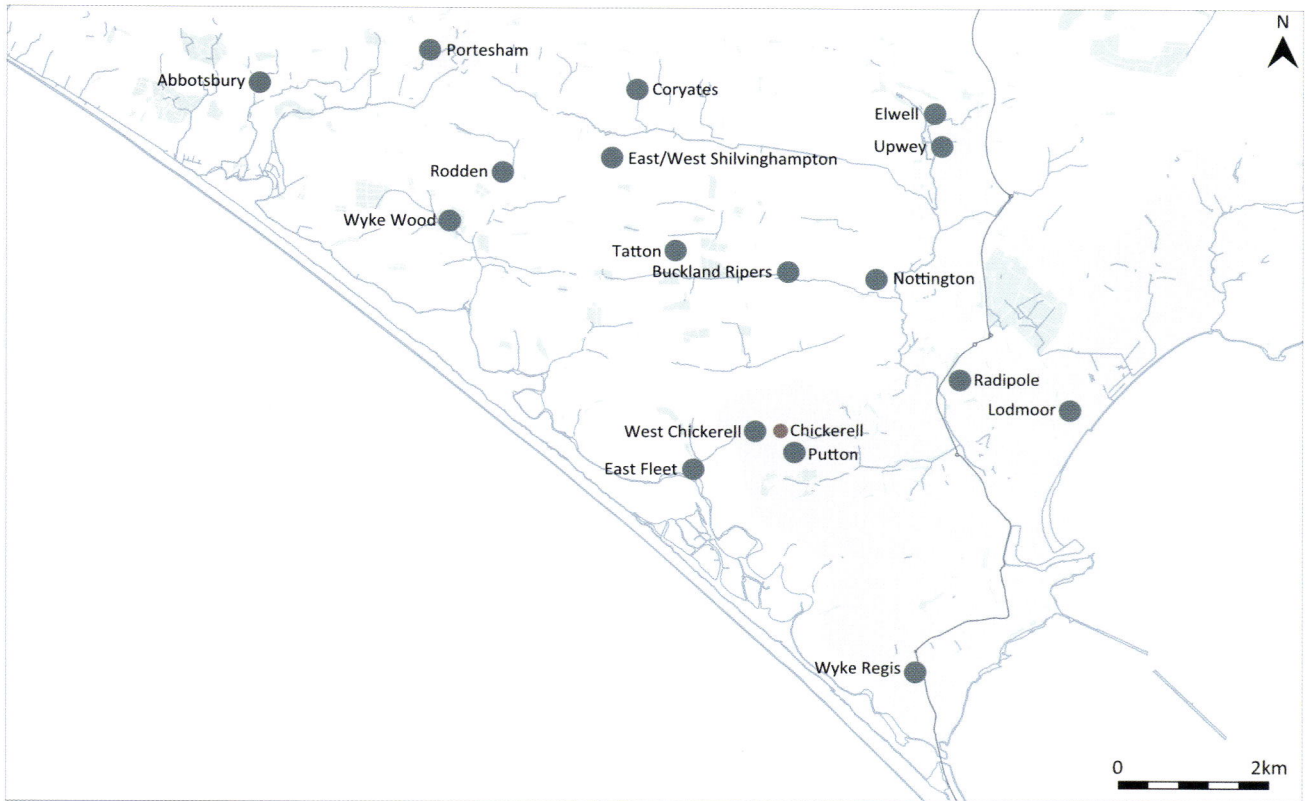

Fig. 5.1   Places mentioned in Chapter 5.

north–south organisation of the area. Clearly, this whole area is ripe for further research.

Holwell, to the north of Buckland Ripers, occurs in Domesday as *Halegewell* derived from Old English 'holy well' (Mills 1998, 89). Elwell, in Upwey, which was part of a liberty from the Cullifordtree Hundred with Wyke Regis, may derive from similar roots. It occurred in 1212 as *Helewill* with an Old English root which implies either health or good luck and can be interpreted as either a healing spring or wishing well (Mills 1986, 247). Situated in an area containing the early ecclesiastical foundations mentioned above, this is intriguing. Radipole, also mentioned in Domesday, derives from Old English 'reed pool' which accurately describes Radipole Lake which creates the eastern boundary of this group of holdings. Tatton, also a Domesday holding, is derived from Old English as the 'Farm of Tata' (Mills 1998, 143), with Nottington similarly the 'farm of Hnotta' from a personal name (Mills 1998, 114). The number of personal name plus *-ingtun* or *-tun* suffix place names in the area is discussed further in Chapter 6.

Charters

To the north of Chickerell, the Domesday holding of Buckland Ripers acquired the second part of its name from the de Rivers or de Ripariis family who held it from the 13th century. 'Buckland' is however Old English in origin, relating to land which was in some way defined by a charter (Mills 1998, 46), although this document does not appear to have survived. It is not therefore clear if the boundary between Buckland and Chickerell originated at this point in time. To the south, Wyke Regis acquired the royal epithet from at least the 13th century (*Kingeswick*) as it was a royal demesne. The original large size of the ecclesiastical parish (now much altered, most dramatically by the development of Weymouth in its north-eastern portion during the medieval and early modern period) may have related to its royal status. Wyke derives from Old English *wīc* which in this case could signify either a specialised (dairy) farming unit, or a harbour/port (Mills 1998, 164), which given its location overlooking the entrance into the Fleet may make more sense. The Wyke charter of 984 (copied in the 14th century) gives details of the charter boundary on its north side (the south was bordered by the sea, overlooking Portland). This boundary is described (Jenkins 2008) as stretching from the 'West Sea' (clearly somewhere on Chesil beach) to 'Saggeloth', to the 'Muldich', to 'Blake Ston', to 'Soreditch', to 'Lodmor' (another Brittonic name [Eagles 2018], possibly from *lutā* 'mud' [Mills 1936,232]), and the 'East Sea', somewhere in Weymouth Bay. This indicates that the total area spanned the entirety of what is now Weymouth as far east as Preston, but the identification of the places named in the western section, which would provide the boundary with Chickerell, remain unclear. 'Saggeloth' and 'Muldich' are obscure, although the latter implies a ditched boundary.

CHICKERELL AFTER THE CONQUEST

The area of 'Chickerell' had apparently been defined by land covered by charters to the south and probably the north by the late Saxon period. The Domesday survey entry for Chickerell, probably in its entirety a vil, was included in the lands of the Kings thanes:

> 'Bolle holds Chickerell. Saewulf held it before 1066. It paid tax for 3 hides and ½ virgate of land. Land for 3 ploughs, which are there, in lordship; four slaves; 1 villager and 6 smallholders. Meadow, 6 acres; pasture 7 furlongs. Value 60s'. (Thorn and Thorn 1983).

Bolle also held Mappowder, which was a more valuable holding. In that entry he is described as Bolle the Priest. He also held Shilvinghampton, part of the lands of Abbotsbury Abbey with a note that 'he cannot withdraw from the church with this land', which refers to the lease arrangement. Bolle also held the churches of Winfrith, Chaldon, Puddletown as well as nearby Fleet. He seems therefore to have been a significant churchman. The rest of the land listed for these places was held by the King (Thorn and Thorn 1983), and several of them were apparently early foundations. This may indicate something about the status of Chickerell. Saewulf, who held the land before 1066 was apparently an independent thane. He had also held a virgate of land at Winterborne Belet (Thorne and Thorne 1983), another now vanished settlement. This chimes with the characterisation of Dorset in general, and

the Weymouth lowlands in particular, as an area dominated by small independent thanes during the late Anglo-Saxon period (Costen 2007). If the Chickerell of the Domesday survey is divided into its three later units, each would be a holding of around 1 hide (120 acres). A respectable amount of ploughland was in the direct control of the lord, with associated tied labour (four slaves) and was supplemented by meadow and pasture. In addition to the land under the direct control of the lord there was one villager and several smallholders who would have held and worked their land independently in addition to their labour obligations to the lord. It is likely that this type of tenure continued into later centuries.

PODINGTON, WEST CHICKERELL AND EAST CHICKERELL – LAND AND FAMILY FORTUNES

The land holding pattern reflected in the 13th to 15th century records associated with Putton is typical of the complex tenanting arrangements of the feudal period. Tenants in chief who held land from the king would settle estates on retainers to cover a fee for service which they owed the king. It was common for these retainers to further sublet their holdings to others often creating multilayered patterns of land holding. It had become common by the middle of the 13th century to regularise arrangements by replacing knight's service with financial payments known as scutage (Bailey 2002). The process of documenting these payments and changes in ownership often resulted in considerable, if incomplete, documentation. The records appertaining to Putton consist mainly of inquisitions post-mortem (an inquest after a death to establish the estate extent and confirm the heirs), feet of fines (judgements concerning title to land) and court rolls (manorial or leet records). An exhaustive examination of the material has not been undertaken but a selection is presented here in order to provide a framework in which to understand the legal complexities of the land holding from the 13th–15th centuries which may have affected the trajectory of development and decline of the Putton manorial complex. Some mentions are made of the scale and proportions of arable, pasture and meadow land. It is however in the descent of the rights to land over the course of three centuries that increasing complexity and fragmentation can be seen and which must have impacted the operation of Putton as a manorial unit.

The Le Walys and 13th century Putton

The earliest mention of Putton (or in this case Poditon) was in a feet of fines of the 21st year of the reign of Henry II (1236–7) (Fry and Fry 1896, 68). Ralph le Walys was the tenant of the fourth of a knight's fee held from Roger de Woth, excepting 40 acres of pasture and 2 acres of meadow. In this document, Roger and his wife Cecelia petitioned Ralph to grant this holding to John de Strode, which he did in return for 10 marcs of silver. The le Walys family already had holdings in the area. Feet of fines indicate that Nichola de Champflower, the widow of William le Walys had by 1235 inherited from him the rights to half a knight's fee in West Chickerell. Nichola had married William after the death of her first husband Thomas de Champflower, and subsequently William's son by a previous wife, married Nichola's step-daughter Joan de Champflower (Baggs et al. 1985), a union which tied together the later descent of Poditon and Huish Champflower in Somerset. It is not clear therefore when the le Walys obtained their rights to Poditon, and it may have been of some standing.

Various le Walys family members held land at Chickerell, in Purbeck and at Stock Gaylard near Sherborne, as well as in Somerset, in various combinations throughout the 13th and 14th centuries and into the 15th century. Other land in West Chickerell was held by the Cifrewast family of Hooke, and Hutchins suggests (1863, 493), probably correctly, that their holding was the principle part of the West Chickerell manor. The records of the 13th century are less frequent, and so neither the descent of the manors nor the familial relationships are entirely clear. Nevertheless, some references to the le Walys holdings in West Chickerell imply their residency at Putton. For example, an inquisition post-mortem in 1338 of land held by Nicholas le Waleys at his death referred to him as 'of Podyngton' (HMSO 1904, 162).

In a close roll of 1242 Joan, wife of Ralph Walys petitioned the king to establish that Ralph, 'said

to be weak', had 'redeemed himself' to his lord Nicholas Poynz (HMSO 1911, 355) of Sutton Poyntz, which was located c. 6km to the east of Putton. Ralph's holding in West Chickerell was affirmed in 1249–52 (Chadwyck-Healey 1897). There is then a break in records regarding Putton until after the death of Nicholas le Walys in 1292, when his widow Margery was endowed with his holdings (HMSO 1904, 95). Nicholas had continued to have an interest in the Somerset lands deriving from the Champfleur's, Huish Champflower, Holeford St Mary and Athelardeston. He had also held a knight's fee at Poditon and a quarter fee in West Chickerell, the former from the Poyntz family and the latter from Philip Harang (the family which named nearby Langton Herring, c. 4km to the west). At this point the Putton manor was apparently divided into three portions. Nicholas le Walys held a knight's fee, 'including a pasture called Gormere', of Sir Hugh Poinz for 40s. scutage. Nicholas de Strode held a fourth part of a knight's fee by royal service, and Sir Ingram le Walleis held a 'fourth part by royal service and by service of a pair of gilt spurs, price 6d'. Identification of places such as Gormere are useful in understanding the resources available to the manor. The -mere element indicates a moor or marsh, which fits with some of the waterlogged and rough grazing in the southern part of the Chickerell area in modern times. The 'gor' element is derived from OE *gāra* and refers to a 'spear-shaped', or triangular, parcel of land (University of Nottingham 2020). This root occurs elsewhere in Dorset, for example at Gore Land/Garland at Kington Magna (Ross 1985, 31); Gore Cove on the Fleet, between West Fleet and Langton Herring could be described as triangular. The identification of Gormere is discussed further below.

Wider interests

Ingram or Ingelram le Walys, who died 1303–1304 (HMSO 1911b, 489), his lands passing to his son John (HMSO 1911b, 494) and widow Alice as dower (Rushton 2002 120–2), had also held Langton in Purbeck since 1264 (Hinton 2002; HMSO 1906, 403). The Le Walys' held a substantial proportion of what was an unusually large manor. This is now referred to as Langton Matravers after the family which held the other portion (and in 1296 held land from Ingram le Waleys [HMSO 1904, 267]), but it was once Langton

Wallis. That name now adheres to an area which was once the heathland associated with the manor on the shore of Poole Harbour, Langton Wallis Heath. An assignment of dower to Alice in 1304 includes, as well as land and rents, reference to the payment of some of the latter in salt. She also received a third part of 'all marble and freestone' and her son John the remaining two thirds (Rushton 2002, 122), a reference to the Purbeck marble quarries near Wilkswood (see Chapter 6). At some stage Ingelram le Walys had also gained an interest in the coastal manor of Melecumbe (Melcombe Regis). Ingelram and his wife gave up Melcombe to Ralph Basset of Drayton in 1276–77 for a payment of one hundred pounds sterling (Fry and Fry 1896, 182), indicating the potential value of trade through Melcombe in the late 13th century. This may be the same Ingram le Waleys who was imprisoned in 'Shereburn' in 1288 for 'a trespass of venison in the forest of Rechyh' until he could find 12 Dorset men to attest that he was not a 'regular evildoer in the King's forests' (HMSO 1911b, 251). In 1316, close rolls record the granting of the Langton manor by John le Walsh to his son John and his wife Isabel, whilst he retained Chickerell and 'Stoke Gaillard' (National Archives C 143/112/16). A Roger le Walys who died in 1375 left the Langton manor, a dwelling house at Stoke (valued at 100s), and the manor of East Chickerell (also valued at 100s) to his daughter Margaret (National Archives D-BKL/A/F/7). 'Langeton in Purbyk' included two salterns in Middelbere. This is probably the same Roger who endowed a religious house at Wilkeswood in Langton in 1373 (Page 1908).

Poditon in the 14th century

The son of Ingelram le Walys, John le Walys of Chickerell, had interests in West Chickerell, 'Podinton' (or 'Pudicots'), 'Estcheckerell' and 'Suthwaye' ([Hutchins 1863, 493] the latter probably in Radipole). Other parties to this land were Robert de Faryndon, Robert de Wodeton, Geoffry de Warmwell, William Crucket and John le Fleming, so the pattern of land holding was already complex. A close roll of 1315 puts the value of Poditon and Chickerell, held by John le Walys as £8 (HMSO 1893). The inquisition on the death of John le Walisshe of Podington in 1333 (HMSO 1909) also acknowledged the interests in Somerset, as well as Podynton and

Westchyckerel. The latter by this point consisted of 40 acres arable, 2 acres meadow, a pasture, and 2s. rent held from Walter Heryng, by service of a quarter knight's fee. The holding at 'Podynton' was referred to as

'a capital messuage, lands and rent held of Roger de Chaundos and Maud his wife as of her dower of the manor of Sutton, of the inheritance of Nicholas Poyntz, by knight's service'.

This reference to the capital messuage is particularly helpful as it confirms the presence of a substantial residential dwelling and manorial administrative centre at Putton. The description of the entire holding was

'a capital messuage with a curtilage, value, per annum 12d. 60 acres of arable, value per annum 10s; six acres of meadow, value per annum, 3s; a certain common pasture, value per annum 3s. 4d.; two cottagers (coterelli) which pay 2s. 10d. at the four terms of the year in equal portions'

This record also confirms the continued presence of peasant tenants within the manor during this period. John le Walisshe's heir was identified as his 25-year-old son Nicholas. However, a further inquisition occurred into the affairs of Nicholas le Walissh of Podynton only six years later, in 1339 (National Archives SC 8/40/1990). His heirs were his daughters Joan, aged 2 years and Elizabeth, one year old. At the time of his death, Nicholas held,

'two parts of a messuage and curtilage value per annum 7d. and forty acres of arable land, 4 acres of pasture, two parts of a common pasture and of two cottagers (coterelli)'.

A third of the interest in the manorial buildings and land, including access to the commons had been disposed of elsewhere at this point (see below). Nicholas had also continued to hold land in West Chickerell. Because of the minority of Nicholas' daughters, the 'messuage and 60 acres of arable' passed into the hands of the king. However, the eldest daughter Joan died on the Feast of St Luke (October) in 1350, 'and Elizabeth died the same day'. They would have been 13 and 12 years old respectively, and given the timing, one has to wonder if they were amongst the final victims of the first wave of the Black Death. Listing of the remaining heirs of Nicholas included his sisters Alice (married to Walter Malet) and Joan, and the children and grandson of his sister Edith St

Clere who was also dead. Edith's daughter Joan was wife of William le Swan, her daughter Lucia the wife of John Cruket, and Cristina, only 12 years old, was the wife of John atte Hulle. These are individuals to whom we will return.

Complications of inheritance

The pattern of management within and between the manors always appears to have been complex, as they are often referred to together, and this seems to have increased as the number of interested parties grew after the death of Nicholas le Walisshe. It was common for widows to retain a dower interest long after their husband's demise, which had to be considered alongside the other heirs to estates. Maud, the widow of Nicholas le Walssh, subsequently married Walter Malet, but by the time that she died in 1358/9, had married Walter Cancy. However, she still had dower rights over 'Podyton and West Chykerel', leaving them to her brother Ralph de Middelneye (HMSO 1921, 562). The inquisition after the death of Rose (or Roesa), widow of John le Walisshe (and probably mother of Nicholas), in 1362 (HMSO 1904, 343) shows that she had held land in Putton as her dower (possibly the third not in the possession of Nicholas) after the death of her husband, before it passed to the descendants of her daughters. There were other complications introduced by land changing hands between those from whom the holdings were tenanted. West Chikerell, Poditon, and Estchickerel were part of the lands associated with Sutton Poyntz which were given up in 1366 by Nicholas Poyntz to Guy de Bryene, chivaler, Martin Moulisshe, clerk and John Seys, clerk, in return for 200 marcs of silver (Fry and Fry 1910, 112). Whilst it is not clear who was in possession of what from the list of manors and parties holding them, Roger le Walishe was mentioned along with Rose de Poditon, Alice de Poditon, and Joan de Poditon, who can be identified as the widow and daughters of John le Walsh.

By 1353, Walter Malet, William le Swan and John Crucket (the husbands of Nicholas le Walsh's sisters and niece) were in control of

'two messuages and one curtilage, 84 acres of arable, 6 acres of meadow, 3 acres of pasture and 5s. and 4d. rent with appurtenances in Podyton and West Chickerell'.

One messuage and curtilage was most likely at Putton. Perhaps another house had been constructed in West Chickerell by this point. Thereafter, the holding seems to have been increasingly sub-divided, and this may have initially supported additional dwellings. By 1362, Joan, the sister of Nicholas le Walsh who had been married to John Crucket, had died (HMSO 1935, 259). At her death she was married to Henry le Frere and held a 'fourth part of two carucates of land in Podyngton....and 20 acres of land in West Chickerell'. Joan's heirs were her sister Alice, her nephew Simon Brutt (son of her sister Matilda), and Christian/Cristina wife of John atte Hulle, daughter of her sister Edith. In 1365, another sister of Nicholas le Walsh, Elizabeth, wife of Robert Salmon, died (HMSO 1938, 23–4). It was claimed that she had held one messuage and 40 acres of land in Podyngton, lands in West Chickerell and other lands in Somerset. It does seem that this was a duplicate claim and three years later her son John Salmon's share of

'seizen of one messuage, of a moiety of one curtilage, of 40 acres of land, of two acres and one rod and one rod and a half of pasture, and of 2s. 4d rent in Podyngton'

was described as 'an eighth part of an eighth part', which by anyone's assessment wasn't a great deal. He was granted a similar proportion of 11 acres of land, of one rod of meadow and of three and a half rods of pasture and 20d. rent in West Chickerell.

Additional levels of complication also originated from the continuing interests of the other descendants of John le Walisshe. An *Inquisition ad quod damnum* of 9. Edward II (1315) has John le Walshe of Chickerell granting the Langton manor to his son John and wife Isabel (PRO 1963, 160). A feet of fines of John le Walsh in 1332 (HMSO 1909) settled two messuages, land and meadow in East Chickerell and Stoke Coillard on himself for life, and afterwards to his son Roger le Walsh, and daughter-in-law Joanna de Chiseldene, and after them to their daughter Margaret, who first married Adam Soidon and then John Filiol. Roger also had a son, John, by a previous wife, who died before his father leaving a nine-month old daughter Johanna, who would become the wife of John Fauntleroy. These complexities meant that there were competing interests within the extended family for the land at East Chickerell. This is indicated in the inquisition post-mortem after the death of Roger le Walsh in 1375 (HMSO 1952, 222). He had held Langton Walish in Purbeck as well as Stock Gaylard and East Chickerell, but this had been held by Alice Malet and Simon Byrt. These were his cousins, who held land in Putton, discussed above. Later disputes over this inheritance occurred between John Filiol, Philip Soydon and Henry Frere, 'clerk' and John Fauntleroy. The first two could claim it by virtue of marriage to and descent from Margaret, daughter of Roger le Walsh, whilst John Fauntlery could claim the inheritance as the husband of the granddaughter of Roger le Walsh. Henry Frere may be either one and the same as, or a son of, the man who had married Nicholas le Walsh's sister Joan. Henry became priest in Chickerell on 28 November 1361 as a result of the death of his predecessor William Stapleford during the second major outbreak of Black Death. His patron was John Maltravers (Hutchins 1863, 497), which indicates the close relationship of these families who held adjacent land. The various claims to the land were still in effect in some respects at the beginning of the 16th century. The Filiols retained interests in the Chickerell manors throughout the 15th century (see below) and by 1514, John Fauntleroy held East Chickerell alongside land at East and West Tatton (Hutchins 1863, 494).

Increasing fragmentation

Within West Chickerell and Putton the increasing complexity, and possible expansion of sub-letting, are suggested by an increase in the number of buildings mentioned. In 1383 four messuages, one carucate of land, fifteen acres of meadow, and forty acres of pasture in Westchikerel and Podyngton were let by William and Alice Colne to Thomas Nitere and John Lunday (Fry and Fry 1910, 196). Six messuages, two carucates of land twenty acres of meadow, 100 acres of pasture and a moiety of messuages, 30 acres of land and 2½ acres of meadow in Westchkerell and Podyngton were granted in 1393 by William Jewe to Alice Malet. These were tenanted by four other tenants, John Fillole, John Ornayne, Katheryn Worth, and John Gyll. The rent was 'two shillings.... one pair of gilt spurs, one pound of cumin and one sparrowhawk' (Fry and Fry 1910, 218–9) which has given this chapter its title.

The fallout of the untimely death of Nicholas le Walsshe continued well into the 15th century. An inquisition held at Dorchester in 1408 into the affairs of Christina wife of John Hulle related to attempts to establish the rightful heirs to

'two messuages, one curtilage, 84 acres of arable, 6 acres of meadow, 3 acres of pasture and 5s.4d. rent in Poditon and Westchickerell'

Nicholas Hulle the son of Christina claimed her eighth share of this holding on the basis that she was the third daughter of Nicholas le Walsh's fourth sister Edith. When Christina died this land was held from William Filiol and dame Alice Bryan (National Archives C 137/68/37 mm. 1, 3). The inquisition in 1415 after the death of the tenant in chief, Elizabeth wife of William de Montacute, Earl of Salisbury, lists Chickerell and West Chickerell as being held by Roger le Walshe and John Jewe by service of a quarter of a knights fee. Parts of West Chickerell and Putton were amongst numerous other manors in Dorset and Devon changing hands between William Carent Esquire, John Fauntleroy, and Thomas Hody, and John Hody in 1430 (Fry and Fry 1910, 307–8). In 1437 the inquisition after the death of Thomas Othe shows that he held a rood of land in Putton from Elizabeth Lovell for a rent of 2d (National Archives C 139/85/16 mm. 1, 3). It seems that some holdings by this time were very small. Hutchins notes (1863, 496), that there was now a break in the records and that Putton was 'divided and subdivided' before appearing again as a single unit in 1473 in the possession of Elizabeth, wife of Sir John Hody of Pillesdon. Elizabeth and her then husband Robert Cappes had rendered the manors of Putton and Chickerell to Walter Moreton and William Parker (Fry and Fry 1910,326). However, in 1497 John Hody, son of Sir John and Elizabeth held four messuages with appurtenances in 'Puttyng and Checkerell' (Hutchins 1863, 497).

THE EARLY MODERN AND POST-MEDIEVAL POPULATION

Several sources can be used to broadly indicate the population of Putton from the 16th to 19th century. The muster roll of 1542 (Stoate 1978) does not differentiate the three manors, referring only to the 'Chyckerell' tithing, within which there were 18 men listed. The Subsidy of 1545 has 14 taxpayers listed for Chickerell, but only four in 1594. The Hearth tax for 1672 has three names and three hearths being taxed in Putton, compared with four in West Chickerell (National Archives E 179/105/352/137). Two years later, the count for Putton had increased to four (National Archives E 179/105/352/139). The population does not appear to have expanded much in the 18th century. The militia list of 1758 for Putton and East Chickerell combined which listed men between the ages of 18 and 50 lists seven men all servants, labourers and a shepherd. In 1774, Edward Beale of Putton and East Chickerell, Yeoman had his militia place substituted, as did Thomas Downton of Putton, Yeoman in 1778. By 1796 (National Archives IR 23/22/59) there were four eligible men in Putton, including William Pond, Gent and Edward Carter, a Yeoman farmer. Whilst this is clearly a partial reflection of the local population, the limited numbers of individuals referred to seems to accord with the lack of evidence for substantial reuse of the manor site during the early modern period.

Putton was still recorded separately in the 1841 census as the 'tything of Putton in the liberty of Sutton Poyntz' with 14 households. Of these, one had their occupation listed as a gardener, one as a carter, and all the others were agricultural labourers. *Lewis's Topographical Dictionary of England* suggests there were 67 inhabitants in 1845. In the 1851 census Charles Rashley was listed as a farmer, with George Brown described as a 'farmer of 250 acres employing seven labourers'. There were a further 16 households, including one headed by a dairyman, two gardeners, two laundresses, a dressmaker, a butcher, and all the others still agricultural labourers. A further three houses were unoccupied, with one being built, and the increase in the number of households seems to indicate the commencement of the modern expansion of settlement. The place of birth of eight heads of households was further afield than Putton or Chickerell and indicates the increasing mobility of the rural population in the mid-19th century. The limited population throughout the 16th to early 19th century, and the agricultural focus of their employment accords with the evidence of insubstantial re-use of the Lower Putton Lane site during this period.

POST-MEDIEVAL LANDHOLDING

The pattern of land holding from the 16th century onward is not entirely clear, although there are several references to holdings within West Chickerell, Putton and East Chickerell. These demonstrate that any relationship which had existed between East Chickerell and Putton was gradually severed in the early modern period. However, greater complexity in land holding appears to have remained between West Chickerell and Putton as the post-medieval pattern of farms was created. The documentation also provides glimpses of the type of agriculture carried out and the wider contacts and concerns of landowners across the district.

William Jesope (or Josoppe) was sued in 1538 by John Bond for 'chasing and rechasing' of sheep and 'other misuse of common of pasture within the manor of Putton in Chickerell, whereof both parties hold shares' (National Archives C 1/950/44-48). In 1547 Podyngton was transferred from Edmund and Elena Fox to John Bonnde for £37. At the time it comprised 160 acres of land, 20 acres meadow, 80 acres of pasture and 200 acres of furze and heath (Hutchins 1863, 497), a similar area to that cited in the medieval sources. This implies that the unit of land may not have been greatly changed from the previous centuries. Neither Fox nor Bonnde are mentioned in the muster roll of 1542 or the Subsidy of 1545, which might suggest neither was resident. By 1556 John and Anne Bond released to William Mescelsey for a payment of 160*l* sterling,

> 'two messuages, 80 acres of land, 30 acres of meadow, 100 acres of pasture, and 200 acres of furze and heath in Podyngton, alias Putton'.

The '200 acres of furze and heath' noted in the 1546 and 1556 description might have encompassed the 'Gormere' pasture referred to as a separate unit in 14th century documents. By 1588, the 'farm or manor' of Putton 'in West Chickerell' and four messuages and 480 acres of land in Putton and West Chickerell had passed into the hands of James Hannam Esq (Hutchins 1863, 496).

Whilst the Jesoppes appear to have had an interest in Putton land in the 1540s, their main holding was

East Chickerell. In the 1542 Chickerell muster roll, William Jesope senior was listed as providing two pairs of harness, two bows and two sheaves of arrows, with William Jesope, junior, having a bow and half a sheaf, and Thomas Jesope a bow and 6 arrows. The picture is of a relatively well off and established family. All three appear in the subsidy rolls for 1545, with William Jesope senior being clearly the most wealthy man in the district with goods worth £60, the other William Jesope the next most wealthy with £5 in goods and Thomas Jesope having £2 of goods. The 1584 will of William Jesope of East Chickerell (National Archives PROB 11/67/334) not only made provision for his four daughters' marriages of a hundred marks a piece, disposed of his silver spoons, and provided his godchildren with four pence each, but ensured that his 'land in East Chickerell and Causewaye' (in Radipole) would provide an income for his daughters. His possessions included 'yokes and ropes' and 'corn and grain....whether it be in the barn or gleanings upon the ground'. He also made bequests of individual heifers to specific beneficiaries. The area was clearly involved in both arable farming and probably dairying. The agricultural economy of the area may well not have changed a great deal from the preceding centuries. The will of Gratuit Jesope, widow of John Jesope of Chickerell, proved in 1604 (National Archives PROB 11/104/191), indicated that she had inherited from her husband an interest in a building let as a parsonage in Southampton, as well as holdings in both West and East Chickerell. Her son John was evidently a minor as she had to appoint a guardian for him. The family was still well off enough for Gratuit to make several cash bequests of around ten pounds.

From the later 17th century it is clear that the affairs of Putton and East Chickerell had been largely disentangled. Thomas Baynard, who died in 1684 (National Archives 11/743/349) owned the farm in East Chickerell (National Archives PROB 11/378/274), where he appears to have lived, as well as holding leased lands in Athelhampton, Burleston and Tolpuddle. He provided cash bequests amounting to thousands of pounds. He left his 'manor capital messuage farm and demesnes of East Chickerell' to his son John as well as other lands in West Chickerell, East Chickerell and Radipole. The will of Christopher Farewell of East Chickerell proved in 1745 is clear

that the East Chickerell farm included lands in East and West Chickerell and 'Radipole Causeway' and Southill, but not Putton.

In contrast, the landholding pattern across West Chickerell and Putton seems to have remained enmeshed throughout the 16th and 17th centuries. A will of 1575 proved August 1576, of William Samwaies 'of Putton within the parish of West Chickerell' (National Archives PROB 11/58/328), also provides an interesting glimpse of the wider connections of landowners in this period. Samwaies bequeathed three shillings and four pence to 'the Cathedral Church of Bristol', as well as the same amount to West Chickerell church. While it does not describe William's holdings in Putton, it does mention that he also owned a tenement in Melcombe. Robert Smarte of West Chickerell's will of 1610 (National Archives PROB 11/115/462) refers to land in both West Chickerell and Putton which was bequeathed his wife Joane, but it does not specify the location of the Putton element. This may be the same Robert Smart as listed in the 1592 Subsidy roll as having goods of £4, suggesting that he was not a major landowner. It may be that the land was then passed on to Nicholas Smarte, who in 1615 was accusing Richard Allen alias Belpit of Weymouth and Melcombe Regis, merchant, John Rake, parson of West Chickerell, his wife Elizabeth Rake, 'and others' of 'riotous resistance to collection of tithe of West Chickerell' (National Archives STAC 8/270/22). Land in Putton was subject to a number of property disputes. William and Edith Bussell brought a complaint in 1648 (National Archives C 8/111/13) against Thomas and Marie Scammell concerning property in Chickerell and Putton. A further complaint was brought in 1652 by John Wallys (National Archives C 3/466/40) against Thomas Risbye and his wife Rebecca regarding property in Putton. Several people evidently had interests in various components of the tithing, although it is not possible to identify what these were.

The emergence of Putton Farm

In 1699 a tripartite assignment of mortgage was raised (Dorset History Centre D-GOO/3097) between James Gould of Dorchester, esq, and Anthony Floyer of Stratton, esq, (the executors of the will of John Gould the elder of Upway, gent) to John Gould of Milborne St Andrew, esq, and Hubert Gould of Upway, gent (two of the sons of John Gould the elder), and to Lawrence Purchase of the Inner Temple, London, gent, and James Gould of Upway, gent (a further son of John Gould the elder) for the 'manor or farm of Putton and Chickerels alias West Chickerell lying in the parish of Chickerell with all messuages, cottages, gardens, orchards, buildings, meadows'. However, Putton soon changed hands again.

The will of Richard Harris proved in 1729 but written in 1714 (Blandford Calendar of Wills) provides a considerably greater amount of detail with respect to what must have been a considerable proportion of the original medieval holding. Harris (described as being 'of Putton in the parish of West Chickerell, Yeoman') left a number of parcels of land to his son John (who was baptised at Chickerell in 1699) 'in the manner [sic] of Putton', with the residue going to his wife Anne. John received a total of 13½ acres of meadow and pasture, along with 'ten ewe sheep and ten hogg sheep', evidently enough to provide a start-up business. The fields are named and in some cases the location described; at least two fields retained their names until the 1839 Tithe Apportionment. None of these fields were large parcels, in several cases only being around half an acre and none more than two acres. The named fields are described in a way which reflects how they appear on the earliest, late 18th century map. This implies that the pattern of land division through this period was stable, and there is no reason to think that the pattern of fields in the early 18th century was not of long standing by that point. The will of Richard Harris helpfully provides a description of the remains of the estate which Anne Harris received. The 'lands and tenements' are described as comprising 'meadow, pasture and arable lands, feedings and commons of pasture'. There was also his 'dwelling house, barn, stables, stalls and outhouses', as well as 'implements and household goods and chattels'. It is against this description that perhaps some of the later buildings within the Lower Putton Lane site and the type and quality of objects disposed of in the area should be considered.

In the mid-18th century, it seems that the farm at Putton had passed into the hands of Roger Wellstead, who is described as 'gentleman, of Putton, Yeoman', when he entered his plea in the quarter sessions in 1768 'for a nuisance' (Dorset History Centre Q/S/M/2/8). A year later it seems that the population or passing trade warranted the establishment of a victualling house in Putton, with James Randall of Putton, victualler, obtaining the licence (Dorset History Centre Q/S/M/2/9). It is not clear where this establishment was situated, although the maps of the earlier 20th century have a building immediately to the east of the Lower Putton Lane site noted as The Fisherman's Arms public house. The land tax returns for the later 18th and early 19th centuries (Dorset History Centre Q/D/E/L0/18/1/10) are helpful in that they clearly indicate that the taxable value of Putton was half that of East Chickerell, which provides a hint of the area of good land available by that time. The exonerated taxation remained static until 1832. By 1780 Putton was in the ownership of William Templeman and let to Edward Beale; there were a number of other people listed within the tything, but it is unclear where they held property, and from the taxation applied some interests were clearly minor. It is possible that the buildings within the former manorial site may relate to some of these individuals.

An Inclosure Act was passed in 1789 for '*dividing and allotting the Open and Common Fields, and other Commonable Lands and Grounds, in Putton alias Podington, in the Village or Tything of Easton, in the Parish of Chickerill alias West Chickerill*' (Parliamentary Archives HL/PO/PB/1/1789/29G3n54), a description which serves to underline the confusion which had probably arisen out of the long and complex relationship between the three manors. Putton Farm was depicted on this map (Fig. 5.2), located to the north of Lower Putton Lane, where the farmhouse still stands. According to the land tax returns Mr Templeman still held Putton in 1800, but by 1805 it was in the hands of a Mr Bowles and let to John Kellaway and Henry Bartlett. Charles Bowls had Putton Farm (now explicitly named) let to Kellaway and Robert Fowler in 1808 and 1810, and to John Flower in 1819. Charles Bowls died in 1822 (his memorial is in St Mary's Church, West Chickerell [Trevarthen and Bellamy 2011]), leaving Putton Farm to his wife, Anne. Between 1826 and 1832 it was let

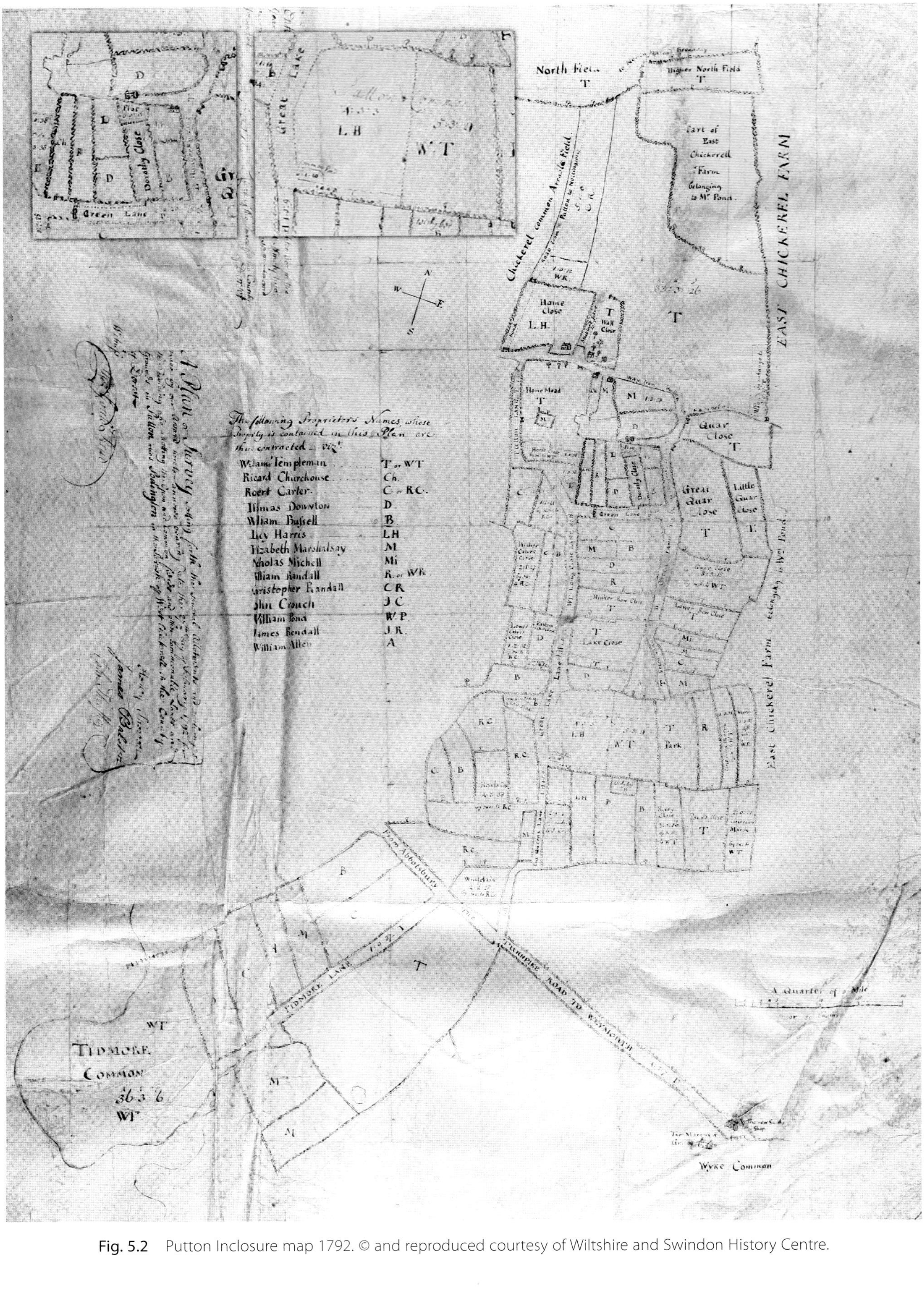

Fig. 5.2 Putton Inclosure map 1792. © and reproduced courtesy of Wiltshire and Swindon History Centre.

to Isaac Rabbetts who was listed as the tenant of Putton Farm in the Tithe Apportionment of 1839. In the 1841 census, Isaac, a yeoman farmer, was living at Putton Farm with his wife and two servants.

THE MANOR AND THE MAPS

The overall area of the ecclesiastical parish (prior to 19th century boundary changes) provides us with the template within which the three medieval Chickerell manors can be ascertained, as parishes were often co-terminous with other administrative units. The three manors developed on differing trajectories. West Chickerell ultimately obtained the present village centre with the late 13th century church of St Mary the Virgin at its core. Putton and East Chickerell became the location of farms. Each had a relationship with the Chickerell brook, which appears to have risen immediately to the south of the West Chickerell village centre and ran east through Putton and East Chickerell to empty into Radipole Lake. The water course ran through the site at Lower Putton Lane. It does not appear on the Inclosure or Tithe maps, but is clearly depicted on the 1st edition Ordnance Survey map crossing the site from west to east, with a couple of right angled dog-legs in the centre of the site which took its original course south of the area originally occupied by the manorial buildings (Fig. 1.28). The 1882 OS map shows a pond in the middle of the northern boundary of the site, opposite the Putton Farm buildings, from which a watercourse runs south to meet the Chickerell brook. The pond appears to have disappeared by the 1930s. On the later 19th and early 20th century maps a well is shown close by which may correspond with the post-medieval well identified during the excavation. This had disappeared from maps between 1902 and 1929. The use of a well may have become necessary as the brook was affected up stream by the development of West Chickerell during the 19th century.

Putton was subject to Inclosure by an act of parliament in 1789. This involved the re-organisation of the 'East Field' 'West Field' and 'Putton Plain' (RCHME 1970, 41), and these elements appear to be the remnants of the medieval land organisation. Luckily both the Putton Inclosure map and assignment (Wiltshire and Swindon History Centre D/375/1/3) (Fig. 5.2)

and the 1804 Inclosure map of West Chickerell (Dorset History Centre Ph.30) survive. The boundary between the tithings of West Chickerell and Putton has in many cases been preserved in the modern road system (including part of what is now Putton Lane and School Hill) and follows features similar to those on the Tithe map and the 1st edition Ordnance Survey map. We can be reasonably confident that this boundary between the tithings is largely that of the medieval arrangement. There is however a slight discrepancy. The Putton Inclosure map shows Putton having its northern extent at the bend in the road at the north end of what is now School Hill, with the Coldharbour road forming the northern boundary. However, the West Chickerell Inclosure map shows its eastern boundary continuing north up to the parish boundary, with a large area of land immediately to the north of West Chickerell village marked as 'part of the tything of Putton'. In general terms there is a north–south orientation of land boundaries across the Chickerell area which is reflected right back to the 1792 Inclosure map. Given the degree of adherence to the north–south arrangement in the central portion of the West Chickerell and Putton tithings, it is possible that the original demarcation between the two continued on a northern trajectory until it met the parish boundary. It may be that this portion of land had by the time of the Inclosure been incorporated with land held by Putton Farm and was regarded by whoever drew up the West Chickerell map as being part of the Putton tithing.

The eastern boundary of the Putton tithing shown on the 1792 Inclosure map (Fig. 5.2) commences at Coldharbour and follows a series of parcels along a generally north–south boundary, situated c. 300m to the west of East Chickerell farm. This ceases at a corner to the south-east of a pond which appears on all of the maps, before running due west, and then turning south west, crossing the turnpike road from Wyke to Abbotsbury and incorporating land either side of a road leading to Tidmoor Point on the Fleet. This arrangement might be original, but as with the discrepancy with West Chickerell at the north end of the tithing, it may be that the original manorial boundary continued its north–south trajectory from the point where it turned to the west (Fig. 5.3). A north–south course would have meant that it met the

N

West Chickerell

suggested
demesne land

Putton

East Chickerell

suggested
demesne land

Putton Common

common
pond

'Gormere'

The Fleet

Boundary of West Chickerell Tithing, 1804

Boundary of Putton Tithing, 1792

Suggested boundary

0   1km

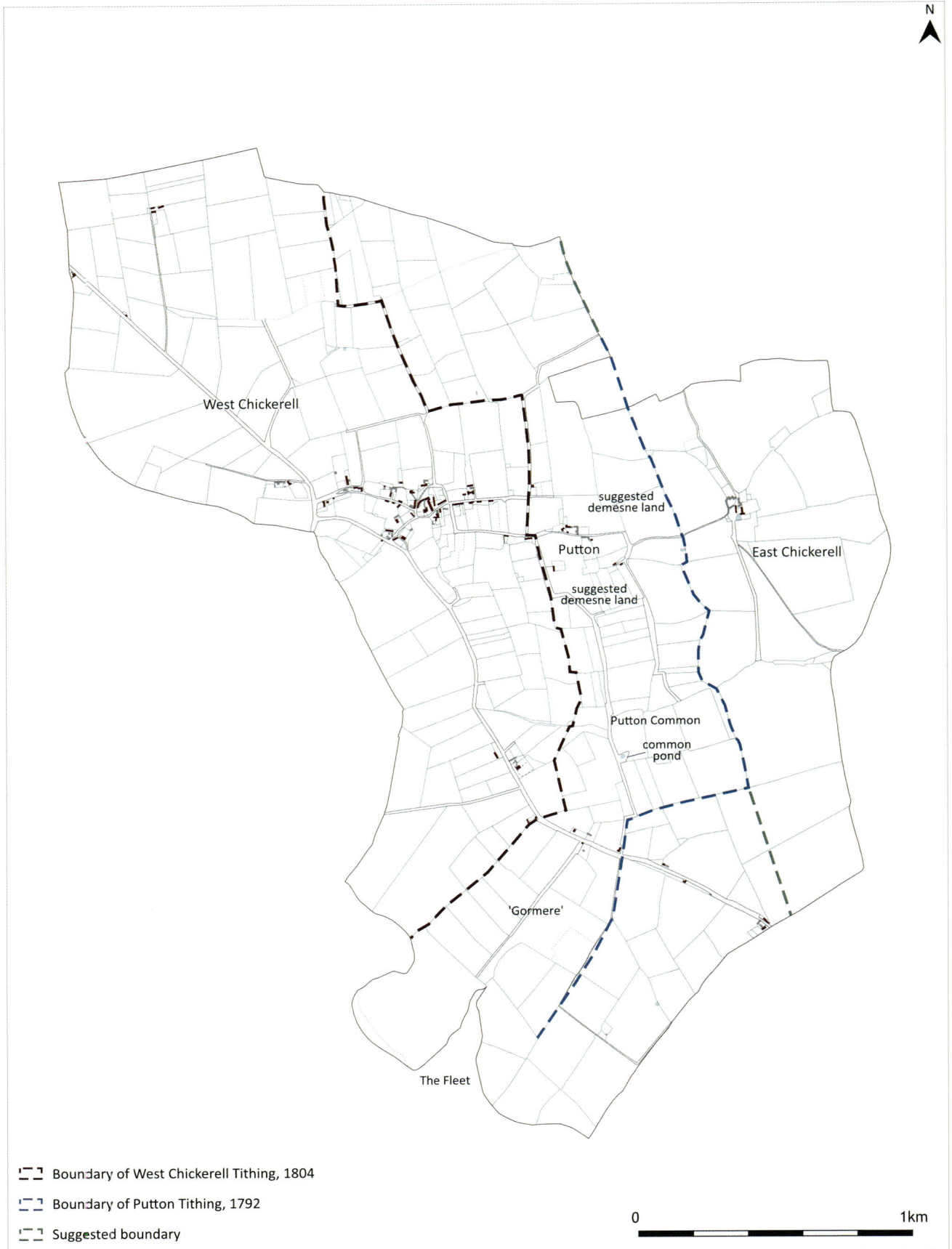

Fig. 5.3   The Putton manor reconstructed from the West Chickerell and Putton Inclosure maps, overlaid on the Chickerell Tithe map.

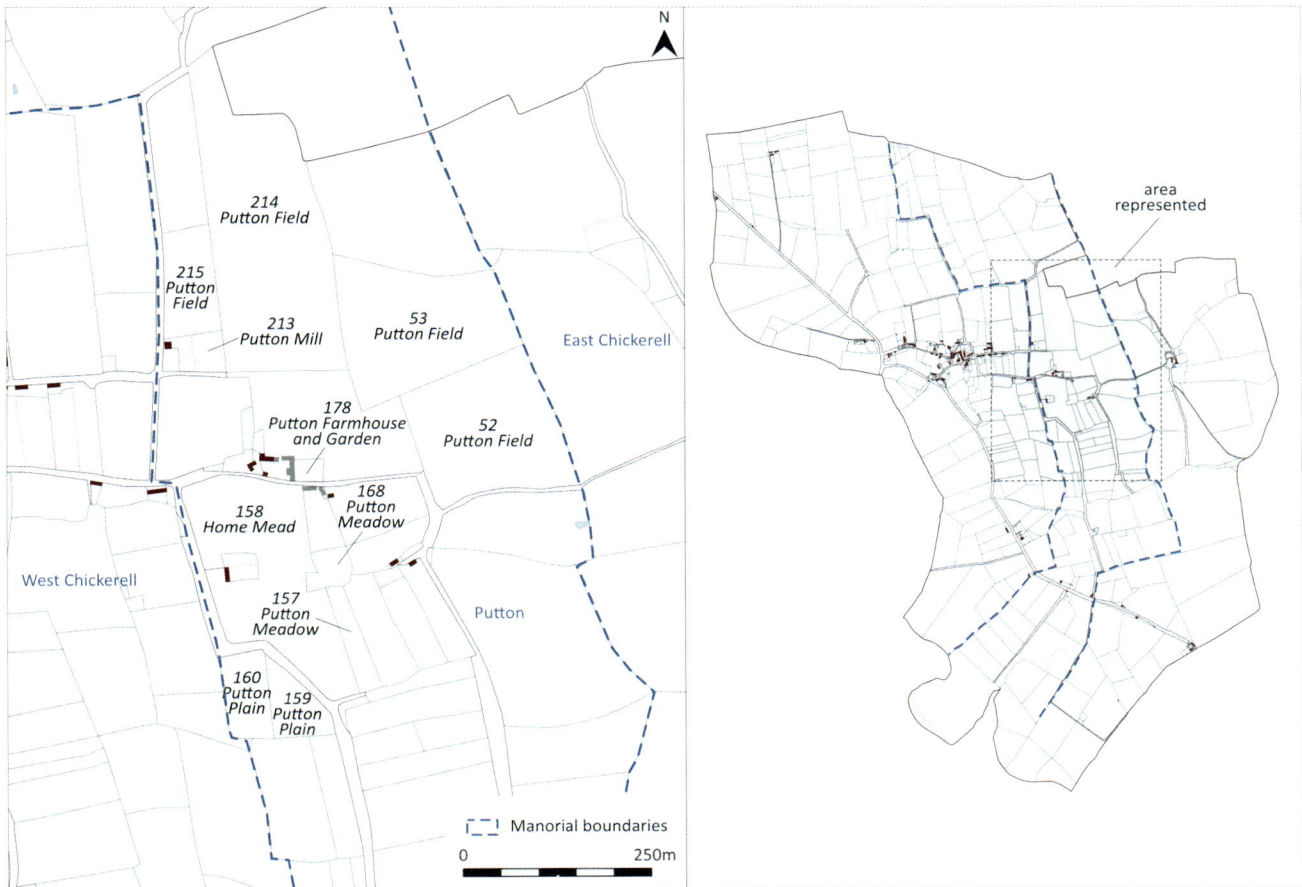

Fig. 5.4   Field names from the Chickerell Tithe map.

Wyke Regis parish boundary near the point where it was crossed by the turnpike road; the fields to the south shown on the Chickerell Tithe map continue a north–south arrangement, if slightly offset. If this was the case, the land noted as being part of 'East Chickerell Farm' may have been acquired during the 17th or 18th century, and by the time of the Putton Inclosure the tithing relationship had disappeared. However, it is notable that the pattern of land parcels within West Chickerell and Putton very clearly reflect numerous small, and often narrow, closes on a north–south and east–west pattern, whilst the Tithe map shows a distinct contrast with the field pattern within East Chickerell. This includes a difference in the pattern between the south-western area shown as part of Putton on the 1792 map, and the land immediately to the east. Perhaps any common fields within East Chickerell were not subdivided to the same extent or were not amalgamated from strip cultivation as appears to be the case at Putton. The East Chickerell field names listed on the Tithe

Apportionment are not particularly helpful being rather generic or related to more recent features (e.g. Lime Kiln Field).

The field names included in both the 1792 Putton Inclosure map and the 1839 Tithe Apportionment (Dorset History Centre D1-LX/9/1) assist with understanding the potential internal layout of the manor. On the Tithe, names include 'Putton Field', 'Putton Mill', 'Putton Meadow' and 'Putton Plain'. 'Putton Field' comprised four larger parcels of land, all to the north of the Putton Farm farmhouse (Fig. 5.4). Comparing the field names in the Tithe Apportionment with the stated intention in the Putton Inclosure Act to enclose the 'East Field' and 'West Field' and 'Putton Plain', it seems that the east and west fields are probably the two halves of the group of fields referred to as 'Putton Field' on the Tithe. These were all arable fields. Putton Plain is the name of two small fields to the south of the farm on the Tithe, on the west side of Putton Lane.

It seems likely that this originally referred to a wider area, possibly including parts of 'Home Mead' which now has a quite generic name, probably relating to its proximity to the buildings of Putton Farm. The numerous small rectilinear closes to the east of Home Mead may preserve some indication of strip cultivation. Two of these parcels were called 'Putton Meadow'. The area covered by these field names would have comfortably accommodated the amount of arable land referred to in the medieval documentation. On the 1792 Inclosure map (Fig. 5.2), an area to the south is identified as Putton Common. The pond beside the north–south road which would become Putton Lane (here somewhat ironically named as Great Lake Lane) is labelled as the 'common pond', whilst to the east a field carries the name 'Pound'. The north–south road, Green Lane, parallel to Putton Lane, but running through the centre of the manorial area terminates where the common began. It clearly provided access for moving livestock around the manor.

If these arrangements were of long standing, and we have no reason to believe that they were not, we can speculate on the location of land farmed directly from the manorial centre and that which was tenanted. The location of demesne land within a manorial unit was highly variable. It depended on the local type of agriculture and organisation as well as regional and topographic considerations (Bailey 2002, 4). However, the proximity of the 'Putton' field names to the now known manorial centre suggests that they may encompass what had originally been the demesne land (Fig. 5.3). The common to the south occupies an area which is open land even today, with some marshy elements. Further to this the south-western extent of the manor which ran from Putton Common down to the Fleet, might reasonably be described as triangular in shape. This may allow its identification with the area mentioned in 1292 as the pasture Gormere and discussed above. The area identified via the Inclosure map is approximately 130 acres in extent. The medieval references to Gormere describe it as comprising 120 acres, so it is strongly suggested that it is to be identified with this area. The road to Tidmoor also may have been of some long standing. It lies axially through the middle of this portion of land and links the rest of the road system within

Putton with the inlet next to Tidmoor Point, which may have represented a good beaching point.

The Putton Inclosure map may also assist in understanding the original location of any peasant settlement associated with the manorial centre. The earthworks to the south of the excavation area at Putton Lane (Fig. 1.28) have been in the past assumed to provide the location of the Putton 'village'. However, they largely comprise a north-south aligned holloway adjoined by two banks on an east–west orientation. Neither on the ground nor in the geophysical survey were there any indications of smaller enclosures within this area (see Chapter 1). Comparing them to the Inclosure map, it is clear that the two east–west lynchets still present to either side of the holloway correspond very well to the boundaries of a parcel called Horse Craft (sic 'Croft'?). It seems from the style of representation on this map that the boundaries were not functional during the late 18th century. The lack of house platforms and limited findings from evaluation trenches in this area (see Chapter 1) does not support this being a settlement centre. However, a possible alternative is presented by the arrangement of roads to the immediate east of the now known location of the manorial centre. These are most clearly depicted on the Inclosure map (Fig. 5.2). Green Lane ran from what is now Lower Putton Lane, due south until it reached Putton Common, providing a spinal routeway through the heart of the Putton tithing, unlike the earthworks which are on the western edge of the holding. Immediately due east of the location of the manor buildings was a more complex and apparently partly curvilinear arrangement of roads which are depicted as having at least two buildings on them, with the road at this point being named as Hungerhill Lane. This area may present a more likely location for any original associated settlement and would have been situated to the east of the main entrance of the manorial complex.

Further insights into the development of the Chickerell settlements are provided by the 1804 West Chickerell Inclosure map and 1839 Tithe map and apportionment. The centre of West Chickerell village has a very irregular road pattern (Fig. 5.5). The oldest buildings in West Chickerell are situated around the curvilinear arrangement of roads (RCHME 1970a, 39–

Fig. 5.5 The centre of West Chickerell village from the West Chickerell Inclosure map 1804. Reproduced with permission of Dorset History Centre.

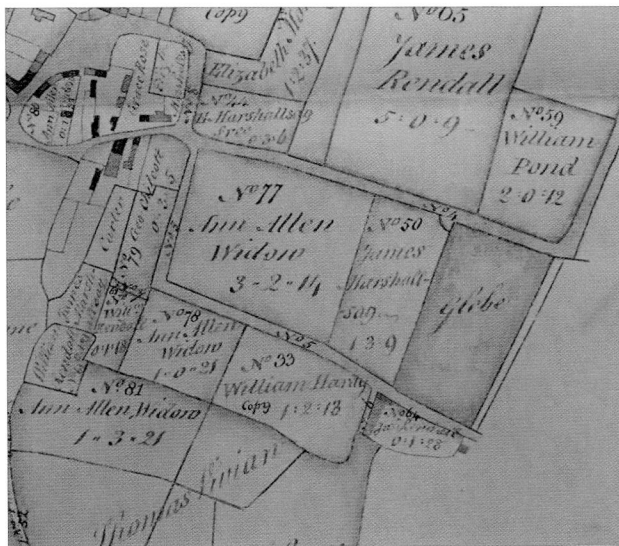

Fig. 5.6 The rectilinear arrangement of roads between West Chickerell and Putton from the West Chickerell Inclosure map 1804. Reproduced with permission of Dorset History Centre.

40) which indicates that this arrangement predates the act of Inclosure. The church sits on the outside of this core. Ricketts (1977) suggested that this reflects a late Saxon settlement. This arrangement appears embedded within a wider north–south organisation of fields. This has created an irregular shape to some land parcels which makes no sense if they were imposed around this curvilinear pattern, but can be explained if the curvilinear arrangement was positioned within an existing rectilinear landscape.

Both the 1804 and 1839 maps indicate further roads to the south of the village centre which appear to have fallen into disuse. The buildings fronting the available roads in 1839 and particularly in 1804 are sparse, and the appearance is reminiscent of a shrunken settlement.

The area between the centre of West Chickerell and Putton Farm shows more roads than are necessary or make sense by way of creating routes between West and East Chickerell (Fig. 5.6). Two parallel west–east roads are present, the southern one being the one on which Putton Farm was constructed, and which led to East Chickerell. However, this was only accessible via a north–south stretch, and there is no obvious obstacle to be avoided. The northern road, leading directly out of West Chickerell, went to a field named on the 1839 Tithe as Putton Mill, but evidently originally continued to the east before being preserved in a field boundary. These two parallel roads were linked by a further north–south section between Putton Mill and Putton Farm, creating a rectangular block. In 1804 this was divided into three parcels; by 1839 it had been further subdivided and buildings constructed facing the northern of the two parallel roads. It is hard to see any practical reason for the creation or preservation of this arrangement during a period when there were no clear structures or destinations, but it appears to have been of similar longstanding as the rest of the road network. It is possible that it might represent medieval expansion of the centre of West Chickerell which had subsequently failed. Its form has similarities with planned settlements elsewhere in the county.

By the time of the 1st edition Ordnance survey maps of the 1880s there had been a degree of infilling around West Chickerell. The Putton brickworks, established in the earlier 19th century, were largely out of use by the 1860s (Smith 2012, 90). Situated c. 400m to the south of Putton Farm they were located on fields listed on the 1869 Tithe as Calves Close (part of the holdings of Putton Farm as early as 1714) and Long Close. Ultimately the clay extraction pits became a Wildlife Trust reserve and Bennett's Water Gardens, whilst the site of the brickworks and the land between it and Putton Farm were developed for residential housing.

6

'A CAPITAL MESSUAGE WITH A CURTILAGE…'

By Clare Randall, with contributions by Cheryl Green

The archaeological study of medieval rural settlement, agriculture and industry in Dorset has to date been relatively limited. Whilst there is some understanding of the development of primary urban centres, monastic and other ecclesiastical sites, both the pattern of modern development in the county and the interests of researchers have resulted in limited archaeological exploration of the rural landscape beyond extant settlements. Important exceptions are outlined in Chapter 1. However, the opportunity had not arisen previously to examine a large area of the core of a medieval manorial complex. In their assessment of the state of the archaeology of the county in the early 1980s, Groube and Bowden (1982) identified medieval fishing and coastal industry, agricultural practice and the full settlement pattern as being issues which needed to be addressed. Where the county has been included in wider analyses (e.g. the Fields of Britannia project [Rippon et al. 2015]), its contribution of data has been limited. Consequently, Dorset now appears within a zone largely defined by data from other parts of that zone. Whilst the high-level nature of the research is acknowledged, the true texture of the county's medieval settlement, agriculture and the wider economy remains largely obscure. Consequently, the site at Lower Putton Lane provides important insights into both the specificities and more general questions about the development of settlement patterns and land use in Dorset and beyond during this period. It also offers the first instance in Dorset

where developments in domestic architecture of the 13th–14th centuries can be seen sequentially on the same site.

THE PRE-MEDIEVAL ARCHAEOLOGY,
By Clare Randall

Prehistoric activity was attested by a general spread of flint across all three excavated areas. This was not associated with any specific features but incorporated into colluvial deposits which both underlay and covered the medieval buildings. The material has not been examined in detail as part of this project, but it fits within a general distribution of worked flint in the area. A Mesolithic convex scraper is recorded as being found at Crook Hill (Fig. 6.1. no. 1), whilst further material of the period came from works at St Mary's church, West Chickerell (Fig. 6.1. no. 2; Trevarthen and Bellamy 2011). Two sherds of later prehistoric pottery were recovered at Lower Putton Lane from deposits near the cross wall of B5. On fabric grounds this has been suggested to be of Late Bronze Age or Early Iron Age date. It was clearly residual (Mepham, Chapter 2), and the location is suggestive of it having travelled before deposition; the area adjacent to the culvert was prone to flooding. Bronze Age pottery was also noted at St Mary's Church (Trevarthen and Bellamy 2011), and at East Chickerell sub-station (Fig. 6.1. no. 3). There is other general evidence of activity of this

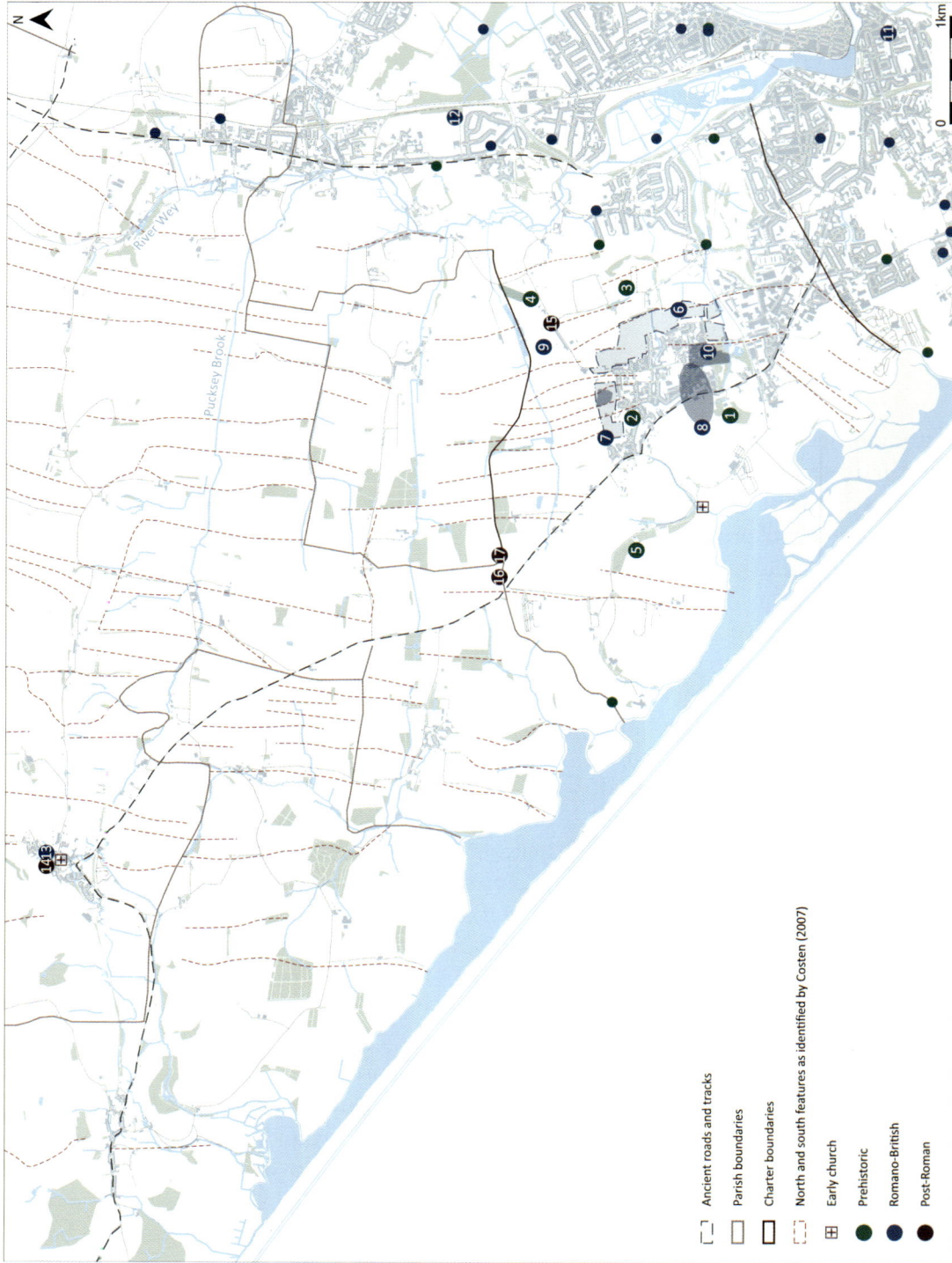

Fig. 6.1 Prehistoric and Romano-British sites and findspots. 1. Mesolithic convex scraper, Crook Hill (MWX 374). 2. Mesolithic flint and Bronze Age pottery, St, Mary's Church (Trevarthen and Bellamy 2011).3. Bronze Age pottery, East Chickerell substation (MWX3550). 4. Later Bronze Age South Buckland linear earthwork (MDO 24772). 5. Late Bronze Age gold neck rings, Chickerell (MWX4830). 6. Romano-British field system (MDO 41992). 7. Romano-British settlement and fields, north of Chickerell village (EDO6262; EDO6579; MDO 41991). 8. Blacklands field names. 9. Coldharbour place name. 10. Romano-British burials and object findspots, Putton brickworks (e.g. MDO24835). 11. Villa, Newberry Road, Weymouth (MDO6655). 12. Romano-British occupation, Redlands, Broadwey (MDO6692). 13. Romano-British occupation, Manor Farm, Portesham (MWX2926). 14. Post-Roman cemetery, Manor Farm, Portesham (MWX2927). 15. Stone lined graves, Coldharbour. 16. Stone lined graves, Tatton Farm (MDO2071). 17. Stone lined graves, Buckland Ripers, Coldharbour.

period in the immediate area, for example the South Buckland linear earthwork which may be late Bronze Age or earlier Iron Age in date (Fig. 6.1. no. 4), and the findspot of the late Bronze Age Chickerell neck rings (Fig. 6.1. no. 5; Woodward 2000) which subsequently produced evidence of a Late Neolithic or Early Bronze Age monument, later Bronze Age settlement and Romano-British occupation (Woodward 2002).

A limited spread of Romano-British material culture probably derived from manuring from nearby settlement during the Romano-British period. The material included 18 Romano-British sherds, a copper alloy needle of Roman type and four coins, three of them of Antoninus Pius (mid-2nd century) and one a rare Antoninianus of Gallienus, dating to AD 268. All of these were residual in later contexts or completely unstratified finds. There was nothing to suggest a substantive Romano-British presence on the site itself. However, there are a number of Romano-British sites nearby (Fig. 6.1). Romano-British material was recovered from a field system during an archaeological evaluation immediately to the east of Putton (Fig. 6.1. no. 6; Wessex Archaeology 2016). The fields were on a similar orientation to the existing field layout. Further evidence for settlement and fields of this period were also identified to the north of Chickerell village centre (Fig. 6.1. no. 7; Cotswold Archaeology 2016). A group of 'Blacklands' field names listed in the 1839 tithe apportionment were located to the west of Putton (Fig. 6.1. no. 8). Blacklands names can be highly suggestive of Romano-British occupation. Coldharbour (Fig. 6.1. no. 9) names tend to have an association with Roman roads (Cooper 2002). The use of the Coldharbour road as the northern boundary of the Putton tithing on the 1792 Putton Inclosure map (see Chapter 5) may be therefore significant.

Considerable evidence of Romano-British activity is known from the area of the Putton Brickworks (Fig. 6.1. no. 10) which was located c. 400–600m to the south of Putton. Numerous burials were recovered (Prideaux 1925; Smith 1934; Farrar 1963; 1965; Winnall 1978; RCHME 1970a). A complete terra nigra dish, apparently from a cist burial provided a date of 50–85 AD (Goodyer 1986). This seems to have been a nucleus of activity, some of it potentially of high status. However, due to extensive 19th century clay extraction and processing, and its subsequent redevelopment for residential housing, the likelihood of ever recovering more detail is slim. It does appear however that in common with other parts of the coastal strip and the Wey valley (e.g. Newberry Road, Weymouth; Redlands; Manor Farm, Portesham [Fig. 6.1. no. 11, no. 12, and no. 13]), Romano-British utilisation of this landscape was widespread. This activity possibly extended into the post-Roman period. There was a cemetery dated to the post-Roman period at Manor Farm, Portesham (Fig. 6.1. no. 14; see below). A pair of east–west burials in stone lined graves at Coldharbour, immediately north of the Lower Putton Lane site (Fig. 6.1. no. 15; Hinton 1998, 23) may be part of a larger cemetery of late Romano-British or post-Roman date (Woodward and Smith 1996), whilst the same may be true of further stone lined graves which occurred at Tatton and Buckland Ripers (Fig. 6.1. no. 16 and no. 17).

With evidence of Romano-British activity on all sides, the scatter of finds at Putton is unsurprising. This material culture probably also relates to the emmer and spelt wheat fragments which were recovered from the site, although they could have been of early medieval date. Not generally cultivated in Britain after the end of the Romano-British period, these fragments were of limited number and spread over different parts of the site, although the majority came from one Phase 2 pit beneath B5 (Carruthers, Chapter 4). They possibly derived from features destroyed or masked by later construction. The underpinning Romano-British activity also informs consideration of the structure of the later landscape which will be discussed below.

THE SEQUENCE OF CREATION OF THE MANORIAL COMPLEX, By Clare Randall

The evidence for the earliest medieval activity at Lower Putton Lane is ephemeral. It primarily relies on the presence of unstratified finds recovered during the metal detecting of the site. The earliest medieval objects are a fragment of a copper alloy strap-end of the 8th–10th centuries, an ansate brooch, dating to the 10th century, and a silver longcross penny of Aethelred II (978–1016) (Schuster, Chapter 3). The ansate brooch is only the second example known from Dorset. The main distribution for this type is in the north-east and down the east coast of England (Ciostaidh Hayward-Trevarthen pers. comm.). Two loops for horse harness cheek pieces or strap distributors belong to a type dated to the first half of the 11th century. Added to this is a high-quality gold and rock crystal brooch of mid-11th to early 12th century date. The construction implies that not only was it a high-status object but that it had continental origins. It was probably produced in central Europe by Italian goldsmiths with a relationship to the imperial court of the Holy Roman Empire (Schuster, Chapter 3). How it travelled to Putton may only be speculated upon, but the Imperial court of that time had links to Empress Matilda. During the Anarchy in 1139 her army invaded south west England via Poole Harbour (Davis 1977). As it was effectively a stray find, it is not possible to say whether it belonged to the earlier period of medieval use of the site, or if it was an heirloom in the possession of the occupants of the 13th–14th centuries. However, it evidently belonged to someone of some substance, and it attests to long distance elite contacts, either directly or indirectly.

The limited selection of Saxo-Norman pottery largely occurred in features and deposits of later date but indicates the likely existence of a predecessor settlement. The pottery provides a date of the 11th–12th centuries into the early 13th century (Mepham, Chapter 2) for the initial features recognised on the site (Phase 2). Activity prior to the main stone construction phase is attested by the ditches which underlay B4 in the southern part of Area 3, and deposits and pits beneath B1 and B5 (Fig. 1.7). The high degree of inter-cutting between the pits under B5 suggests that there may have been a relatively protracted period of activity prior to the first stone building construction. However, the small-scale and poor chronological resolution of the ceramic assemblage is unhelpful in determining the precise period over which these features were created, or indeed their function. With much of these earlier levels cut away by the later buildings, it was not possible to postulate any structural role for them, although that cannot be entirely discounted. A single post-hole was sealed beneath B1 which may hint at earlier timber structures. However, it seems that the pits in the area of B5

may have been intended more for the removal of clay, potentially analogous to a series of 12th century pits at Ower Farm which was suggested as related to the extraction of the raw materials for cob walling (Cox et al. 1991a, 85). The Putton pits apparently had a limited role in receiving refuse, although F107 did contain a high concentration of fish bones and scales. One pit, F76, stood open for some time. It accumulated a significant deposit of adult and juvenile frog bones, attesting to the damp nature of this part of the site (Randall, Chapter 4).

It was during this early period that the boundary around the complex was first created. It may have in part utilised the course of the Chickerell stream. The route of the stream is shown on later 19th and earlier 20th century maps as running across the field generally west to east but in the middle of the field turning to the south of the location of the complex of buildings; in modern times it has been altered to create a culvert which cut through the southern part of the excavated area. If the course of the stream shown on the 1st edition Ordnance Survey map reflected its route during the medieval period, then it would have passed on the west and south sides of the southern end of B5 and to the south of B4. A further channel, still extant, but possibly altered, is shown on the 1st edition Ordnance survey map running north–south from the location of a pond located on the northern boundary of the site opposite Putton Farm farmhouse, down the west side of the building complex to meet the main stream course. In other places, a ditched boundary was created around the occupied area during Phase 2. The substantial ditch (F85) on the east side of Area 3 included a terminal suggesting an eastern entrance. A matching ditch terminal was not seen but this is probably because there had been recent terracing into the rise relating to the modern culvert. The initial fills of F85 contained pottery of the 12th century with the later fills accumulating 13th–14th century material as it went out of use. It may have been accompanied by a fence, or, because no post-holes were seen, a cob wall. Documentary references of the early 15th century at Kingston Lacy refer to a cob court wall with a thatched cover (Papworth 1998, 47). Something similar may have been employed at Putton. It is probable that F80 provided part of the circuit on the west side of the complex. The series of ditches beneath B4 may also have demarcated the southern side of a pre-Phase 3 court. Ditch F85/F80 has similarities with a substantial linear feature seen at Ower Farm, on the south side of Poole Harbour. At Ower, during the earliest 12th century phase, a ditch 1.1m wide and 1.75m deep with steep sides and a flat base, was constructed which was interpreted as either a drainage or boundary ditch around the buildings (Cox et al. 1991a, 83–85). Providing a physical boundary to settlements was clearly an established practice by this time.

The first stone buildings were constructed during Phase 3 (Fig. 1.11). The nature of these is discussed below. Direct evidence for the date of B2 is limited, but the pottery sealed beneath it seems to indicate a point no earlier than the early 13th century. This would accord with similarly limited dating available for the construction of B1 to the north-east, and probably B4 to the south. If these three structures were constructed or existed at the same time, they formed three sides around the outside of the enclosed space. The next major act of construction involved the demolition of B5 and construction of B2 (Phase 4; Fig. 1.29). This seems to have happened in the later 13th century or early 14th century. The expansion of the church of St Mary in West Chickerell via a 13th century rebuild has been suggested to relate to an expanding population (Trevarthen and Bellamy 2011), which would coincide with the changes at Putton. B2 was on a similar alignment as its predecessor (albeit skewed slightly to the north-west), but involved a shift to the north, effectively upslope. This moved the building onto the limestone bedrock, possibly partly quarried in the earlier period, and which provided a platform. This was clear of the area apparently most prone to flooding (and demonstrated to be wet from the amphibians in pit F76). The elaborate east facing porch retained the general orientation of the complex whilst it seems that B1 and B4 continued in use throughout the life of B2.

One significant effect of the construction of B2 to the north of its predecessor was that it opened out onto a space on the north side of B1, rather than into the original court. The overburden in this area was much thinner than further down the slope so there was little indication of contemporary features. However,

it does seem that during this second incarnation of the site arrangement, it was not enclosed with a ditch, and the original enclosure ditch was filling up. The original court may have remained in use, but its control and seclusion were evidently less important. However, at the southern end of B2, W7 continued the alignment of the building to the south. It had the character of a boundary wall rather than an extension to the house structure and would have had the effect of attempting to maintain an enclosure of the space between B2 and B4 from the western side. The less substantial wall, W17, also provided what may have been an enclosed garden. This suggests that there was still a concern to create private space.

Whilst there were few deposits which could be directly associated with the buildings themselves, the large humic deposits in the base of the valley, identified as a midden, along with the vast majority of material overlying the buildings, had a date range covering the 13th–14th centuries. It seems reasonable to assume that this encompasses the life of the buildings. Part of a holloway was also seen, filled with this material. It was on the same alignment and appeared to represent a continuation to the north of the earthwork holloway situated to the south of the site. In addition, a network of field boundaries on the western slope of the site appears to have been in use throughout the same period. As discussed in Chapter 1, it is impossible to assign individual features to a specific main site phase, although the suggested sequence is discussed further below in relation to the farming regime. The boundaries appear to have been almost constantly reworked, with a number of re-diggings and re-orientations, but the material filling them had accumulated in the fields during the same period as the use of the buildings, presumably refuse derived from the manorial muck heap.

THE FORMATION OF THE MANOR,
By Clare Randall

Aside from the complex of manorial buildings, a manor was in essence a 'territorial unit of lordship' (Bailey 2002, 3). The buildings, apart from providing a residence were the location of activities associated with this basic unit of administration. Within an estate, some of the land, the demesne, was the lord's own. It could be leased or directly farmed. Other areas of the manorial holding would have been allocated for the use of the manor's dependent unfree workers, and peasant tenants. The manor was also the jurisdiction for the regulation of various services, fees and rents which were due to the lord. A range of other resources were often included, often a mill but including rights over woodland, fisheries or other raw materials such as salt or minerals (Bailey 2002, 3). Consequently, understanding the scale and nature of the land associated with the Putton manor assists us in fitting the manorial buildings within their productive and tenurial landscape.

The landscape into which the Chickerell manors came into being was already well portioned out by Domesday. To the north settlements were recorded at Bucklanc and Tatton (where both can be related to extant earthworks), with Holwell to the north-east; Wyke, Radipole and Nottington existed to the south and east, with Fleet and Portesham, with its various small settlements to the west (Fig. 6.2). The three Chickerell manorial centres were distributed closely along the line of the Chickerell brook, West Chickerell close to its source, and East Chickerell on its north bank further downstream. The scale and layout of these units, and the boundaries of Putton have been suggested in Chapter 5. However, it is also possible to consider how this arrangement came into being.

The area around the site was clearly well utilised during the Romano-British period (see above). In general terms, the pollen record for the west of England implies a lack of woodland regeneration and continuity of agriculture in the immediate post-Roman period (Dark 2000, 172) which would facilitate a degree of continuity. There are hints of activity in the local area during the post-Roman period. Possible post-Roman burials occurred at Coldharbour (Fig. 6.1. no. 15), just to the north of Putton. Similar burials in stone lined graves occurred at Tatton (Fig. 6.1. no. 16). Unfurnished east–west graves dating to the 6th–8th centuries also occurred at Manor Farm, Portesham (Fig. 6.1. no. 17) on a site previously used for burial in the Romano-British period (Chandler and Valentin 2003). Portesham has been suggested as an early minster site, probably

pre-dating the foundation of Abbotsbury Abbey (Hall 2000, 19–20, 72–3; see Chapter 5). Excavation located a ditch which may represent the *vallum* of an early foundation (Chandler and Valentin, 2003).

Survival of some place names with pre-English roots has been noted in Chapter 5. Stray finds such as the Style I animal ornament pendant of the 6th century from Weymouth (PAS – SOMDOR-A8DD87) reinforce the use of this part of the coast during this period. The distribution of Frisian coinage of the 7th–8th century AD in the Weymouth lowlands, including within Chickerell parish (Costen and Costen 2016, 17; fig. 6), convincingly demonstrates that this was a key locale in early medieval trade. This supports the possibility of a large royal estate in the area, linked to the royal centre at Dorchester (Costen and Costen 2016, 9–10, 16). Chickerell forms the western limit of the Cullifordtree hundred, which it has been argued may have early origins as an estate. During the medieval period, there was an enduring tenurial relationship between Putton and Sutton Poyntz, where there may also have been an important early church (Hall 2000), and royal vill (first recorded in 891). If the Cullifordtree unit was an early medieval estate (Turner 2006, 68) it encompassed both good arable and grazing ground. Importantly it also appears to have included locations, such as Wyke, which provided coastal connectivity.

The north–south pattern of field boundaries around West Chickerell and Putton has been discussed in Chapter 5. The alignment of the holloway earthworks, and its extension and parallel track excavated within the Lower Putton Lane site can be added to this. Aerial photographs (HER reference MDO25713) and geophysics (Stratascan 2016) of the field to the north of Putton Farm farmhouse immediately to the north of the excavated area (Fig. 5.4) indicate the presence of further boundaries or cultivation marks replicating the same arrangement. This landscape structuring does not appear dependent on topography and is largely terrain oblivious. The area falls within a zone of England where a large proportion of later boundaries respect the alignments of earlier Romano-British systems (Rippon et al. 2014). In several parts of Dorset rectilinear field systems relating to medieval manorial arrangements had their origins in the later prehistoric or Romano-

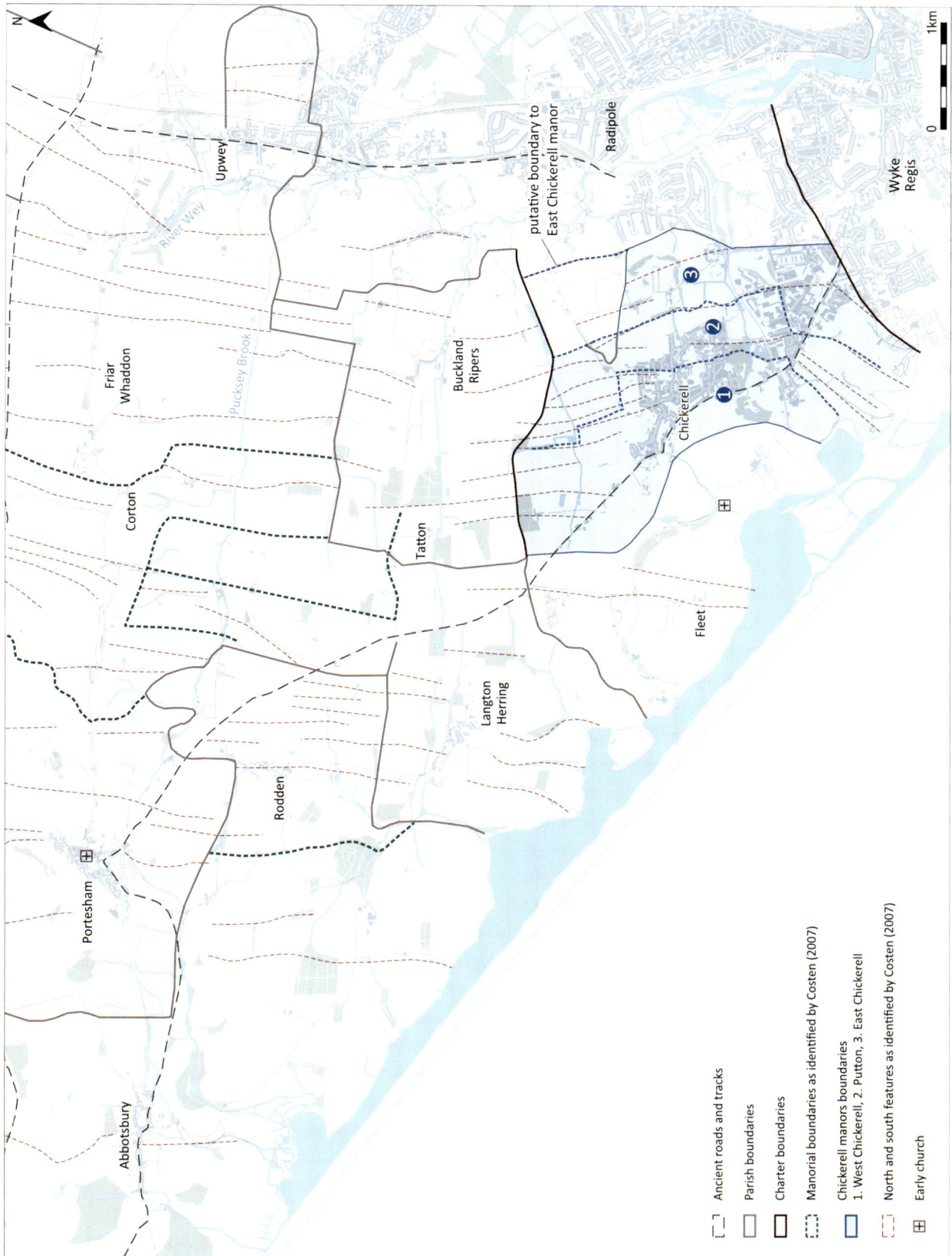

Fig. 6.2 The early landscape of the Chickerell manors.

British landscape (Davey 2013).The Chickerell area sits within an area which Costen (2007) has noted as having a large-scale relict landscape pattern of this type. Roads, tracks and boundaries run in a north to south arrangement across the grain of the landscape and across parish boundaries. This appears to originate as a right-angled offset from the Dorchester-Exeter Roman road, possibly during the late Roman period (Costen 2007, 66–7). It seems highly likely therefore that there was no period of wholesale disruption and re-organisation of the type seen in Devon (Rippon et al. 2006) in the later part of the first millennium AD or in the establishment of an open field system.

Within this existing landscape structure, the Chickerell manors took shape, and evidence of medieval settlement and farming is widespread (Fig. 6.3). By the time of Domesday the landscape had been divided into vills. These were often coterminous with parishes, but frequently contained more than one manor, being the fragments of larger estates (Rippon et al. 2014, 198), which is certainly feasible in the case of Chickerell. The single location referred to as the three hide unit of Chickerell in Domesday seems to describe the group of three later manors. The Old English origin of the name Putton is discussed in Chapter 5. The form of the West Chickerell road layout next to St Mary's Church has been suggested to reflect a late Saxon settlement (Fig. 5.5; Ricketts 1977) although there is no direct evidence for this. With West and East Chickerell, located to either side of Putton, perhaps 'Podington' was inserted into an existing unit. There is evidence elsewhere locally that small late Saxon holdings were inserted into existing larger units. This can be clearly seen in the boundaries and records of Portesham and Buckland Ripers (Costen 2007, 68–69), immediately to the north-west and north of Chickerell. Buckland was a four hide unit at Domesday, held by four thegns indicating a similar unit size as the Chickerell block.

Conversely, the Putton unit could have been early and the two other elements divided from it. Costen believes that place names comprising a personal name with an -ington suffix were being established in the 8th–9th centuries and were therefore one of the earliest creations of new settlement (Michael Costen pers. comm.). As far as the chronology is concerned,

there are a considerable number of -ington suffix names in the area between the Wey, the Ridgeway and the sea (e.g. Nottington; see Chapter 5), and this suggests that there was a phase of some considerable additional partitioning or granting of land. The small selection of early medieval objects from Putton dating between the 8th and 11th century seem to indicate that the creation of the manorial area was part of this process. Locally this was probably followed by the creation of places with a name made up of a personal name with a -tun suffix (e.g. Tatton) which were created in the 9th–10th century (Michael Costen pers. comm.).

A degree of planning in the allocation of land is suggested. Each of the Chickerell manors appears to have originally comprised a similar area of land arranged in long, narrow blocks (Fig. 6.3). These blocks incorporated the Chickerell watercourse running broadly through the mid-point of each block. The local geology also means that each of the units covered two different soil types. Topographically they incorporated better drained ridges and slopes, with more water-logged areas. Each unit provided land usable for arable cultivation, rough pasture as well as connectivity and fisheries via access to the Fleet. These were all factors which seem to have affected exploitation during the main period of activity at Putton during the 12th–14th centuries.

THE BUILDINGS AND ARCHITECTURE, By Cheryl Green

The nine identifiable stone buildings revealed at Lower Putton Lane fall across four main phases of activity (Fig. 6.4), the most conspicuous and significant being within the medieval period and therefore the focus of this discussion. The four large buildings of this date were constructed across a fairly limited timeframe during the 13th century and possibly into the early 14th century, although the site was occupied prior to this with several pits and deposits yielding pottery dated to between the 10th and 12th centuries (see above). There may have been timber antecedents to the stone buildings, as at West Cotton, Raunds, Northamptonshire where the early 12th century buildings gradually replaced timber predecessors (Chapman 2010, 79). At Putton,

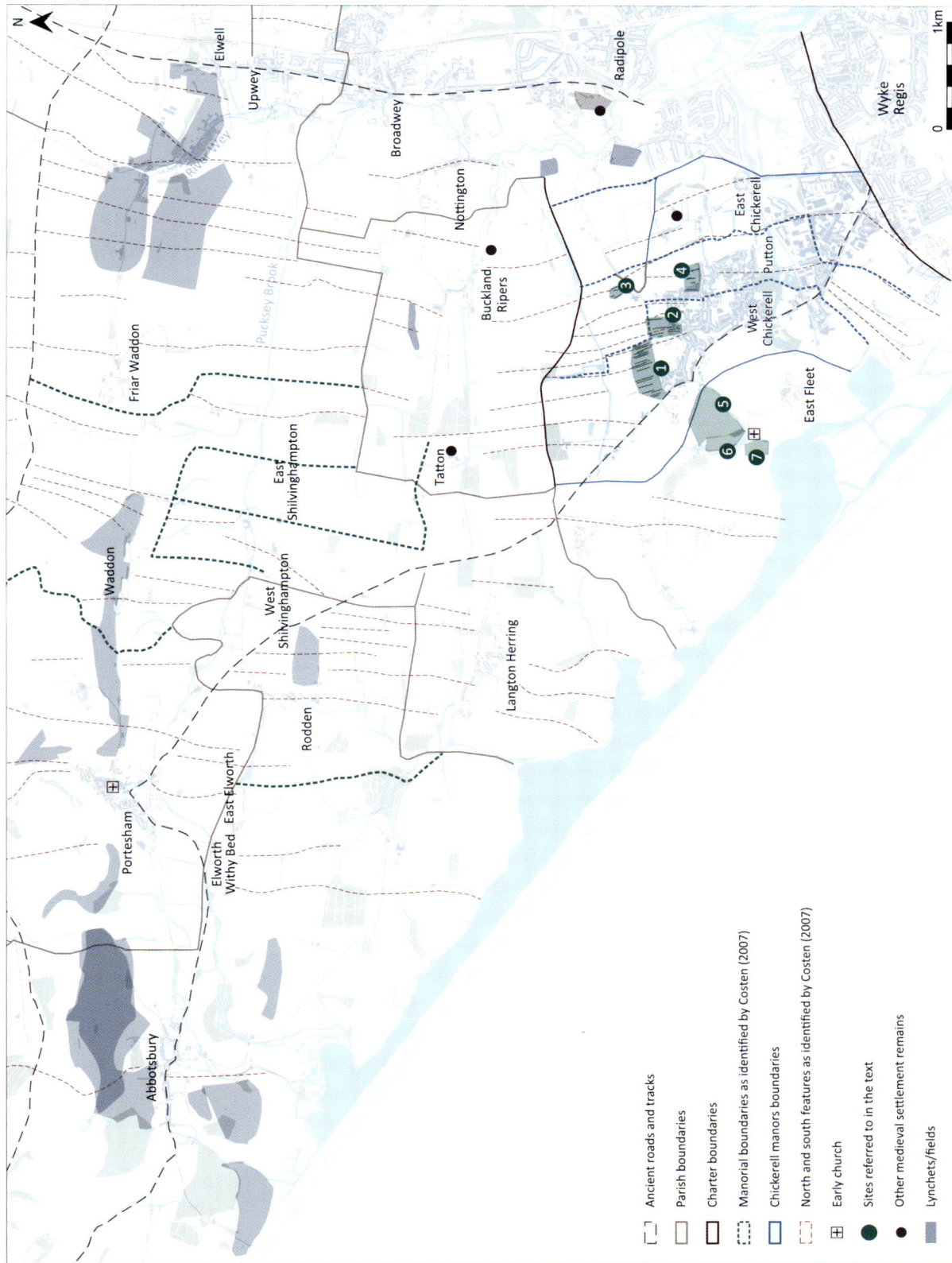

Fig. 6.3   Medieval sites in the Chickerell environs. 1. Medieval field system (MDO25718). 2. Medieval-post-medieval field boundaries (MDO25716). 3. Medieval-post-medieval field boundaries (MDO25715). 4. Medieval-post-medieval field boundaries and cultivation marks (MDO25713). 5. Fleet Common, field system (MDO25808). 6. Medieval strip lynchets, Fleet (MDO1116). 7. East Fleet, Medieval strip field boundaries (MDO25803).

Fig. 6.4 Overall phased plan of buildings.

no firm evidence was found for an earlier phase of construction, except perhaps for a single post-hole beneath B1. Three structures formed the primary components of the medieval manor, and during the decades that followed one of these buildings was replaced by a new dwelling. This not only shifted the spatial focus of the complex but also indicates that the functions of the surviving original buildings would have evolved.

Of the five remaining buildings, two were situated towards the eastern side of Area 1 and occupied the western slope of the site, and three were located on the eastern side of Area 3 clustered both in and around the medieval B1. Both sets of buildings are thought to represent later re-occupation of the manor, with the two western buildings (B8 and B9) tentatively ascribed a late medieval date while the three eastern buildings (B3, B6 and B7) are more likely to be post-medieval. One building (B9) may have been sufficiently robust to have been a dwelling, while the remaining structures are more characteristic of agricultural buildings. All these structures cannibalised building materials from the medieval manor.

The Phase 3 manorial buildings

One of the three stone buildings dated to this phase (B5) is demonstrably earlier than the Phase 4 building (B2) situated immediately to the north, both stratigraphically and in terms of its form and character. This building is interpreted as a 13th century ground-floor open hall and was contemporary with a slightly smaller building (B4) of unknown function to the south-east (Fig. 6.5). Although they were not quite positioned corner-to-corner, they shared the same orientation (north–south and east–west respectively) and the south wall of B5 was aligned with the north wall of B4. Together these two buildings delineated the south-west corner of an inner courtyard, which retained an extensive area of cobbling. The third building B1 of this phase was ranged along the north side of this courtyard, again following the same orientation. Interpreted as a 13th century two-storey chamber-block, it must also pre-date B2 which would have absorbed the functions of both hall and chamber-block under one roof (see below).

B1 – the chamber-block

The external plan of B1 outlines a rectangular building with thick walls. These were certainly of sufficient strength to have carried the weight of a first floor, with two post-pits possibly relating to additional supports (either original or added later). A doorway was situated in the centre of the long south wall, and therefore directly accessible from the inner courtyard. External stairs to the first-floor accommodation were the norm for storeyed chamber-blocks and have been preserved at numerous extant buildings of this type; for example, at Boothby Pagnell Manor House (Lincolnshire) dated c. 1200, the stairs are situated at one end of the long wall and projecting at right-angles (Fig. 6.6). At Putton, the stairs were probably located within the confines of the inner courtyard and close to the postulated main entrance, represented by the termination of the enclosure ditch (see above). A less likely possibility is that the first-floor was accessed via an internal wooden stair from the ground-floor, however as undercrofts served as storage facilities this would not have provided such an auspicious approach for visitors to the manorial abode.

There is no evidence for internal partitions within the undercroft, in keeping with the functional use of these spaces, although the ground-floor doorway probably relates to the loading and unloading of goods. The discovery of the infant burial F74 close to this doorway, within a 13th century pottery vessel inserted into a beaten earth floor, provides a fascinating dimension to the building. Similar burials have been discovered within medieval domestic contexts (see Randall, Chapter 3), and it seems to have had a particular protective meaning. At Putton, while this pot burial remained within the domestic sphere it was vertically removed from day-to-day activities.

Two-storey stone blocks survive particularly well as a medieval building type and several extant versions are known throughout the country, with Boothby Pagnell being one of the more famous examples. In the 1950s and 1960s, architectural historians Margaret Wood and Patrick Faulkner identified these buildings as first-floor halls, as opposed to the open ground-floor halls of the earlier and later medieval periods (Wood 1950; 1965; Faulkner 1958).

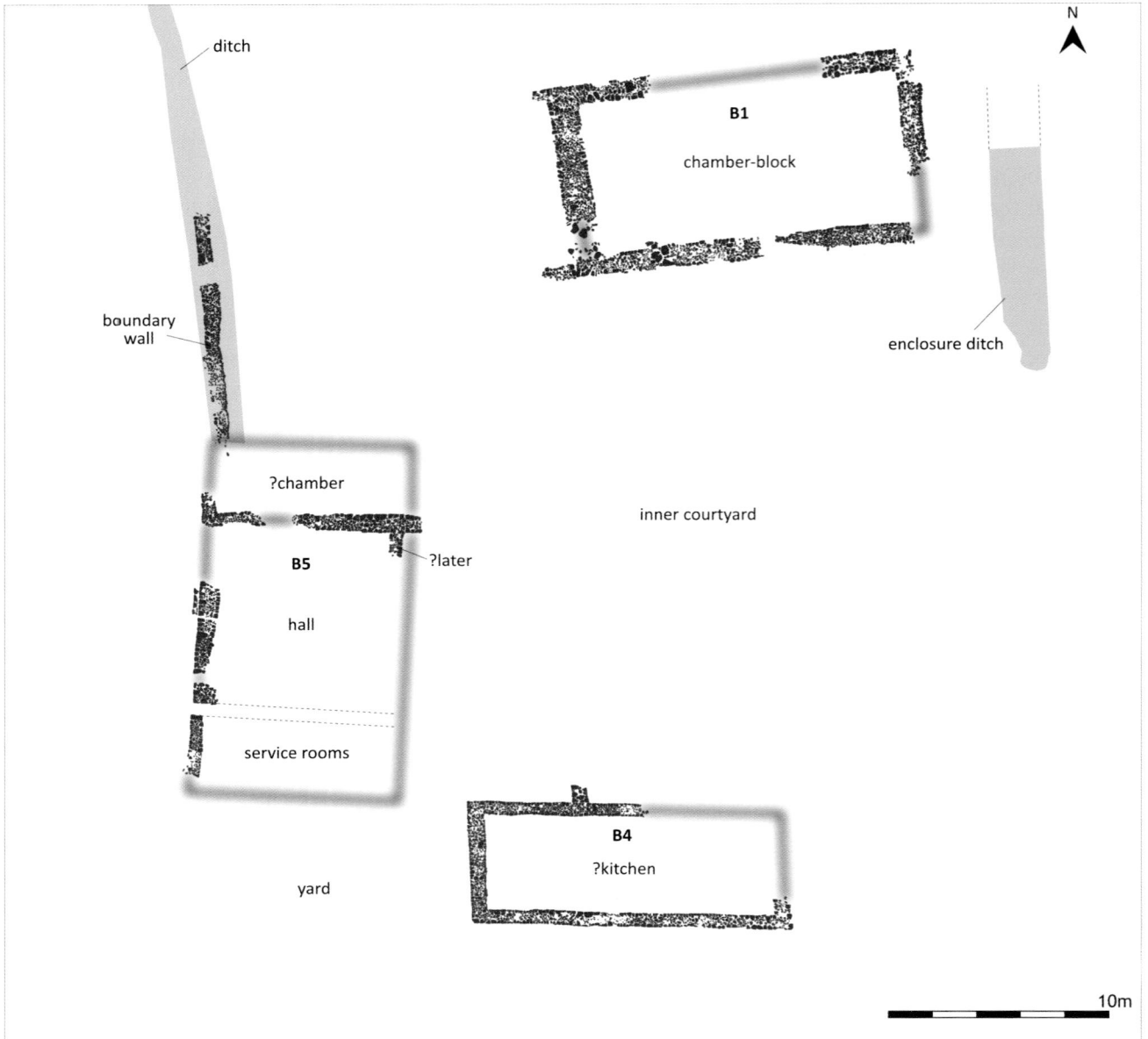

Fig. 6.5   Interpretation of Phase 3 buildings.

Fig. 6.6   Chamber-block, Boothby Pagnell (Lincolnshire) (after Turner 1851, between pp. 52-3).

As the extant versions of these buildings generally exist in isolation from other structures, it was a reasonable hypothesis that several functions of a medieval household would be absorbed under one roof. In 1993, John Blair contended that the first-floor hall model was inappropriate to normal manorial buildings in England between the 11th and 13th centuries, because the storeyed stone buildings are in fact chamber-blocks which were accompanied by detached ground floor halls (Blair 1993, 2). In other words, this recognised that the two-storey stone block only tells part of the story, providing accommodation on the first floor with an undercroft below, existing in close juxtaposition with a separate ground-floor open-hall where communal gatherings took place. As part of this work, Blair also reconsidered two innovations between the mid-12th century and the mid-13th century, heralding the development of the widely recognised late medieval English house:

1) the development of services and a cross-passage at the lower end of the open hall;
2) the attachment of the previously free-standing chamber-block to the upper end of the hall (Blair 1993).

Most surviving houses of the Boothby Pagnell type date from c. 1170–1220 (Blair 1993, 8), with the Putton example sharing the same length to width ratio of 2:1 (not including the additional end room, which Putton lacks). Within the south west, Jacobstow (Cornwall) had a late 12th century two-storey chamber-block, subsequently absorbed within a courtyard arrangement (Fig. 6.7). A row of post-bases were found in the undercroft and a plinth for a possible fireplace heating the great chamber above (Blair 1993, 7). Several extant examples are also known from Dorset. Moigne Court, Owermoigne, dates to the late 13th century; this has a stack embrasure on the west elevation relating to a former chimney, and three 13th century windows within the first floor (two trefoiled lights and a quatrefoil in plate tracery under a two centred head) (RCHME 1970b, 184). Barnston Manor, Church Knowle, retained a first-floor screens passage but no services, a solar at the opposing end with blocked 13th century lancet windows, and a large projecting chimney stack (Historic England List Entry no. 1120351).

Until recently, Blair's comment still held true that no ordinary English manor-house had been discovered with substantial and unambiguous remains of both hall and separate chamber-block (Blair 1993, 9). At the time, Blair identified Alsted, Merstham (Surrey) as a small early 13th century stone chamber-block alongside the platform of a timber building, providing a simple version of the detached hall and chamber plan (Blair 1993, 7). The juxtaposition can also be recognised for the 13th century North Manor at the deserted medieval settlement of Wharram Percy (Yorkshire), based on interpretations of

earthwork surveys and limited excavation evidence (Fig. 6.7). Closer to home, recent excavations by Wessex Archaeology at Longforth Farm, Wellington (Somerset), seem to present a different and more complex arrangement, the excavators identifying a rectangular hall possibly of two-storeys in the centre of the main axial range probably dating from the early 13th century (Fig. 6.7). This was flanked by a storeyed chamber-block to one end and services at the other and bears little resemblance to Putton, probably reflecting Longforth's possible association with the Bishops of Bath and Wells (Flaherty et al. 2016). Indeed, this might also explain the more monastic refectory-type plan for the hall, perhaps with the first floor above an undercroft. Putton on the other hand provides a convincing example of the chamber-block and separate ground floor open-hall model, and it is this building to which we now turn.

B5 – the open hall

Although the remains of B5 are the most fragmentary of the medieval buildings, resulting from at least partial demolition and truncation from modern services, the plan is decipherable and there is enough evidence to allow interpretation of its function. This stems from two opposing faced returns towards the south end of the single surviving side wall, and structural evidence that this led into a cross-passage between the main room (hall) and a rectangular southern room (services) (Fig. 6.5). This resembles the classic open hall of the 13th century, comprising a cross-passage between the hall and the service rooms at the low-end (Fig. 6.8). Opposed doorways adjacent to service ends and providing the main access, are thought to have become a standard feature around the beginning of the early 13th century (Grenville 1997, 93), with houses of c. 1190 onwards having an entrance towards the lower end as opposed to the centre of the side wall (Blair 1993, 13). Separation of hall and chamber continued in lesser houses well after c. 1200 however from about the 1220s or 1230s, and increasingly common thereafter, surviving or excavated houses demonstrate that the main chamber-block was usually attached directly to the upper end of the hall (Blair 1993). This would support an early 13th century date for the Putton hall.

The surviving walls of the service end are narrower than those attributed to the hall, suggesting a less-

Fig. 6.7 Comparative sites for Lower Putton Lane, West Cotton, Raunds: the manor house, later 12th century (after Chapman 2010, fig. 5.3); Wharram Percy: interpretation of the 13th century North Manor (after Oswald 2012, fig. 11); Jacobstow: phasing plan of manor (after Blair 1993, fig. 5; Grenville 1997, fig. 4.9); Longforth Farm: interpretation of 13th century manor (after Flaherty et al. 2016, fig. 3.5).

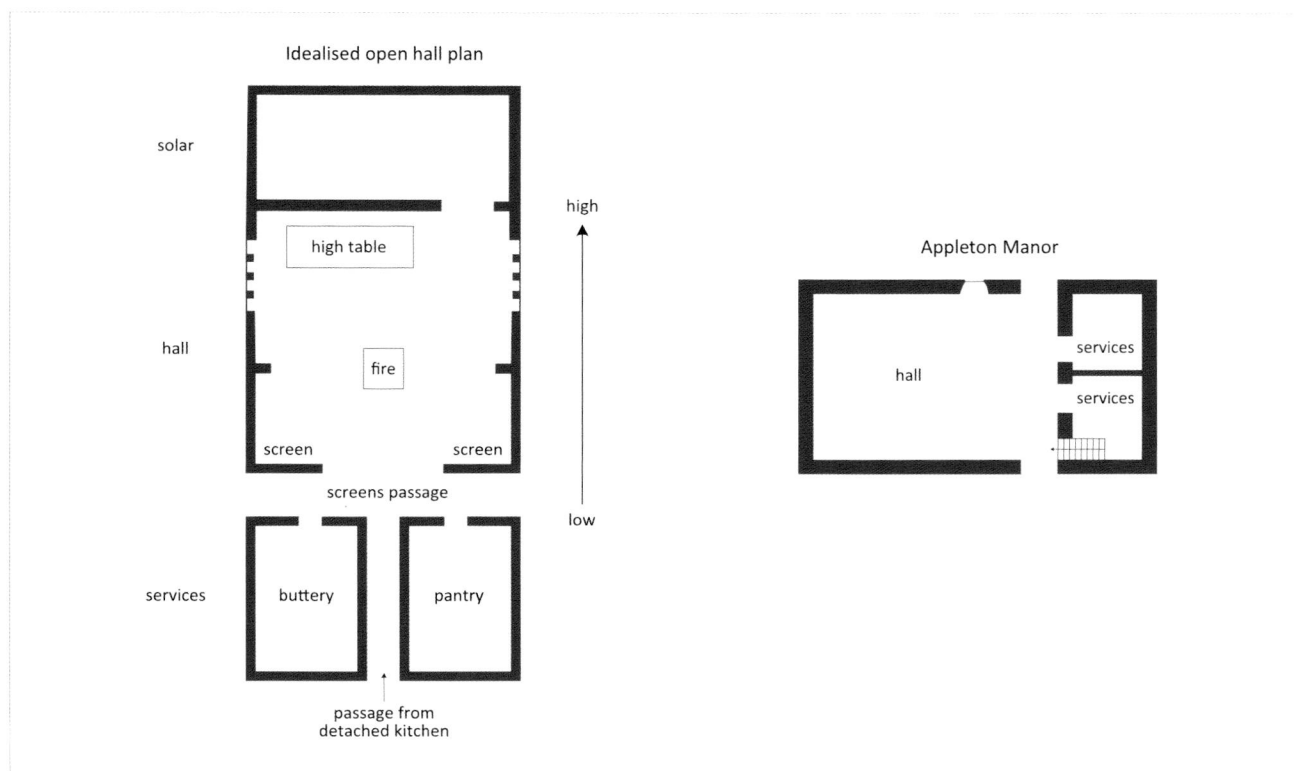

Fig. 6.8 Idealised open hall plan of the 13th century; Appleton Manor (Berkshire) (after Grenville 1997, fig. 4.4a).

substantial structure such as a lean-to. The main doorway to the hall must have been on the east side of the cross-passage, and wider than the narrow doorway in the west wall. Further clues that this building represents an open hall is derived from evidence that the northern part of the main room was distinguished. The north end was slightly raised, the north wall (W18) of the main room resting directly on ground above the floor level identified further south. This would be in keeping with the presence of a raised dais at the high end of the square hall where the lord of the manor and his family would be seated, allowing space for the seating of guests and other household members. A widening of the external plinth foundation perhaps relates to the location of a lateral fireplace or structural support for a more ornate west facing window providing additional light for the high table.

The absence of foundations for the north wall (W18) of the main room contrasts with the substantial foundations for the west wall (W39). This might suggest that the north wall was an internal partition as opposed to a gable end. There is space for a north

room between W18 and the contemporary boundary wall (W42) to the north, with the physical evidence resting solely on a short stub (W6) which might represent the west wall of this room. Argument against the existence of a north room is provided by the swathe of cobbling F51 that sweeps in from the inner courtyard and abuts the north face of W18. Nevertheless, this cobbling is in itself only dated by association and might relate to subsequent use of the area. If a north room existed, its location adjacent to the high end would suggest it was a small chamber providing additional private accommodation to the main chamber-block B1. A similar scenario was seen at the 13th century manor-house at Harwell (Oxfordshire), with a compartment at the end of the hall called the 'wardrobe' or *extrema camera* in addition to a detached chamber-block (Blair 1993, 15). However, an alternative explanation for B5 might be a 'prototype' tripartite plan, as postulated for Appleton Manor (Berkshire) (Fig. 6.8). This consisted of two service doorways at the end of the hall with a narrow rectangular service area behind an internal wall, accessed through two separate doorways (Grenville 1997, 95).

As discussed above, open-halls of the 13th century have recently been recognised as being predominantly ground-floor structures (Blair 1993). Indeed, if W18 was the north wall of the building then the absence of foundations means it was unlikely to have been of sufficient strength to have supported a floor. Conversely, the surviving side wall with foundations may have supported a superstructure of reasonable height. Nevertheless, the very nature of open halls is that they were open to the roof perhaps with a central hearth, although in this case there is tentative evidence for a lateral fireplace on the west side. The floor itself did not survive even though the level was identifiable from the horizon between the foundation and wall, therefore no trace of a hearth was found.

The ground-floor open hall B5 appears to be a rare new example of this building type, where a contemporaneous date with a stone-built chamber-block proves that they served a different function. The spatial separation between the two Lower Putton Lane buildings may seem unusual; most examples seem to have ensured that the lordly household could stagger safely home after entertaining their guests. However, these complexes varied enormously and there may have been other reasons; for example, the location of B1 on higher ground would certainly have proven to be dryer. At Wharram Percy (Yorkshire), the solar block of the 13th century North Manor lay at right-angles to the hall, with the kitchen at right angles to the service end, arranged continuously around a 3-sided inner courtyard (Fig. 6.7). Within the South Manor, the late 12th century camera was thought to have been associated with a ground-floor hall and although no traces were identified during the excavations, a position to the south and east of the camera has been suggested (Everson and Stocker 2012, 264).

In terms of how the hall functioned, the position of the cross-passage (albeit with a very narrow west doorway) strongly suggests the rectangular room at the south end of the building housed the services. A stone wall positioned throughout the west side of this room may have supported a counter, which would fit with the buttery or pantry being housed here. Alternatively, the wall may have supported a stair, as at Appleton Manor (Berkshire) (Fig. 6.8) where a full-height quoined opening between the

hall and service end probably contained a straight stair from the hall to the chamber above (Blair 1993, 14). This provides a tantalizing alternative for the 'counter' but would require an upper floor above the service end, which seems doubtful in this case. Alternatively, the stair may have provided access to a balcony across the south end of the hall. As a final note, it might seem somewhat unusual to have the service end within the southern, warmer part of the building and the possible private chamber at the north, colder end (if indeed this existed). However, in this case the ground became progressively wetter towards the south and it may have been deemed unsuitable for accommodation. Ultimately, it might also explain why B5 was destined for demolition after less than a century of use.

B4 – the ancillary building

The external plan of B4 outlines a narrow rectangular building with well-constructed walls of one phase, and although these may have been quite high, they are unlikely to have carried the weight of a first floor. Although the floor level was identifiable from the horizon between the foundation and walling above, no floor deposits were present. As with B5, this suggests that any flooring materials may have been removed during the removal of architectural stone following abandonment. A small porch structure appears to have been added to the north side of the building; this would make sense for an entrance opening directly onto the inner courtyard, allowing a straight path to the postulated east door of the open hall (B5). However, there is also tentative evidence for a blocked south door, which may have provided access to a possible yard area between B4 and B5, or a back route to the narrow west door of B5.

With the services thought to be located at the south end of the open hall, a detached kitchen should be sought nearby. These buildings were kept separate due to the high risk posed by fire and could be replaced frequently. It is possible that B4 served this purpose, although the distinct length in relation to width might suggest that it also served other purposes, such as servant accommodation. Certainly, a kitchen should be expected in this general area, with refuse taken directly to the rear of the complex and eventually contributing towards the large spread (10-108) to the west derived from household middens. The kitchen/bakehouse at West Cotton, Raunds (Northamptonshire) was also rectangular, with an internal space measuring 8.25m by 4.35m (Chapman 2010, 102; fig. 5.22), with an oven in one corner and two hearths. We are missing part of the building at Putton and the floor had been removed, which might explain the absence of similar features.

The precise east–west orientation raises the question of whether this might have been a manorial chapel, however this can now be discounted on several grounds. The area was covered by the same kinds of domestic refuse as the rest of the site, with no distinct ecclesiastical items. Such a high-status building would not be positioned immediately adjacent to the service end of the hall, but in a more esteemed part of the manor. Where chapels were provided on small manors they tended to be accommodated within an existing building, sometimes above a porch. For comparison, excavation at Sutton Poyntz revealed part of a possible chapel of the 12th–14th century (Rawlings 2007). This rectangular building had internal measurements of 9.90m by 4.70m and the walls measured 0.90m deep (Blair 1993, 26), whereas B4 is disproportionately long (internal measurements of 11.90m by 4.10m) and the walls narrower (maximum of 0.77m). At Sutton Poyntz, a stone plinth or platform measuring 1.5m long and 0.90m wide was positioned against the east wall, thought to represent the base of an altar and one of the factors in interpreting the building as having an ecclesiastical function (Blair 1993, 29). Nevertheless, as the excavations were not extensive enough to locate other complete buildings in the supposed complex, the chapel identification remains uncertain. Another consideration against Putton having its own chapel is that St Mary's church, Chickerell, would probably have met the spiritual needs of the manor. Although the current building was constructed in the later 13th century, parts of the font have carved decoration indicative of a 12th century date (RCHME 1970b, 38), and observations during work on the floors revealed walls of an earlier building probably dating to the 11th–12th centuries (Trevarthen and Bellamy 2011).

The Phase 4 manorial buildings

A single building B2 was attributed to this phase and was designed to take primacy as the most significant manorial building within the complex (Fig. 6.9). The form typifies later 13th to 14th century ambitions which sought to incorporate the former functions of chamber, hall and service rooms, and was very à la mode. The classic three-part house crystalized as a plan form in the later 13th century and endured for three centuries; broadly this comprised a hall flanked by an upper end with a great chamber, perhaps over a parlour, with the services at the lower end and either with or without a lesser chamber above (Blair 1993, 15). However, there were a range of iterations and as Margaret Wood commented, 'in fact almost every 13th century house seems to be differently planned!' (Wood 1950, 103).

Although the construction of B2 saw the demolition of the open-hall B5, it is interesting that the site was not chosen for the new manor house. This might be because some of the walling of B5 was retained and re-used for other purposes, perhaps as stabling or animal pens. However, the over-riding factor was probably avoidance of the wet ground that must have been a nuisance for the users of both B4 and B5. The choice of higher, dryer ground to the north of B5 involved quarrying a shallow terrace into the undulating bedrock. This shift in focus meant that the main approach into the complex would now have be on the north side of B1, and although the northern extent of the enclosure could not be established for either phase it was probably not far north of B2. The construction of B2 also dictated that the west boundary needed to be re-positioned, with the Phase 3 boundary W42 now shifted slightly to the west (W7) and aligned on B2 as opposed to B5.

The plan of the building is relatively complete, with two equally sized rooms separated by a substantial stone wall which formed the north side of a cross-passage, the south side probably formed by a less substantial timber partition. An imposing porch enclosed the eastern cross-passage doorway, while the narrower opposing western doorway led straight onto a cobbled path which ran around the outside of the northern part of the building. Heavy footfall along the cross-passage was evident from the particularly compacted ground through this area. The porch foundations overlapped the foundations of the main building, revealing it was an original component, and the recess along

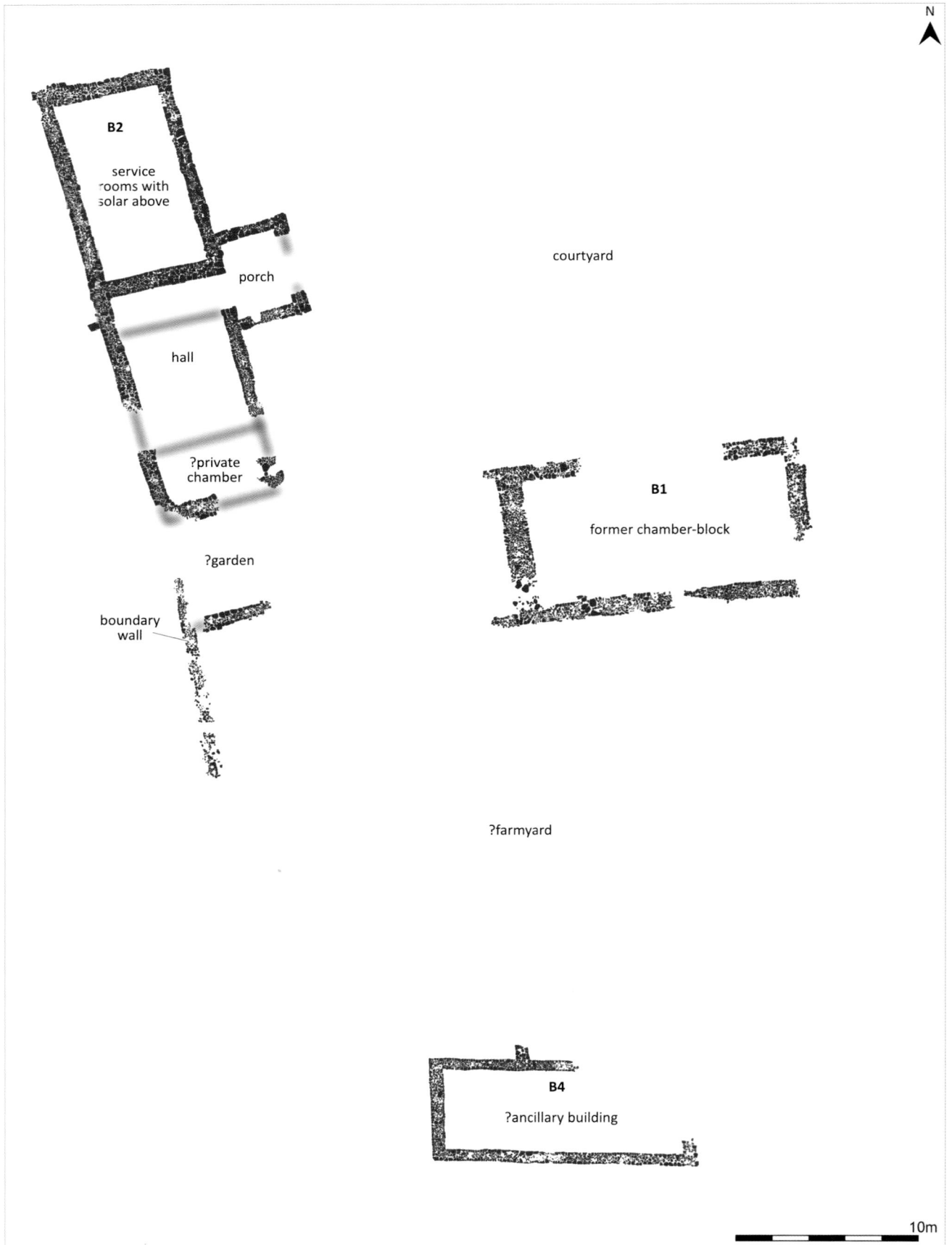

N

B2

service rooms with solar above

porch

hall

?private chamber

?garden

boundary wall

courtyard

B1

former chamber-block

?farmyard

B4

?ancillary building

10m

Fig. 6.9 Interpretation of Phase 4 buildings.

the north side is sufficiently wide to have housed a bench for those waiting for an interview with the lord of the manor. With the exception of the compacted surface noted above, no other flooring materials were evident and once again it is possible that flagstones were removed during the wholesale removal of architectural stone.

There are no other physical clues as to the internal organisation of the building, but these types of structures followed a familiar pattern. The cross-passage would have provided access into an open-hall to the south. This probably would have been further sub-divided with private rooms ranged over two-storeys at the south end, providing a more intimate dining or entertaining space, an increasingly popular pursuit during the 14th century. The north room must have housed the service rooms, although detached or semi-detached kitchens remained almost universal in the 14th century (Grenville 1997, 118), probably with private chambers above. The access between the services and cross-passage was not evident within the substantial cross-passage wall, however this might be explained by the rise in ground level towards the north end of the building suggesting there may have been steps up from the cross-passage. This arrangement is evident at later houses, including the Elizabethan Montacute House (Somerset), the steps leading up to a small private dining room from which the service rooms were accessed.

Dendrochronology survey in Somerset has identified 11 houses of the tripartite plan (from different contexts), six of which have been dated to the late 13th–14th centuries (Penoyre 2005, 37). As the service ends of these types of houses were extra-long they were also used for other purposes, and often seemed to have incorporated a kitchen (Blair 1993). However, they could also be used for 'industrial' purposes such as trade or weaving (Blair 1993, 37) and this is certainly an interesting consideration for the long service end at Putton. A good comparative example is the 14th century Court House at Long Sutton, (Somerset) dated 1328, which had a large porch leading to the cross-passage, with open hall and opposing service end with solar over (Fig. 6.10). Within Dorset, although the tripartite plan is widely recognised in a number of extant properties dating between the 15th and 17th centuries, the earliest example is from Hooke Court. A

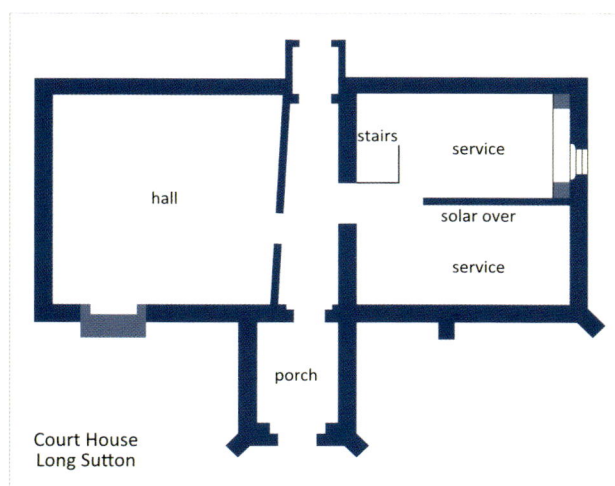

Fig. 6.10   Court House, Long Sutton (after Penoyre 2005, fig. 5.5).

major building interpreted as a first-floor hall possibly of 14th century date dominated the centre of the partly moated enclosure (Wessex Archaeology 2006, 27–28). The 14th century first floor hall at Fiddleford Manor, near Sturminster Newton comprised a large hall associated with a chamber-block of two floors at the western end and service rooms throughout the remainder of the ground floor, above which was a large chamber probably accessed via an external staircase (HE List entry 1013372). At Putton, the service end of B2 was certainly of sufficient length to have incorporated and internal stair, probably at the north end, or possibly adjacent to the cross-passage wall.

There can be little doubt that the lord and his family would have occupied the new dwelling quarters of B2. Yet however progressive this building was in its conception, it was too small to have incorporated all the functions of the manor, and the kitchen should once again be sought elsewhere. Indeed, B1 was retained as a functioning building, possibly still extant in the post-medieval period, and would have been re-purposed. It was probably too far distant to have served as the kitchen, which may have been situated immediately north of B2, but perhaps was utilized for guest or servant quarters. Similarly, there is no reason to suggest that B4 was not retained, but perhaps now served the farmyard which is thought to have occupied the former inner courtyard, as opposed to tasks directly associated with the household.

Overview of the manor complex

The three buildings of the Phase 3 manor probably date to the early 13th century, with the chamber-block (B1), ground-floor open hall (B5) and possible kitchen (B4) organised around a loose three-sided courtyard arrangement, similar to the late 12th century remains excavated at West Cotton, Raunds (Northamptonshire) and the 13th century North Manor at Wharram Percy (Yorkshire) (Fig. 6.7). Closer to home, at Longforth Farm, Wellington, Somerset, the key buildings were arranged axially, with a free-standing kitchen and a barn forming the other two sides of a courtyard, and possibly surrounded by enclosing ditches (Fig. 6.7). The predominantly axial arrangement may reflect an ecclesiastical influence, as the manor was possibly under the ownership of the Bishops of Bath and Wells (Flaherty et al. 2016). Another high-status site often quoted in the literature for the south west is Jacobstow (Cornwall), which had a particularly complex development. The plan published by Beresford in 1974 shows a stand-alone late 12th century chamber (Fig. 6.7), to which a 'wardrobe' with garderobe was added in the 13th century. Over the next century this was flanked by additional buildings (including a hall, services, kitchen and chapel), eventually forming a completely enclosed courtyard.

At Putton, the area occupied by the buildings was enclosed by a boundary ditch F85 running north–south to the east of B1 and a boundary wall (W42) running north from B5, within a possible earlier boundary ditch. Both ditches therefore shared the same orientation as the building and courtyard layout. It is possible that further buildings were present within this enclosure, and indeed a fragment of wall (F48) to the south-east of B4 may possibly relate to an ancillary building outside of the inner courtyard.

The cross-passage house (B2) of the Phase 4 manor may have been constructed in the later 13th century or perhaps the early 14th century. Simultaneously, the courtyard would have been switched from the area encompassed by the Phase 3 buildings, to the area east of B2 and north of B1. The western boundary was re-orientated in order to accommodate B2, with a new boundary wall (W7) slightly to the west. A similar shift in focus is apparent at the North Manor, Wharram Percy (Yorkshire), when the manor was extended eastward and northward with the provision of an enclosed courtyard on the east side of the solar (Oswald 2012, 23). By comparison, with only two large buildings, B1 and B2, occupying this area and at some distance from each other, once again the courtyard arrangement at Putton appears to have been quite loose. A sense of enclosure was most likely provided by fencing and the stream to the west.

Fig. 6.11   Interpretive painting.
© JG O'Donaghue.

A moment in time

An interpretative painting (Fig. 6.11) commissioned as part of the project integrates the excavation plan of the complex with evidence from the recovered material and comparative sites, shaping an impression of how the upstanding remains may have looked. The scene was brought-to-life through the excavated finds, which provide evidence of the range of activities that took place both within the manor complex and the immediate environs. Throughout the process, discussions with the artist, JG O'Donoghue, helped shape an understanding not just about how the site may have appeared but also how the people who lived there moved around and utilised the spaces. It is acknowledged that this painting can only provide an impression and it is not designed to be an accurate depiction, but the following account describes how it came about.

The painting captures a moment in time in the late 13th or early 14th century, after B2 had been constructed. The survival of the lowest part of the walls suggests they were entirely constructed in coursed local limestone, utilising the cornbrash that underlay the site with Portland limestone for the dressings. An abundance of stone tiles, roughly shaped from Portland limestone, were found overlying and around B2, with some also recovered from B1 and B5. The ready availability of this material suggests that all the stone buildings were roofed with stone tiles as opposed to thatch, and although B4 is also

Fig. 6.12   Decorative ridge tiles.

depicted with this roofing material the absence of tile here might suggest otherwise. Similarly, several fragments of ceramic glazed crested ridge tiles and roof furniture (Fig. 6.12) were recovered from B2 alone, although the painting shows them providing ornamentation to all three buildings. Otherwise, stone dressings and architectural elements had been completely removed from the buildings, along with any flooring materials (presumably flagstones) that are assumed to have been present. Given the damp conditions on the site, particularly towards B5 and B4, it seems unlikely that beaten earth floors would have sufficed as a flooring material. The recovery of a few segments of window came and some tiny fragments of late medieval window glass suggest some glazing, however these were not precisely dateable and therefore the painting shows simple unglazed 13th century lancet windows. Similarly, the doors are shown with simple two-centred arches, although the main entrances are likely to have been elaborated with moulded surrounds as in extant 13th century houses.

B1 is shown with a north facing ground floor door even though this part of the wall was missing (Fig. 6.13). It is suggested that the original first floor access was on the south side, together with the door to the undercroft, but once the courtyard was switched to the north side of this building it is possible that B1 was provisioned with an additional doorway on this side. The cross-passage house (B2) is shown dominating the complex (Fig. 6.14), with the boundary wall extending southwards and possibly containing a garden within the angle formed by a cross-wall. Further south, B4 is shown as a simple porched structure within a part of the site given over for the penning of animals, with the former inner courtyard now utilised as a farmyard (Fig. 6.15).

Given the solidity of the stone walls, the roof structure was likely formed by base crucks imbedded in the top of the walls, as opposed to cruck trusses which would be evident within the surviving walling. Fireplaces were common in chamber blocks from the Norman Conquest onwards, surviving in extant buildings as lateral stone stacks, however in the absence of firm evidence for these

Fig. 6.13   Close-up of B1 on interpretive painting © JG O'Donaghue.

Fig. 6.14   Close-up of B2 on interpretive painting © JG O'Donaghue.

features all the buildings are shown with central louvres for open hearths. Indeed, hearth tiles were recovered from the area of B4, and a fragment from a roof-finial, louver or chimney pot came from rubble deposits near B2 with another found elsewhere.

The additional functions of the manor are more likely to have been accommodated within wooden structures which have left no discernible trace, and therefore have not been depicted. At West Cotton, Raunds (Northamptonshire) extensive excavations have allowed a greater understanding of the non-stone buildings and it was possible to closely identify the function of individual structures (Chapman 2010). In Dorset, repair records at Kingston Lacy found that stone buildings were supplemented by cob and timber (Papworth 1998, 50). This demonstrates that buildings of cob, timber framing with wattle and daub, and thatched roofs cannot be discounted, and it is inevitable that we are lacking a full appreciation of the various ancillary buildings and structures. An enclosing wattle fence is depicted on the painting following the line of the eastern enclosure ditch F85, however there is no evidence to support the location of the north and south sides and this is purely based on the fact that no further buildings were found in either direction. The western side is shown as being formed by the stream and holloway, with the manorial fields on the opposing slope.

In order to bring the painting to life, evidence of activities represented within the finds assemblage have been woven in. This includes the delivery of a sealed scroll, known from a seal matrix; carts pulled by horses delivering produce and hay, indicated by traction fittings; tending of a garden, evidenced by plants grown for medicinal purposes; penning of farmyard animals, suggested by chicken and pig remains; a farm dog, although cat bones were also recovered; storage of firewood; and the primary role of the house as a family home. The surrounding landscape gives a general impression of cultivation and pasture, with grazing cattle and sheep/ goat. In the far distance is the sea off the Fleet, with exploitation of the marine resource evidenced by lead net weights or sinkers, fish bone, oyster, scallops and other marine molluscs. A small group of peasant dwellings is depicted to the left, representing the tofts and crofts assumed to have occupied the earthworks; although this volume has called this interpretation into question, it does at least refer to the peasants and tenants who lived outside of the manorial centre.

Fig. 6.15   Close-up of B4 on interpretive painting © JG O'Donaghue.

ACCESS TO THE PUTTON COURT,
By Clare Randall

Whilst it may not be obviously classified as a 'moated' site, the combination of a substantial enclosing ditch, and evidence in other areas for similarly substantial walling falls into the continuum of enclosure of manors and other settlements. These spaces were created in a wide variety of ways and occur on sites at all status levels. The majority appear to have come into being between c. 1200 and c. 1325 (Johnson 2015, 234) The aetiology of such features in a need for defence has long been questioned. Moated sites have been suggested as indicating fear of crime and violence, but these problems seem to have been endemic and there was no apparent increase in creation of boundaries (Hinton 2012, 131). Ideas relating to fashion or the need to indicate status have superseded this as an explanatory framework. Johnson (2015, 235–6) suggests that beyond this debate, the act of creating the enclosure changed both the physical and social landscape. By creating a boundary, it delimited the way in which space could be moved through. Thereby 'moated sites may have reinforced economic and social stratification in a landscape' (Johnson 2015, 237). This is related to the manorial role both as the home of an elite (of whatever level) in a society where hosting other elite families was common, and the administrative and legal hub for the manorial unit. A manor such as Putton was therefore the focus of various levels of society.

Several moated sites in the Weald suggest that the presence of the boundary increased the effort and time taken to access the site (Johnson 2015, 238). This is worth considering for the Lower Putton Lane court. The assumption has been that the earthworks to the south-west of the excavated site represents the location of further (lower status) settlement. The earthworks aligned with the remnant of a holloway which passed along the west side of B5/B2, along the current route of the stream and the exterior of the court boundary wall. Whilst the fragmentary nature of the structures and deposits in the low lying south-western corner of the court does not preclude there being an entrance perhaps between B5 and B4, the positioning of a quite clear terminal to the enclosure ditch F85 on the eastern side suggests that during

Phase 3 at least, the main entrance was on the east side. If any settlement lay to the south-west, it would certainly require a degree of circumnavigation of the perimeter in order to gain access. This would also be the case for anyone approaching from West Chickerell and could potentially reinforce the social differences of those living within and those living without. However, as has been discussed in Chapter 5, there are reasons to suggest that any associated settlement may have been to the east of the manorial complex whilst the features associated with the holloway earthwork are field boundaries. If associated settlement was located outside the main entrance during the first organisation of the court, it would have facilitated relatively easy access; it may however have necessitated a clear boundary. Also, we should consider the potential for reinforcing the gradations in status between classes of peasants and tenants. Those holding rights to land in the more outlying parts of the manor, probably beyond the central area which most likely contained the demesne land, may have had to approach via a more circuitous route, whereas those who were resident close to the centre may have experienced relatively privileged access.

To the east, lay East Chickerell manor. The axis of approach was along the Chickerell brook from the east, where ultimately it met Radipole Lake and provided access via Melcombe Regis to the sea. It may not be accidental that viewed from this easterly perspective the midden, which was accumulating during Phases 3 and 4, would have been screened from the view of any approaching visitors by the buildings. Johnson (2015, 248) indicates that enclosed sites are one feature of an increasingly bounded and regulated landscape, and the class specific experience of them relates to the regulation of societal relationships. If the innermost space is regarded as being the place of highest status, with connotations of feminine seclusion relating ultimately to security of inheritance (Gilchrist 1997; Fairclough 1992), at Putton, the positioning of the entrance on the east side of the court space would emphasise the status of B5, especially to elite visitors approaching from Melcombe.

Whilst the plan of the Putton court is incomplete in both main phases, and the existence of structures in more ephemeral materials cannot be discounted, it seems that the emphasis on separation of space changed over time. With the silting of the ditch, there is little evidence for substantial demarcation of a 'new' courtyard on the north side of B1 after the construction of B2. However, given the design of B2 including a substantial porch, new ways of indicating status via architecture may have superseded the strict control of movement through space. However, moving the approach to the 'main' building, if the original court was still in use for agricultural or craft activities, may also reflect a desire to separate the house from the activity of the demesne farm. If a peasant settlement was situated to the east of the original court, this could also have moved the axis of arrival away from that settlement. This would have provided a different type of social segregation and perhaps introduced an element of privacy for the higher status individuals from the hurly burly of the farmyard. This change in segregation is similar in some ways to the increased separation between the servants and gentry at the moated site of Barentin in Oxfordshire, which occurred during the 13th century (Page et al. 2005). In Dorset, excavation at Hooke Court determined that whilst the moat may have been constructed by the 13th century, it was never a complete circuit (Wessex Archaeology 2006), perhaps suggesting a screening function or control of movement. In that case the layout of pre-15th century structures remains obscure. These examples raise questions as to how widespread these concerns and practices were in Dorset during this period, and why attitudes changed over time.

HOUSE AND HOME, By Clare Randall

A capital messuage and curtilage at Putton is referred to in documents in 1333 (see Chapter 5). This was generally the dwelling place of the manorial lord, although they may not be in residence in all cases (Miller and Hatcher 1978, 87). Where a lord had several holdings it is likely that one would have been the principle residence. Each manor was however the administrative centre of a lord's demesne and included the farmyard and farm buildings necessary for its operation (Miller and Hatcher 1978, 87). As such we expect to see a range of domestic, personal and other activities reflected in the material culture.

As far as assigning specific activities to particular locations, the evidence from Putton is limited by the nature of the deposits. For the most part, material was derived from contexts which did not accumulate in their final form and location contemporaneously with the various phases of buildings. However, the material dating largely between the 13th and 14th centuries gives us a general view of life on the manor.

The plant remains at Putton (Carruthers, Chapter 4) all appear to derive from domestic waste where crop processing residues were utilised as fuel. A range of cereals, as well as peas and beans, were being consumed at Putton from Phase 2 onward, either by people or animals. Accidentally burnt grain was present along with crop cleaning waste, so these crops probably derived from the immediate surroundings. Both bread and rivet wheat were present; one being suitable for bread making, the other a lower gluten wheat more suitable to biscuits. There was a lack of sprouted grains, apparently indicating low levels of spoilage, or at least not supplying any evidence of malting. The presence of burnt fodder or animal bedding is also hinted at, locating livestock within the immediate area, but there was no evidence for burning large amounts of bedding. Horses were the most likely animal to have been housed close at hand. Black mustard was cultivated and provided a condiment for food, and there is a possibility of the use of wild carrot and maybe even turnip. Hazelnut shells attest to modest use of other local wild plant resources.

The meat diet was based around the three main livestock species, cattle, sheep and pigs (Randall, Chapter 4). There was no evidence for keeping goats, but the diet appears to have been supplemented by chicken and small numbers of domesticated geese, but very little in the way of game. There are hints that the cattle may have also been used for dairying as well traction. Pigs were clearly a minority contribution to the diet, perhaps being kept at the household level and providing meat for special occasions. There is some slight evidence that pigs and cattle were perhaps kept at close hand, at least being slaughtered on or near the site. Draught animals nearby are indicated by the presence of an ox shoe (Schuster, Chapter 4). A considerable number of horseshoes dating to the 12th–14th centuries, numerous horseshoe nails, as well as buckles for horse harness, suggest draught and riding horses were available, although there is no indication that horses were eaten. Sheep appear to have become the most abundant livestock, probably by the 13th century. The age profile suggests their use for wool, their meat contributing mutton rather than lamb, with the body parts represented suggesting that some of this meat may have been brought in after slaughter. All of these animals were subject to the same type of butchery which does not appear systematic, so there may not have been an expert butcher available. Shellfish and fish may have contributed more to the diet than at first glance the numbers suggest. Bones and scales of fish and fragments of marine shell were present in almost all the soil samples taken, which hints at their ubiquity. Fish were an important part of the medieval diet, particularly when fast days are taken into account (Hammond 1993, 19). A fair range of species were represented. All of these could be feasibly obtained from the Fleet, or the open water beyond the Chesil bank to which the manor had access (Fig. 4.11). Some of the shellfish may have provided bait and a number of fishing net weights indicate that people from the manorial centre were engaged in this pursuit.

Around the manor court and its buildings we can imagine a daily routine of pig and chicken feeding and caring for horses. Dogs were present throughout the use of the site, probably guard dogs and companion animals; cats would have been vital for pest control in a place where grain storage took place. Some of the plants present not only attest to the diet, but also the potential workload of some of the inhabitants. Flax seeds appear from Phase 3 (Carruthers, Chapter 4) suggesting cultivation of what can be a medicinal, oil (linseed) as well as a fibre crop which would have needed considerable processing. The flax industry in west Dorset was well established by the early 13th century. Centred on Bridport, it utilised similar topography and soils to those at Putton, with sailcloth being supplied to the crown in some quantity by 1211. The industry continued through the medieval and into the modern period, with exports via West Bay (Williams 2006, 7–9). The finding of flax seed at Putton prompts us to consider whether this industry spread into other suitable parts of the county.

The potential for textile working within the manor complex is also suggested by the availability of wool (Randall, Chapter 4), a pair of shears, as well as lead and chalk spindle whorls (Schuster; Green, Chapter 3). Other aspects of the plant remains attest to the workload. Contaminants of crops were present (Carruthers, Chapter 4). These would have needed to have been picked out of the grain by hand to prevent human or animal illness and future crop health, no doubt a laborious, time-consuming task. However, there are also indications of a range of plants being available which would have been efficacious to the health of the inhabitants and may have been cultivated in a garden setting. These included wild carrot and henbane as well as the medicinal uses of mustard and linseed. Two spade shoes, of medieval or post-medieval type, one with the characteristics of a weeding tool, may relate to gardening within the complex. The number of iron objects, and the presence of partly worked iron, albeit difficult to date, suggests smithing somewhere on the site.

Trade and the administrative functions of the manorial centre are attested by a small number of finds (Schuster, Chapter 3). Aside from fourteen coins covering the period of the 12th to 15th centuries (including an early 15th century Venetian soldino), a group of lead weights suggests a concern for accurate measurement of goods, potentially being bought or sold. A 13th century weight of just under two pounds would have been useful in the measurement of a wide range of foodstuffs. Commercial activities at Putton are reflected in a sale of 200 quarters of corn, part of which appears to have taken place there (and in Wyke) by Nicholas Knottesford of London in 1428, although the source of the crop is not clear (National Archives E 210/11037). A seal matrix of the 13th–14th century provides a glimpse of the administrative function of the manor. However, it is an 'off the shelf' example, so does not identify the person using it. There was a concern to safeguard valuables; at least two keys were of a type which came into use in the 13th century (Schuster, Chapter 3).

A brass spoon bowl, possibly dating as early as the 14th century, and fragments of copper alloy sheeting which may derive from late medieval metal dishes (Schuster, Chapter 3), suggests a degree of refinement in dining. The pottery from the site included the expected range of locally produced coarse ware domestic vessels, jars, jugs and a possible dish. However, there was also finer tableware (Mepham, Chapter 2). This comprised glazed Poole Harbour White Ware jugs and imported pottery. Saintonge whiteware from France provided the majority of this, with some Normandy gritty ware and Iberian fabrics, indicating access to a wider network of goods. These may have come directly through Melcombe or Weymouth, which were trading with France and Spain during this period (Forrest 2017b), or via coastal links to other international ports such as Poole and Southampton. The connections of the area with long distance trade are also shown by tiles from St Mary's Church, which were imported from northern France and the Low Countries during the 15th century (Trevarthen and Bellamy 2011; Keen n.d.). The stone used on the site, both architecturally and for objects (Green, Chapters 2 and 3) attests to a range of connections within Dorset, including with Purbeck, and further afield. A piece of lava stone, likely to have been originally used as a quern, was from Germany.

Decorated pottery would have played an important role in social display (Gilchrist 2012, 144). The volume of both local pottery and that from further afield discarded at 13th century sites like West Mead, Bere Regis, and Holworth, Chaldon Herring, have been seen to indicate a degree of commercial success (Hinton 2012, 129). If this is also the case for Putton, it was at least for a time a thriving community. The lesser component of imports at Putton than at Sutton Poyntz has been commented on (Mepham, Chapter 2). It is particularly interesting given the tenurial relationship between the two manors; Sutton was a more important local centre, although the Poyns family who were of some importance may not have been often resident. The differences between the two sites may reflect their relative wealth and status in the local manorial hierarchy. This may also be reflected in the relative abundance of food animals, with domestic birds featuring, but pig, and particularly wild species, a limited contribution (Randall, Chapter 4).

The relative wealth of some of the inhabitants is shown in both the small collection of building materials and fittings which leant an air of higher

status to the buildings themselves, but also in the range of personal objects from the site (Schuster, Chapter 3). This includes two brooches of the 13th–14th centuries, as well as twelve buckles dating between the 12th and 15th centuries and five strap ends of similar dates. Two strap-ends of the 13th–14th centuries, one from the midden, bear part of the inscription 'Maria'. These are typical of the inclusion of devotional mottos on personal items during this period and they often carried an apotropaic meaning (Gilchrist 2012, 163). A copper alloy button of the 13th–14th centuries and lace chapes of probably similar date (Schuster, Chapter 3) hint at dress styles. A copper alloy rumbler bell of the 13th–15th centuries could have also been worn on clothing, but equally may have worn by a dog or been part of horse harness. Two whetstones, one of Kimmeridge shale, and one of a non-local siltstone may have been part of a personal toolkit (Green, Chapter 3). This collection of objects contrasts with the relative scarcity of personal objects from sites such as Ower Farm where they were scant (Farwell 1991). The burial of an infant in the floor of B1 was a personal act in an intimate space. It also perhaps provides an insight into the mindset of the inhabitants, and their real concerns. Their space was structured supernaturally as well as socially and economically.

A variety of people would have lived at, worked in, and visited Putton. The term 'household' is therefore useful in understanding the potential dynamics between a range of individuals whatever their biological relationship. It accommodates the core familial and wider labour force within a complex of domestic and other buildings (Crawford 2014, 28). We can consider how people moved through and utilised the space. Whilst an equation between the domestic and feminine space should not be automatic, we may speculate to a degree on where various members of the community spent their time. Most of the finds from Putton are not gendered (cf Schuster, Chapter 3); even personal dress items were to a degree unisex, and the distribution across the site is not helpful. Anthropological considerations of French peasantry and English medieval documentary evidence have suggested that for the peasant classes at least, the house was a largely female domain, with men spending much more of their time in fields and on outdoor occupations (Gilchrist 1997, 55; Johnson 1997, 146). At Putton there may be potential for gendered and age-derived areas of activity, if concepts of women and children being associated with the inner, private areas (Gilchrist 1997, 54), such as the houses and gardens are considered. However, given the multiplicity of tasks apparently undertaken, and the limitations in understanding areas associated with them, a much more fluid model of interaction is likely, even if certain jobs were 'woman's work'. More complex and potentially of greater interest is the likely interplay of people of differing status within the household and the surrounding landscape. It is within this framework that it is worth considering the potential for a garden to be situated within the most secluded and higher status area. The evidence for this is scant, but it would explain the more ephemeral walls attached to the southern end of B2 (and possibly a similar use in the same area whilst at the northern end of B5). The location would be appropriate for this type of use, and more prosaic activities are perhaps less likely immediately adjacent to the most high-status building in the complex.

If there was a garden present, it is likely to have been a practical space but have carried other functions and meanings. People in both urban and rural settings grew a range of fruit, vegetables and herbs for flavouring (Hammond 1993, 59, 100). The range of foods consumed by the gentry would have made a garden or gardens a necessity. Medicinal plants were frequently cultivated, alongside an increasing conviction in the beneficial effects of beauty and attractive scents as a defence against disease (Rawcliffe 2008), and there is the hint of these types of plants being present at Putton. Medieval gardens were highly variable in size and form (Taylor 2000, 38), so a small walled space is feasible. Enclosed gardens generally appear to have been located adjacent to high status buildings, which might be suggested for Putton. They were often designed to be viewed from above from private spaces (Harvey 1981, 44), and of course we do not know where window openings were positioned, although it seems B2 had an upper storey. Gardens also had connotations of feminine space, evoking love and sexual relationships but

were also often spiritual spaces used for religious contemplation (Noble 2000). The lives of medieval women, and noble women in particular, were highly bounded, both in terms of behaviour and space; their physical freedom and movement was highly controlled (Seaborne 2011, 4). The garden itself, and some of the plants which it contained, specifically the rose, became symbolic of female chastity (Dodson 2018, 595, 599). The provision of an enclosed space within the more private areas of the manorial court at Putton would be an expression of these understandings and also a demonstration of status.

At Barentin, Oxfordshire use of the garden by elite children has prompted questions as to whether they were segregated from the children of the servants and peasants (Crawford 2014, 32). There are no indications at Putton as to whether and how children's lives were regulated and affected by the activities on the site and the arrangement of spaces. However, the interment of a neonate within B1 (Randall, Chapter 3) is an ephemeral reminder of the multi-generational nature of the household. It also seems that in particular circumstances the remains of infants could continue to play a role after their deaths, being involved in apotropaic practices which were concerned with family safety. This gives us a glimpse into the everyday concerns and fears of the people who inhabited the chamber block. It is notable that the location of the deliberate deposition was close to what was probably the principle access to the private space of the family. It was deployed at the most effective location of protection.

THE FAMILY AND THE LAND,
By Clare Randall

As outlined in Chapter 5, Putton was held by the le Walys or le Walsshe family throughout the 13th and 14th centuries when the main buildings were in use. Whilst we cannot be certain whether or which members of the family may have inhabited the buildings themselves, their involvement with the place would have been a key influence on its development and demise. It is not possible to entirely reconstruct the familial relationships and descent. However, the transactions we know of indicate that

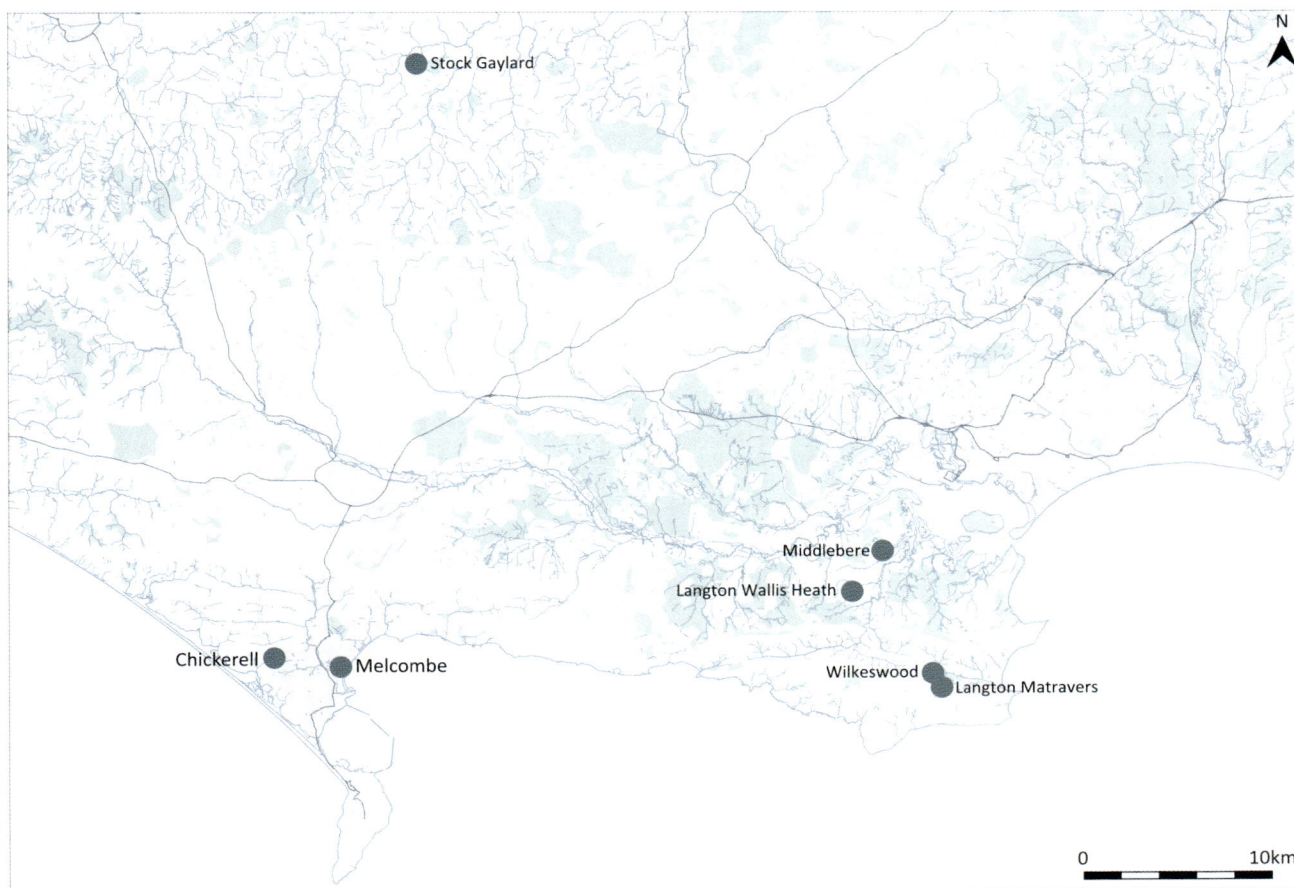

Fig. 6.16   The Dorset manorial holdings of the le Walys family.

this was one extended family with interests not only within one manor, but across a block of neighbouring land, and further afield. We should perhaps consider Putton not alone but as part of the wider 'family business'.

Whilst Putton was in possession of a 'capital messuage and curtilage' which can be equated with the buildings at Lower Putton Lane, no mentions are made of anything similar at West or East Chickerell. It is possible that, only one of the manors received a substantial dwelling which may have been a principle residence of a senior family member and served the needs of the manorial administration for the district. Also, whilst the family held lands in Somerset, and in north Dorset (acquired by marriage), their own original holdings appear to show an interest in coastal access (Fig. 6.16). The Langton holding was a particularly large unit, which appears to have preserved a late Saxon estate and ran inland from the Purbeck coast in

the south to encompass land on the edge of Poole Harbour (Taylor 1970, 62). This included saltworks at Middlebere (see Chapter 5). Langton became a centre of Purbeck marble production, with quarries at Wilkswood, some in the control of the Priory, others within the purview of the Langton manor (Hinton 2002, 98). As this fossiliferous limestone weathers poorly it was predominantly used for the production of tombs, coffin lids and fonts (RCHME 1970b, xl) such as a slab in St Mary's Church Chickerell with the incised figure of a priest of probable 15th century date (RCHME 1970a, 38). It was also used for decorative internal features of many major public buildings of the period such as Salisbury Cathedral (Tatton-Brown 1991; Williams 2002, 126). These uses may explain why there was only a single bowl fragment identified at Putton, although the subsequent removal of architectural stone may also have contributed (see Green, Chapter 2). However, it is worth noting that the extraction and use of Purbeck marble was increasing rapidly during the 13th century, reaching its zenith in the 14th century (Drury 1949). It was used as far afield as Durham Cathedral where it was regarded as having come from 'overseas parts' (Blair 1991, 43), and at Lisieux and Bayeux cathedrals (Williams 2002, 129), underlining the importance of transportation by sea.

The predominantly coastal pattern of the le Walys interests is further enhanced by the fact that for at least part of the 13th century, Melcombe Regis was in the control of Ingelram le Walys. This would have given the family not only control of either side of the Wey valley across Radipole Lake but the county's main trading port at this time (Forrest 2017b), as well as contact via the sea with Langton with its stone and salt resources. Perhaps we should begin to see the choices at work in the establishment of particular sites as relating to wider entrepreneurialism and familial economic strategy. Marriage choices may have related to these business strategies. Deliberate acquisition of blocks of manors has been noted elsewhere (Bailey 2002, 10) and there is no reason not to think that it did not occur in Dorset. There was certainly an interest in trade. Langton was granted a market in 1277 (Hinton 2002, 100). We can also speculate as to what they did with the money. Ingelram le Walys gave up Melcombe in 1276, receiving 100 pounds sterling. This later 13th century date might coincide with the rebuilding of the Putton manorial building and with the expansion of the church at West Chickerell. The apparent relative poverty revealed by taxation records for the Isle of Purbeck in the 14th century has been suggested to relate to the skill of the local landed families in manipulating the taxation system and controlling supplemental industries to the exclusion of most of the population (Hinton 2002). A kind description might suggest this was an entrepreneurial approach to the opportunities provided by specific manors. It was certainly more than an accumulation of agricultural land.

The slight indications of military equipment at Putton (Schuster, Chapter 3) might also imply that some members of the family were not averse to supplying their military service obligations themselves rather than converting it to a cash payment. A tomb, said to represent Sir Ingelram le Walys at Stock Gaylard

(RCHME 1970b, 138) dating to the second half of the 13th century shows him in mail with a sword. The buildings at Putton show that they were people of taste and refinement, aware of their social standing and the le Walys' were certainly well connected during the 14th century. For instance, they had an association with the Maltravers family (see Chapter 5). Sir John Maltravers was one of Edward III's bannerets fighting in northern France in the lead up to the battle of Crecy in 1346 (Hefferan 2019, 29). The Maltravers were related to the Cifrewast family of Hooke (Wessex Archaeology 2006) who probably held the greater portion of West Chickerell (see Chapter 5). These associations brought them into contact with the most elevated strata of society. The Wilkswood Priory Cartulary of 1370 (Nottingham University Middleton Collection PM/LM1/1167:20) describes the preparations by Roger Walesch in advance of a visit to the Wilkswood Chantry by Edward III (Papworth 1996). At some point after the early 12th century, someone at Putton came into the possession, and subsequently lost, a rare and exquisite gold and rock crystal brooch which had originated at the court of the Holy Roman Emperor. Either by wealth or social connections they had access to fine things and long-distance networks.

FARMING AND FISHING, By Clare Randall

The medieval landscape

Putton is in an area where pollen analysis consistently suggests low tree cover from the late Romano-British period throughout the later 1st millennium (Rippon et al. 2014). Other information about the local environment is scant. Calculations from Domesday Book suggest that around 13% of Dorset was covered in woodland (Rackham 1980,114). Woods and their products regularly featured in Dorset manorial records (Horsfall 1997). As for the area under plough in the medieval period there is widespread earthwork evidence throughout south Dorset, but it has not received detailed study. Many examples remain undated. In addition, many of the known earthwork sites survive due to what might be regarded as their more peripheral locations, positioned on steep valley slopes. For example, the medieval terraces of the Portesham and Abbotsbury area (RCHME 1952, 11) survive by dint of their inaccessibility for modern plough equipment. The area around Putton contains plenty of probably medieval examples (e.g. Fig. 6.3. nos. 1–7). In addition, cultivation marks and boundaries which are probably medieval occur to the north of Putton Farm, in irregular boundaries around the location of East Chickerell and in a series of fields to the north of Chickerell village between Chickerell Hill and Barr Lane. These are probably part of the main fields of the Chickerell manors. A further medieval field system is present at East Fleet and on Fleet common to the south west, and there are extensive agricultural and settlement earthworks to the north at Tatton and Buckland Ripers (RCHME 1970a, 41), as well as boundaries at South Buckland. The addition of information on the sequence of boundaries at Putton is helpful to understanding the potential chronological and functional complexity of these systems.

The fields

The classic arrangements of strip cultivation within a series of open fields, facilitating communal rotations and stinting, was not ubiquitous in Dorset. South Dorset is at the periphery of a central English zone where villages and open fields developed (Rippon 2008; Rippon et al. 2014, 195), but the pattern of adoption is not clear. Enclosure of both open downland and arable appears to have begun in the county during the 15th century. Strip cultivation still occurred in the early modern period being finally extinguished in the late 18th and early 19th centuries with a major re-orientation associated with the Inclosures (Taylor 1970, 150). The extensive Fordington open field system surrounding Dorchester may have post-Roman or later Saxon origins (Keen 1984, 236), and extended within the Roman town using earlier boundaries (Woodward et al. 1993, 376). Documentary and earthwork evidence suggest an open field system in operation at Melbury Abbas (Ross 1993, 115). However, to what degree these examples reflect classic centralised systems is debatable. The trajectory of development, or association with particular activities, soils or topographies, remains obscure largely due to the lack of systematic study. Dorset may possess some areas of nucleation with large open field systems. However, the dispersed settlement patterns of the south west

and smaller scale open fields within closes (Rippon 2008; 2012) may prove a better model.

Few medieval field boundaries in Dorset have been excavated, so their chronology and form are poorly understood. Lynchets are a common feature of the parts of the Dorset landscape where steep sided valleys predominate. However, lynchets were not always part of classical open fields (RCHME 1970b, xlvii; 1970a, xxxix). Whilst some may have their origins in the earlier medieval period (Taylor 1966; 1970, 88) they are generally assumed to be medieval in date although clear chronologies can prove elusive (Table 6.1). For example, at Bincombe (Fig. 6.17), which Taylor suggested (1966, 282) may have early medieval origins, the date of creation of the lynchets remained unclear after excavation. They were however apparently formed as a by-product of ploughing rather than deliberate construction (Heyden et al. 2014, 284). Lynchets excavated at Rope Lake Hole, Purbeck produced abraded pottery dated to the 12th–14th centuries (Woodward 1986), although it has been noted that Purbeck may have already been 'marginal' by the 12th and 13th centuries (Hinton 2002, 84). Strip fields expanded to fill every available part of Worth Matravers parish (McOmish 2002), whilst documentary evidence implies that almost all workable land in Langton Wallis was in use during this period (Hinton 2002, 92). In recent years, around Dorset, field boundaries have been excavated which survive only as ditches (Table 6.1). These all have a similar date and display a variety of morphologies. They seem to support an increase or change in agricultural exploitation during the 12th–14th centuries. Expansion into new areas, including heathland occurred during this period (Taylor 1970, 86). This was probably related to population increase (Hinton 2002, 90). The addition of these previously unknown or underappreciated fields indicates that expansion and intensification had wide and deep effects on areas which were already used as well as those which had not been previously cultivated.

The date of inception of the Putton Area 2 enclosures remains unclear, but the ditches filled with material, most likely derived from a manuring regime between the 12th and 14th centuries. This broad period coincides with the extensive midden deposit in the

Table 6.1 Excavated/dated medieval field boundaries in Dorset.

Site	Date	Description	Reference
Rope Lake Hoe, Kimmeridge	12th–14th century	Lynchets.	Woodward 1986
Bincombe valley	Undated	Lynchets. Suggested to perhaps be of earlier medieval date, but not demonstrated by excavation.	Taylor 1966; Hayden et al. 2014
Hanglands, Poyntington	Undated	Lynchet.	Randall 2020
East of the Corfe River	Medieval	Four parallel ditches c. 30m apart; parallel modern field boundary.	Cox and Hearne 1999,42
West Mead, Bere Regis	13th century	Rectilinear arrangement of shallow ditches.	Hearne and Birbeck 1999, 79–84
Chantry Fields, Gillingham	12th–13th centuries	Shallow boundary ditches; recutting/ re-creation; complex series of small land parcels; overlying earthworks and on the edge of a town.	Heaton 1992, 111–3, 125
Broad Mead, Kington Magna	12th–14th centuries	Earthworks of small rectilinear fields associated with pottery (fieldwalked).	Ross 1992
Curtis Fields, Weymouth	13th–14th centuries	Rectilinear arrangement of shallow ditches.	Randall 2019

valley base (see below). The numerous episodes of apparent alteration and re-imposition of boundaries described in Chapter 1 may relate to the shallowness and ease of silting of the ditches. Boundaries of the 13th–14th centuries at nearby Curtis Fields, Weymouth (Randall 2018) exhibited multiple re-establishments of shallow ditches. Situated on similar clays to those at Lower Putton Lane, it may indicate that erosion was an issue on these soils. However, the dynamic nature of relatively ephemeral boundaries is seen on other excavated sites in western England. Numerous ditched boundaries were repeatedly re-established on similar alignments between the 12th and 14th centuries at King's Stanley, Gloucestershire (Hardy and Wright 2013, 64). At least three phases of medieval fields occurred at Tinker's Close, Moreton-in-Marsh (Langton et al. 2000). At Lower Putton Lane, during the span of Phases 3 and 4, there was apparently, a considerable change in layout (Fig. 1.27). In this case it appears to have been a functional alteration.

The suggested original form of boundaries at Putton may represent land parcels of some size alongside a corral. The rectilinear enclosure, an apparently trampled pathway around its exterior, and an adjacent terrace, also seemingly trampled,

represent an area where there was a high traffic of livestock. It may represent a specialised animal handling complex. Whilst penning sheep might be beneficial at certain times, this arrangement would be equally suitable to cattle husbandry. The proximity to the main manorial buildings would be appropriate for dairying, whilst the immediately adjacent water source would be suitable, given the significant water requirements of cattle (Smith Thomas 2005). It may also have contributed to the extensive humic deposits in the valley base. Furthermore, it lies adjacent to the main trackway, which is certainly of a scale to facilitate stock handling, and if followed to the south would provide access to grazing on what was probably the common and the pasture known as Gormere (see Chapter 5). The inception of these features may coincide with the slight indications of a more significant proportion of cattle remains in earlier contexts (Randall, Chapter 4).

The organising principle of the later Area 2 boundaries was apparently a central spinal trackway. This was parallel with the holloway track seen in Area 1, and the earthworks to the south of the excavated area. It seems that at some point there was a re-orientation, with a change to small rectilinear

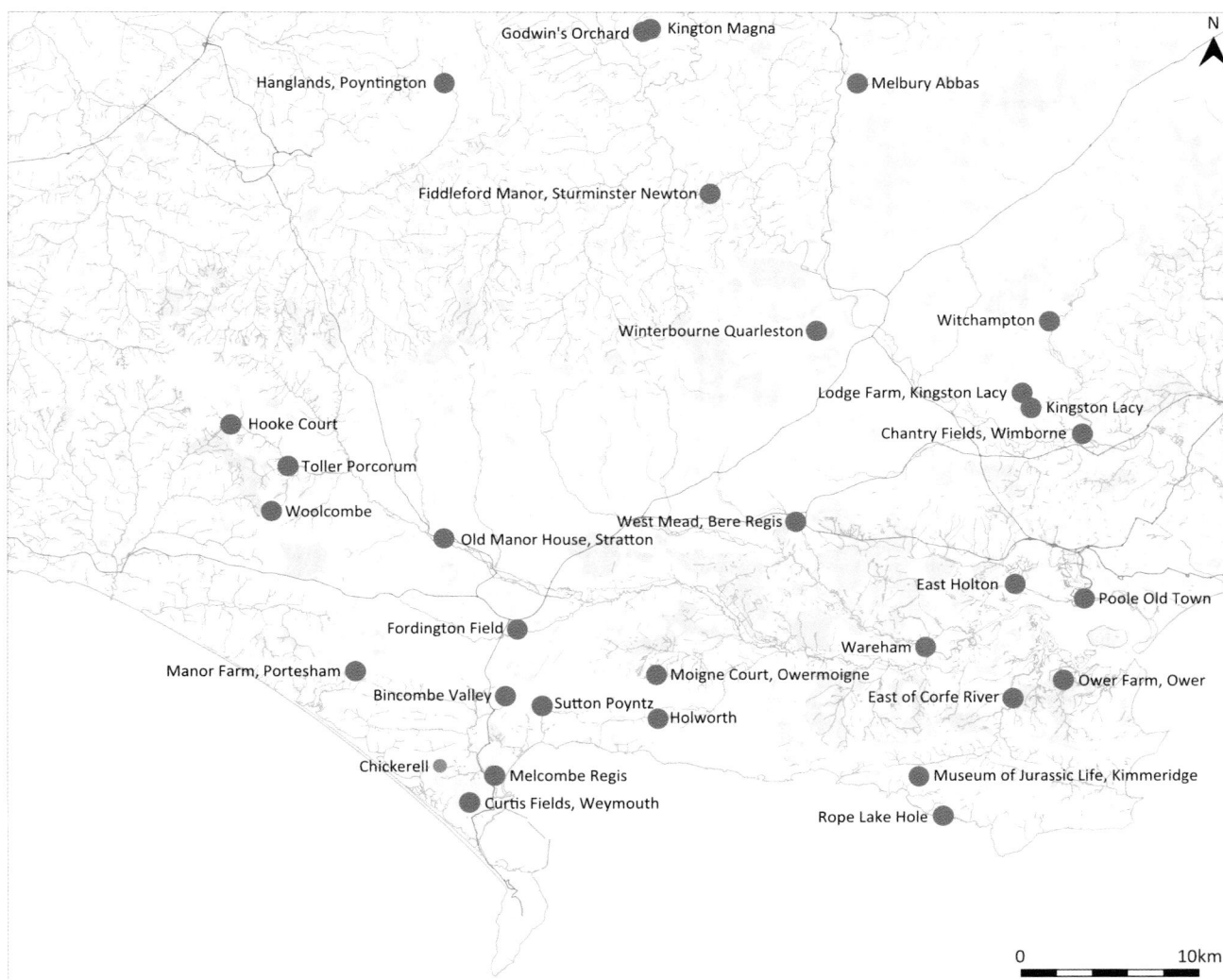

Fig. 6.17 *Places mentioned in Chapter 6.*

closes, and ultimately what appear to be strips. The reason for this change is explored further below, but clearly systems were not immutable but dynamic. The freedom with which they were altered over a relatively short period of time suggests a responsive approach to using the land. This may have been in relation to practical issues, but also probably associated with either a freedom from tenurial considerations, if it was part of the manor demesne, or resulted from tenurial complexity amongst peasant tenants. This complexity is worth considering in future. Creative methods were being used to possibly maximise the output of what was becoming a more limited resource, land.

Middens

The extensive midden at Lower Putton Lane appears to have been an integral part of the organisation of the manor and its agricultural regime (see below). The plant remains and the microartefacts appear to indicate that there was a degree of churn within the deposit (Carruthers; Randall, Chapter 4). It is likely that it was constantly added to and had material extracted from it. Large humic deposits and middens have been identified in a number of locations (Table 6.2). West Mead, Bere Regis comprised domestic and agricultural waste indicating storage of refuse before manuring the nearby fields (Hearne and Birbeck 1999, 231–2). This interpretation fits the Lower Putton Lane midden deposit well.

Table 6.2 Medieval midden and potential midden sites in Dorset

Site	Date	Description	Reference
Ower Farm, Corfe Castle	13th century	Humic soil accumulation; fish and mammal bone.	Cox et al. 1991a, 85
West Mead, Bere Regis	13th century	Extensive humic deposit with pottery and iron objects; associated with agricultural boundaries.	Higgins 1995; Hearne and Birbeck 1999, 79–84; Mepham 1999; Loader 1999
Curtis Fields, Weymouth	13th–14th centuries	Dark humic deposit with pottery; associated with field boundaries.	Randall 2019
Woolcombe Farm, Toller Porcorum	13th–14th centuries	Humic deposit with abundant pottery	Hunt 1985
Museum of Jurassic Marine Life, Kimmeridge	12th–13th centuries	Substantial deposit; associated yard surface.	Robinson et al. 2018
Beside the River Strichel, Melbury Abbas	12th–14th centuries	Scatter of pottery; adjacent strip lynchets.	Ross 1993
Godwin's Orchard, Kington Magna	12th–14th centuries	A 'lower soil horizon' with a very substantial amount of pottery.	Richards 1991

All of these middens date to around the 13th century. The curation of refuse, especially where associated with field systems, indicates a deliberate practice focussed on the maintenance of arable fertility. New settlements, farms and manors were appearing in Dorset at this time on previously marginal land, such as the Dorset heaths (Taylor 1970, 92). The effort involved in creating lynchets has been regarded as symptomatic of land pressure due to settlement expansion in the 12th–13th centuries. This period of agricultural expansion and intensification appears to have come to an end in the 14th century. The indications are that there were land pressures and concerns over soil fertility. Potential middens where other settlement evidence is otherwise unknown may prove a useful marker of occupation and agricultural exploitation. They also may be indicators of developing awareness of the need for inputs to maintain the system.

The farming regime

Types of farming regimes compared with the underlying geologies have been considered in various regions (Thirsk 1987). However, documentary sources suggest localised variations of approach within these zones (Campbell 2000). Any successful farming community will have recognised the opportunity to work with the properties of the locale (Rippon et al. 2014, 197). Examples from the south of England suggest mixed farming where most produce was consumed within the household with a small surplus sold on. This appears to be echoed by the great estates, with the only variation being on the chalk with its greater emphasis on sheep production (Hinton 2012, 127). This approach is likely to hold true for Dorset, and indeed for Putton. The utilisation of land necessarily depends on the physical parameters which it offers to the needs of crops and livestock (Randall 2010). There is however plenty to be done in understanding the local interplay of land, topography, soils and available markets to approach questions of specialisation and choices by landowners and tenants. As far as Putton is concerned Fig. 6.18, provides some putative suggestions as to how the available landscape may have been utilised.

The arable economy (Carruthers, Chapter 4) from Phase 2 onwards appears to have been relatively diverse, with bread and rivet wheat, barley as a lesser component, and the possibility of cultivation of oats and some rye, although these may have been weeds within cereal crops. Peas and beans were grown, and it seems that cultivated vetch and flax were present from at least Phase 3. The former would have largely been used as animal fodder, whilst the latter, albeit present in very small numbers would have been a valuable source of both oil and fibre. The weed seeds present suggest that crops were being grown on various different soils. It is worth noting here the differences in geology between the northern part of the manor, on limestone, and the heavier clays in the southern half. Barley may have been more appropriate to grow on the freer draining soils in the north, whilst rivet wheat may have been suited to the heavier clays. Use of both nutrient rich and poor areas are indicated by variation in arable weeds.

The likelihood is that the material which arrived at the centre of the manor was derived from both the demesne land and as tithes from tenants. As has been suggested above, it seems likely that the original manor demesne arable land was situated on the slightly better land to the north of the excavated area. Other parts of the Putton manor do not have such efficacious soils, and it is in those locations that some of these crops may have been produced. Crops, with the addition of a few other plants, appear to have provided useful residues, both in the provision of bedding or fodder for livestock, and for burning. Cultivated vetches appear to have also become a useful crop and would largely have been used for animal feed. This supplies scant evidence for housing of large numbers of livestock in the vicinity, but provision for plough animals and riding horses may have been needed on site.

There appears to have been a shift in the crop husbandry regime over time. There are indications that there were issues of declining soil fertility with an inability to rotate crops sufficiently. There was an increase in small seeded leguminous weeds over time. Clover and vetch were valuable nitrogen fixers and the increase in their presence may have been an attempt to counteract the effects of continual arable use of land. The presence of peas and beans implies a rotation, and as the proportions seemed to be stable between Phase 2 and later material, it is likely that the same regime was in force. However, the greater use of leguminous weeds may show that it was increasingly strained. There is further evidence of a lack of opportunity for rotation in the presence of wheat nematode gall, which greater land rotation would have managed effectively. The pressure on land may be possible to discern in the apparently changing field layouts. If the earliest version of the boundaries in Area 2 of the site is

interpreted as a stock corral then there is a clear change from a specialised use of that area perhaps in the 13th century to one which seems more suited to cultivation than animal handling. There may have been an imperative to bring more of what was probably the demesne land into the arable rotation. This also potentially underlines the efficacy of establishing the midden which developed in the middle of the site from the 13th century onwards. Most material culture making its way into the ditches on the western slope in this period probably derived from manuring of the land with compost taken from this heap. The practice probably accounts for the degree of churn seen in those deposits.

The interdependence of arable cultivation and livestock is clearly apparent in this regime where maintenance of income was constrained by the proportion of suitable land within the manorial boundaries. The information on animal husbandry is somewhat limited but it may have been that sheep were lambed away from the manor centre, whilst those most beneficial on a daily basis (domestic birds, milking cattle and pigs) were part of the household regime. Cattle, especially used for dairying, have a significant water requirement (Smith Thomas 2005, 16), so are better kept near water sources, whilst sheep get most of their water from what they eat (Goodwin 1979, 169). Both could utilise the areas of the manor less suitable for arable, including wetland grazing. Information on the herd and flock structures is not good enough to comment in detail on the approach used in flock/herd maintenance or development and there is virtually no metrical information to tell us about the size of animals, only to say that they were small, and not akin to 'improved' animals in the post-medieval period. This however probably made handling them easier.

At Putton, the faunal remains from Phases 2–4 suggest a move from a greater relative abundance of cattle to that of sheep (Randall, Chapter 4) and this change probably occurred during the main period of use of the buildings. The layout of the enclosures within Area 2 may have provided facilities for specialised cattle production (see Chapter 1). Whilst Putton does not seem to offer the specific features of vaccaries as defined in the northern uplands of

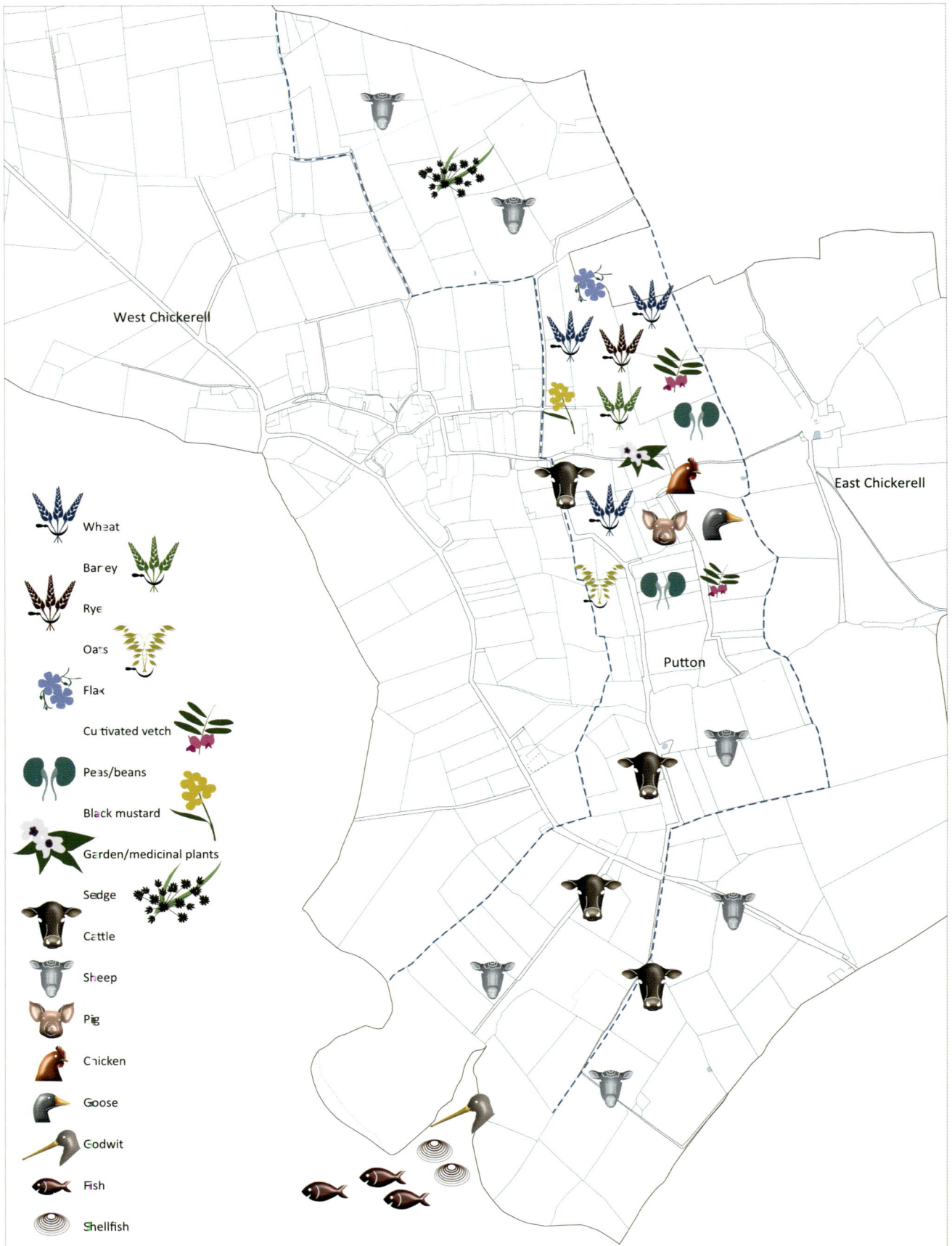

Fig. 6.18 Possible location of resources within the Putton manor.

England, and identified in the south of England at sites like The Hayworth in the Weald (Margetts 2017), it has some elements in common. Specialised stock handling features and access to extensive rough grazing via tracks are apparently present. The southern part of the Putton manor stretching down to the north shore of the Fleet would provide rough grazing. Some place names in the local area suggest specialised, probably dairy farms. Whilst the *wic* element of Wyke Regis might more properly be related to its role as a trading hub, Wyke Wood, Abbotsbury, with a reference as early as 1269, refers to a dairy farm. Another example is Wyke Oliver, first mentioned in 1327 (Mills 1998,164) originally within the Sutton Poyntz manor. This might suggest the establishment of specialised dairying in this part of Dorset. Pressure on land for arable use may have contributed to a change.

The Domesday survey for Dorset had a general high predominance of sheep with smaller numbers of pigs and goats, and very few recorded cattle (Darby and Finn 1967, 123). Despite the heavy clay soils of the Weymouth Lowlands, there was a reliance on sheep. The account rolls of Wyke Regis for 1242–3 note 500 sheep on the demesne farm, with 700 in the preceding year (Taylor 1970, 100). The proximity of a wool exporting port at Melcombe Regis may have provided a local impetus to change. Nevertheless, if there had been some specialisation in cattle at Putton, the shift to a greater relative abundance of sheep may also have been part of wider economic trends. That this occurred on the English chalk and limestone is supported by analysis of the documentary sources (Rippon et al. 2014, 223), and this is reflected in limited Dorset data (Randall, Chapter 4). It is however worth considering that a decline in cattle keeping may have been related to other issues. The widespread outbreak of disease in cattle, probably Rinderpest, during the earlier 14th century resulted in some areas in losses of over 50% of cattle (Newfield 2009; Slavin 2012). We do not know how this affected Dorset.

We may consider then how the evidence of fields, livestock and crops comes together to suggest a husbandry regime. In the south west peninsula, the landscape is dominated by small and irregular groups of fields which developed during the early medieval period with the inception of the practice of convertible husbandry (Rippon et al. 2006). Small parcels of land or closes were used for arable cultivation on a rotational basis of around four years, in between which they are used for pastoral husbandry. This is a lower intensity regime than the classic rotation between arable and fallow within a large scale open-field system. It also leads to the pattern of isolated farms and small hamlets. At Putton, the forms of some of the fields (both excavated and perhaps preserved in the 18th–19th century mapping) might suggest something similar was being used at least part of the time.

The marine resource

Marine resources were also an important component of the household and manorial economy of Putton. There appear to be similarities between small scale coastal sites such as Ower Farm, on the southern fringe of Poole Harbour, whilst having demonstrable differences with urban trading centres such as Poole itself. Both Ower and Putton produced fish bone assemblages dominated by local coastal species which could have been obtained from the shore or by small boats. Exploitation at Putton appears to have focussed on provision of a range of easy to obtain species which were consumed locally. There does not appear to be evidence that there was active management of the oyster fishery. By contrast the 13th century shell midden at Ower Farm was comprised of species which would have been readily available from the adjacent mudflats but showed preferences for particular species which were not immediately nearby. In that case oysters only occurred at a low level, and it is possible that they were harvested and transported to the landholder, Milton Abbey (Cox et al. 1991a, 90). It provides a direct contrast to the pattern of distribution of marine shell at Putton. A similar range of species including cockles, winkles and oysters was present on both sites, but at Ower Farm they were in very considerable numbers and were also present in the midden in dumps of single species, implying that they were being systematically harvested (Winder 1991, 213). At Putton the absolute numbers were much lower, and the material more widely distributed. All could have been obtained from the parts of the Fleet which the manor bordered. Certainly, the shellfish of preference were oysters. The other species are all perfectly edible, but it should also be considered that they may have been useful as bait for line or net fishing from the shore. Many of the fish species present are readily line caught, and ten fishing weights were recovered (Schuster, Chapter 3).

PUTTON AND THE DORSET MANORIAL HIERARCHY, By Clare Randall

As outlined in Chapter 1, excavation of Dorset houses and settlements has been limited in both scale and number, and few relate to manorial complexes. Limited work has been undertaken at known village sites where there has been shrinkage or settlement shift (see Table 6.3). Many buildings are only known because they are incorporated into later structures or located within their grounds (e.g. Kingston Lacy [Papworth 1997]). However, in general terms Dorset seems to follow the pattern of the 13th century marking the point of greatest expansion of the manorial system (Bailey 2002, 16), and the contemporary developments at Putton place it in this milieu. Some local investigations have indicated 13th century expansion into new areas. Activity of the 13th–14th centuries at Curtis Fields, Weymouth, probably represents new tenanting of a previously under-used area of the large Wyke Regis estate (Randall 2018).

Some investigations have examined possible planted or specialised settlements, such as Holworth, Chaldon Herring, which comprised seven tofts along a trackway. Excavation of one structure revealed stone foundations which would have supported timber and cob walls. The substantial ceramic assemblage indicated inception by the 12th century and reorganisation as a planned settlement in the 13th century. This was probably instigated by Milton Abbey. Holworth demonstrated the local building style for lesser tenants and showed that even within a single toft, structures had differing functions (Rahtz 1959). Another holding of Milton Abbey was at Ower Farm on the south side of Poole Harbour. Possible specialised exploitation of local shellfish suggested a role in supply to the Abbey. A substantial timber building parallel to a trackway was superseded in the 13th–14th centuries

by buildings of stone or with stone footings. The generally modest nature of the buildings, including lack of ceramic tile roofing, has been related to its status as an ecclesiastical holding. (Cox et al. 1991a, 86–90). It may be however that these differences were a reflection of its general position in the local hierarchy of settlement.

Few investigations have examined manorial sites, and then in a limited fashion. However, there are initial indications of not only differences between them and the settlements of lesser tenants and peasants, but between manors of differing social standing. A manor house of some social importance with royal connections was in use at Kingston Lacy from the 12th to the 15th century (Papworth 1997; 1998). Manor Farm, Portesham, produced slight evidence of the manorial centre which had been a possession of Abbotsbury Abbey. A capital messuage and farm is referred to in documentation of 1594 (Valentin 2003, 61–63). Sutton Poyntz has been discussed above (Green, this Chapter), although the full plan was not seen (Rawlings 2007, 37, 39). Information on the size, arrangement and nature of the capital buildings would be interesting as Sutton was in the possession of the landlords of the Putton manor, the Poyns family. Whilst they may not have resided there (Chandler 2007), the connection between the manors was of longstanding and Sutton was, relatively speaking, further up the social scale. Mepham (Chapter 2) has noted the greater number of imported ceramic vessels at Sutton Poyntz than at Putton, which supports this. Whilst the corpus of sites is small, it hints at the potential variety of arrangements and status within Dorset manors which deserves more exploration. Putton itself might be regarded as being of the 'middling sort'.

THE PROCESS OF ABANDONMENT, By Clare Randall

Whilst the deposits overlying the buildings at Lower Putton Lane had been dispersed and re-worked, all the evidence suggests that the complex had fallen into disuse or been dismantled probably by the end of the 14th century. Dumps of building stone and broken limestone tiles contain material dating to the 13th–14th century reflecting the lifespan

Table 6.3 Excavated medieval settlements in Dorset

Site	Date	Description	Reference
Kington Magna	12th–14th centuries	Settlement earthworks by church; house platforms.	Ross 1985
Witchampton	10th–13th centuries	Earthworks; 20 tofts on lane north of the village.	Hall 1993, 125
Quarleston Farm, Winterborne Stickland	10th–13th centuries	Earthworks of Winterborne Quarleston; excavated pits of 12th–13th centuries.	Butterworth 2003
East Holton, Wareham St Martin	11th–12th centuries	Two buildings of probable cob construction arranged on a trackway.	Hewitt et al. 2002, 2003, 2004
Holworth, Chaldon Herring	12th–13th centuries	Planned series of seven tofts with associated areas for cultivation, arranged along a trackway.	Rahtz 1959
Ower Farm, Corfe Castle	12th–14th centuries	Timber and later, stone buildings, shell midden, track, enclosure ditch.	Cox et al 1991a, 86-90
Godwin's Orchard, Kington Magna	12th–14th centuries	Pottery scatter/potential midden.	Richards 1999
Curtis Fields, Weymouth	13th–14th centuries	field boundaries/potential midden.	Randall 2018
Hooke Court, Hooke	11th–14th centuries	Partly moated manorial site with 14th century building; earlier activity and nearby earthworks associated with 12th century pottery.	Wessex Archaeology 2006
The Old Manor, Stratton	13th–14th centuries	Parts of manorial curtilage buildings and fishponds.	Maw 2015
Woolcombe Farm, Toller Porcorum	13th–14th centuries	Earthwork platforms; stone buildings, floors and cut features; boundaries.	Poulson 1983; Hunt 1984; 1985; 1986; 1990; 1991;1992
Church Mead, Toller Porcorum	12th–14th centuries	Boundaries, buildings and possible industrial activity.	Gale 1991;1992; 1993
Kingston Lacy	12th–15th centuries	Earthworks; stone buildings to the north of the post-medieval mansion; documentary description.	Papworth 1997
Manor Farm, Portesham	13th–14th centuries	Early medieval and Saxo-Norman activity; flint constructed wall foundation; pits. Identified as manorial centre.	Valentin 2003
Sutton Poyntz Water Treatment Works	13th–14th centuries	Substantial stone building, probably a chapel; part of a stone built domestic building; possible pond, boundary ditches.	Rawlings 2007
Village Hall, West Stafford	13th century	Small group of pits containing 13th century pottery.	Draper 1975
The Leaze, Wimborne	12th–14th centuries	Earthworks of street, lanes, houses and fields. Planned and then failed expansion of the town.	Field 1973

of the buildings. Deposits overlying these contain some post-medieval material, derived from later buildings, adjacency to the Putton Farm farmhouse and agricultural use of the area. There is however a clear break in the dates of the material between the 14th and 17th centuries.

Whilst it is possible that the buildings were abandoned and fell down, they seem, at least in part, to have been deliberately dismantled. A notable feature, given the scale of the main buildings, is the lack of identifiable architectural stonework. Areas such as the porch of B2 which must have had an ornate door surround appear to have been robbed, and whilst faced stones occurred in the lowest remaining levels around the doorways in B1 and B2, squared off blocks were absent. The rubble largely comprised unworked, irregular and smaller elements which had been used to create the cores of the walls. This suggests that the better building stone had been entirely removed from the site. Some of the material, particularly from the more easily exposed elements of B1, may well have been re-used in the creation of the post-medieval structures which partly overlay it. Some of the material was probably incorporated into later buildings such as Putton Farm farmhouse located immediately to the north of the excavation site. However, it is also likely that the more valuable components were removed not long after the complex ceased to function.

Various explanations can be advanced for the ending of the Putton manorial complex. It is suggested in Chapter 5, that there was also expansion and shrinkage in West Chickerell, although this is undated. The date of Putton's disuse falls within the continuum of abandonment in the county. Dorset has more than 250 known deserted or considerably shrunken settlements dating from the medieval period onward (Viner 2002, 10), but understanding the chronology of settlement failure is limited. The point of Holworth's abandonment in the 14th or 15th century is not clear (Hinton 2012, 121). It is presumed that medieval sites within Kington Magna parish went out of use by the 15th century due to a combination of climatic deterioration and the Black Death (Ross 1992). Across central southern England however the evidence generally indicates shrinkage rather than complete desertion (Hinton 2012, 131). The abandonment and contraction of settlements in Dorset was geographically widespread and did not just affect more marginal land (Taylor 1970, 111). Taylor notes (1970, 115) that it was the smaller settlements which were most affected. The replacement of a former settlement or estate centre with a single farmstead is a common occurrence (Viner 2002, 10). Holworth, for example remained as a farm (Rahtz 1959) and locally Buckland Ripers and Tatton offer examples of remnant communities (RCHME 1970a, 41). Putton, with its successor farm, fits well within this picture with its demise coming probably by the end of the 14th century. Like other

small medieval manors in the county it was affected by much wider forces as well as more local events, all of which combined to hasten its end. The more significant of these forces are considered further below.

Climate change

The trend towards a warmer and drier climate had begun in the later first millennium AD (Dark 2000, 171). The Medieval Climate Anomaly, or Medieval Warm Period was a warm interlude, which appears to have been in effect between the 10th and mid-14th centuries, after which the climate began to cool again probably affected by changes originating in the Pacific (Graham et al. 2011). In northern Europe this had the effect of providing warm springs and dry summers. Cooling in the first half of the 14th century was accompanied by an increase in rainfall. However, the regional and local effects of these changes were variable (Hughes and Diaz 1994). These events may well have contributed to the Great Hunger of 1315–19 and the Great Bovine Pestilence of 1319–21. Widespread flooding and very cold winters in 1314–1317 led to three consecutive years of failed harvests, with dramatically reduced yields (Dawson et al. 2007; Campbell 2010). Widespread sheep liver-fluke between 1315 and 1317, would have been exacerbated by the wet weather. The disease seen in cattle between 1319 and 1321 was probably an outbreak of rinderpest resulting in high cattle mortality (Newfield 2009; Slavin 2012). This was followed by further crop failures in the 1320s (Campbell 2010).

The Black Death

'In 1348 two ships, one of them from Bristol, landed at Melcombe in Dorset a little before Midsummer. In them were sailors from Gascony who were infected with an unheard of epidemic illness called pestilence. They infected the men of Melcombe, who were the first to be infected in England. The first inhabitants to die from the illness did so on the Eve of St John (23 June) after being ill for three days at most' (translated from Gransden 1957 by Forrest 2010).

While there is no contemporary account of the spread of the plague in Dorset, there are two main sources of information, the bishops registers in which the appointment of clergy to parishes is recorded and manor court documents which record deaths and subsequent changes to tenancies within a manor (Forrest 2010, 3). Examination of a sample of manor court rolls from Gillingham, Charlton Marshall and Fordington for the mid-14th century indicate the scale of mortality amongst tenants. In Gillingham recorded deaths went from four in the nine months preceding the plague's arrival there in early autumn 1348, to 166 between October 1348 and February the following year. There was a similar impact at Fordington (Forrest 2010, 4, 7). Multiple transfers of tenancies occurred as family members succumbed and tenements passed back into the hands of the lord of the manor (Forrest 2010, 5, 7); this held true as well in the further outbreak in 1361. The implications are that the outbreak had killed possibly more than 50% of the population within five months (Forrest 2010, 6–7). The accounts of the Reeve at Abbotsbury at Michaelmas 1349 recording the heriots paid in livestock by deceased tenants implies a mortality of around 18% of the tenants in the early months of 1349 (Forrest 2010, 8). The impact the preceding year can only be guessed at.

The mortality rate amongst the clergy also gives some indication of the progress and impact of the disease. Huge numbers of parish priests were replaced during 1348–9 across Dorset (Forrest 2010, 9). The abbot of Abbotsbury and the parish priests of Abbotsbury and Portesham all died of the disease in December 1348 (Forrest, 2010, 8). More particularly, the priest of Chickerell itself was one of the earliest to have succumbed, recorded as being replaced on 30 September 1348. This was Adam de Nyweton who had been installed in 1332, and his replacement was John de Stapleford (Hutchins 1863, 497). Unfortunately, another replacement had to be sought on 6th March the following year (Fletcher 1923, 7), named as William Stapleford (Hutchins 1863, 497). Large numbers of clergy were to succumb again in 1361 (Forrest 2010, 9), including at Chickerell where William Stapleford's replacement was instituted on 28 November 1361. This was Henry Frere (Hutchins 1863, 497), a descendent of the le Walys family via his mother (see Chapter 5). These individual deaths are merely an indicator of the impact on the local

population. A probable effect of the 1348 outbreak was the most likely related deaths of the two young heiresses, Joan and Elizabeth le Walys which was to lead to a century of legal disputes (Chapter 5). Whilst we cannot guess at the impact on the manor workforce, the level of mortality and the clear involvement of the Chickerell manors early in the pandemic placed Putton at the epicentre of the crisis in 1348–9.

The contemporary economy

It is still arguable whether the Black Death created new problems or exacerbated those which had already come into being (Hinton 2012, 131). The full impact of the plague on the county was probably not immediate, and most likely did not lead directly to settlement abandonment (Forrest 2010, 12). Shrinkage and desertion were a longer-term process as population contraction and related economic change combined at the local scale. The Dorset economy was changing prior to 1348. The manor as an economic unit was declining nationally by this point as incomes from land diminished, and there was an increase in letting out elements of holdings, such as fisheries or the mill (Bailey 2002, 17). There appears to have been a widespread change to pasture on the chalk downlands of Dorset during the 14th and 15th centuries and this seems to have been matched by an increase in sheep farming (Taylor 1970, 118–9). Economic change was well in train across the south west of Britain by the 14th and 15th centuries, but this was variable and in some cases highly localised (Forrest 2017a). The indications are that nationally the population trend was downward in the early 14th century (Smith 1991). The Great Famine of 1316–1320 claimed numerous lives in various parts of the country (Twigg 2003). In addition, elsewhere in Dorset the labour services due to the lord had by *c.* 1300 begun to be largely commuted to monetary payment (Forrest 2010, 12). A reduction occurred in the numbers of rural dwellers who were 'unfree' in some sense, that is, bonded to a lord or piece of land in a fashion that was hereditary rather than contractual or temporary. Around 1300 about half of the rural population of England, were smallholders and landless labourers, and in some respect servile. This figure had halved by around 1400, through a variety of processes (Bailey 2014, 3–4). Whilst the wool price began to decline in the later 14th century, this was in part mitigated by a burgeoning Somerset cloth trade (Forrest 2010, 12), so there was still some incentive to move into the less labour intensive wool production.

The impact of the broader economic picture was, in south Dorset, related to the fortunes of trading centres and this must in turn have had an impact on the trajectory of local settlements and manorial units. For the Chickerell manors, the proximity of Melcombe Regis was obviously significant. Towns were increasingly important in local commerce in this period, and market-based exchange with sites in the immediate rural area would have had notable economic benefits to both (cf. Perring 2002, 29). In the late 13th century Melcombe, along with Lyme Regis was recognised as the principle port for the county (Forrest 2017b, 20) a fact further underlined in the 14th century when Melcombe was made a Staple Port. That meant that it was responsible for customs dues on wool and other goods, and most of the other ports in the county were regarded as subordinate to it. The most significant exports were wool and cloth throughout the 14th and 15th centuries. In the year before the Black Death, Melcombe was exporting wool to France and imported linen, wine and other goods (Forrest 2017b, 20). There was some evidence of expansion in the mid-14th century, taking business from Southampton, before a clear decline in the later 14th century (Forrest 2017b, 20–21). By 1377 Melcombe was receiving a large rebate on taxation, which continued into the 15th century, whilst Poole was able to expand and invest and became a Staple Port in 1433 (Forrest 2017b).

The central Dorset chalk was particularly affected by the price reductions for wool and cloth in the mid-15th century with evidence of considerable reductions in numbers of people eligible to pay tax and in an increase of rebates of taxation (Forrest 2017a, 434–435, 2017b). Associated with these changes, Dorset ports, particularly Melcombe received large and subsequently permanent reductions to taxation in the later 14th and 15th centuries (Forrest 2017a, 441–444) reflecting their waning importance. Settlement on the central Dorset chalklands, which would have contributed to the wool and cloth trade partly dependent on Melcombe, was contracting in the 15th century (Forrest 2013). Sheep flocks still

increased from the 15th century on the chalk, but other areas of the county concentrated on arable and dairying (Forrest 2017b). Chickerell (it is not subdivided in taxation records) does not appear to have received substantial reductions to its rate in the later 15th century, but it is worth noting that its original assessment in 1334 was actually the lowest of all the land units in the Cullifordtree Hundred at 112 ½ pence compared with adjacent Radipole at 224 ½ pence, and Broadwey at 614 pence (cf Forrest 2013, 79). This implies that it was relatively impoverished already in the earlier 14th century.

Personal reasons

One element which is not often considered in the trajectory of specific locales and the way in which they changed over time is the impact of the personal circumstances of individuals and families and the events which befell them. The financial situation at Wharram Percy, Yorkshire was rendered insecure in the 13th and early 14th centuries by legal disputes following an unclear inheritance and contributed to its decline (Wrathmell 2012, 239). In the case of Putton, we have a selection of documents available to us for the 13th–15th centuries (see Chapter 5) which give us an outline of the le Walys family's fortunes. The Putton manor was in the family possession from at least the first half of the 13th century. The point at which this ended is more complex. What is clear is that the land that made up the manor continued in use. The demise of the buildings did not lead to abandonment of the land. The death of Nicholas le Walsshe in 1339 (prior to the Black Death) precipitated a complex legal situation. He was survived by two daughters, both minors who died, still below the age of majority on the same day in 1350, possibly in the final stages of the first Black Death pandemic. Deaths as a result of plague were still common in 1350 (Ziegler 1991). Ultimately the holding appears to have been divided amongst various heirs, passing to a variety of families by marriage. The effect of this may have been to keep the land in use but removed the necessity for there to be a residential or administrative centre, especially if other functions of the manor were then assumed by West and East Chickerell. The house may have come to be seen by numerous heirs as an asset with no use greater than its value as a source of re-usable materials and this may well have contributed to its deliberate demolition.

Reuse and reconstitution

That the land continued in use is attested by the probable reoccupation in the 15th and 16th centuries with what may be two late medieval buildings on the western slope facing the original manorial centre. These were however much reduced in scale and quality, and indeed it is difficult to discern function. It may have been a modest farmstead comprising a possible dwelling and an agricultural building or more likely had an agricultural use. The possibility of activity in this period covering a slightly wider area is suggested by the presence of pottery dating to the 14th–15th centuries in the deposits overlying the north end of the earthwork holloway (Cotswold Archaeology 2003, 7) and noted in broadly the same area in an earlier service trench (RCHME 1970a, 41). A more substantial reconstitution occurred later on the highest part of the eastern slope, where three fragments of a building or buildings were built adjacent to and overlying part of B1. These seem to have utilised rubble from the site and were of notably lesser quality. It is assumed that they must have had some domestic function, possibly as an earlier incarnation of Putton Farm, as this area is associated with 17th and 18th century pottery and other artefacts.

The documentary information shows that the Putton tithing during the later 17th and 18th century had a limited population, and there is scant evidence of numerous dwellings. However, Putton Farm is documented as a named unit from the end of the 17th century (see Chapter 5), and there are a substantial number of finds of 17th and 18th century date which probably derive from rubbish disposal on what was probably now an adjacent parcel of land. There is a degree of continuity in the field names between the early 18th and mid-19th century, as well as little alteration of boundaries between the late 18th century Inclosure map and the 1839 Tithe map and apportionment. Although not conclusive, this does suggest a degree of stability in the arrangement of the land. The

likelihood is that it was physically arranged around the farmhouse and buildings on the north side of Lower Putton Lane, which are apparent on maps from the later 18th century. The description and taxation levels associated with the farm in the 18th and early 19th century suggests a substantial but relatively modest holding. The remains of the later phase buildings within the site at Lower Putton Lane would fit with the picture of modest dwellings associated with farming and housing agricultural workers. However, these structures were not depicted on the Inclosure map of 1792 or the 1839 Tithe map, suggesting that they predated this or that they were not substantial enough to depict. The status of the owners and tenants of the farm in the 18th and 19th century is however attested by some of the post-medieval objects found. Considering that much of this was found in Areas 1 and 3 it was probably the result of rubbish disposal from the farm buildings across the lane.

CONCLUSIONS, By Clare Randall

The site at Lower Putton Lane has provided the opportunity to understand the gradations of status which existed within the structure of the wider manorial landscape of Dorset. Putton also provides the first excavated example in south west England of a contemporaneous open hall and chamber block arrangement. Furthermore, it is significant in demonstrating a re-orientation of space to accommodate new domestic architectural developments and social concerns in the later 13th century.

The buildings themselves represent two overall phases of development. The Phase 3 manor includes two distinct building types that were common in the early 13th century. They provide a rare and important example of a separate chamber-block and ground-floor open-hall, supplemented by an additional stone building which might have been a kitchen. Although a number of chamber-blocks have been recognised across the south west region as standalone structures, nowhere else have they been excavated alongside the contemporary halls which would have accompanied them. The only other extensive excavation of a previously unknown

13th century manor took place at Longforth Farm (Somerset), with the axial arrangement probably reflecting an ecclesiastical influence. At Putton, the single building attributed to Phase 4 is a cross-passage house encompassing hall, chamber and services under one roof, a type that became widespread from the later 13th century into the early 14th century. Numerous extant examples survive across the region although very few pre-date the 15th century, and it is only through the excavation at Lower Futton Lane that the displacement of the earlier open-hall can be observed. The layout and form of the buildings at Putton will feed into regional and indeed national debate about secular manorial complexes, as opposed to royal or ecclesiastical examples, particularly as more of these sites are excavated or subject to reinterpretation.

Putton also suggests that we should not consider manors in isolation or as a homogenous 'class'. Manors did not exist in social or practical isolation. Gradations in status between holdings which sat at differing levels in the hierarchy of landholding and tenancy is clear in historical sources but should play a role in archaeological interpretation. The subtle differences in material culture between Putton and its social 'superior' at nearby Sutton Poyntz demonstrates this. Also, Putton sat within a block of landholding between which there would have been regular economic, social and familial exchanges. The effect of wider interests is often referred to in respect to the motivations behind activities on the holdings of large royal or ecclesiastical estates (e.g. Ower Farm and Holworth). However, the wider network of secular landholders' interests would have been equally influential on localised developments. Furthermore, the ability to place the site in the context of the documentary record and consider the connections and motivations of the controlling personalities, provides the opportunity for an interpretive framework to include the fortunes and actions of individuals, families and groups. The indications of the controlling family's wider interests and contacts provides some explanation as to the adoption of fashionable styles of architecture as well as contributing nuance to the explanation of the decline of the manor.

Excavation and study of Putton has demonstrated that there is rich potential within the medieval archaeology of Dorset. There is the possibility to inform broader considerations of regional land use, adoption of architectural style, as well as development of trade and long-distance contacts. The ceramic assemblage has made an important contribution to the corpus for Dorset and southern Britain, which will assist in future research. The burial of an infant in a pot in a building floor has opened the door to considerations of medieval beliefs within the county and beyond. The identification of field boundaries as an example of the dynamic approaches to agriculture in the county during the 12th to 14th centuries, and the identification of middens as a potential indication of significant settlement, should be born in mind in future projects. Considerations of how spaces were used and inhabited raise questions with respect to family, household and social dynamics which have not been previously considered from a regional perspective and deserve more attention. Linking the manorial centre with understanding of how the land unit which it administered and served came into being and of what it comprised has enabled a greater understanding of the residues of the production of that estate. This would not have been possible without knowing the scope of landscape resources which were available to the inhabitants. In addition, the effects of wider economic and societal changes as well as international events can be identified at a local level. Within the complex at Putton we can see elements of the effect that people's social role had in patterning the archaeology, and the beliefs which permeated medieval society. All these contributions should be borne in mind in future research in the region and underlines the desirability of bringing unpublished local sites into the light of day.

When the cross-passage house was constructed, sometime in the late 13th or early 14th century, probably at the peak of the Le Walys family's fortunes, it would have been an imposing building. For a time, it probably served as one of the principle homes of the family. They would not have foreseen the decline in fortunes which would lead to its abandonment. They could not have guessed at the chain of events unleashed by the untimely deaths of an only son and his young daughters, or that its fate would be sealed by the marriages of four sisters. The desertion and deconstruction of the manor buildings of Putton are a reminder that the reasons for the creation and abandonment of archaeological sites will always be multi-factoral. In this case, the full effects of great events such as the Black Death are difficult to discern, but present. The underlying economic realities of long-term processes such as changes in the supply and control of agricultural labour will have played their part. However, ultimately it was the actions of individuals within the social and legal strictures of their day which delivered the coup de grace.

In the end Putton was about the land, and the land remained largely intact as a unit. It perhaps had its origins in the late Roman period and endured through the 16th and 17th centuries, emerging in the 18th century as Putton Farm. Parts of its layout have been preserved in the remaining field boundaries and even today in the alignment of roads and homes. The land has always been in use, it is just the way that it has been managed and lived within that has changed. The creation of the impressive manorial centre at Putton was the result of a moment in time when the 13th century lords deemed it suitable to be a centre of their estates, and it declined as that suitability waned. However, it was, 'anciently a manor', and its echo remains.

BIBLIOGRAPHY

Alexander, J.S. 1995. 'Building Stone from the East Midlands Quarries: Sources, Transportation and Usage', *Medieval Archaeology* **39**, 107–131.

Allan, J.P. 1983. 'The importation of pottery to southern England, *c.* 1200–1500', in P. Davey and R. Hodges (eds) *Ceramics and Trade: the production and distribution of later medieval pottery in north-west Europe.* University of Sheffield, 193–207.

Allan, J.P. 2003. 'A group of early 13th-century pottery from Sherborne Old Castle and its wider context', *Proceedings of the Dorset Natural History and Archaeological Society* **125**, 71–82.

Allan, J.P., Hughes, M.J. and Taylor, R.T. 2010. 'Saxo-Norman pottery in Somerset: some recent research', *Proceedings of the Somerset Archaeological and Natural History Society* **154**, 165–84.

Anon, 1911. 'Thursday, 23rd February, 1911', *Proceedings of the Society of Antiquaries of London* **23**, 363–69.

Ashley, S. 2002. *Medieval Armorial Horse Furniture in Norfolk.* East Anglian Archaeology 101, Archaeology and Environment, Norfolk Museums and Archaeology Service, Dereham.

Austermann, M. 1999. 'Haarschmuck, Nähnadeln und Maultrommeln – Funde vom spätmittelalterlichen Jahrmarkt am Kloster Arnsburg in der Wetterau', *Germania* **77 (1)**, 307–19.

Ayres, K. and Serjeantson, D. 2002. 'The animal bones', in T.G. Allen and J. Hiller *The excavation of a medieval manor house of the bishops of Winchester at Mount House, Witney, Oxfordshire.* Thames Valley Landscapes Monograph 13, Oxford Archaeology, Oxford, 169–178.

Baggs, A.P., Bush R.J.E. and Siraut, M.C. 1985. 'Parishes: Huish Champflower', in R. W. Dunning (Ed.) *A History of the County of Somerset: Volume 5.* Victoria County History, London, 81–88.

Bailey, G. 2004. *Buttons and fasteners 500BC-AD1840.* Greenlight Publishing, Witham.

Bailey, M. 2002. *The English manor c. 1200-c. 1500.* Manchester University Press, Manchester.

Bailey, M. 2014. *The decline of serfdom in medieval England – from bondage to freedom.* The Boydell Press, Woodbridge.

Baker, J. and Brothwell, D. 1980. *Animal diseases in archaeology.* Academic Press, New York.

Barclay, A., Knight, D., Booth, P., Evans, J., Brown, D. H. and Wood, I. 2016. *A standard for pottery studies in archaeology.* Historic England, London.

Barton, K.J., Cartwright, L., Jarvis, K.S. and Thomson, R.G. 1992. 'Catalogue of the pottery', in I.P. Horsey, *Excavations in Poole 1973-1983.* Dorset Natural History and Archaeological Society Monograph 10, Dorset Natural History and Archaeology Society, Dorchester, 65–128.

Bartosiewicz, L. and Gál. E. 2013. *Shuffling nags, lame ducks: the archaeology of animal disease.* Oxbow Books, Oxford.

Bass, J. 1986. 'Fishes of the Fleet', *Porcupine Newsletter* **3 (6)**, 147–148.

Bass, W. 1995. *Human osteology: a laboratory and field manual.* (4th Edn) Missouri Archaeological Society, Columbia.

Beckmann, B. 1966. 'Studien über die Metallnadeln der Römischen Kaiserzeit im freien Germanien', *Saalburg-Jahrbuch* **23**, 5–100.

Bell, R., Archibald, M. and Knight, B. 2004. 'Coins, jettons and tokens', in K. Rodwell and R. Bell (eds) *Acton Court: The evolution of an early Tudor courtier's house.* English Heritage, London, 359–65.

Bellamy, P.S. 1993. 'The clay and stone roof tile', in P. J. Woodward, A. H. Graham and S. M. Davies *Excavations at Greyhound Yard, Dorchester 1981-4.* Dorset Natural History and Archaeological Society Monograph 12, Dorset Natural History and Archaeology Society, Dorchester, 172–6.

Beresford, G. 1974. 'The medieval manor of Penhallam, Jacobstow, Cornwall', *Medieval Archaeology* **18**, 90–145.

Beresford, G. 1979. 'Three deserted medieval settlements on Dartmoor: a report on the late E. Marie Minter's excavations', *Medieval Archaeology* **23**, 98–158.

Biddle, M. 1990. *Object and economy in medieval Winchester: artefacts from medieval Winchester.* Winchester studies 7.ii. Clarendon, Oxford.

Biddle, M. 2005. *Nonsuch Palace: the material culture of a noble restoration household.* Oxbow, Oxford.

Biddle, M. and Barclay, K. 1990. 'Sewing pins and wire', in M. Biddle (Ed.) *Object and economy in medieval Winchester: artefacts from medieval Winchester.* Winchester studies 7.ii. Clarendon, Oxford, 560–71.

Biddle, M., Hiller, J., Scott, I. and Streeten, A. 2001. *Henry VIII's coastal artillery fort at Camber Castle, Rye, East Sussex: an archaeological, structural and historical investigation.* Oxford Archaeological Unit, Oxford.

Biggs, N. 1990. 'Coin-weights in England – up to 1588', *British Numismatic Journal* **60**, 65–79.

Bishop, C.M. 2000. *Quarr stone: an archaeological and petrological study in relation to the Roman, Anglo-Saxon and Medieval stone building industries of Southern England.* Unpublished PhD thesis, University of Reading, Reading.

Blair, J. 1991. 'Purbeck marble', in J. Blair and N. Ramsay (eds) *English Medieval Industries.* Hambledon, London, 41–56.

Blair, J. 1993. 'Hall and chamber: English domestic planning 1000–1250', in G. Meirion-Jones and M. Jones (eds) *Manorial Domestic Buildings in England and Northern France.* Society of Antiquaries Occasional Papers 15, London, 1–21.

Blair, J. 2005. *The church in Anglo-Saxon society.* Oxford University Press, Oxford.

Blinkhorn, P. n.d. *Pottery from Pound Lane, Wareham, Dorset.* Unpublished report for Bournemouth University.

Blockley, K., Blockley, M., Blockley, P., Frere, S.S. and Stow, S. 1995. *Excavations in the Marlowe Car Park and surrounding areas.* Archaeology of Canterbury 5, Canterbury Archaeological Trust, Canterbury.

Borg, A., 1991. 'Arms and armour', in P. Saunders and E. Saunders (eds) *Salisbury Museum medieval catalogue. Part 1.* Salisbury and South Wiltshire Museum, Salisbury, 79–92.

Bourdillon, J.M. 1994. 'The mammal and bird bones', in D.R. Watkins *The Foundry excavations on Poole Waterfront 1986/7.* Dorset Natural History and Archaeological Society Monograph 14, Dorset Natural History and Archaeology Society, Dorchester, 75–82.

Bowles Barret, W. 1910. 'Weymouth and Melcombe Regis in the time of the Great Civil War', *Proceedings of the Dorset Natural History and Antiquarian Field Club* **31**, 204–29.

Brickley, M. and McKinley, J.I. 2004. *Guidelines to the standards for recording human remains.* IFA Paper No 7 BABAO/IFA, Reading.

British Geological Survey (BGS) 2020. *Geology of Britain Viewer.* http://mapapps.bgs.ac.uk/geologyofbritain/home.html [Accessed 1 July 2020].

Brothwell, D. 1972. 'Palaeodemography and earlier British populations', *World Archaeology* **4 (1)**, 75–87.

Brown, D.H. 2002. *Pottery in Medieval Southampton c.1066–1510.* Southampton Archaeological Monograph 8, Council for British Archaeology Research Report 133, Southampton.

Bullock, A. 1994. 'The fish remains', in D.R. Watkins *The Foundry excavations on Poole Waterfront 1986/7.* Dorset Natural History and Archaeological Society Monograph 14, Dorset Natural History and Archaeological Society, Dorchester, 82–85.

Buora, M. 2018. 'Alcune osservazioni sui chiodi per ferratura in uso nel Medioevo', *Instrumentum* **48**, 27–31.

Butler, L.A.S. 1974. 'Medieval finds from Castell-y-Bere, Merioneth', *Archaeologia Cambrensis* **123**, 78–112.

Butler, R., Green, C. and Payne, N. 2009. *Cast copper-alloy cooking vessels.* Finds Research Group Datasheet 41, Finds Research Group AD700–1700.

Butler, R.U. 1910. 'St. Hugh of Lincoln', *The Catholic Encyclopedia.* Robert Appleton Company, New York.

Butterworth, C. 2003. 'Multi-period finds from Quarleston Farm, Winterborne Stickland, 1994–5', *Proceedings of the Dorset Natural History and Archaeological Society* **125**, 147–150.

Campbell, B.M.S. 2000. *English Seigniorial Agriculture 1250–1450.* Cambridge University Press, Cambridge.

Campbell, B.M.S. 2010. 'Nature as historical protagonist: environment and society in pre-industrial England', *Economic History Review* **63 (2)**, 281–314.

Campbell, G. and Robinson, M. 2009. 'Plant and invertebrate remains', in M. Auduoy and A. Chapman *Raunds: the origin and growth of a midland village AD 450-1500.* Oxbow Books, Oxford, 222–244.

Campbell, G. and Robinson, M. 2010. 'The environmental evidence', in A. Chapman *West Cotton, Raunds: a study of medieval settlement dynamics AD450-1450.* Oxbow Books, 427–515.

Carruthers. W. 2009. 'The Charred Plant Remains', in M. Brett, M. Collard and E. McSloy *Excavation of 10th and 5th century BC settlement at Hartshill Copse, Upper Bucklebury, Berkshire, 2003.* Cotswold Archaeology ADS (doi:10.5284/1000365).

Carruthers, W. 2010. 'The Plant Remains', In C. Harding, E. Marlow-Mann and S. Wrathmell *The Post-Medieval Farm and Vicarage Sites. Wharram: A study of Settlement on the Yorkshire Wolds, XII.* York University Archaeological Publications **14**, 287–313.

Carruthers, W. 2020. 'The charred plant remains,' in A. Young *Eckweek, Peasedown St. John, Somerset: Survey and Excavation at a Shrunken Medieval Hamlet 1988-90.* The Society for Medieval Archaeology Monograph 40, Routledge, London.

Carruthers W. J. and Hunter Dowse K. L. 2019. *A Review of Macroscopic Plant Remains from the Midland Counties.* Historic England Research Report No. 47/2019.

Chadwyck-Healy, E.H. 1897. *Somersetshire Pleas (Civil and Criminal), from the Rolls of the Itinerant Justices.* Somerset Record Society vol. XI, London.

Chandler, N. 2007. 'The documentary evidence', in M. Rawlings *By a crystal brook. Early riverside settlement and a medieval chapel at Sutton Poyntz, Dorset.* Wessex Archaeology Ltd, Salisbury, 80–85.

Chandler, J. and Valentin, J. 2003. 'Discussion', in J. Valentin, 'Manor Farm, Portesham, Dorset: excavations on a multi-period religious and settlement site', *Proceedings of the Dorset Natural History and Archaeological Society* **125**, 60–61.

Chapman, A. 2010. *West Cotton, Raunds: a study of medieval settlement dynamics AD450-1450.* Oxbow Books, Oxford.

Cherry, J. 1991a. 'Harness pendants', in P. Saunders and E. Saunders (eds) *Salisbury Museum medieval catalogue. Part 1,* 17–28. Salisbury and South Wiltshire Museum, Salisbury.

Cherry, J. 1991b. 'Seal matrices', in P. Saunders and E. Saunders (eds) *Salisbury Museum medieval catalogue. Part 1.* Salisbury and South Wiltshire Museum, Salisbury, 29–39.

Christie, N. and Stamper, P. 2012. *Medieval Rural Settlement Britain and Ireland AD800-1600.* Windgather Press, Oxford.

Clark, J. 2004. *The medieval horse and its equipment, c.1150-c.1450.* Medieval finds from excavations in London 5, Boydell, Woodbridge.

Coleman-Smith, R. and Pearson, T. 1988. *Excavations in the Donyatt Potteries.* Phillimore, Chichester.

Coles, C. 2018. 'The animal bone', in S. Robinson, E. Firth, C. Coles and W. Carruthers 'Excavations on the site of the Museum of Jurassic Marine Life, Kimmeridge, 2013', *Proceedings of the Dorset Natural History and Archaeological Society* **139**, 190–191.

Cooper, G. 2002. 'Fieldname survey', in R. Tabor *South Cadbury Environs Project Interim Fieldwork report 1998-2001.* University of Bristol, Bristol, 15–25.

Costen, M. 1992. *The Origins of Somerset.* Manchester University Press, Manchester.

Costen, M. 2007. 'Anonymous thegns in the landscape of Wessex 900–1066', in M. Costen (Ed.) *People and places. Essays in honour of Mick Aston.* Oxbow Books, Oxford, 61–75.

Costen, M. and Costen, N. 2016. 'Trade and exchange in Anglo-Saxon Wessex, *c.* AD 600–780', *Medieval Archaeology* **60/1**, 1–26.

Cotswold Archaeology 2003. *Land at Lower Putton Lane, Chickerell, Dorset, Archaeological Evaluation.* Unpublished report 03167, Cotswold Archaeology.

Cotswold Archaeology 2005. *Land at Lower Putton Lane, Chickerell, Dorset, Archaeological Desk-Based Assessment.* Unpublished report 05048, Cotswold Archaeology.

Cotswold Archaeology 2016. *Land at Chickerell, Weymouth, Dorset. Archaeological Evaluation.* Unpublished report No 16444, Cotswold Archaeology.

Courtney, P. 1993. 'The medieval and post-medieval objects', in P. Ellis (Ed.) *Beeston Castle, Cheshire: Excavations by Laurence Keen and Peter Hough, 1968-85.* English Heritage Archaeological Report 23, Historic Buildings and Monuments Commission for England, London, 134–61.

Courtney, P. 2004. 'Small finds', in K. Rodwell and R. Bell (eds) *Acton Court: The evolution of an early Tudor courtier's house.* English Heritage, London, 365–97.

Courtney, P., Egan, G. and Gilchrist, R., 2015. 'Small finds', in R. Gilchrist and C. Green (eds) *Glastonbury Abbey: Archaeological Investigations 1904-79.* Society of Antiquaries of London, London, 293–311.

Cox, P. and Hearne, C. 1991a. *Redeemed from the Heath The archaeology of the Wytch Farm Oilfield (1987-90).* Dorset Natural History and Archaeological Society Monograph 9, Dorset Natural History and Archaeology Society, Dorchester.

Cox, P., Hearne, C. and Farwell, D.E. 1991b. 'Ower Farm', in P. Cox, and C. Hearne *Redeemed from the Heath The archaeology of the Wytch Farm Oilfield (1987-90).* Dorset Natural History and Archaeological Society Monograph 9, Dorset Natural History and Archaeology Society, Dorchester, 82–90.

Coy, J. 1992. 'The animal bone', in I.P. Horsey *Excavations in Poole 1973-1983.* Dorset Natural History and Archaeological Society Monograph 10, Dorset Natural History and Archaeology Society, Dorchester, 186–193.

Craig-Atkins, E. 2014. 'Eavesdropping on short lives: Eaves-drip burial and the differential treatment of children one year of age and under in early Christian cemeteries', in D.M. Hadley and K.A. Hemer (eds) *Medieval Childhood. Archaeological approaches.* Oxford, Oxbow Books, 95–113.

Cranfield Soil and Agriculture Institute (CSAI) 2020. *Soilscapes.* http://www.landis.org.uk/soilscapes/ [Accessed 1 July 2020].

Crawford, S. 2014. 'Archaeology of the medieval family', in D.M. Hadley and K.A. Hemer (eds) *Medieval Childhood. Archaeological approaches.* Oxbow Books, Oxford, 26–38.

Crawforth-Hitchins, D., 2005. 'Weights', in J. Gardiner (Ed.) *Before the mast: life and death aboard the Mary Rose.* The Archaeology of the Mary Rose 4. Mary Rose Trust, Portsmouth, 330–34.

Crummy, N. 1983. *The Roman small finds from excavations in Colchester 1971-9.* Colchester Archaeological Report 2, Colchester Archaeological Trust, Colchester.

Cunningham, C.M. and Drury, P.J. 1985. *Post-medieval sites and their pottery: Moulsham Street, Chelmsford.* CBA Research Report No 54, Chelmsford Archaeological Trust Report 5, London.

Darby, H.C. and Finn, R.W. 1967. *The Domesday geography of south-west Britain.* Cambridge University Press, Cambridge.

Dark, P. 2000. *The environment of Britain in the first millennium AD.* Duckworth, London.

Davey, J. 2013. 'Rectilinear landscapes in Dorset', *Proceedings of the Dorset Natural History and Archaeological Society* **134**, 175–190.

Davis, R. 1977. *King Stephen.* Longman, London.

Dawson, A.G. Hickey, K., Mayewski, P.A. and Nesje, A. 2007. 'Greenland (GISP2) ice core and historical indicators of complex North Atlantic climate changes during the fourteenth century', *The Holocene* **17 (4)**, 427–434.

Dawson, D., Andersen, J. and Rollinson, G. 2018. 'Characterising post-medieval pottery production centres in Somerset', *Medieval Ceramics* **39**, 29–42.

Dodson, K. 2018. The Price of Virtue for the Medieval Woman: Chastity and the Crucible of the Virgin', *English Studies* **99 (6)**, 593–608.

Draper, J. 1975. 'A group of 13th century pottery from West Stafford', *Proceedings of the Dorset Natural History and Archaeological Society* **97**, 60–62.

Draper, J. 1982. 'An 18th-century kiln at Hole Common, Lyme Regis, Dorset', *Proceedings of the Dorset Natural History and Archaeological Society* **104**, 137–42.

Drury, G. 1949. 'The use of Purbeck marble in medieval times', *Proceedings of the Dorset Natural History and Archaeological Society* **70**, 74–98.

Dungworth, D. 2002. *Analysis of post-medieval lead-tin alloy, copper alloy and glass artefacts from Southwark, London.*

Centre for Archaeology Reports 64/2002, English Heritage, Portsmouth.

Dütting, M.K. and Hoss, S. 2014. 'Lead net-sinkers as an indicator of fishing activities', *Journal of Roman Archaeology* **27**, 429–42.

Eagles, B. 2018. *From Roman civitas to Anglo-Saxon shire.* Oxbow Books, Oxford.

Ecchevarría Aruaga, A. 2007. 'The shrine as mediator: England, Castile and the pilgrimage to Compostela', in M. Bullón-Fernández (Ed.) *England and Iberia in the Middle Ages 12th-15th century. Cultural, Literary and cultural exchanges.* Palgrave Macmillan, Basingstoke, 47–66.

Egan, G. 2001. 'Lead/tin alloy metalwork', in P. Saunders (Ed.) *Salisbury Museum medieval catalogue part 3.* Salisbury and South Wiltshire Museum, Salisbury, 92–118.

Egan, G. 2007a. 'Later medieval non-ferrous metalwork and evidence for metalworking: AD 1050–1100 to 1500–50', in D. Griffiths, R.A. Philpott and G. Egan (eds) *Meols: the archaeology of the North Wirral coast: discoveries and observations in the 19th and 20th centuries, with a catalogue of collections.* Oxford University School of Archaeology Monograph 68, School of Archaeology, Oxford, 77–188.

Egan, G. 2007b. 'Post-medieval non-ferrous metalwork and evidence for metalworking: AD 1500–50 to 1800–50', in D. Griffiths, R.A. Philpott and G. Egan (eds) *Meols: the archaeology of the North Wirral coast: discoveries and observations in the 19th and 20th centuries, with a catalogue of collections.* Oxford University School of Archaeology Monograph 68, School of Archaeology, Oxford, 213–28.

Egan, G. 2010. *The medieval household: daily living c.1150–c.1450.* Medieval finds from excavations in London 6, Boydell Press, Woodbridge.

Egan, G. and Pritchard, F. 2002. *Dress accessories c.1150 – c.1450.* Medieval finds from excavations in London 3, Boydell & Brewer, Woodbridge.

Ellenberg, H. 1988. *Vegetation Ecology of Central Europe.* Cambridge University Press, Cambridge.

Ellis, B. 1993. 'The spurs', in P. Ellis (Ed.) *Beeston Castle, Cheshire: Excavations by Laurence Keen and Peter Hough, 1968-85.* English Heritage Archaeological Report 23, Historic Buildings and Monuments Commission for England, London, 165–169.

Evans, D.E. and Loveluck, C. 2009. *Life and economy at early medieval Flixborough, c. AD 600-1000: the artefact evidence.* Excavations at Flixborough 2, Oxbow Books, Oxford.

Everson, F. and Stocker, D. 2012. 'Who at Wharram', in S. Wrathmell *Wharram. A Study of Settlement on the Yorkshire Wolds, XIII. A History of Wharram Percy and its neighbours.* The University of York, York, 262–277.

Fabiš, M. 2005. 'Pathological alterations of cattle skeletons: Evidence for the draught exploitation of animals?', In J. Davies, M. Fabis, I. Mainland, M. Richards, and R. Thomas (eds) *Diet and Health in Past Animal Populations.* Oxbow Books, Oxford, 58–62.

Fägersten, A. 1978. *The place names of Dorset.* EP Publishing.

Fairclough, G. 1992. 'Meaningful constructions — spatial and functional analysis of medieval buildings', *Antiquity* **66**, 348–366.

Farrar, R.A.H. 1963. 'Recent discoveries and acquisitions', *Proceedings of the Dorset Natural History and Archaeological Society* 85, 100–101.

Farrar, R.A.H. 1965. 'Roman inhumation burials at Burton Bradstock and Chickerell', *Proceedings of the Dorset Natural History and Archaeological Society* **87**, 114–118.

Farwell, D.E. 1991. 'Ower Farm', in P.W. Cox and C.M. Hearne *Redeemed from the Heath The archaeology of the Wytch Farm Oilfield (1987-90).* Dorset Natural History and Archaeological Society Monograph 9, Dorset Natural History and Archaeology Society, Dorchester, 82–90.

Faulkner, P. A. 1958. 'Domestic planning from the twelfth to the fourteenth centuries', *Archaeological Journal* **105**, 150–83.

Field, N.H. 1966. 'A thirteenth-century kiln at Hermitage, Dorset', *Proceedings of the Dorset Natural History and Archaeological Society* 88, 161–75.

Field, N.H. 1973. 'The Leaze, Wimborne: An excavation of a deserted medieval quarter of the town', *Proceedings of the Dorset Natural History and Archaeological Society* **94**, 49–62.

Fitzpatrick, A. 2017. "The famous volcanic rock of the Eifel', was it imported to Britain in Prehistory?', in R. Shaffrey, R (Ed.) *Written in Stone: Papers on the function, form and provenancing of prehistoric stone objects in memory of Fiona Roe.* The Highfield Press, St Andrews, 195–214.

Flaherty, S. Andrews, P. and Leivers, M. 2016. *A medieval manor house rediscovered. Excavations at Longforth Farm, Wellington, Somerset.* Wessex Archaeology Occasional Paper 10, Salisbury.

Fletcher, J.M.J. 1923. 'The Black Death in Dorset (1348–1349)', *Proceedings of the Dorset Natural History and Archaeological Society* **43**, 1–14.

Foard, G. 2008. *Integrating documentary and archaeological evidence in the investigation of battles: A case study from seventeenth-century England.* PhD-Thesis University of East Anglia, Norwich.

Foard, G. 2009. *Guidance on recording lead bullets from early modern battlefields.* http://www.heritagescience. ac.uk/Research_Projects/projects/Projectposters/ Conservation_of_Battlefield_Archaeology_project_ report_-_Appendix_3 University College London, London.

Forrest, M. 2010. 'The Black Death in Dorset: the crisis of 1348–1349', *Proceedings of the Dorset Natural History and Archaeological Society* **131**, 3–13.

Forrest, M. 2013. 'Economic change in late medieval Dorset: an analysis of evidence from the Lay Subsidies', *Proceedings of the Dorset Natural History and Archaeological Society* **134**, 68–82.

Forrest, M. 2017a. 'Economic change in the southwest: an analysis of the reductions to the Lay Subsidies', *Economic History Review* **70**, 423–51.

Forrest, M. 2017b. 'The development of Dorset's harbours in the fourteenth and fifteenth centuries', *Proceedings of the Dorset Natural History and Archaeological Society* **138**, 17–33.

Fox-Davies, A.C. 1949. *A complete guide to heraldry.* Nelson, S.l.

Frick, H.-J. 1992. 'Karolingisch-ottonische Scheibenfibeln des nördlichen Formenkreises', *Offa* **49/50**, 243–463.

Fry, E.A. and Fry, G.S. 1896. *Full abstracts of the Feet of Fines relating to the County of Dorset, remaining in the Public Record Office, London, from their commencement in the reign of Richard I.* Dorset Records 5.

Fry, E.A. and Fry, G.S. 1910. *Full abstracts of the Feet of Fines relating to the County of Dorset, remaining in the Public Record Office, London, from the commencement of the reign of Edward III to the end of the reign of Richard III. 1327-1485.* Dorset Records 10

Gale, J. 1991. 'Toller Porcorum excavations 1991', *Proceedings of the Dorset Natural History and Archaeological Society* **113**, 178–180.

Gale, J. 1992. 'Toller Porcorum', *Proceedings of the Dorset Natural History and Archaeological Society* **114**, 244–5.

Gale, J. 1993. 'Toller Porcorum excavations 1993', *Proceedings of the Dorset Natural History and Archaeological Society* **115**, 158.

Gardiner, J. 2005. *Before the mast: life and death aboard the Mary Rose.* The Archaeology of the Mary Rose 4, Mary Rose Trust, Portsmouth.

Geddes, J. 1985. 'The small finds', in J. Hare (Ed.) *Battle Abbey: the Eastern range and excavations of 1978-80.* English Heritage Archaeological Reports 2, Historic Buildings and Monuments Commission for England, London, 147–77.

Geophysical Surveys Bradford (GSB) 2003. *Lower Putton Lane, Chickerell, Dorset, Geophysical Survey.* Unpublished GSB report 2003/67.

Gerrard, C.M., Gutierrez, A., Hurst, J.G. and Vince, A.G. 1995. 'A guide to Spanish medieval pottery', in C.M. Gerrard, A. Gutierrez, and A.G. Vince (eds) *Spanish Medieval Ceramics in Spain and the British Isles*, British Archaeological Report International Series 610, Oxford, 281–95.

Gies, F. and Gies, J. 1989. *Life in a Medieval Village.* Harper & Row, New York.

Gilchrist, R. 1997. 'Ambivalent bodies: gender and medieval archaeology', in J. Moore and E. Scott (eds) *Invisible people and processes. Writing gender and childhood into European Archaeology.* Leicester University Press, London, 42–58.

Gilchrist, R. 2008. 'Magic for the Dead? The Archaeology of Magic in Later Medieval Burials', *Medieval Archaeology* **52 (1)**, 119–159.

Gilchrist, R. 2012. *Medieval life, archaeology and the life course.* Boydell, Woodbridge.

Gilchrist, R. and Green, C. 2015. *Glastonbury Abbey: Archaeological Investigations 1904-79.* Society of Antiquaries of London, London.

Gilchrist, R. and Sloane, B. 2005. *Requiem: the medieval monastic cemetery in Britain.* Museum of London Archaeology Service, London.

Good, R. 1987. *Lost Villages of Dorset.* Dovecot Press, Dorchester.

Goodall, A. 1981. 'The medieval bronzesmith and his products', in D.W. Crossley (Ed.) *Medieval industry.* CBA research report 40, Council for British Archaeology, London, 63–71.

Goodall, A. 1985. 'Household equipment', in C.M. Cunningham and P.J. Drury (eds) *Post-medieval sites and their pottery: Moulsham Street, Chelmsford.* CBA Research Report No 54, Chelmsford Archaeological Trust - Report 5, London, 45.

Goodall, A. 2005. 'Objects of copper alloy', in P. Page, K. Atherton and A. Hardy (eds) *Barentin's Manor: Excavations of the moated manor at Harding's Field, Chalgrove, Oxfordshire 1976-9.* Thames Valley Landscape Monograph 24. Oxford Archaeology, Oxford, 78–88.

Goodall, A. 2012. 'Objects of copper alloy', in P. Saunders (Ed.) *Salisbury Museum medieval catalogue. Part 4.* Salisbury and South Wiltshire Museum, Salisbury, 90–142.

Goodall, I.H. 1990. 'Knives', in M. Biddle (Ed.) *Object and economy in medieval Winchester: artefacts from medieval Winchester.* Winchester studies 7.ii. Clarendon, Oxford, 835–60.

Goodall, I.H. 1993. 'Iron knives', in S.M. Margeson (Ed.) *Norwich households: The medieval and post-medieval finds from Norwich Survey Excavations 1971-78.* East Anglian Archaeology 58, University of East Anglia, Norwich, 124–33.

Goodall, I.H. 2005a. 'Iron objects', in M. Biddle (Ed.) *Nonsuch Palace: the material culture of a noble restoration household*, Oxbow, Oxford, 373–411.

Goodall, I.H. 2005b. 'Iron objects', in P. Page, K. Atherton and A. Hardy (eds) *Barentin's Manor: Excavations of the moated manor at Harding's Field, Chalgrove, Oxfordshire 1976-9.* Thames Valley Landscape Monograph 24, Oxford Archaeology, Oxford, 92–105.

Goodall, I.H. 2011. *Ironwork in Medieval Britain: an archaeological study.* Society for Medieval Archaeology Monograph 31, Society for Medieval Archaeology, London.

Goodwin, D.H. 1979. *Sheep management and production.* (2nd Ed) Hutchinson, London.

Goodyer, R.I. 1986. 'A terra nigra platter from Chickerell', *Proceedings of the Dorset Natural History and Archaeological Society* **108**, 177.

Gordon, S. 2015. 'Domestic magic and the walking dead in medieval England: a diachronic approach', in C. Houlbrook and N. Armitage (eds) *The materiality of magic.* Oxbow Books, Oxford.

Gover, J.E.B., Mawer, A. and Stenton, F.M. 1939. *The place names of Wiltshire.* English Place Name Society 16, Cambridge.

Graham, A.H. 1984. 'Wimborne Minster, Dorset – excavations in the town centre 1983', *Proceedings of the Dorset Natural History and Archaeological Society* **106**, 77–86.

Graham, N.E., Ammann, C.M., Fleitmann, D., Cobb, K.M. and Luterbacher, J. 2011. 'Support for global climate reorganization during the "Medieval Climate Anomaly"', *Climate Dynamics* **37**, 1217–1245.

Gransden, A. 1957. 'A fourteenth-century chronicle from the Grey Friars at Lynn', *English Historical Review* **72**, 270–278.

Greep, S. 1995. 'Objects of bone, antler and ivory from C.A.T. sites', in K. Blockley, M. Blockley, P. Blockley, S.S. Frere and S. Stow (eds) *Excavations in the Marlowe Car Park and surrounding areas*. Archaeology of Canterbury 5, Canterbury Archaeological Trust, Canterbury, 1112–52.

Grenville, J. 1997. *Medieval Housing*. Leicester University Press, Leicester and London.

Grieve, M. 1931. *A Modern Herbal*. Tiger Books International, London.

Grimm, G.V. and Hoss, S. 2017. 'Catalogus metaalvondsten', in S. Depuydt and F. Delporte (eds) *Plan Nieuwe Bierkaai te Hulst, gemeente Hulst. Archeologische begeleiding, protocol Opgraven en Opgraving scheepsresten. Deel I: Rapport.* Arcadis Archeologische Rapport 93, s-Hertogenbosch, 281–363.

Groube, L.M. and Bowden, M.C.B. 1982. *The archaeology of rural Dorset past, present and future.* Dorset Natural History and Archaeological Society Monograph 4, Dorset Natural History and Archaeological Society, Dorchester.

Halbout, P., Pilet, C. and Vaudour, C. 1987. *Corpus des objets domestiques et des armes en fer de Normandie du Ier au XVe siècle*. Cahier des Annales de Normandie 20. Centre archéologique de Normandie, Caen.

Hall, R.A. and Whyman, M. 1996. 'Settlement and Monasticism at Ripon, North Yorkshire, From the 7th to 11th Centuries A.D', *Medieval Archaeology* **40**, 62–150.

Hall, T. 1993. 'Witchampton: village origins', *Proceedings of the Dorset Natural History and Archaeological Society* **115**, 121–132.

Hall, T. 2000. *Minster churches in the Dorset landscape.* British Archaeological Reports 304, BAR, Oxford.

Hamilton-Dyer, S. 1991. 'Animal bone,' in P.W. Cox and C.M. Hearne *Redeemed from the Heath The archaeology of the Wytch Farm Oilfield (1987-90)*. Dorset Natural History and Archaeological Society Monograph 9, Dorset Natural History and Archaeological Society, Dorchester, 209–212.

Hamilton-Dyer, S. 2007. 'The animal remains', in M. Rawlings *By a crystal brook. Early riverside settlement and a medieval chapel at Sutton Poyntz, Dorset* Wessex Archaeology Ltd, Salisbury, 80–85.

Hammond, P.W. 1993. *Food and Feast in medieval England*. Stroud, Sutton.

Harding, C., Marlow-Mann E. and Wrathmell S. 2010. *The Post-Medieval Farm and Vicarage Sites. Wharram: A study of Settlement on the Yorkshire Wolds, XII.* York University Archaeological Publications 14, York.

Harding, P. Mepham, L. and Smith, R. 1995. 'The excavation of 12th-13th century deposits at Howard's Lane, Wareham', *Proceedings of the Dorset Natural History and Archaeological Society* **117**, 81–90.

Hardy, A. and Wright, J. 2013. 'Medieval enclosures and a fishpond at Rectory Meadows, Kings Stanley: excavations in 2011', in M. Watts (Ed.) *Prehistoric, Romano-British and medieval occupation in the Frome Valley, Gloucestershire.* Bristol and Gloucestershire Archaeological Report No. 8, 59–82

Hare, J. 1985. *Battle Abbey: the Eastern range and excavations of 1978-80.* English Heritage Archaeological Reports 2, Historic Buildings and Monuments Commission for England, London.

Harte, J. 2020. *Dorset Survey.* http://www.apotropaios.co.uk/dorset-survey.html# [accessed 12 September 2020].

Harvey, J. 1981. *Medieval Gardens.* Batsford, London.

Harvey, P.D.A. and McGuinness, A. 1996. *A Guide to British Medieval Seals.* British Library/Public Record Office, London.

Hayden, C., Hughes, V., Cotter, J., Stafford, E. and Score, D., 2014. 'Bincombe Valley contour survey and excavation', in L. Brown, C. Hayden, and D. Score *'Down to Weymouth town by Ridgeway' Prehistoric, Roman and later sites along the Weymouth Relief Road.* Dorset Natural History and Archaeological Society Monograph 23, Dorset Natural History and Archaeological Society, Dorchester, 283–6.

Hearne, C.M. and Birbeck, V. 1999. *A35 Tolpuddle to Puddletown bypass DBFO, Dorset, 1996-8.* Wessex Archaeology Report No. 15, Trust for Wessex Archaeology, Salisbury.

Heaton, M.J. 1992. 'Two mid-Saxon grain-dryers and later medieval features at Chantry Fields, Gillingham, Dorset', *Proceedings of the Dorset Natural History and Archaeological Society* **114**, 97–126.

Hefferan, M. 2019. 'Edward III's household knights and the Crécy campaign of 1346', *Historical Research* **92**, 24–49.

Heindel, I. 2019. *Früh- und hochmittelalterliches Werkzeug zwischen Elbe, Saale, Weichsel und Bug.* Materialien zur Archäologie in Brandenburg 12, VML Verlag Marie Leidorf, Rahden/Westf.

HMSO 1893. *Calendar of the Close Rolls preserved in the Public Record Office Edward II AD 1313-1318.* HMSO, London.

HMSO 1904. *Calendar of Inquisitions post-mortem in the Public Record Office London Edward III AD 1327-1336.* HMSO, London.

HMSO 1909. *Calendar of Inquisitions post-mortem in the Public Record Office London Edward III AD 1327-1336.* HMSO, London.

HMSO 1911a. *Calendar of the Close Rolls preserved in the Public Record Office. Henry III AD 1237-1242.* HMSO, London.

HMSO 1911b. *Calendar of Fine rolls preserved in the Public Record Office Edward I AD 1272-1307.* HMSO, London.

HMSO 1921. *Calendar of Inquisitions post-mortem in the Public Record Office London Edward III AD 1352-1361.* HMSO, London.

HMSO 1935. *Calendar of Inquisitions post-mortem in the Public Record Office London Edward III AD 1361-1365.* HMSO, London.

HMSO 1938. *Calendar of Inquisitions post-mortem in the Public Record Office London Edward III AD 1365-1370.* HMSO, London.

HMSO 1952. *Calendar of Inquisitions post-mortem and other analogous documents in the Public Record Office London Edward III 1374-1377*. HMSO, London.

Hewitt, I., Cheetham, P. and Chartrand, J. 2002. 'East Holton, Wareham St Martin', *Proceedings of the Dorset Natural History and Archaeological Society* **124**, 120–1.

Hewitt, I., James, B. and Cheetham, P. 2004. 'East Holton, Wareham St Martin', *Proceedings of the Dorset Natural History and Archaeological Society* **126**, 180.

Hewitt, I., James, B. and Parham, D. 2005. 'East Holton (Holton Lee), Wareham St Martin', *Proceedings of the Dorset Natural History and Archaeological Society* **127**, 148–9.

Hicks, J. and English, J. n.d. *Earthworks at Newark Priory, Ripley, Surrey: an archaeological survey*. Surrey Archaeological Society, Guildford.

Higgins, D. 1995. 'A medieval site at Bere Regis', *Proceedings of the Dorset Natural History and Archaeological Society* **117**, 143–147.

Higgins, P. 1998. *Summary report on an archaeological watching brief on a gas pipeline from Littlemoor to Chickerell*. Unpublished report, Southern Archaeological Services.

Hildburgh, W. 1942. 'Cowrie shells as amulets in Europe', *Folklore* **53**, 178–95.

Hill, M.O., Mountford, J.O., Roy, D.B. and Bunce, R.G.H. 1999. *Ellenberg's indicator values for British plants*. ECOFACT Volume 2: Technical Annex, HMSO, London.

Hilton, R.H. and Rahtz, P. 1966. 'Upton Gloucestershire, 1959–1964', *Transactions of the Bristol and Gloucestershire Archaeological Society* **85**, 70–146.

Hinton, D. 1968. 'A medieval cistern from Churchill', *Oxoniensia* **33**, 66–70.

Hinton, D.A. 1998. *Saxons and Vikings*. Dovecote Press, Wimborne.

Hinton, D.A. 2002. 'A `marginal economy'? The Isle of Purbeck from the Norman Conquest to the Black Death', in D.A. Hinton *Purbeck Papers*. University of Southampton Monograph 4, 84–117.

Hinton, D.A. 2012. 'Central Southern England 'Chalk and Cheese'', in N. Christie and P. Stamper (eds) *Medieval rural settlement Britain and Ireland AD 800-1600*. Windgather Press, Oxford, 118–134.

Hinton, D.A. and Hodges, R. 1977. 'Excavations in Wareham, 1974–5', *Proceedings of the Dorset Natural History and Archaeological Society* **99**, 42–83.

Horsey, I.P. 1992. *Excavations in Poole 1973-1983*. Dorset Natural History and Archaeological Society Monograph 10, Dorset Natural History and Archaeology Society, Dorchester.

Horsfall, A. 1996. 'Domesday woodland in Dorset', *Proceedings of the Dorset Natural History and Archaeological Society* **118**, 1–6.

Horsfall, A. 1997. 'Woodland in medieval Dorset', *Proceedings of the Dorset Natural History and Archaeological Society* **119**, 59–64.

Hübener, W. 1972. 'Gleicharmige Bügelfibeln der Merowingerzeit in Westeuropa', *Madrider Mitteilungen* **13**, 211–69.

Hughes, M.K. and Diaz, H.F. 1994. 'Was there a 'Medieval Warm Period', and if so, where and when?', *Climatic Change* **26**, 109–142.

Humphreys, O.J. 2018. *Craft, Industry and Agriculture in a Roman City: The Iron Tools from London*. PhD Thesis, University of Reading, Reading.

Hunt, A. 1984. 'Woolcombe Farm', *Proceedings of the Dorset Natural History and Archaeological Society* **106**, 155–159.

Hunt, A. 1985. 'Woolcombe Farm', *Proceedings of the Dorset Natural History and Archaeological Society* **107**, 172–173.

Hunt, A. 1986. 'Woolcombe Farm', *Proceedings of the Dorset Natural History and Archaeological Society* **108**, 186–187.

Hunt, A. 1990. 'Woolcombe Farm', *Proceedings of the Dorset Natural History and Archaeological Society* **112**, 125–127.

Hunt, A. 1991. 'Woolcombe Farm', *Proceedings of the Dorset Natural History and Archaeological Society* **113**, 175–178.

Hunt, A. 1992. 'Woolcombe Farm', *Proceedings of the Dorset Natural History and Archaeological Society* **114**, 245.

Hutchins, J. 1863. *History of the County of Dorset*.

Jackson, C.J. 1892. 'The spoon and its history; its form, material, and development, more particularly in England', *Archaeologia* **53**, 107–46.

Jacomet, S. 2006. *Identification of cereal remains from archaeological sites*. (2nd Edn) Archaeobotany Lab IPAS, Basel University.

James, T.B. and Knight, B. 1988. 'Lead and lead-alloy objects', in T.B. James and A.M. Robinson (eds) *Clarendon Palace: the history and archaeology of a medieval palace and hunting lodge near Salisbury, Wiltshire*. Reports of the Research Committee of the Society of Antiquaries of London 45, London, 224–29.

Jarvis, K.S. 1992a. 'Introduction to the pottery', in I.P. Horsey *Excavations in Poole 1973-1983*. Dorset Natural History and Archaeological Society Monograph 5, Dorset Natural History and Archaeological Society, Dorchester, 62–5.

Jarvis, K.S. 1992b. 'The ridge tiles and other clay finds', in I P Horsey *Excavations in Poole 1973-1983*. Dorset Natural History and Archaeological Society Monograph 10, Dorset Natural History and Archaeological Society, Dorchester, 131.

Jarvis, K.S. 1994. 'The roof tile', in D.R. Watkins *The Foundry: excavations on Poole Waterfront 1986/7*. Dorset Natural History and Archaeological Society Monograph 14, Dorset Natural History and Archaeological Society, Dorchester, 55–6.

Jenkyns, J. 2008. 'The litigious afterlife of an Anglo-saxon charter: Wyke Regis, Dorset', in O.J. Padel and D.N. Parsons (eds) *A commodity of good names. Essays in honour of Margaret Gelling*. Donnington, 55–78.

Jessup, O. 1996. 'A new artefact typology for the study of medieval arrowheads', *Medieval Archaeology* **40**, 192–205.

Johnson, E.D. 2015. 'Moated sites and the production of authority in the Eastern Weald of England', *Medieval Archaeology* **59**, 233–254.

Jones, D. 2014. 'Arrows against mail armour', *Journal of the Society of Archer-Antiquaries* **57**, 62–70.

Katzenburg, A.M. and Saunders S.R. 2008. *Biological Anthropology of the human skeleton.* Wiley.

Keen, L. 1984. 'The towns of Dorset' in J. Haslam (Ed.) *Anglo-Saxon towns in southern England.* Phillimore, Chichester, 203–248.

Keen, L. n.d. *Three tile pavements: the evidence of late-medieval and sixteenth-century Continental floor-tile imports.* Unpublished report.

Klein, K.L. 2005. 'Buckles', in J. Gardiner (Ed.) *Before the mast: life and death aboard the Mary Rose.* The Archaeology of the Mary Rose 4, Mary Rose Trust, Portsmouth, 99–105.

Kowaleski, M. 2016. 'The early documentary evidence for the commercialisation of the sea fisheries in medieval Britain', in J.H. Barrett and D.C. Orton (eds) *Cod and Herring. The archaeology and history of medieval sea fishing.* Oxbow Books, Oxford, 23–41.

Langton, B., Ings, M., Walker, G. and Oakey, N. 2000. 'Medieval Field Systems at Tinker's Close, Moreton-in-Marsh, Gloucestershire. Excavations in 1995–6', in N.J. Oakey (Ed.) *Three Medieval Sites in Gloucestershire: Excavations at Ebley, Moreton in Marsh and Stonehouse.* Cotswold Archaeological Trust Occasional Paper 1, Cotswold Archaeological Trust, Cirencester, 15–23.

Leary, E. 1983. *The building limestones of the British Isles.* Building Research Establishment Report HMSO, London.

Leonard, A. 2008. 'Late Iron Age and Romano-British burials and associated activity at the former allotments, Church Knap, Wyke Regis, Weymouth', *Proceedings of the Dorset Natural History and Archaeological Society* **129**, 115–126.

Lewis, M. 2000. 'Non-adult palaeopathology: current status and future potential', in M. Cox and S. Mays *Human Osteology in archaeology and forensic science.* Greenwich Medical Media Ltd, London, 39–57.

Loader, E. 1999. 'Iron Objects', in C.M. Hearne and V. Birbeck *A35 Tolpuddle to Puddletown bypass DBFO, Dorset, 1996–8.* Wessex Archaeology Report No. 15, Trust for Wessex Archaeology, Salisbury, 106–109.

Locker, A. 1998. 'Faunal Remains', in M. Papworth 'The medieval manorial buildings of Kingston Lacy: survey and excavation results with an analysis of the medieval account rolls 1295–1462', *Proceedings of the Dorset Natural History and Archaeological Society* **120**, 59–60.

Mainman, A.J. and Rogers, N.S.H. 2000. *Craft, industry and everyday life: Finds from Anglo-Scandinavian York, The archaeology of York: The small finds 17/14.* Published for the York Archaeological Trust by the Council for British Archaeology, York.

Maltby, M 1993. 'Animal bones', in P.J. Woodward, S.M. Davies and A.H Graham *Excavations at Greyhound Yard, Dorchester 1981–4.* Dorset Natural History and Archaeological Society Monograph 12, Dorset Natural History and Archaeological Society, Dorchester, 315–340.

Manning, W.H. 1985. *Catalogue of the Romano-British iron tools, fittings and weapons in the British Museum.* British Museum Publications, London.

Mansell-Pleydell, J.C. 1898. *The molluscs of Dorset.* Dorchester.

Margeson, S.M. 1993. *Norwich households: The medieval and post-medieval finds from Norwich Survey Excavations 1971–78.* East Anglian Archaeology 58. University of East Anglia Centre of East Anglian Studies, Norwich.

Margetts, A. 2017. 'The Hayworth: a lowland vaccary site in south-east England', *Medieval Archaeology* **61 (1)**, 117–148.

Maw, R. 2015. 'The Old Manor, Stratton', *Proceedings of the Dorset Natural History and Archaeological Society* **136**, 149–50.

Maw, R. and Mepham, L. in prep. 'Medieval pottery from the Old Manor, Stratton', *Proceedings of the Dorset Natural History and Archaeological Society.*

McOmish, D. 2002. 'Report on the survey of the strip lynchets at Worth Matravers, Dorset', in D.A. Hinton *Purbeck Papers.* University of Southampton Monograph 4, 132–138.

Medieval Pottery Research Group (MPRG) 1998. *A Guide to the Classification of Medieval Ceramic Forms.* MPRG Occasional Paper 1.

Mepham, L. 1999. 'Medieval pottery from West Mead Objects', in C.M. Hearne and V. Birbeck *A35 Tolpuddle to Puddletown bypass DBFO, Dorset, 1996–8.* Wessex Archaeology Report No. 15, Trust for Wessex Archaeology, Salisbury, 127–131.

Mepham, L. 2000a. 'Pottery', in M. Rawlings, 'Excavations at Ivy Street and Brown Street, Salisbury, 1994', *Wiltshire Archaeological and Natural History Magazine* **93**, 29–37.

Mepham, L. 2000b. 'Pottery', in D. Godden, J. Grove and R.J.C. Smith, 'Medieval and post-medieval Bridport: excavations at 43 South Street, 1996', *Proceedings of the Dorset Natural History and Archaeological Society* **122**, 115–9.

Mepham, L. 2003. 'The pottery', in C. Butterworth, 'Multi-period finds from Quarleston Farm, Winterbourne Stickland, 1994–5', *Proceedings of the Dorset Natural History and Archaeological Society* **125**, 147–50.

Mepham, L. 2007. 'The medieval pottery', in M. Rawlings *By a Crystal Brook: Early riverside settlement and a medieval chapel at Sutton Poyntz, Dorset.* Wessex Archaeology, Salisbury, 58–66.

Mepham, L. 2012. *The Ceramic Building Material [from Corfe Castle].* unpublished report for National Trust.

Mepham, L. 2015. 'The pottery', in P. White and A. Cook *Sherborne Old Castle, Dorset: Archaeological investigations 1930–90.* Society of Antiquaries of London, 158–85.

Mepham, L. 2018. 'Town and country: production and consumption of Laverstock ware', *Medieval Ceramics* **39**, 17–28.

Merrifield, R. 1987. *The archaeology of ritual and magic.* Batsford, London.

Miller, E. and Hatcher J. 1978. *Medieval England – Rural society and economic change.* Routledge, London.

Mills, A.D. 1986. *The place names of Dorset.* English Place Name Society Vol. 52, English Place Name Society, Nottingham.

Mills, A.D. 1998. *Dorset place names Their origins and meanings*. Countryside Books, Newbury.

Milward, J. 2017. 'Results of an archaeological excavation at Pound Lane, Wareham', *Proceedings of the Dorset Natural History and Archaeological Soci*ety **138**, 96–101.

Moffat, B. 1987. 'A curious assemblage of seeds from Waltham Abbey: a study of Medieval Medication', *Essex Archaeology and History* **18**, 121–4.

Moffett, L. 1991. 'The archaeobotanical evidence for free-threshing tetraploid wheat in Britain', in Ing. Eva Hajnalová (Ed.) *Palaeoethnobotany and Archaeology*. Acta Interdisciplinaria Archaeologica VII, Nitra, 233–243.

Monckton, A. 2002. *Charred plant remains from Cawston DMV, Dunchurch, Rugby, Warks (DC99)*. ULAS Report 2002–111.

Moore, P. 2000. 'Tilbury Fort: a post-medieval fort and its inhabitants', *Post-Medieval Archaeology* **34**, 3–104.

Moorhouse, S. 1971. 'Finds from Basing House, Hampshire (c. 1540–1645): Part Two', *Post-Medieval Archaeology* **5**, 35–76.

Moorhouse, S. 1978. 'Documentary evidence for the uses of medieval pottery: an interim statement', *Medieval Ceramics* **2**, 3–21.

Moorhouse, S. and Goodall, I.H. 1971. 'Iron', in S. Moorhouse 'Finds from Basing House, Hampshire (c. 1540–1645): Part Two', *Post-Medieval Archaeology* **5**, 35–76.

Moreland, J. and Hadley, D. 2020. *Sheffield Castle. Archaeology, Archives, Regeneration, 1927-2018*. White Rose University Press, York.

Morley, B. and Gurney, D. 1997. *Castle Rising Castle, Norfolk*. East Anglian Archaeology 81, Field Archaeology Division, Norfolk Museums Service, Norwich.

Moss, S. 2004. 'The Broadbank long-term experiment at Rothamstead: what has it told us about weeds?', *Weed Science*, **52**, 864–873.

Müller-Wille, M. 2005. 'Zwei Bergkristallfibeln aus Mecklenburg-Vorpommern', *Germania* **83 (2)**, 373–85.

Murdoch, T.V. 2006. *Noble households: eighteenth-century inventories of great English houses. A tribute to John Cornforth*. J. Adamson, Cambridge.

Musty, J., Algar, D.J. and Ewence, P.F. 1969. 'The medieval pottery kilns at Laverstock, near Salisbury, Wiltshire', *Archaeologia* **102**, 83–150.

Nash, G. 2003. 'Archaeological Investigations at the Southern Electricity Depot, High Street, Shaftesbury, Dorset', *Proceedings of the Dorset Natural History and Archaeological Soci*ety **125**, 83–92.

Neubecker, O. 1980. *Wappenkunde*. Battenberg Verlag, München.

Newfield, T.P. 2009. 'A cattle panzootic in early fourteenth-century Europe', *Agricultural History Review* **57 (1)**, 155–190.

Noble, C. 2000. 'Spiritual practice and designed landscape: monastic precinct gardens', *Studies in the History of Gardens and Designed Landscapes* **20 (3)**, 197–205.

Ortner, D. 2000. *Identification of pathological conditions in human skeletal remains.* (2nd Edn). Academic Press, London.

Oswald, A. 2012. 'A New Earthwork Survey of Wharram Percy', in S. Wrathmell *Wharram. A Study of Settlement on the Yorkshire Wolds, XIII. A History of Wharram Percy and its neighbours*. York University Archaeological Publications 15, York, 23–43.

Oswald, G. 1984. *Lexikon der Heraldik*. VEB Bibliographisches Institut, Leipzig.

Ottaway, P. 1996. 'The ironwork', in R.A. Hall, and M. Whyman 'Settlement and Monasticism at Ripon, North Yorkshire, from the 7th to 11th Centuries AD', *Medieval Archaeology* **40**, 62–150.

Ottaway, P. 2009. 'Iron domestic fixtures, fittings and implements', in D.H. Evans and C. Loveluck (eds) *Life and economy at early medieval Flixborough, c. AD 600-1000: the artefact evidence*. Excavations at Flixborough 2. Oxbow Books, Oxford, 166–87.

Ottaway, P. and Rogers, N.S.H. 2002. *Craft, industry and everyday life: finds from medieval York, The archaeology of York: The small finds 17/15.* York Archaeological Trust, York.

Page, P. Atherton, K. and Hardy, A. 2005. *Barentin's Manor: excavations of the moated manor at Harding's Field, Chalgrove, Oxfordshire 1976-9.* Thames Valley Landscapes Monograph 24, Oxford University School of Archaeology, Oxford.

Page, W. 1908. A History of the County of Dorset: Volume 2. London.

Papworth, M. 1994. 'Lodge Farm, Kingston Lacy Estate, Dorset', *Journal of the British Archaeological Association* **147**, 57–121.

Papworth, M. 1996. 'Excavations at Wilkswood Farmhouse, Langton Matravers', *Proceedings of the Dorset Natural History and Archaeological Soci*ety **118**, 157–159.

Papworth, M. 1997. 'Kingston Lacy medieval manorial buildings', *Proceedings of the Dorset Natural History and Archaeological Soci*ety **119**, 161.

Papworth, M. 1998. 'The medieval manorial buildings of Kingston Lacy: survey and excavation results with an analysis of the medieval account rolls 1295-1462', *Proceedings of the Dorset Natural History and Archaeological Society* **120**, 45–62.

Parkhouse, J. 1997. 'The distribution and exchange of Mayen lava quernstones in Early Medieval Northwestern Europe', in G. De Boe and F. Verhaeghe (eds) *Exchange and trade in medieval Europe: Papers of the Medieval Europe Brugge Conference, Vol 3.* lAP Rapporten 3. Instituut voor het Archeologisch Patrimonium, Zellik, 97–106.

Pascoe, W.H. 1979. *A Cornish armory.* Lodenek Press, Padstow.

Pastoureau, M. 1984. *Quel est le roi des animaux ?, Actes des congrès de la Société des historiens médiévistes de l'enseignement supérieur public, 15e congrès, Toulouse, 1984. Le monde animal et ses représentations au moyen-âge (XIe-XVe siècles).* Toulouse, 133–42.

Pearce, J. 2016. 'Down at the old Ship and Ball – taverns, trade and daily life in the London Borough of Southwark', *Post-Medieval Archaeology* **50**, 181–226.

Pearson, T. 1982. ‘The post-Roman wares’, in P. Leach (Ed.) *Ilchester, Vol. 1: Excavations 1974-5*. Western Archaeological Trust Excavation Monograph 3, 169–217.

Pelling, R. and Robinson, M. 2000. ‘Saxon emmer wheat from the upper and middle Thames Valley, England’, *Environmental Archaeology* 5, 117–119

Penny, W.E.W. 1911. ‘The medieval keys in Salisbury Museum’, *Connoisseur* 29, 11–16.

Penoyre, J. 2005. *Traditional Houses of Somerset*. Somerset Vernacular Building Research Group.

Perring, D. 2002. *Town and country in England: Frameworks for Archaeological research*. CBA Research Report 134, Council for British Archaeology, York.

Pitt-Rivers, A.H. 1890. *King John’s House, Tollard Royal, Wiltshire*. Privately published.

Platt, C.P.S. and Coleman-Smith, R. 1975. *Excavations in Medieval Southampton 1953-1969*. Leicester University Press, Leicester.

Pohl, M. 2010. *Quern-stones and tuff as indicators of medieval European trade patterns*. Papers from the Institute of Archaeology 20, 148–53.

Poole, A.L. 1955. *From Domesday book to Magna Carta, 1087-1216*. (2nd Edn) Oxford University Press, Oxford.

Poulsen, J. 1983. ‘Excavations on a medieval settlement at Woolcombe Farm, Toller Porcorum 1966-1969’, *Proceedings of the Dorset Natural History and Archaeological Society* 105, 75–81.

Prideaux, C.S. 1925.’ A Romano-British foodbowl recovered from a burial place near Chickerell’, *Proceedings of the Dorset Natural History and Archaeological Society* 47, xlvi–lxix.

Pritchard, F. 1991. ‘Small finds’, in A. Vince (Ed.) *Aspects of Saxo-Norman London 2. Finds and environmental evidence*. London and Middlesex Archaeological Society, Special Paper 12, London, 120–278.

Public Record Office (PRO) 1963. *List of Inquisitions ad quod damnum preserved in the Public Record Office*. Public Record Office, London.

Rackham, O. 1980. *Ancient Woodland*. Harper Collins, London.

Rahtz, P. 1959. ‘Holworth medieval village excavation 1958’, *Proceedings of the Dorset Natural History and Archaeological Society* 80, 127–147.

Rahtz, P. 1969a. *Excavations at King John’s Hunting Lodge, Writtle, Essex, 1955-57*. Society of Medieval Archaeology Monograph 3, London.

Rahtz, P. 1969b. ‘Upton Gloucestershire, 1964–1968’, *Transactions of the Bristol and Gloucestershire Archaeological Society* 88, 74–126.

Rahtz, P. 1979. *The Saxon and Medieval Palaces at Cheddar*. British Archaeological Report 65, Oxford.

Randall, C 2010. *Livestock and landscape: Exploring animal exploitation in later prehistory in the south west of Britain*. Unpublished PhD Thesis, Bournemouth University.

Randall, C. 2018. ‘The human remains – prehistoric human remains, Romano-British infants and the post-Roman cemetery’, in L. Ladle *Excavations at Football Field, Worth Matravers, Dorset: Prehistoric and Romano-British settlement and a post-Roman cemetery*. BAR British Series 643, 221–233.

Randall, C. 2019. ‘Evidence of medieval agriculture and settlement: Excavation at Curtis Fields, Chickerell, Weymouth’, *Proceedings of the Dorset Natural History and Archaeological Society* 140, 85–98.

Randall, C. in prep. ‘The human remains’, in L. Ladle *Druce Farm Roman Villa, Dorset: excavations 2012-17* BAR.

Rawcliffe, C. 2008. “Delectable Sightes and Fragrant Smelles’: Gardens and Health in Late Medieval and Early Modern England’, *Garden History* 36 (1), 3–21.

Rawlings, M. 2007. *By a Crystal Brook Early riverside settlement and a medieval chapel at Sutton Poyntz, Dorset*. Wessex Archaeology, Salisbury.

Read, B. 2010. *Metal buttons: c.900 BC–c.AD 1700*. Portcullis Publications, Huish Episcopi.

Rees, H., Crummy, N., Dunn, G. and Ottaway, P.J. 2008. *Artefacts and Society in Roman and Medieval Winchester: Small finds from the suburbs and defences, 1971-1986*. Winchester Museums, Winchester.

Rees, S.E. 2011. ‘Agriculture’, in L. Allason-Jones (Ed.) *Artefacts in Roman Britain. Their purpose and use*. Cambridge University Press, Cambridge, 89–113.

Renn, D.F. 1959. ‘Steelyard Weights: A Postscript’, *Proceedings of the Dorset Natural History and Archaeological Society* 81, 148–49.

RGZM 1992. *Das Reich der Salier, 1024-1125: Katalog zur Ausstellung des Landes Rheinland-Pfalz*. Jan Thorbecke, Sigmaringen.

Richards, J. 1991. ‘Godwin’s Orchard, Kington Magna, Dorset’, *Proceedings of the Dorset Natural History and Archaeological Society* 113, 190–192.

Ricketts, E. 1977. *The Buildings of Old Weymouth. Part Three: The Villages*. Longmans, Weymouth.

Rietstap, J.B. 1884. *Armorial general, precede d’ un dictionnaire des termes du Blason*. Gouda.

Rippon, S. 2008. *Beyond the medieval village*. Oxford University Press, Oxford.

Rippon, S. Fyfe, R. and Brown, A. 2006. ‘Beyond open fields: the origins and development of a landscape characterised by dispersed settlement in south-west England’, *Medieval Archaeology* 50 (1), 31–70.

Rippon, S., Smart, C. and Pears, B. 2015. *The Fields of Britannia*. Oxford University Press, Oxford.

Rippon, S., Wainwright A. and Smart, S. 2014. ‘Farming regions in medieval England: the archaeobotanical and zooarchaeolical evidence’, *Medieval Archaeology* 58 (1), 195–255.

Roberts, C. and Cox, M. 2003. *Health and disease in Britain from prehistory to the present day*. Sutton, Stroud.

Robinson, S., Firth E., Coles, C. and Carruthers, W. 2018. ‘Excavations on the site of the Museum of Jurrassic Marine Life, Kimmeridge, Dorset, 2013’, *Proceedings of the Dorset Natural History and Archaeological Society* 139, 177–196.

Rodwell, K. and Bell, R. 2004. *Acton Court: The evolution of an early Tudor courtier's house.* English Heritage, London.

Ross, M.S. 1985. 'Kington Magna: A parish survey', *Proceedings of the Dorset Natural History and Archaeological Society* **107**, 23–46.

Ross, M.S. 1992. 'Medieval settlement at Kington Magna, Dorset', *Proceedings of the Dorset Natural History and Archaeological Society* **114**, 261–263.

Ross, M.S. 1993. 'Melbury Abbas: medieval pottery in perspective', *Proceedings of the Dorset Natural History and Archaeological Society* **115**, 111–119.

Royal Commission on Historic Monuments England (RCHME) 1952. *An inventory of the historical monuments in the County of Dorset Vol I West.* RCHME, London.

Royal Commission on Historic Monuments England (RCHME) 1960. 'Excavations in the West Bailey at Corfe Castle', *Medieval Archaeology* **4**, 29–55.

Royal Commission on Historic Monuments England (RCHME) 1970a. *An inventory of the historical monuments in the County of Dorset Vol II South-east Part 1.* RCHME, London.

Royal Commission on Historic Monuments England (RCHME) 1970b. *An inventory of the historical monuments in the County of Dorset Vol III Central Part 1.* RCHME, London.

Rushton, D. 2002. 'Some Pre-Black Death surveys and extents of Purbeck', in D.A. Hinton *Purbeck Papers.* University of Southampton Monograph 4, 118–125.

Salzman, L.F. 1952. *Building in England Down to 1540.* Oxford University Press, Oxford.

Saunders, P. 2001. *Salisbury Museum medieval catalogue. Part 3.* Salisbury and South Wiltshire Museum, Salisbury.

Saunders, P. and Saunders, E. 1991. *Salisbury Museum medieval catalogue. Part 1.* Salisbury and South Wiltshire Museum, Salisbury.

Scheuer, L. and Black, S. 2000. *Developmental juvenile osteology.* Elsevier Academic Press, London.

Schmidt, O., Wilms, K.-H. and Lingelbach, B. 1999. 'The Visby Lenses', *Optometry and Vision Science* **76**, 624–30.

Schulze-Dörrlamm, M. 1990. 'Bemerkungen zu Alter und Funktion der Alsengemmen', *Archäologisches Korrespondenzblatt* **20**, 215–26.

Schulze-Dörrlamm, M. 2020. 'Neues zum Mainzer Goldschatz des 11. Jahrhunderts (Teil 2)', *Archäologisches Korrespondenzblatt* **50**, 285–305.

Schuster, J. 2006. *Die Buntmetallfunde der Grabung Feddersen Wierde: Chronologie, Chorologie, Technologie, Probleme der Küstenforschung im südlichen Nordseegebiet 30.* Feddersen Wierde 6. Isensee, Oldenburg.

Schuster, J. 2010. 'Metalwork', in P. Andrews 'West Thurrock: Late prehistoric settlement, Roman burials and the medieval manor house. Channel Tunnel Rail Link Excavations 2002', *Essex Archaeology and History* **40**, 1–77.

Schuster, J. 2014. *Court Farm, Wookey, Somerset – Metalwork Report.* AsF Report 0010.01, ARCHÆOLOGICALsmall FINDS, Salisbury. DOI: 10.13140/2.1.5121.4086.

Schuster, J. 2015. *Weatleigh Close, Taunton, Somerset –*

Metalwork Report. AsF Report 0013.01, ARCHÆOLOGICAL smallFINDS, Salisbury. DOI: 10.13140/RG.2.1.1316.2969.

Schuster, J., Saunders, P. and Algar, D. 2012. 'Objects of iron', in P. Saunders (Ed.) *Salisbury Museum medieval catalogue. Part 4*, Salisbury and South Wiltshire Museum, Salisbury, 143–99.

Scott, I. 2011. 'Southampton French Quarter 1382. Specialist Report Download F6: Metal Objects', in R. Brown and A. Hardy (eds) *Trade and prosperity, war and poverty. An archaeological and historical investigation into Southampton's French Quarter.* Oxford Archaeology Monograph 15, Oxford.

Seaborne, G. 2011. *Imprisoning medieval women: The non-judicial confinement and abduction of women in England c. 1170-1509.* Routledge, London.

Seaward, D.R. 1978. 'The marine molluscs of the Fleet, Dorset', *Proceedings of the Dorset Natural History and Archaeological Society* **100**, 100–108.

Seaward, D.R. 1986. 'The Fleet, Dorset – A saline lagoon with special reference to its molluscs', *Porcupine Newslettter* **3 (6)**, 140–146.

Serjeantson, D. 1993. 'The animal bone and shell', in M. Ross 'Melbury Abbas: medieval pottery in perspective', *Proceedings of the Dorset Natural History and Archaeological Society* **115**, 119.

Shorrocks, D.M.M. 1974. 'Medieval deeds from the Walker-Heneage Manuscripts', in *Medieval Deeds of Bath and District.* Somerset Records Society 73.

Shortt, H. 1982. 'A thirteenth-century 'steelyard' balance from Huish', *Wiltshire Archaeological and Natural History Magazine* **63**, 61–66.

Slavin, P. 2012. 'The Great Bovine Pestilence and its economic and environmental consequences in England and Wales, 1318-9', *Economic History Review* **65(4)**, 1239–1266.

Smith, D. 2012. 'Brickyards and claypits, a Dorset industry', *Geoscience in South-West England* **13**, 84–92.

Smith, H.P. 1934. 'Local historical research and the school curriculum', *Proceedings of the Dorset Natural History and Archaeological Society* **56**, 15.

Smith, R.M. 1991. 'Demographic developments in Rural England, 1300–48: a survey', in BMS Campbell (Ed.) *Before the Black Death: studies in the 'Crisis' of the Early Fourteenth Century.* Manchester, Manchester University Press, 25–77.

Smith Thomas, H. 2005. *Getting started with beef and dairy cattle.* Story Publishing, North Adams (MS).

Sørensen, A.B. 2005. 'Ein Prachtfund aus der mittelalterlichen Siedlung Østergård bei Hyrup in Sønderjylland, Dänemark', *Germania* **83 (2)**, 337–71.

Spoerry, P. 1988. 'Documentary and other evidence for medieval and post-medieval ceramic production in Dorset', *Proceedings of the Dorset Natural History and Archaeological Society* **110**, 29–35.

Spoerry, P.S. 1990. 'Ceramic production in medieval Dorset and the surrounding region', *Medieval Ceramics* **14**, 3–17.

Stace, C. 2010. *New Flora of the British Isles.* (3rd Edn) Cambridge University Press.

Steane, J.M. and Foreman, M. 1988. 'Medieval fishing tackle', in M. Aston (Ed.) *Medieval fish, fisheries, and fishponds in England.* British Archaeological Reports. British Series 182, Oxford, 137–86.

Stoate, T.L. 1978. *Dorset Tudor Muster Rolls, 1539, 1542 and 1569.* West Country Books, Newton Abbot.

Stratascan 2016. *Chickerell, Dorset. Geophysical Survey Report.* Unpublished report, Stratascan, Upton on Severn.

Ströbele, F. and Schuster, J. 2019. *The London protected wreck, The Nore, off Southend-on-Sea, Thames Estuary, Essex: Compositional analyses of copper alloy and pewter objects.* Research Report Series 04-2019. Historic England, Portsmouth.

Sykes, E.R. 1892. 'On some monstrosities of *Littorina rudis*, Maton', *Proceedings of the Dorset Natural History and Archaeological Society* **8**, 191.

Sykes, N. 2003. 'Animal remains', in J. Valentin, 'Manor Farm, Portesham, Dorset: excavations on a multi-period religious and settlement site', *Proceedings of the Dorset Natural History and Archaeological Society* **125**, 63.

Tabor, R. 2013. 'Sherborne House, Sherborne', *Proceedings of the Dorset Natural History and Archaeological Society* **134**, 160.

Tatton-Brown, T. 1991. 'Building the tower and spire of Salisbury Cathedral', *Antiquity* **64**, 74–96.

Taylor, C.C. 1966. 'Strip lynchets', *Antiquity* **40 (160)**, 277–83.

Taylor, C.C. 1970. *Dorset.* Hodder and Stoughton, London.

Taylor, C.C. 2000. 'Medieval ornamental landscapes', *Landscapes* **1**, 38–55.

Thirsk, J. 1987. *Agricultural Regions and Agrarian History in England, 1500- 1750.* Macmillan Education, Basingstoke.

Thomas, G. 2000. *A survey of late Anglo-Saxon and Viking-Age strap-ends from Britain.* PhD thesis, University of London, London.

Thörle, S. 2001. *Gleicharmige Bügelfibeln des frühen Mittelalters.* Universitätsforschungen zur prähistorischen Archäologie 81. Bonn.

Thorn, C. and Thorn, F. 1983. *Domesday Book Dorset.* Phillimore, Chichester.

Thuaudet, O. 2015. *Les accessoires métalliques du vêtement et de la parure de corps en Provence du XIe au XVIe siècle. Archéologie, techniques et économie d'une industrie méconnue.* Thèse de doctorat d'archéologie médiévale, Aix-Marseille Université, Aix-en-Provence.

Trevarthen, M. and Bellamy, P. 2011. *St Mary's Church Chickerell. Observations and recording.* Unpublished report Terrain Archaeology Report 53329/3/1.

Truc, M.C. 1997. 'Les fibules ansées symétriques en Normandie', *Archéologie Médiévale* **27**, 1–58.

Turner, S. 2006. *Making a Christian landscape. The countryside in early medieval Cornwall, Devon and Wessex.* University of Exeter Press, Exeter.

Turner, T. H. 1851. *Some Account of Domestic Architecture in England from the Conquest to the End of the Thirteenth Century.* Oxford.

Twigg, G. 2003. 'The black death: a problem of population-wide infection', *Local Population Studies* **71**, 40–52.

University of Nottingham 2020. *Key to English Place Names.* http://kepn.nottingham.ac.uk/ [Accessed 1 July 2020].

Valentin, J. 2003. 'Manor Farm, Portesham, Dorset: excavations on a multi-period religious and settlement site', *Proceedings of the Dorset Natural History and Archaeological Society* **125**, 23–69.

Verhulst, A. 2002. *The Carolingian economy.* Cambridge University Press, Cambridge.

Vince, A.G. 1984. *The medieval ceramic industry of the Severn Valley.* Unpublished PhD thesis, University of Southampton, Southampton.

Viner, L. 2002. *Lost Villages.* The Dovecote Press Ltd, Wimborne.

Waldron, T. 2009. *Palaeopathology.* Cambridge University Press, Cambridge.

Walton Rogers, P. 2007. *Cloth and clothing in early Anglo-Saxon England, AD 450-700.* CBA Research Report 145, Council for British Archaeology, York.

Warman, S. 2008. 'Animal bone', in T. Carew 'An early Bronze Age timber Structure, a Saxon kiln and Saxon and medieval occupation at Coppice Street, Shaftesbury, Dorset', *Proceedings of the Dorset Natural History and Archaeological Society* **129**, 85–88.

Wastling, L. 2009. 'Iron nail typology', in D.H. Evans and C. Loveluck (eds) *Life and economy at early medieval Flixborough, c. AD 600-1000: the artefact evidence.* Excavations at Flixborough 2, Oxbow Books, Oxford, 143–44.

Watkins, D.R. 1994. *The Foundry: excavations on Poole Waterfront 1986/7.* Dorset Natural History and Archaeological Society Monograph 14, Dorset Natural History and Archaeology Society, Dorchester.

Webster, C. 2008. *The Archaeology of South West England South West Archaeological Research Framework Resource Assessment and Research Agenda.* Somerset County Council, Taunton.

Weetch, R. 2014. *Brooches in Late Anglo-Saxon England within a North West European Context. A study of social identities between the eighth and eleventh centuries.* PhD thesis, University of Reading, Reading.

Wells, N.A. 1993. *Ceramic Roof tile [from Sherborne Old Castle].* Unpublished report for English Heritage.

Wells, N.A. 2007a. 'Ceramic Building Material', in M. Rawlings *By a Crystal Brook: Early riverside settlement and a medieval chapel at Sutton Poyntz, Dorset.* Wessex Archaeology, Salisbury, 66–9.

Wells, N.A. 2007b. 'Worked Stone', in M. Rawlings *By a Crystal Brook: Early riverside settlement and a medieval chapel at Sutton Poyntz, Dorset,* Wessex Archaeology, Salisbury, 55–57.

Wessex Archaeology 2006. *Hooke Court, Hooke, Dorset.*

Archaeological Evaluation and Assessment of the Results. Unpublished report Ref: 62502.01, Wessex Archaeology, Salisbury.

Wessex Archaeology 2016. *East Chickerell, Weymouth, Dorset. Archaeological Evaluation Report.* Unpublished report Ref. 73312.03, Wessex Archaeology, Salisbury.

White, T.D. and Folkens, P.A. 2000. *Human osteology.* (2nd Edn) Academic Press, San Diego.

Williams, D. 2018. *Copper-alloy Purse Components: A new classification using finds from England and Wales recorded by the Portable Antiquities Scheme.* Finds Research Group Datasheet 50, Finds Research Group AD700–1700.

Williams, D.F. 2002. 'Purbeck marble in Roman and medieval Britain', in D. Hinton *Purbeck Papers.* University of Southampton Monograph 4, Oxbow Books, Oxford, 126–131.

Williams, M. 2006. *Bridport and West Bay: the buildings of the flax and hemp industry.* English Heritage, London.

Williams, V. 1997 'The small finds', in B. Morley and D. Gurney (eds) *Castle Rising Castle, Norfolk.* East Anglian Archaeology 81, Norfolk Museums Service, Norwich, 87–100.

Williamson, G.C. 1889. *Trade tokens issued in the seventeenth century in England, Wales and Ireland by corporations, merchants, tradesmen, etc., vol. 1.* Elliot Stock, London.

Wilson, C.A. 1973. *Food and Drink in Britain. From the Stone Age to the 19th Century.* Academy Publishers, Chicago.

Winder, J. 1991. 'Marine Mollusca', in P.W. Cox and C.M. Hearne *Redeemed from the Heath The archaeology of the Wytch Farm Oilfield (1987–90).* Dorset Natural History and Archaeological Society Monograph 9, Dorset Natural History and Archaeological Society, Dorchester, 212–216.

Winder, J. 1992. 'The oysters', in I.P. Horsey *Excavations in Poole 1973–1983.* Dorset Natural History and Archaeological Society Monograph 10, Dorset Natural History and Archaeological Society, Dorchester, 194–200.

Winder, J. 1994. 'The marine mollusc shells', in D.R. Watkins *The Foundry excavations on Poole Waterfront 1986/7.* Dorset Natural History and Archaeological Society Monograph 14, Dorset Natural History and Archaeological Society, Dorchester, 85–88.

Winder, J. 2017. 'Oysters in archaeology', in M.J. Allen (Ed.) *Molluscs in Archaeology* Oxbow Books, Oxford, 238–258.

Winnall, F.A. 1978. 'Chickerell Burials', *Proceedings of the Dorset Natural History and Archaeological Society* **100**, 112.

Wolters, J. 1985. *s.v. Filigran.* Reallexikon zur Deutschen Kunstgeschichte 8.9, Beck, München, 1062–1184.

Wood, M.E. 1950. '13th century domestic architecture in England', *Archaeological Journal* **105**, Supplement.

Wood, M.E. 1965. *The English Medieval House,* Dent, London.

Woodward, J. and Luff, P. 1983. *The Field Guide: A Farmland Companion.* Blandford Press, Blandford.

Woodward, P.J. 1983. 'Wimborne Minster, Dorset – excavations in the town centre 1975–80', *Proceedings of the Dorset Natural History and Archaeological Society* **105**, 57–74.

Woodward, P.J. 1986. 'The excavation of an Iron Age and Romano-British settlement at Rope Lake Hole, Corfe Castle, Dorset', in N. Sunter and P.J. Woodward *Romano-British Industries in Purbeck* Dorset Natural History and Archaeological Society Monograph Series 6, Dorset Natural History and Archaeological Society, Dorchester, 125–180.

Woodward, P.J. 2000. 'The Late Bronze Age Gold neckrings from Chickerell: an interim note', *Proceedings of the Dorset Natural History and Archaeological Society* **122**, 145–148.

Woodward, P.J. 2002. 'A Late Neolithic/Early Bronze Age triple ring monument and a Late Bronze Age house near Chickerell: An interim note', *Proceedings of the Dorset Natural History and Archaeological Society* **124**, 109–10.

Woodward, P.J., Davies, S.M. and Graham, A.H. 1993. *Excavations at Greyhound Yard, Dorchester 1981-4* Dorset Natural History and Archaeological Society Monograph Series 12, Dorset Natural History and Archaeological Society, Dorchester.

Woodward, P.J. and Smith, R. 1996. 'Coldharbour, Chickerell', *Proceedings of the Dorset Natural History and Archaeological Society* **118**, 145–6.

Wrathmell, S. 2012. *Wharram. A Study of Settlement on the Yorkshire Wolds, XIII. A History of Wharram Percy and its neighbours.* The University of York, York.

Wyles, S. 2007. 'The animal remains', in M. Rawlings *By a crystal brook. Early riverside settlement and a medieval chapel at Sutton Poyntz, Dorset.* Wessex Archaeology, Salisbury, 85–87.

Yalden, D. and Albarella, U. 2009. *The history of British Birds.* Oxford University Press, Oxford.

Ziegler, P. 1991. *The Black Death.* Sutton, Stroud.

Zohary, D., Hopf, M. and Weiss, E. 2013. *Domestication of Plants in the Old World.* (4th Edn) Oxford University Press, Oxford.

INDEX